NORBERT SZÁMVÉBER

ILLUSTRATED HISTORY OF THE STURMGESCHÜTZ-ABTEILUNG 202

peko
PUBLISHING

PUBLISHED BY
PeKo Publishing Kft.
8360 Keszthely, Bessenyei Gyorgy utca 37.
Email: infp@pekobooks.com
Website: www.pekobooks.com
Facebook: www.facebook.com/PeKoPublishing

AUTHOR
Norbert Számvéber

Edited by Derik Hammond
Translated by Tímea Tóthné Vágó
Color plates designed by Felipe Rodna
Cover designed by Ádám Nagy (www.nadam.hu)

Photos: Péter Kocsis, Thomas Anderson, Archive of Modern Conflict

FIRST PUBLISHED
2016

ISBN 978-615-80072-6-9

TABLE OF CONTENTS

Seventy years after the end of World War Two there are still many issues of historical interest that have not been researched and described in sufficient detail.

When the managing director of Peko Publishing House called upon me to write the detailed combat history of one of the most successful German assault gun units in World War II, *Sturmgeschütz-Abteilung 202,* I suddenly found myself in a difficult situation. To the best of my knowledge, no detailed history has ever been penned about this outstanding unit which destroyed more than 1,000 confirmed Soviet AFVs (armoured fighting vehicles) during the savage war fought in the eastern theatre. Only a generalized overview of its outstanding achievements is available in excerpts of war diaries (long out-of-print) written by veterans who served in the unit and in some excellent general works on the German assault artillery.

Moreover, I unfortunately had to face the fact that some of the German divisions that, according to evidence in archival documents, owed much to this assault gun-unit often forgot to mention its name and accomplishments in their own formal histories. The lack of contemporary sources must have played a great part in this.

To my best knowledge, *Sturmgeschütz-Abteilung 202*'s own records have not survived the hell of war. So, without any guide, my work was exactly like a criminal investigation: each and every 'suspicious' archival and bibliographical source had to be collected and examined minutely for details concerning this unit. I wouldn't say that I found all traceable sources, nor that my work is a perfect unit history of *Sturmgeschütz-Abteilung 202.* However, I did my best to write the combat history of the third most decorated assault gun unit in the German land forces in the most detailed way. So if you, dear reader, have any archival record, document or photo relating to this unit or can correct any shortcoming in the content of this work, I would be interested to hear from you through the publisher's e-mail-address so that any new information might be included in a new, extended edition of the history of this outstanding formation.

In the course of my work I received invaluable help from my friends Péter Barnaky, Péter Kocsis and Mátyás Pánczél. Mr Thomas Anderson helped me in a way he may not know about. Thank you all! But as always my greatest gratitude goes to my wife and my two sons, who endured, smiling, all that went with this work.

Budapest, in May, 2015
The author

INTRODUCTION

Armoured Support for the German Infantry

During World War I, the attacking infantry – within the last one-or-two hundred metres from the enemy trenches – always found themselves facing the fire of machine guns and other firearms that survived friendly preparatory fire, as well as the resistance of the remaining elements of fortification. For this reason the Germans developed a light 3.7 cm gun that, moving forward in the infantry's order of battle, could knock out remaining defensive elements by direct fire, clearing the way towards the enemy's positions. A new infantry arm of service was formed around this weapon: assault troops heavily equipped with hand grenades. The combination worked perfectly well.

However, the manually portable gun proved too clumsy in the field and its crew was exposed to the defensive fire. Because of this emerged the idea of the mechanically propelled (self-propelled) gun carriage which, with the realization of the necessity for anti-tank defence, soon appeared on the battlefield.

Refreshing the concept of the accompanying artillery piece, the Germans mounted a 7.7 cm field gun on a tracked towing vehicle and put it to service with the *Reichswehr*. However, its 50 hp engine was not powerful enough to propel the 6.8-ton vehicle. Later they tried to 'crossbreed' a 7.5 cm field gun with a 100 hp chassis, but it wasn't accepted for use either. Finally, in 1932 Germans ceased experimenting with self-propelled accompanying guns.

In 1935, Erich von Manstein – who was a colonel at that point in time – raised the issue of the need for mechanized accompanying guns. The well-known term of the 'assault artillery' *(Sturmartillerie)* originated with him, though the word itself is not a German 'invention'. In World War I, the French referred to heavy tanks employed to support their infantry as *l'artillerie d'assaut.* A year later Manstein worked out the principles of its employment. German ground forces backed the idea and, on 15 June 1936, they commissioned the development of a prototype assault gun.

Developed as a self-propelled 'accompanying gun' for the infantry, and manufactured with a short barrelled (L/24) 7.5 cm main armament that was very effective against personnel and field fortifications, the StuG. III assault gun was first employed in May 1940, during the western campaign. At that time the six-gun battery was the largest formation of these weapons. Eighteen combat vehicles were deployed in three batteries then, in mid-June, a fourth battery joined them with an additional six assault guns. In 1941, three assault gun battalions (each with three batteries of six guns) participated in the Balkans Campaign. Until 1943, German assault artillerymen were trained at Jüterbog near Berlin with *Artillerie-Lehr-Regiment 2 (mot.).* After that, work continued at Burg, near Magdeburg, at the so called assault-gun school.

Between 1940 and 1942, 826 StuG. IIIs were produced. These were equipped with the short-barrelled, 7.5 cm main gun (*Kampfwagenkanone 37 L/24*). However, to achieve a more effective anti-tank defence – due to the mass appearance of modern Soviet tanks – these assault vehicles were subsequently equipped with longer barrelled 7.5 cm guns (*L/43s* then *L/48s*) with higher armour penetration capabilities that enabled them to operate as self-propelled anti-tank reserves in combat focal points.

When Germany attacked the Soviet Union on 22 June 1941, its *Heer* (army) had 11 assault gun battalions and seven independent assault gun batteries. The assault gun units (each subordinated to a corps) effectively supported the German infantry during attacks, counterattacks and in defence but mostly provided 'back up' against the Soviet AFVs that usually appeared in superior numbers. Orders were issued to set up the staff of *Sturmgeschütz-Abteilung 202* on 29 August 1941. On 10 September 1941, the staff of *Sturmgeschütz-Abteilung 202* was formed at Jüterbog *(Wehrkreis III)* with three assault-gun batteries under its command.[1] The replacement unit became *Sturmgeschütz-Ersatz-Abteilung 200*[2] when it was relocated to Schweinfurt (*Wehrkreis VIII*).

Seven StuG. III assault guns made up a battery each of which consisted of the assault gun of the battery commander and six other guns divided equally into three platoons. Battalions were equipped with three batteries giving them a total complement of 21 assault guns. The battalion commanders led their assault guns from half-track armoured vehicles.

The period of time between raising the unit and its arrival in the theatre was unusually short (just three weeks) and it is therefore it is highly probable that the personnel of these units were assembled from officers, NCOs and enlisted men who had already undergone training as assault artillery troops. Consequently, after their transfer to *Sturmgeschütz-Abteilung 202*, there wasn't a lot more to be done in terms of training until their departure for the front line apart from developing team spirit and familiarising themselves with their vehicles by conducting exercises in different formations and practising live-fire manoeuvres.

1 The staff battery of *Sturmgeschütz-Abteilung* 202 was set up on 20 September 1941.

2 It was changed on 1 May 1942. From then on, *Sturmgeschütz-Ersatz-Abteilung 300,* located in Neisse, was tasked with the replacement of personnel.

In September 1941, units of the German *Heeresgruppe Mitte* (Army Group Centre) fighting in the area of Smolensk were significantly reinforced before the launch of Operation 'Typhoon' against Moscow in early October 1941. The assigned forces were rested and losses in equipment partly replaced. Infantry divisions with reduced strength were reinforced with heavy artillery and assault artillery guns. One of *Wehrmacht's* youngest assault artillery units, *Sturmgeschütz-Abteilung 202,* was ordered to join the attack without delay.

PART I

IN *HEERESGRUPPE MITTE*

CHAPTER 1

In the sector of the German *4. Armee* near Moscow

1941

Operational Background
Sturmgeschütz-Abteilung 202 was introduced under the command of the *4. Armee* into the sector of *Heeresgruppe Mitte*. It fought in the area south-west of Wjasma in October 1941 for the first time during Operation 'Typhoon'.

16 SEPTEMBER 1941

The German *Armeeoberkommando 4* informed the staff of *IX. Armeekorps* that transportation of *Sturmgeschütz-Abteilung 202* was to begin on 20 September 1941 and ordered it move from Jüterbog to Smolensk where it would be temporarily subordinated to the *IX. Armeekorps.*[3]

19 SEPTEMBER 1941

The headquarters of the *IX. Armeekorps* issued orders according to which the infantry divisions would receive support from the arriving assault gun battalion. Two-thirds of the unit were assigned to *183. Infanterie-Division,* but one battery was put under the corps' direct command.[4]

3 National Archives and Records Administration (Washington). Henceforward: NARA. T314, R406 (*IX. Armeekorps*), F000346.

4 NARA T315, R1416 (*137. Infanterie-Division*), F000264.

20 SEPTEMBER 1941

Sturmgeschütz-Abteilung 202 came under the command of *IX. Armeekorps.*[5]

22 SEPTEMBER1941

The staff of the *IX. Armeekorps* planned to subordinate the whole of *Sturmgeschütz-Abteilung 202*, which presumably began arriving from 25 September, to the *183. Infanterie-Division.*[6]

26 SEPTEMBER 1941

The *IX. Armeekorps* drew up plans for the deployment of the assault artillery battalion. According to the order of battle, which came into effect on 28 September, one assault gun battery would be attached to each of the *263.* and *292. Infanterie Divisionen* with the battalion staff and the remaining battery remaining subordinated to *183. Infanterie-Division.*[7]

27 SEPTEMBER 1941

At 1120 hours[8] the staff of *IX. Armeekorps* informed the *4. Armee* by telegram that the promised *Sturmgeschütz-Abteilung 202* (along with other army units) still hadn't arrived. However, the battalion commander reported to the corps that the transport of his unit was in progress.[9]

29 SEPTEMBER 1941

At 2202 hours, the *IX. Armeekorps reported* to the staff of the *4. Armee* that *Sturmgeschütz-Abteilung 202* had arrived in the sector of the corps.[10]

30 SEPTEMBER 1941

The batteries of the assault gun battalion finally arrived at the infantry divisions of *IX. Armeekorps.*[11] On the same day the *263. Infanterie-Division* issued orders for its own attack across the Ustrom River at 0630 hours on 3 October as part of Operation 'Typhoon'. According to this plan, its most important task was to contain the Soviet troops in positions facing them.

During the attack, the division's reinforced *Infanterie-Regiment 483* would advance to Hill 247.6 and Hill 260.7 north-west of Sadki, jumping off from the area of Mal. Tischowo North–Bossjawo public bridge in an easterly direction then

---

5 NARA T314, R409 (*IX. Armeekorps*), F000022.

6 NARA T315, R1416 (*137. Infanterie-Division*), F000329.

7 NARA T315, R1416 (*137. Infanterie-Division*), F000386.

8 Unless otherwise indicated, times and dates quoted according to the German documents are given in Berlin time and not in local time.

9 NARA T314, R406 (*IX. Armeekorps*), F000792.

10 NARA T312, R147 (*Armeeoberkommando 4*), 7686891.

11 NARA T314 R407 (*IX. Armeekorps*), F000482.

turning northwards, together with the *2. Batterie/Sturmgeschütz-Abteilung 202, III. Bataillon* and the regimental pioneer platoon of *Infanterie-Regiment 463, 1. Kompanie/Pionier-Bataillon 263,* and the *1. Kompanie / Panzerjäger-Abteilung 263.* The hill was to be reached by the group in one phase by taking advantage of terrain thickly overgrown with mountain pines.[12]

The staff and *1. Batterie* of the assault gun battalion waited for the order to launch the offensive operation under the command of *Infanterie-division 183* while *3. Batterie* was subordinated to *Infanterie-Division 292.*[13]

Infanterie Division 292 had already been advised of the detailed plan of the imminent offensive in a divisional order the day before, on 29 September. According to this, most of the *3. Batterie/Sturmgeschütz-Abteilung 202* was subordinated to *Infanterie-Regiment 508* and one section of the battery was put under the command of *Infanterie-Regiment 507.* The plan was for the assault gun battery to be brought forward across a bridge that would be built at Oserensk.[14]

1 OCTOBER 1941

According to an oral report submitted at 0650 hours by the adjutant of the assault gun *Abteilung,* the staff battery and the maintenance squad were stationed in the area of Metwedewa from 1300 hours. The advance message centre *(Meldekopf)* was set up at Rukino, in the corps' ammunition dump. In the evening the command post of *Sturmgeschütz-Abteilung 202* was located near the command post of *Infanterie-Division 183* in the western part of Berniki.[15]

3 OCTOBER 1941

At 0500 hours, the four divisions of *IX. Armeekorps*[16] launched their attack. The three infantry divisions (a total of nine battalions in the first echelon) attacking in the main direction along the 10 km frontline were supported by 50 artillery batteries and *Sturmgeschütz-Abteilung 202.*[17]

At night the assault guns were drawn forward to their jump-off positions so that they could participate in the attack in the area of Wjasma. The batteries of *Sturmgeschütz-Abteilung 202* assigned to the infantry divisions received orders to attack at daybreak. The AFVs rolled forward to open the way for the German infantry through the Soviet defence. However, in the sector of the *1. Batterie,* which was subordinated to *183. Infanterie-Division,* the German attack collapsed in an hour. By that time six out of the seven assault guns had struck mines and been had been

---

12 NARA T315, R1416 (*137. Infanterie-Division*), F000449.

13 NARA T315, R1416 (*137. Infanterie-Division*), F000458.

14 NARA T315, R1919 (*292. Infanterie-Division*), F000156.

15 NARA T314, R407 (*IX. Armeekorps*), F000482.

16 The forth division of *IX. Armeekorps, 137. Infanterie-Division* didn't receive any assault guns.

17 NARA T315, R1923 (*292. Infanterie-Division*), F000592.

disabled. None of the AFVs were destroyed, but their tracks and suspensions were damaged. *Oberleutnant* Hans-Gerhard Maurischat, platoon leader of *1. Batterie*, left to bring forward towing vehicles to rescue the immobilized assault guns, but disappeared in the area of Nowo Tischowo without a trace. Despite a thorough search, he was never found.[18]

By around noon, only one assault gun remained operational. Its commander was *Leutnant* Heise. However, by then the AFV had almost used up its ammunition. When the assault gun turned to collect more ammunition, a Soviet anti-tank gun fired on it from the edge of a nearby forest. The German assault gun then fired on the supposed Russian firing position with its last three shells which had been reserved to meet any unforeseen contingency. However the attempt failed: neither Heise (the commander of the assault gun) nor *Unteroffizier* Barth (the gunner), was able to spot the Soviet anti-tank gun. After a half-turn, the German assault gun started back on its quest to rearm but at that moment it was hit by a Russian shell that struck its armour with a deafening crash. The StuG was able to make it to a depression where nonetheless it became disabled. The Soviet anti-tank shell had damaged one of its road wheels and its track, which luckily for the crew only became detached after they had reached cover.

The first action of the other two batteries was equally unsuccessful. For example, the *2. Batterie* lost its commander and his entire crew, all of whom were killed by a direct hit.[19]

The assault guns of *Sturmgeschütz-Abteilung 202* had failed to provide the required support for the infantry. The attack was described in the war diary of the *292. Infanterie-Division*:

The attack is launched at 0530 hours. The infantry attacks with a great dash – the artillery fire is accurate. The attack is making progress despite the very stubborn resistance and the well-directed, violent Russian artillery fire, even though most of the assault guns strike mines or get stuck.[20]

4 OCTOBER 1941

Sturmgeschütz-Abteilung 202 had only four combat-ready assault guns left. These came under the command of *Leutnant* Heise, who was given the task of conducting reconnaissance with *Radfahr-Schwadron 219* (219 Bicycle Squadron) of the *183. Infanterie-Division* towards the division fighting on their left flank because a gap had opened up between them. The leader of the bicycle-squadron was *Rittmeister* Hans-Hermann Sachenbacher. *Leutnant* Heise recalled the action:

---

18 Kurowski, Franz – Tornau, Gottfried: *Sturmgeschütze – Die Panzer der Infanterie*. Würzburg, 2008. p. 76. The authors of the book cover the battles of *Sturmgeschütz-Abteilung 202* fought in October 1941 with a day's delay, compared to the data of contemporary operational documents. It has been corrected in the present text.

19 Kurowski, Franz – Tornau, Gottfried: *Sturmgeschütze – Die Panzer der Infanterie*. Würzburg, 2008. p. 76.

20 NARA T315, R1918 (*292. Infanterie-Division*), Kriegstagebuch Ia vom 3. Okt. 1941.

We fought our way forward a couple of hundred metres to high ground from where a wide view opened up. We recognised at once that this wasn't a 'no man's land' anymore. Russians were lying everywhere in the surrounding cornfields, masterfully camouflaged. It was extremely difficult to identify their machine-gun nests, not to mention their nasty mortars, which were impossible to hit most of the time. While we were busy cleaning up our immediate surroundings with fire, I received a radio message from Leutnant Sch., leader of the Second Platoon. He reported that the other assault gun had slipped into a Soviet trench along the total length of one of its tracks. The hull was trapped on the edge of the trench. Since I was fully aware of the difficulties of the required towing operation, I radioed him to wait till I could come to his aid. Because Rittmeister Sachenbacher had just informed me that he considered the mission accomplished and was pulling back his men, I asked him to stay and provide fire support for us while we recovered the stuck assault gun. Obviously he was not able to inform his men about this, because when I looked back shortly afterwards, I only saw the last helmets of his infantry disappearing far in the rear behind us.

Meanwhile Leutnant Sch. tried to tow out the assault gun with his own vehicle, but it too was trapped – just like the other one – two metres behind it. Neglecting our own defence I then had to pull out Leutnant Sch.'s gun with my second gun. The enemy fired at us with infantry weapons. We suffered casualties. When at last Leutnant Sch. broke free, he provided fire support for us with his gun. The group returned with the sad balance of several dead from this mission, at the end of which my own gun struck a mine, too![21]

5 OCTOBER 1941

At 0700 hours two infantry regiments *(Infanterie-Regimente 507* and *508)* of the *292. Infanterie-Division* received two assault guns each (supposedly repaired during the night) from *3. Batterie/Sturmgeschütz-Abteilung 202* for the attack planned to be launched in the morning across the area of Jelnja in a north-easterly direction.[22]

Infanterie-Regiment 508 advanced with two StuG. III assault guns. The regiment encountered minimal resistance and were soon fighting 1.5 km north-east of Leonidow. At the same time *Infanterie-Regiment 507* and two of its assault guns met considerable Soviet resistance in the area of Leonowo on Hill 236.1. The Hill was eventually taken at around 1400 hours because the '*Russians had to be smitten one by one in their foxholes*'.[23]

German pioneers cleared passages through a minefield allowing the assault guns from the *1. Batterie/Sturmgeschütz-Abteilung 202,* together with elements of

---

21 Kurowski, Franz – Tornau, Gottfried: *Sturmgeschütze – Die Panzer der Infanterie*. Würzburg, 2008. p. 77.

22 NARA T315, R1919 (*292. Infanterie-Division*), F000163-164.

23 NARA T315, R1918 (*292. Infanterie-Division*), Kriegstagebuch Ia vom 5. Okt. 1941.

183. Infanterie-Division to reach the railway north Jelnja. During this action, the German AFVs participated mainly in fighting down Soviet artillery batteries that had presented difficulties not only for the infantry but for the assault guns as well.

6 OCTOBER 1941

The *1. Batterie* of the assault gun battalion could deploy only two of its StuG. IIIs. Under the command of *Leutnant* Heise and *Leutnant* Pickert, they set off to seize Dorogobusch 30 km east of their position together with an advance detachment of the *183. Infanterie-Division.*

Following preparation by the 21 cm mortars of *Schwere Artillerie Bataillon 833* (833 Heavy Artillery Battalion), elements of *292. Infanterie-Division* took Jelnja at 0845 hours. If the *3. Batterie/Sturmgeschütz-Abteilung 202* still had combat-ready assault guns they too might have participated in capturing the town.[24]

7 OCTOBER 1941

Following the two assault guns of *Sturmgeschütz-Abteilung 202,* an advance detachment of *183. Infanterie-Division* (*Rittmeister* Sachenbacher's bicycle squadron), pressed forward, passing through a number of Soviet settlements without significant contact with the enemy. During their advance they encountered Soviet supply columns which they fired on and destroyed.

As the Germans pushed forward, 20 aircraft appeared in the sky above a settlement. Luckily for the German ground troops these were Ju 87 'Stuka' dive bombers. Having evidently seen the unfolded marking panels on the German assault vehicles they swung around in a wide circle before flying further to the east.

The two StuG. III assault guns were only 800 m from Dorogobusch when *Leutnant* Heise looked through his periscope binoculars and saw vehicles and throngs of enemy soldiers milling around in front of the settlement and a significant Soviet force retreating towards the town. However, the bicycle riflemen of the German advance infantry detachment had dropped behind leaving the assault guns without infantry support.

At around 1400 hours, the advance detachment of *183. Infanterie-Division* with the two assault guns of the *1. Batterie* at their head, broke into Dorogobusch before the main forces of *IX. Armeekorps* and, during continuous action, established a bridgehead on the north bank of the Dnieper. This bridgehead was successfully defended together with two bridges that had been captured intact despite the fact that Soviet troops were still fighting in the settlement (until the next morning).[25] *Leutnant* Heise wrote the following about the fighting:

24 NARA T315, R1923 (*292. Infanterie-Division*), F000592.

25 NARA T315, R1923 (*292. Infanterie-Division*), F000593.

My first thought was that I start at full throttle and take the entrance to the settlement by surprise. At that moment my loader reported: 'Herr Leutnant! We have almost no ammunition left!' I stopped to discuss the situation with my friend, Pickert, who stayed right behind me. The ammunition situation was no better with him. We had 20 shells altogether so a private action would have been too risky.

Meanwhile the Soviets had noticed us. The enemy set up an anti-aircraft battery at the entrance of the place in a hurry, and its guns were aimed at us. Using up some of our valuable shells we destroyed the battery while it was still unlimbering.

It soon it became clear to me that we had to exploit the confusion among the Russians. We had to dash forward or else the enemy would complete the establishment of its defensive position and our advance detachment would be too weak to breach that.

Following a brief check with my driver, Wachtmeister Frenzel, we headed for the settlement at full throttle behind an enemy column that turned away to the right, inside the locality. All at once indescribable confusion broke out. Russians were swarming around us, lurking behind house walls and hedges. I saw frightened faces but also fists grasping Molotov cocktails. It was clear to me that we mustn't stop for a moment. If the Russians found out that we were all by ourselves, we would be dead meat.

We fired our few remaining shells into the column ahead of us at point-blank range. That must have been a terrible shock to the enemy because they didn't even attempt to knock out Pickert's vehicle or my own, or shoot at us, as we stood in our the open entrance hatches.

Clanking and crashing, literally shooting our way clear, our two assault guns drove through the rubble. The street was more or less clear. It was then that I noticed a side road turning at right angles towards a valley and directly towards a long timber bridge. It had to be the bridge over the Dnieper, the upper reaches of which flowed through Dorogobusch. I abruptly turned in that direction because we needed to take that bridge while it was still undamaged!

A guard stood in the middle of the 100 m long bridge. Our shell – the last one, according to the report of the loader – swept him away. With butterflies in our stomachs we dashed across the bridge. Then we found ourselves alone, on the opposite bank of the Dnieper, discussing what to do. Meanwhile Leutnant Pickert had driven straight on. Obviously he hadn't noticed when we had turned.

Now we were attracting the fire of the Soviet infantry. Then we saw the enemy closing on us from the opposite bank of the river. 'Get the submachine guns out – one for the loader and the other for me!' I yelled.

We opened fire but both guns failed to feed after the first shots. They were covered with sand and had jammed. The same thing happened to my P08 pistol. Then a dozen egg-grenades came to our rescue. This is how we used them: we stuck our head out of the entrance hatch for a moment, then pulled it back; the enemy shot at us revealing his position. We threw the grenades in their direction, and gained a moment's peace.

The whole thing lasted for about 10 minutes, but for us it seemed an eternity. We could hardly wait for the bicycle riflemen to arrive. Before they showed up, a low-silhouetted vehicle appeared on the opposite bank of the Dnieper and raced across the bridge towards us at breakneck speed. We didn't believe our eyes – it was our ammunition vehicle. The driver had calculated that we must have run out of ammunition. Luckily enough they had been able to push their way through the Russian units despite their absurdly soft-shelled vehicle.

As we stacked our ammunition, we could hear the din of bicycle riflemen arriving at the entrance to the settlement, and see Pickert's gun. He had found us at last. He drove across the bridge and picked up his ammunition. After this we established radio-contact with Rittmeister Sachenbacher. The cyclists reached us and with this, Dorogobusch was ours.

Towards evening, the Russians tried once again to recapture Dorogobusch with artillery support. By the light of the burning houses the struggle for the town continued. By dawn, 7 October [correctly: 8 October (Author)], *the settlement was securely in our hands. For capturing Dorogobusch Rittmeister Sachenbacher was awarded the Knight's Cross of the Iron Cross. The crews of the assault guns were decorated with Iron Cross 1 Class.*[26]

8/9 OCTOBER 1941

Elements of *Infanterie-Regiment 509* were drawn into a savage woodland battle by the Soviet troops south of Potschinok in the sector of *Infanterie-Division 292.* The hard-pressed infantry were pulled out of the hole by the assault guns of the *3. Batterie/Sturmgeschütz-Abteilung 202.* Nevertheless, Soviet soldiers put up strenuous opposition, and fought skilfully.[27]

On 9 October, the staff of the *IX. Armeekorps* decided – based on the battle order that was about to come into force the following day – that the whole of *Sturmgeschütz-Abteilung 202* would operate under the command of *137. Infanterie-Division.*[28] The reason for this was that as from 10 October the *183. Infanterie-Division* would be detached from the corps and although the assault gun battalion had been supplied through the latter division till 11 October, from 12 October it was assigned to *137. Infanterie-Division.*[29]

During its attack covering the period 3 to 9 October 1941, the *IX. Armeekorps* clashed with elements of a total of 13 Soviet divisions. In the course of the fighting the forces of the German corps – besides others – took 20,908 prisoners and destroyed or captured 108 various guns and five AFVs. The Soviet AFVs fought exclusively in the sector of the *183. Infanterie-Division.*[30]

12 OCTOBER 1941

The Quartermaster General of the German Land Forces (*Heer*) issued a general order that applied to every assault gun unit in relation to requests for additional

---

26 Kurowski, Franz – Tornau, Gottfried: *Sturmgeschütze – Die Panzer der Infanterie.* Würzburg, 2008. pp. 77-78.

27 NARA T315, R1918 (*292. Infanterie-Division*), Kriegstagebuch Ia vom 8. Okt. 1941.

28 NARA T315, R1416 (*137. Infanterie-Division*), F000642.

29 NARA T314, R409 (*IX. Armeekorps*), F000423.

30 NARA T315, R1923 (*292. Infanterie-Division*), F000593.

assault guns. According to this order, the growing need for assault guns could only be partially covered by AFVs from the production lines and from repair. In such circumstances, the Quartermaster General emphasized again the importance of the recovery of assault guns knocked out or broken down, as well as their transport to the army tank equipment depot at Magdeburg–Königsborn, because the ability to provide additional vehicles decisively depended on this. Requests for the supply of assault guns had to be submitted to the Quartermaster General of the *Heer* in two copies that included the following content:

- The chassis number of the assault gun damaged or knocked out.
- The location of the assault gun damaged or knocked out (a sketch-map was requested in the case of unrecovered AFVs and in the case of recovered vehicles the location of the unit accommodating them).
- For assault guns already transported to the rear area, the place and time of their dispatch and the number transported.[31]

15 OCTOBER 1941

From noon, the assault gun battalion should have been allocated to the *268. Infanterie-Division,* subordinated to *IX. Armeekorps,* but it didn't come to that.[32] *Sturmgeschütz-Abteilung 202* was relieved from its assignment with *IX. Armeekorps* that morning and dispatched to the sector of the German *Panzerarmeekommando 2* together with other independent artillery units. The forces were to reach the area of Karatschew (40 km south-east of Brjansk) as soon as possible, following the Spass-Djemenskoje–Kirow–Brjansk route prescribed for them.[33]

31 NARA T314, R409 (*IX. Armeekorps*), F000443.

32 NARA T314, R409 (*IX. Armeekorps*), F000602-604.

33 NARA T314, R406 (*IX. Armeekorps*), F001062.

CHAPTER 2

In the Sector of the German *2. Panzerarmee*, in the area of Orel, Tula and Bolchow 1941

Operational Background:
From the second half of October 1941, Sturmgeschütz-Abteilung 202 fought in the southern foreground of Orel then, from early November, they were operating south-west of Tula under the command of the 2. Panzerarmee in the German offensive against Moscow. The assault gun unit was driven back into the area of Bolchow during the counter-offensive launched by the Soviet Red Army on 5 December, 1941.

18 OCTOBER 1941

Shortly before midnight, *Panzerarmeekommando 2* (the command of the 2 Panzer Army) informed the staff of *XXXXVII. Panzerkorps* by telephone, that *Sturmgeschütz-Abteilung 202* had arrived to Orel and had been subordinated to the corps, together with other units. There was a good reason for that: the *XXXXVII. Panzerkorps* had been assigned the task of launching an attack on Fatesh from a northerly direction with the available forces of the *18. Panzer-Division* (without *Panzer-Regiment 18).* because one of the armoured divisions of *XXXXVIII. Panzerkorps* had been halted by Soviet counter-attacks and needed help to reach the Kursk–Kromy highway.[34] The assault gun battalion was needed to compensate for the lack of tanks.

19 OCTOBER 1941

The plan for the attack was drafted by the staff of the *XXXX. Panzerkorps* according to which, jumping off from the area of Karatschew, a motorcycle rifle battalion, a towed artillery battalion, an armoured pioneer company, a tank destroyer company and an anti-aircraft artillery battery of the *18. Panzer-Division* would launch an attack through the area of Kromy, along the road to Fatesh the following day. As an enforcement, the *II. Bataillon/ schwere Artillerie-Regiment 71* (with 15 cm field howitzers and 10 cm field guns), the *III. Bataillon* of the motorized *Infanterie-Regiment 60,* the whole of *Sturmgeschütz-Abteilung 202* plus a bridge column were subordinated to the division.[35]

---

34 NARA T314, R1100 (*XXXXVII. Panzerkorps*), F000113.

35 NARA T314, R1100 (*XXXXVII. Panzerkorps*), F000115.

21 OCTOBER 1941

The *18. Panzer-Division* finally commenced its attack on Fatesh. From 1745 hours the town was shelled by the artillery of the German division.[36]

22 OCTOBER 1941

German troops together with the assault guns of *Sturmgeschütz-Abteilung 202* took the town of Fatesh. The forces of the *18. Panzer-Division* and the StuG. III assault guns clashed with elements of the Soviet 29 Cavalry Division, the 38 Motorcycle Regiment and the AFVs of the 133 Tank Brigade. According to their reports, the Germans destroyed nine Soviet heavy tanks during the fighting. During the night, four more Soviet AFVs were reported as destroyed; two had been hit by StuG. III assault guns after nightfall and another two had struck mines.[37] The Germans reported a total of 18 AFVs destroyed (15 of them heavy AFVs) and the capture of 110 POWs and 30 motorcycles [38] in the course of occupying the town and mopping up the surrounding area.

23 OCTOBER 1941

Part of the assault gun battalion moved back from the area of a bridge being built as a substitute for one that had been blown up in the northern part of Fatesh at around 1010 hours.[39]

26 OCTOBER 1941

The assault gun battalion was subordinated to *2. Panzerarmee* in theory, but practically it hadn't yet been relieved from assignment with the *XXXXVII. Panzerkorps.*[40]

3 NOVEMBER 1941

At 1445 hours, the *LIII. Armeekorps* made a request by telegram to the headquarters of the *2. Panzerarmee* for, amongst things, an assault gun battalion to be subordinated to them. The operational staff officer of the corps made this request because the corps, which formed the southern flank of the army, was fighting along vital railroads that would undoubtedly be employed by the Soviets to deploy new formations to get behind the southern (right) flank of the army which was without artillery cover. Should this happen, the horse-drawn artillery of the subordinate infantry divisions would not be able to intervene because they had been immobilized by the poor condition of the roads. To this end, the assault artillery was badly needed.[41] At

36 NARA T315, R710 (*18. Panzer-Division*), F001060.

37 NARA T315, R710 (*18. Panzer-Division*), F001060.

38 NARA T314, R1100 (*XXXXVII. Panzerkorps*), F000127.

39 NARA T315, R710 (*18. Panzer-Division*), F000042.

40 NARA T314, R1312 (*LIII. Armeekorps*), F000017.

41 NARA T314, R1311 (*LIII. Armeekorps*), F001032.

2315 hours the HQ of the *2. Panzerarmee* informed the staff of *LIII. Armeekorps* by telephone that the assault-gun unit under the command of *18. Panzer-Division* – stationed in Orel at that time – had been subordinated to the corps.[42]

4 NOVEMBER 1941

Sturmgeschütz-Abteilung 202 was relieved from its assignment with the *XXXXVII. Panzerkorps* and attached to *LIII. Armeekorps.*[43] At 1900 hours the latter corps informed *167. Infanterie-Division* by telegram that it had already received one of the batteries of the assault-gun battalion.[44] That battery was stationed in Tschern at that time and under the direct command of the division commander who was allowed to deploy the assault guns only in an emergency.[45]

5 NOVEMBER 1941

The *LIII. Armeekorps* issued orders according to which the assault gun battalion (without its *1. Batterie* which was subordinated to *167. Infanterie-Division*) should temporarily remain in corps reserve in Plawsk, though it was planned to deploy it later in the sector of *112. Infanterie-Division.*[46]

The *1. Batterie* meanwhile, under the direct command of the *167. Infanterie-Division*, was to be used in the focal point of the attack by the division's infantry – a matter in which even the artillery commander of the corps did not have a voice.[47]

6 NOVEMBER 1941

The representative of the commander of *Sturmgeschütz-Abteilung 202* received the mission of observing routes of march for a possible deployment around Teploje, as well as to provide direct security to Plawsk.[48]

Until the 11 November 1941, the assault gun battalion fought defensive battles in the area south-east of Plawsk and took part in the destruction of the Soviet troops encircled there.[49]

The commander of the *LIII. Armeekorps, General der Infanterie* Karl Weisenberger, visited the commander of the *112. Infanterie-Division* and proposed deploying *Sturmgeschütz-Abteilung 202* in the focal point of the division's infantry.[50]

---

42 NARA T314, R1310 (*LIII. Armeekorps*), F000422.

43 NARA T314, R1100 (*XXXXVII. Panzerkorps*), F000147. In contrast, according to the documents of *LIII. Armeekorps* the shift in subordination had already taken place by 3 November 1941. NARA T314, R1312 (*LIII. Armeekorps*), F000808.

44 NARA T314, R1310 (*LIII. Armeekorps*), F000424.

45 NARA T314, R1311 (*LIII. Armeekorps*), F000695.

46 NARA T314, R1311 (*LIII. Armeekorps*), F000694.

47 NARA T314, R1313 (*LIII. Armeekorps*), F000226 and T315, R1477 (*167. Infanterie-Division*), F000827.

48 NARA T314, R1310 (*LIII. Armeekorps*), F000434.

49 NARA T314, R1310 (*LIII. Armeekorps*), F000032.

50 NARA T314, R1313 (*LIII. Armeekorps*), F000221.

7 NOVEMBER 1941

General der Infanterie Karl Weisenberger visited the commander of the *167. Infanterie-Division,* who wanted to attach the *1. Batterie/Sturmgeschütz-Abteilung 202* – subordinated to the division at that time – to *Infanterie-Regiment 331* for the next day's attack which was to be launched from the area of Wassiljewskaja towards Bororodizkoje. A *Leutnant* from the battery reported that they had only two combat-ready assault guns at that moment but that two more would be operational by the next morning.[51]

However, the war diary of the *167. Infanterie-Division* recorded at 1715 hours shows that the *1. Batterie*, subordinated to the division, was still not deployable because only two of the six assault guns had so far arrived at Roshestwenno. Moreover, even those two StuG. IIIs were in need of repairs due to technical defects.[52]

After nightfall, a total of three assault guns of the battery were operational and these were attached to *Infanterie-Regiment 331* for deployment, on the right flank of the regiment, at the focal point of the attack.[53]

For the next day's attack a battery was relieved from its assignment with *Sturmgeschütz-Abteilung 202* and attached to *Infanterie-Regiment 339.*[54]

According to the war diary of the *167. Infanterie-Division*, the *2.* and *3. Batterien* of the assault gun battalion were subordinated to the division in the evening.[55]

8 NOVEMBER 1941

At 0700 hours the aforementioned bridge collapsed under one of the three assault guns and it fell into the Plawa River. This forced the other two assault guns to cross the river through a ford a little further to the north, at Ostrowki. Due to the accident, the assault guns were now to be deployed not on the right flank of the infantry regiment but on the left. The regiment launched the attack at 0830 hours, and the infantry – with the support of the two assault guns – took Oserki Nishnije at around 1100 hours.[56] Following that *Leutnant* Heise encircled Teploje with two StuG. III assault guns and two infantry companies.[57]

Fresh units from two Soviet rifle divisions[58], brought up to full strength, launched a forceful attack on the troops of the *167. Infanterie-Division* south of Nowosselki,

---

51 NARA T314, R1313 (*LIII. Armeekorps*), F000218.

52 NARA T315, R1477 (*167. Infanterie-Division*), F000832.

53 NARA T315, R1477 (*167. Infanterie-Division*), F000833.

54 NARA T315, R1477 (*167. Infanterie-Division*), F000833.

55 NARA T315, R1477 (*167. Infanterie-Division*), F000837.

56 NARA T315, R1477 (*167. Infanterie-Division*), F000833.

57 On the night from 10 to 11 November, the Soviet troops ceased their attacks on the encircled German battle group. One of the gun commanders was killed in action. Horst Kudicke, a war correspondent from the *Luftwaffe,* joined the assault guns in action. He replaced the loader in *Leutnant* Heise's AFV, and proved himself worthy of the task. *See* Kurowski, Franz – Tornau, Gottfried: *Sturmgeschütze – Die Panzer der Infanterie.* Würzburg, 2008. p. 79.

58 According to data obtained by German reconnaissance, those were the 6 Guards- and 283 Rifle Divisions. In the course of the interrogation of the POWs, the Germans were told that there were also '25-ton' tanks subordinated to the 6 Guards-Rifle Division (probably from an independent tank brigade that was assigned to them). Soviet tanks are distinguished by weight in German reports of the first months of the campaign against the Soviet Union. The T-34 tanks were designated as '26-ton' tanks.

along the railroad. The commander of *Sturmgeschütz-Abteilung 202, Hauptmann* Marder, reported the following to the *LIII. Armeekorps* at 1915 hours:

The enemy is very stout and gives the impression of being impeccable. Russians obviously use tanks as guns. Battle is fierce at the railway-embankment.[59]

Forces of the *LIII. Armeekorps* reported 10 Soviet AFVs knocked out or captured.[60] More were knocked out by assault guns. At 2015 hours, the *167. Infanterie-Division* gave orders by radio to *Infanterie-Regiment 315* to launch an attack from Pokrowskoje towards Sergejewka the following day with its forces arranged in echelon to the right. For this mission one battery (six assault guns) of *Sturmgeschütz-Abteilung 202* was subordinated to the regiment.[61]

9 NOVEMBER 1941

The Soviets continued their attack on the *167. Infanterie-Division.* At 0730 hours the assault guns of *Sturmgeschütz-Abteilung 202* arrived at the division command post and were dispatched to *Infanterie-Regiment 315.*

The regiment was to attack from Pokrowskoje area in a north-easterly direction. At 1530 hours the infantry division reported that its infantry regiment had taken the small forest north-east of Pokrowskoje and had observed Soviet AFVs south-east of the settlement. This prompted the division's commander to order *Infanterie-Regiment 315* to stop in the sector they had reached and to take and hold the sector Pokrowskoje–small forest–Sergejewka–2.5 km west. However *Sturmgeschütz-Abteilung 202* – which had been tasked with providing support – had only eight combat-ready StuG. III assault guns left.[62]

At 1750 hours, *Hauptmann* Marder reported to the corps that his assault guns would stay ahead of the infantry and about 300 m behind the main combat line for the night.[63] The drivers slept in their vehicles.[64]

In the day's fighting, *Leutnant der Reserve* Schneider, a platoon leader of the assault gun unit, was killed in action and *Hauptmann* Meißner, a battery commander, was wounded.[65]

Sturmgeschütz-Abteilung 202 was not the only formation equipped with AFVs that had been subordinated to *LIII. Armeekorps* that day. In the two armoured

59 NARA T314, R1310 (*LIII. Armeekorps*), F000448.
60 NARA T314, R1311 (*LIII. Armeekorps*), F000669.
61 NARA T315, R1477 (*167. Infanterie-Division*), F000836.
62 NARA T314, R1310 (*LIII. Armeekorps*), F000452.
63 NARA T314, R1310 (*LIII. Armeekorps*), F000454.
64 NARA T315, R1479 (*167. Infanterie-Division*), F000375.
65 NARA T313, R108 (*Panzerarmeeoberkommando 2*), F7352704.

regiments of *Panzer-Brigade 5* there were a total of nine Panzer IIs, 31 Panzer IIIs and six Panzer IVs in combat-ready condition.[66]

At 2350 hours *Panzer-Regiment 18* received orders from the corps to assemble in the area of Kondyrjowka and to refuel its AFVs at the supply base of *Sturmgeschütz-Abteilung 202,* which was subordinated to *112. Infanterie-Division.*[67]

10 NOVEMBER 1941

The right flank of *Infanterie-Regiment 315* launched an attack at 0700 hours with the support of the assault guns of *Sturmgeschütz-Abteilung 202.* It soon it became apparent that the southern flank of the *112. Infanterie-Division* in the area of Mochowaja was threatened by three newly arrived Soviet cavalry regiments. Because of this, *I. Bataillon* of the infantry regiment was ordered there.[68]

11 NOVEMBER 1941

Elements of *Sturmgeschütz-Abteilung 202* (with 12 assault guns) in cooperation with the forces of the strengthened *Infanterie-Regiment 331/167. Infanterie-Division,* annihilated the 107 Cavalry Regiment of the Soviet 29 Cavalry Division during their vigorous advance in Nikitinskoje area. During the battle the Germans took 400 POWs, captured eight guns, and shot a Soviet political officer (commissar) dead.[69]

In the course of the attack *Leutnant* Heise drove his assault gun immediately behind that of his battery commander who advanced at the point of the *Kampfgruppe* (battle group). The leading assault gun stirred up the powder snow reducing the visibility for those travelling behind. *Leutnant* Heise's StuG caught up with the leading AFV from the left so that he could see more clearly. He recalled this mission as follows:

Getting a clear view, I soon became aware of a closed settlement about 1 km from us. It had to be Nikitinskoje if the map was reliable. I wondered why my battery commander wasn't heading there – instead, he was sweeping round the settlement to the left. A little later I asked him if we weren't moving in the wrong direction. We stopped and soon we realized that we had gone around Nikitinskoje. My battery commander, seeing me overtaking him on the left, thought that I knew the area better and wanted to take the lead. So he followed me to the left, and I, trying to keep the distance needed, came more and more to the left, and by so doing, the whole Kampfgruppe moved in the wrong direction.

So then we turned right and rolled towards Nikitinskoje at high speed from an entirely different direction from the one we had planned. We fanned out as we approached the place and launched our attack on the partly abandoned positions. We were able to

66 NARA T314, R1312 (*LIII. Armeekorps*), F000016.

67 NARA T314, R1310 (*LIII. Armeekorps*), F000456.

68 NARA T315, R1477 (*167. Infanterie-Division*), F000838.

69 NARA T314, R1312 (*LIII. Armeekorps*), F000732.

capture almost the whole enemy formation together with their horses and heavy weapons without suffering any casualties. Only a few of them managed to escape on horseback.[70]

The Cossack unit was alarmed but when they saw that the *Kampfgruppe* had passed the settlement the alarm was called off. Due to that, even the commander of the cavalry regiment fell into German captivity.

The assault guns participating in the attack were withdrawn to the supply base of *Sturmgeschütz-Abteilung 202* in Roshestwenno after 2100 hours to draw ammunition and refuel their AFVs.[71]

The assault gun-formation knocked out six of the twelve Soviet medium tanks destroyed between 6 and 11 November 1941 in the sector of the *167. Infanterie-Division.*[72]

12 NOVEMBER 1941

The assault guns of *Sturmgeschütz-Abteilung 202* knocked out another '25-ton' Soviet tank in the sector of *167. Infanterie-Division* (presumably in the area of Nikitskoje).[73]

The assault gun unit continued to pursue the Soviet troops until 26 November, finally encircling them in the area of Bogorodizk–Jepifan–Stalinogorsk.[74]

During the day the assault-gun battalion came under the direct command of the corps but after discussions between the division commander and *Hauptmann* Marder certain assault gun platoons remained with the units of *167. Infanterie-Division.*[75]

13 NOVEMBER 1941

Most of *Sturmgeschütz-Abteilung 202* (without the *Kampfgruppe* subordinated to *167. Infanterie-Division*) was stationed temporarily at Plawsk.[76] Only five assault guns under the command of *Oberleutnant* Lechens remained with the infantry division.[77] In accordance with the day's orders issued by the *167. Infanterie-Division,* the five assault guns remained in Roshestwenno for maintenance work in preparation for their move to the area of Ogarewo on 15 November.[78]

15 NOVEMBER 1941

In the evening elements of the *112. Infanterie-Division* were fighting in the middle of Bogorodizk. One battery (probably the *3.*) of *Sturmgeschütz-Abteilung 202* was

70 See Kurowski, Franz – Tornau, Gottfried: *Sturmgeschütze – Die Panzer der Infanterie.* Würzburg, 2008. p. 79.

71 NARA T315, R1479 (*167. Infanterie-Division*), F000383.

72 NARA T315, R1479 (*167. Infanterie-Division*), F000386.

73 NARA T314, R1312 (*LIII. Armeekorps*), F000725.

74 NARA T314, R1310 (*LIII. Armeekorps*), F000032.

75 NARA T314, R1311 (*LIII. Armeekorps*), F000683.

76 NARA T314, R1311 (*LIII. Armeekorps*), F000668.

77 NARA T315, R1477 (*167. Infanterie-Division*), F000845.

78 NARA T315, R1479 (*167. Infanterie-Division*), F000379.

sent to the southern exit of the settlement through Lomowka, and from midnight it was attached to that infantry division.[79]

The staff of the *167. Infanterie-Division* subordinated another battery (probably that of *Kampfgruppe 'Lechens'*) with five assault guns to *Infanterie-Regiment 315* and ordered them to arrive at the division command post in Nowowoskressenskoje by 0730 hours.[80]

17 NOVEMBER 1941

To support the attack of the reinforced *Infanterie-Regiment 33* on Nikitskoje, the staff of the *167. Infanterie-Division* attached three assault guns of *Sturmgeschütz-Abteilung 202* to the regiment. They were to move out from Lewino at 0600 hours and then report to the commander of the *II. Bataillon/ Infanterie-Regiment 331*.[81]

In the sector of the *112. Infanterie-Division*, the *3. Batterie* of the arriving assault-gun unit was promised to *Infanterie-Regiment 110* at 1345 hours.[82]

18 NOVEMBER 1941

At 2100 hours the assault guns in the rear were brought forward to the sector of the *167. Infanterie-Division* because there were only two combat-ready AFVs left with *Infanterie-Regiment 315*. Ammunition supply for the assault guns arrived at Gorbartschewo.[83]

Leutnant Vetter from the *3. Batterie/Sturmgeschütz-Abteilung 202* reported the following in his dispatch about the day's fighting in the sector of the *112. Infanterie-Division:*

I arrived at around 1530 hours on 18 November 1941 with three combat-ready assault guns at the III. Bataillon of Infanterie-Regiment 110 (Leutnant von Gammingen), north of Iwanowskoje. I was immediately briefed by Hauptmann Meißner and I joined the attack that was launched from a narrow valley. The gun of Oberwachtmeister Schramm failed to fire after the first shots because, due to decreased air pressure, the barrel was unable to recoil in its cradle. Wachtmeister Pirklbauer and I supported the infantry attack that was to be carried out on a hill in front of us. We shelled the Russian infantry and machine-gun nests from 100–300 metres. It was marvellous how little influence our fire had on the Russian infantry. Despite the effect of the fire of our machine guns, mortars and guns, the Russian infantry was closing on us, unfaltering. In the thickening darkness the attack was brought to a halt. The guns were withdrawn to the jump off position next to a kolkhoz [collective farm] *and we were set the task of securing it.*[84]

---

79 NARA T314, R1310 (*LIII. Armeekorps*), F000478.

80 NARA T315, R1479 (*167. Infanterie-Division*), F000402.

81 NARA T315, R1479 (*167. Infanterie-Division*), F000409.

82 NARA T315, R1269 (*112. Infanterie-Division*), F000671.

83 NARA T314, R1310 (*LIII. Armeekorps*), F000490.

84 NARA T314, R1313 (*LIII. Armeekorps*), F000374.

According to the war diary of the *112. Infanterie-Division*, *Leutnant* Vetter reported to the staff of the division at 1830 hours that he used his only combat-ready assault gun in the gap between *Infanterie-Regiment 110* and *Infanterie-Regiment 256* to cover the interface of the two regiments.[85]

19 NOVEMBER 1941

The elements of the assault gun battalion that had not been subordinated to the divisions were stationed at Bogorodizk under the command of the *LIII. Armeekorps.*[86]

However, the *3. Batterie/Sturmgeschütz-Abteilung 202* was still fighting in the sector of the *112. Infanterie-Division:*

On 19/11/1941 we were subordinated to Infanterie-Regiment 256, and received the mission of accompanying the assault there. On the way, one of the assault guns suffered track damage and the other two, soon after the infantry launched their attack, were bogged down in the marshy terrain. In the afternoon the assault gun with the track damage was brought forward (by Wachtmeister Pirklbauer) to the infantry and deployed there. On the same afternoon, three prime movers were placed at our service from Mörser-Abteilung 735[87] *for our attempts to recover the stuck assault guns. One of the guns could be partly pulled out but our recovery efforts proved unsuccessful.*[88]

Having had its track damage repaired, the lone assault gun knocked out a Soviet AFV in the sector of *Infanterie-Regiment 256*, in the area of Weljminowa, at around 1400 hours.[89]

20 NOVEMBER 1941

Of the five assault guns of *Kampfgruppe 'Lechens'* deployed in the sector of the *167. Infanterie-Division,* three were allocated to *Infanterie-Regiment 339* to support its attack. The other two remained subordinated to *Infanterie-Regiment 315.*[90]

Infanterie-Regiment 339 launched its attack at 1010 hours towards Krutaja with the support of the assault guns of *Sturmgeschütz-Abteilung 202*. Soviet resistance was encountered for the first time 1.5 km south of the settlement at 1150 hours. The Germans reached the outskirts of the village but their attack was halted there by Soviet mortar and machine-gun fire. At 1330 hours, following an effective artillery preparation, the Germans resumed their attack and, with the support of three StuG. III assault guns, they broke into Krutaja at around 1400 hours.

---

85 NARA T315, R1269 (*112. Infanterie-Division*), F000679.

86 NARA T314, R1311 (*LIII. Armeekorps*), F000649.

87 Correctly: *schwere Artillerie-Abteilung 735.*

88 NARA T314, R1313 (*LIII. Armeekorps*), F000374.

89 NARA T315, R1269 (*112. Infanterie-Division*), F000685.

90 NARA T315, R1479 (*167. Infanterie-Division*), F000414.

The vicious battle lasted until 2000 hours. The Germans suffered 333 dead and 104 wounded.[91]

At *Infanterie-Regiment 315,* only one assault gun remained available to carry out tasks the following day.[92]

The *3. Batterie,* attached to the *112. Infanterie-Division,* was still to meet its trials. *Leutnant* Vetter's dispatch read:

The towing vehicles of the Mörser-Abteilung should have been put at our disposal for the recovery attempts but were retained instead on the corps' orders. I kept on trying to recover our vehicles with the pioneers of the infantry and with my men. On that day Oberwachtmeister Schramm went on the mission instead of Wachtmeister Pirklbauer. I placed guards next to the guns that had been bogged down. At around 1800 hours I reported to the command post of Infanterie-Regiment 256 to be briefed about the situation. I was informed that the Russians had attacked our infantry positions with strong forces but the positions were still held. After an hour I observed that white flares[93] *streaking across the sky were quickly drawing nearer to us. I joined my assault guns and ordered them to load the radio sets and all demountable equipment onto the field kitchen and the ammunition trailers, and to move off in the direction of Iwanowskoje under the command of Wachtmeister Ring. The field kitchen received enemy machine-gun fire as soon as it started off. I stayed with my men at the gun and provided cover. My gun was set up between the eastern exit from Kuliski and the western exit from Mal. Jemanowka, in a ravine. Everything had been silent so far.*

I stopped some infantrymen who arrived at my gun from Jemanowka and asked them about the situation. They told us that they had been at Jegorjewskoje with the I. Bataillon when the Russian attack was launched. Russians came hard and fast. There was an enormous artillery preparation prior to the attack and murderous heavy machine-gun fire all the while, so the few men of our side were unable to stand their ground in the face of the attack. They had to leave about 30 wounded behind when they crawled out from a barn and broke through to us by a round-about route after nightfall.

We were running short of ammunition. We were a bit loud while talking, and from the west part of Mal.Jemanowka, from a kolkhoz about 150 m away, an anti-tank gun opened fire at us. Upon that we retreated towards Koliski. The Russians didn't let us alone all through the way there. I found more infantrymen from the I. Bataillon, who arrived rather confused, and I sent them to the regimental command post.

I moved behind the houses with my men, parallel to the direction to the command post. On the way, I met some officers from the regiment who tried to flock the foot soldiers together. Oberstleutnant von Dobinick, commander of Infanterie-Regiment 256, ordered

91 NARA T315, R1477 (*167. Infanterie-Division*), F000856.

92 NARA T315, R1479 (*167. Infanterie-Division*), F000420.

93 The German troops indicated the position of their forces by the use of flares.

the soldiers to stand in line and had them counted. Finally, the soldiers had to line up according to their respective companies and battalions. Having ordered them to form a U-shape around himself, the Oberstleutnant called their attention to the graveness of the situation. He made clear that we had to retreat, but we also had to prevent the Russians from any further advance by any means. To this end, the artillery took up positions with two batteries in front of the houses to deliver direct fire on the enemy. The infantry present would be deployed to defend the settlement which was to be held under any circumstances. Should they fail, he said, it would be a shameful memory for all of us. Finally, the Oberstleutnant issued the order that the settlement had to be defended. The infantrymen's ammunition was supplemented from the artillery's stock and infantry soldiers were deployed to defend the settlement. I was assigned to the commander of the staff company with my men and took over the task of providing cover in its sector.

The Russians ceased their attacks for the night. The commander's calm and thoughtful style and exemplary attitude gave new vigour and purpose to the soldiers. At the decisive moment, he assembled the remains of the infantry that had been forced to retreat in panic from the gang of greedy marauders that afternoon and early evening, leaving some anti-tank guns, a light infantry gun, a heavy infantry gun and a lot of heavy machine guns behind.[94]

According to the war diary of the *112. Infanterie-Division,* not long before 1400 hours, two more assault guns of *Sturmgeschütz-Abteilung 202* were held in divisional reserve in the area of Iwanowskoje together with the *II. Bataillon / Infanterie-Regiment 258* and elements of *Panzerjäger-Abteilung 112.*[95]

By evening, with the support of just one assault gun, the *II. Bataillon/Infanterie-Regiment 258* had seized and held the hill in the north-eastern foreground of a kolkhoz 2 km north-east of Iwanowskoje.[96]

21 NOVEMBER 1941

In the early morning the assault guns of the *3. Batterie/Sturmgeschütz-Abteilungen 202,* became trapped in the mud but had not been secured. *Leutnant* Vetter wrote in his dispatch:

On 21 November 1941, in the early morning hours, I started off on the road to Iwanovskoje to meet Herr Hauptmann Meißner who was supposed to arrive with a towing vehicle to recover the assault guns and to take the recovery vehicle to the guns by a roundabout route to hide it from the eyes of the Russians. I couldn't catch sight of the recovery vehicle but at around 0730 I met Hauptmann Meißner to whom I reported the critical situation. The Russians tried to press forward that day but our

94 NARA T314, R1313 (*LIII. Armeekorps*), F000374-375.

95 NARA T315, R1269 (*112. Infanterie-Division*), F000693.

96 NARA T315, R1269 (*112. Infanterie-Division*), F000695.

artillery used ricochet-fire against them so wonderfully that they gave up all desire for further advance. However they still occupied the hill to the north and from there they shot towards Kuliski with mortars and towards Iwanowskoje with even heavier calibre guns. We had to give up our recovery attempts because our recovery equipment was insufficient.[97]

The commander of the *LIII. Armeekorps, General der Infanterie* Weisenberger, visiting command post of the *112. Infanterie-Division,* pointed out:

> […] *assault guns assigned to the division and dropped out* [of battle] *must be recovered and towed away. The assault guns must be prevented from falling into the hands of the enemy.*[98]

23 NOVEMBER 1941

Three assault guns of the assault-artillery unit of *Kampfgruppe 'Lechens'* received orders to be in the area of Kamenzy by 0930 hours where they would be subordinated to *Infanterie-Regiment 315.*[99]

Later, the assault guns provided support for the elements of *Infanterie-Regiment 339* during their successful attack to take Urwanki. The infantry, together with the assault guns, were soon halted and withdrawn because the *112. Infanterie-Division* did not join in the successful advance. However, the staff of the *167. Infanterie-Division* only became aware of this when *Oberleutnant* Lechens reported the matter to them in the evening.[100]

At 1540 hours, the *112. Infanterie-Division* informed the staff of the *LIII. Armeekorps* that the attack it had planned to carry out in the direction of Donskoj railway station could not be launched for the time being because there were Soviet snipers operating in the surrounding industrial area and there was only one combat-ready assault gun left under the division's command.[101] This assault gun was fighting with the *II. Bataillon/Infanterie-Regiment 258* at an industrial plant 1 km south-east of Wassiljewskaja at around 1640 hours then, at 1755 hours, it intervened at Hill 113.3. At 1900 hours *Infanterie-Regiment 258* reported that its *II. Bataillon* – with the decisive help from the assault gun – had taken the plant.[102]

97 NARA T314, R1313 (*LIII. Armeekorps*), F000375.
98 NARA T314, R1313 (*LIII. Armeekorps*), F000204.
99 NARA T315, R1479 (*167. Infanterie-Division*), F000445.
100 NARA T315, R1477 (*167. Infanterie-Division*), F000862.
101 NARA T315, R1269 (*112. Infanterie-Division*), F000713.
102 NARA T315, R1269 (*112. Infanterie-Division*), F000715.

24 NOVEMBER 1941

Sturmgeschütz-Abteilung 202 submitted a request to the corps to withdraw all of its assault guns from the front line because they were inoperable without ice cleats installed on their tracks.[103]

Elements of the assault gun battalion unsubordinated to the divisions were still located in Bogorodizk.[104] At 0045 hours, in the sector of the *112. Infanterie-Division, Infanterie-Regiment 258* was given the task, together with the subordinated assault-gun battery of *Sturmgeschütz-Abteilung 202,* of joining the attack of *167. Infanterie-Division* that was to launched at 0900 hours with the aim of seizing the hills 1.5 km north-east of Wassiljewskaja.[105] The war diary of the infantry division recorded:

Shortage of assault guns, dropped out due to the lack of ice-cleats and maintenance in the workshops.[106]

25 NOVEMBER 1941

At this point in time there were only three assault guns left in each of the three batteries of *Sturmgeschütz-Abteilung 202.*[107]

In the recent battles, the infantry that the assault guns had supported had also sustained significant losses. For example, the combat strength of the rifle companies of *167. Infanterie-Division* amounted to, on average, about 52 men and the rifle divisions of the *112. Infanterie-Division* had been reduced to around just 33 soldiers.[108]

27 NOVEMBER 1971

From 27 November until 5 December 1941, the assault gun battalion fought in the battle of Tula and participated in the drive towards Rjasan and Kashira.[109]

On the first day, five StuG. III assault guns of *Sturmgeschütz-Abteilung 202* provided support for *Infanterie-Regiment 339* in the sector of the *167. Infanterie-Division* in the battle for Olchowez. Deployable elements of the regiment were assembled into assault squads (with at least 20 infantrymen per assault gun).[110] Following a short artillery preparation, the settlement went into German hands at around 1400 hours. German forces took at least 200 prisoners inside the settlement and an additional 500 prisoners in its vicinity. They also captured, among other items, 15 medium and light AFVs.[111]

103 NARA T314, R1310 (*LIII. Armeekorps*), F000510.
104 NARA T314, R1311 (*LIII. Armeekorps*), F000637.
105 NARA T315, R1269 (*112. Infanterie-Division*), F000717.
106 NARA T315, R1269 (*112. Infanterie-Division*), F000721.
107 NARA T314, R1312 (*LIII. Armeekorps*), F000013.
108 NARA T314, R1312 (*LIII. Armeekorps*), F001347.
109 NARA T314, R1310 (*LIII. Armeekorps*), F000032.
110 NARA T315, R1479 (*167. Infanterie-Division*), F000458.
111 NARA T314, R1312 (*LIII. Armeekorps*), F001333.

The corps called the attention of its subordinate infantry divisions to the special circumstances of employing the assault guns:

We are pointing out that assault guns, despite the ice cleats received, are not able to advance in the midst of the present weather and road conditions. Unit commanders, with whom the assault guns are to be deployed, are advised to keep this circumstance in mind when reconnoitring an area and to always involve the commanders of the assault guns when determining the route of march.[112]

28 NOVEMBER 1941

The corps put the assault guns from elements fighting under the command of the *112. Infanterie-Division* under the direct control of the battalion staff again with immediate effect.[113]

However, assault-gun *Kampfgruppe 'Lechens'*, which was deployed in the sector of the *167. Infanterie-Division,* remained in Olchowez where it was subordinated to *Infanterie-Regiment 339.*[114]

2 DECEMBER 1941

Assault-gun *Kampfgruppe 'Lechens'* was under direct command of *167. Infanterie-Division* at Gribowka.[115]

3 DECEMBER 1941

The assault-gun *Kampfgruppe* was subordinated to *Infanterie-Regiment 331* and was brought forward from the area of Wasiljewskoje to the regiment.[116]

4 DECEMBER 1941

Assault-gun *Kampfgruppe 'Lechens'*, now under direct command of the staff of the *167. Infanterie-Division*, was sent to the command post of *Infanterie-Regiment 315* and ordered to be ready for immediate action on both regimental front lines.[117]

From 6 December until 26 December 1941, *Sturmgeschütz-Abteilung 202* fought a defensive battle in the area of Tula and Jefremew against Soviet units carrying out the Moscow counter-offensive.[118]

112 NARA T314, R1311 (*LIII. Armeekorps*), F000632.
113 NARA T314, R1311 (*LIII. Armeekorps*), F000630.
114 NARA T315, R1479 (*167. Infanterie-Division*), F000464.
115 NARA T315, R1479 (*167. Infanterie-Division*), F000483.
116 NARA T315, R1479 (*167. Infanterie-Division*), F000486.
117 NARA T315, R1479 (*167. Infanterie-Division*), F000490.
118 NARA T315, R1479 (*167. Infanterie-Division*), F000490.

11 DECEMBER 1941

The whole of *Sturmgeschütz-Abteilung 202* was subordinated to the *112. Infanterie-Division* from 1200 hours.

The forces of the *LIII. Armeekorps* were given the task of defending positions along the Don and Shat between Michailowka and Stublenka, and to prepare for withdrawal towards the south-west.[119]

12 DECEMBER 1941

At 1025 hours, the assault guns of the assault-artillery unit and the *3. Kompanie/ Panzerjäger-Abteilung 112* were subordinated to *Infanterie-Regiment 258.* At 1130 hours the regiment reported that two combat-ready assault guns had arrived.[120]

At 1510 hours *Infanterie-Regiment 256* reported by telephone that a Soviet attack had been launched from the area of Koshanka and to defend against that they needed the two assault guns.[121] However they still had not arrived by daybreak.[122]

THE NIGHT OF 12/13 DECEMBER 1941

In the sector of *Infanterie-Regiment 258* (*112. Infanterie-Division*) an assault gun of *Sturmgeschütz-Abteilung 202* had to be blown up at around 0235 hours because it slid off the road and couldn't be made combat-ready because the German units had already begun their withdrawal.[123]

At 0745 hours assault guns were ordered into the area of Weljminowa and put under direct command of the division. Their deployment might have been requested by *Infanterie-Regiment 256.* In the afternoon at 1345 hours the StuG. III combat vehicles were ordered into the area of Pritonj with their march to be carried out before nightfall.[124]

15 DECEMBER 1941

After 0700 hours, during the retreat of the *112. Infanterie-Division*, two assault guns of *Sturmgeschütz-Abteilung 202,* several recovery vehicles and anti-tank guns of *Panzerjäger-Abteilung 112* as well as the heavy artillery of the division became hopelessly stuck due to snowdrifts and ice-covered roads and consequently had to be blown up. The other assault guns were ordered into a blocking position with a pioneer platoon and anti-aircraft heavy machine guns on the northern part of Jewlewo to prevent Soviet units from the crossing the river there.[125]

---

119 NARA T314, R1311 (*LIII. Armeekorps*), F000229-230.

120 NARA T315, R1269 (*112. Infanterie-Division*), F000767.

121 NARA T315, R1269 (*112. Infanterie-Division*), F000769.

122 NARA T315, R1269 (*112. Infanterie-Division*), F000771.

123 NARA T314, R1312 (*LIII. Armeekorps*), F001209.

124 NARA T315, R1269 (*112. Infanterie-Division*), F000773.

125 NARA T315, R1269 (*112. Infanterie-Division*), F000781.

At 1545 hours, the assault guns were subordinated to *Panzerjäger-Abteilung 112* and were ordered to take up position at Oserki to be available for the division next morning in the area of Tjoploje.[126]

16 DECEMBER 1941

At 0940 hours the *LIII. Armeekorps* placed the assault gun battalion under its own direct command, with effect from the day before, that is from 15 December.[127] The commander of the assault guns said farewell to the division at around 1500 hours.[128]

17 DECEMBER 1941

In the afternoon, three assault guns of *Sturmgeschütz-Abteilung 202* were again subordinated to the *112. Infanterie-Division* and ordered to its command post.[129] At 1830 hours the assault guns were attached to *Panzerjäger-Abteilung 112* and given security tasks at the railway junction south of Tjoploje.[130]

18 DECEMBER 1941

The *LIII. Armeekorps* issued orders to its subordinate units to retreat behind the Oka River because the Soviet troops advancing westwards from the area of Tula threatened the northern flank of the *2. Panzerarmee.* In relation to that, *Sturmgeschütz-Abteilung 202* had to retreat to the northern foreground of Bolchow. The unit had to dispatch the assault guns subordinated to *112. Infanterie-Division* (providing support for *Infanterie-Regiment 258*) in time – around noon – to allow them to use the Plawsk–Tschen route.[131] In the evening the three assault guns were put back under the direct command of the *LIII. Armeekorps.*[132]

20 DECEMBER 1941

Apart from the corps units, and besides *Sturmgeschütz-Abteilung 202,* three infantry divisions *(112., 167., 296. Infanterie-Divisionen),*one motorized infantry regiment (*Grossdeutschland)*[133], a horse-drawn infantry regiment *(Infanterie-Regiment 171)* and *schwere Artillerie-Abteilung 735* (armed with 21 cm mortars), fought under subordination to the *LIII. Armeekorps.*[134]

On that day measures were taken by the headquarters of the *2. Panzerarmee* to ensure that of the 64 replacement tanks and 13 replacement assault guns

126 NARA T315, R1269 (*112. Infanterie-Division*), F000783.
127 NARA T314, R1311 (*LIII. Armeekorps*), F000219.
128 NARA T315, R1269 (*112. Infanterie-Division*), F000787.
129 NARA T314, R1311 (*LIII. Armeekorps*), F000589.
130 NARA T315, R1269 (*112. Infanterie-Division*), F000796.
131 NARA T314, R1311 (*LIII. Armeekorps*), F000217.
132 NARA T315, R1269 (*112. Infanterie-Division*), F000802.
133 This regiment had own assault guns in his 16th *Kompanie.*
134 NARA T314, R1312 (*LIII. Armeekorps*), F000005.

arriving from Charkow to Kursk, the latter should be sent to Orel and delivered to *Sturmgeschütz-Abteilung 202.*[135] This implies that that the total losses of the unit were equal to that number and thereby to its shortage of combat vehicles compared to its original TOE (Table of Organization and Equipment) strength at the time of its first deployment on 3 October 1941.

25 DECEMBER 1941

Ten cubic metres of fuel and 0.4 cubic metres of engine oil were issued from the Orel railway station to the assault gun unit.[136]

27 DECEMBER 1941

The defensive battle, in which *Sturmgeschütz-Abteilung 202* also participated, of the *LIII. Armeekorps* began north-east of Orel,[137]

28 DECEMBER 1941

In the late afternoon, Soviet troops crossed the Oka River south-east of Tolkatshi, penetrated into the defences of the *112. Infanterie-Division* and pushed towards Bolchow.

At 0845 hours, the German infantry division had requested the corps to send the three assault guns promised to them earlier into the area of Chmelewaja and to direct the commander to report to the regimental command post of *Infanterie-Regiment 256* in Kolodesi. Due to the deteriorating situation the division would have deployed the assault guns to *Infanterie-Regiment 258* in the area of Kriwzowa at 1130 hours.[138]

At 1320 hours the *LIII. Armeekorps* held out the prospect of transferring five assault guns to the division.[139]

At 1630 hours the adjutant of *Sturmgeschütz-Abteilung 202* reported to the staff of *112. Infanterie-Division* by telephone.[140]

But the corps had other plans for the assault guns. To contain the Soviet advance, two companies from *Schützen-Regiment 33,* belonging to the *4. Panzer-Division's* order of battle, were dispatched on vehicles provided by the *LIII. Armeekorps* to delay the Russian advance. When, in the late afternoon, the four assault guns of *Sturmgeschütz-Abteilung 202* reached Bolchow they were sent after the motorized infantry companies.[141]

---

135 NARA T314, R1310 (*LIII. Armeekorps*), F001030.

136 NARA T313, R108 (*Panzerarmeeoberkommando 2*), F7352492.

137 NARA T314, R1310 (*LIII. Armeekorps*), F000033.

138 NARA T315, R1269 (*112. Infanterie-Division*), F000857.

139 NARA T315, R1269 (*112. Infanterie-Division*), F000859.

140 NARA T315, R1269 (*112. Infanterie-Division*), F000861.

141 NARA T315, R195 (*4. Panzer-Division*), F000747.

According to the war diary of the *112. Infanterie-Division,* the commander of *LIII. Armeekorps* only announced that the assault guns had begun to move off at 2215 hours.[142]

29 DECEMBER 1941

The Soviet troops continued their attack in the sector of the *112. Infanterie-Division.* They pressed forward from the penetration at Kriwzowa to reach the area 7 km south-east of Kriwzowa–Bloschnja–5 km north of Bloschnja–Kolodesi–northern foreground of Kolodesi.

Kampfgruppe 'Marder' – consisting of elements of the *4. Panzer-Division* (the *6.* and *8. Kompanien* of the motorized *Schützen-Regiment 3*); the assault guns of *Sturmgeschütz-Abteilung 202* with seven StuG. IIIs led by the commander and the *6. Kompanie/ Schützen-Regiment 33* – set off at around 0400 hours from Bolchow to join forces with the *8.Kompanie/112. Infanterie-Division* that had been forced to retreat from Bogrinowa, 7 km south-west of Kriwzowa. The plan was to carry out an attack from a south-westerly direction to retake Bogrinowa before capturing Chmelewaja, a settlement 2 km north-west of Kriwzowa.[143]

The StuG. III assault guns and the motorized rifle company reached the area of Kischkino between 0400 and 0500 hours. At around 0900 hours, the *Kampfgruppe* launched an attack together with the *I. Bataillon/ Infanterie-Regiment 258* and had mopped up the village in heavy fighting against weakening Soviet resistance by 1700 hours.[144]

During the day *Kampfgruppe 'Marder'* successfully pushed back the Soviet units fighting southwest of Kriwzowa to the sector 3 km west of the settlement.[145]

The medical officer of *Sturmgeschütz-Abteilung 202, Unterarzt der Reserve* Dr Scheuer, was wounded in the course of the day's fighting.[146]

At 1935 hours *Kampfgruppe 'Marder'* reported to the corps, that although they had cleared the Soviet troops from Bogrinowa, the situation was still extremely dangerous because the enemy threatened to breakthrough in the direction of Bolchow.[147]

30 DECEMBER 1941

Hauptmann Dr Hans Marder, commander of *Sturmgeschütz-Abteilung 202,* was killed in action together with his driver in the area of Kriwzowa. A salvo from a Soviet machine-gun shot them dead.

142 NARA T315, R1269 (*112. Infanterie-Division*), F000863.

143 NARA T314, R1312 (*LIII. Armeekorps*), F001088.

144 NARA T315, R195 (*4. Panzer-Division*), F000747, and also T315, R1269 (*112. Infanterie-Division*), F000871.

145 NARA T314, R1312 (*LIII. Armeekorps*), F001081.

146 NARA T313, R108 (*Panzerarmeeoberkommando 2*), F7352731.

147 NARA T314, R1310 (*LIII. Armeekorps*), F000644.

The staff of the *LIII. Armeekorps* ordered its subordinate divisions by telegram that from the following morning they – among others – should include in their report the number of combat-ready assault guns and tanks attached to them on the basis of the information obtained the previous evening.[148]

1942

Operational Background:

After the Soviet counter-offensive slowly ground to a halt, Sturmgeschütz-Abteilung 202 fought a mainly static war until September 1942. The only exception to this occurred between 5 and 12 July 1942 when the three armies of the Soviet Western Front attacked elements of 2. Panzerarmee between Kirow and Bolchow.

2 JANUARY 1942

In the morning, Soviet troops launched several attacks in the sector of the *4. Panzer-Division.* One of these was followed by a counter-thrust led by the assault guns of *Sturmgeschütz-Abteilung 202* in the direction of Tolkatshi during which the Germans reached the houses on the perimeter of the settlement. Part of the retreating Soviet forces tried to find cover in the ravine south-west of the settlement.[149]

At 0910 hours the Soviets launched an attack with significant rifle forces in a westerly direction, south of the ravine lying to the south-west of Butyrki. They were subjected to German artillery and rocket-launcher fire but the Soviet infantry continued their advance. Several German machine guns were frozen up and were unable to halt the attack. However, a counter-thrust was launched by a German company in reserve with the support of the assault guns of *Sturmgeschütz-Abteilung 202.*

Elements of the assault gun unit had just jumped off when, at around 1030 hours, the officer leading the attack, *Generalmajor* Dietrich von Saucken (commander of *4. Panzer-Division*), was wounded in his right eye.[150] Nevertheless, the assault guns pushed back the Soviet attackers inflicting serious losses on them. The Germans captured several mortars and machine guns.

Following this, the assault guns conducted armed reconnaissance against the village 1.5 km south-west of Butyrki. During that mission, the assault artillerymen found that the Soviets had evacuated the settlement and most of the houses had been burnt down. However, when the assault guns tried to push on towards the

148 NARA T314, R1312 (*LIII. Armeekorps*), F001069.

149 NARA T315, R195 (*4. Panzer-Division*), F000757.

150 NARA T315, R195 (*4. Panzer-Division*), F000756.

Oka River, Soviet anti-tank and anti-aircraft guns opened fire at them, preventing their further advance.[151]

3 JANUARY 1942

At around 1100 hours *Oberst* Smilo von Lüttwitz, commander of *Schützen-Regiment 12*, was planning to attack and take Kargaschinka with an assault group in company strength supported by the assault guns of *Sturmgeschütz-Abteilung 202.* He had the distinct impression that the village had already been partly evacuated by the Soviets. At around 1200 hours, following a violent battle, Kargaschinka was indeed occupied by the German group which was led by the regimental commander.[152]

4 JANUARY 1942

Elements of the *25. Infanterie-Division (mot.)* occupied the western half of Ssinkowa in a fierce fighting but due to their own heavy losses they burnt down and evacuated that part of the settlement. The assault was repeated by the forces of *Infanterie-Regiment 20 (mot.)* with the support of the assault guns of *Sturmgeschütz-Abteilung 202* with the aim of levelling the whole locality to the ground.[153]

At around noon, with the support of the assault guns, the Germans took the settlement 1.5 km south-west of Butyrki. This had been reconnoitred by the assault guns two days before. The houses still standing were set on fire.[154]

5 JANUARY 1942

At 1530 hours, the *4. Panzer-Division* reported to the *LIII. Armeekorps* that the planned attack of *Infanterie-Regiment 20 (mot.)* to destroy Ssinkowa could not be carried out because *Sturmgeschütz-Abteilung 202* had only one combat-ready assault gun left and that they would only be combat-ready again after a few day's rest.[155]

6 JANUARY 1942

Sturmgeschütz-Abteilung 202 had 13 StuG. III assault guns and 23 machine guns distributed as follows:

- four machine guns to the staff *Batterie*
- four assault guns and eight machine guns to the *1. Batterie*
- four assault guns and nine machine guns to the *2. Batterie*
- five assault guns and two machine guns to the *3. Batterie*[156]

151 NARA T315, R195 (*4. Panzer-Division*), F000758.
152 NARA T315, R195 (*4. Panzer-Division*), F000759.
153 NARA T315, R195 (*4. Panzer-Division*), F000761.
154 NARA T315, R195 (*4. Panzer-Division*), F000762.
155 NARA T315, R195 (*4. Panzer-Division*), F000763.
156 NARA T314, R1314 (*LIII. Armeekorps*), F000638.

7 JANUARY 1942

According to valid information that day, *Sturmgeschütz-Abteilung 202* was the only assault gun unit subordinated to the *2. Panzerarmee.*[157]

8 JANUARY 1942

The *Kampfgruppe* of *Oberstleutnant* Oskar Munzel[158] was ordered into the sector of the *296. Infanterie-Division* and subordinated to it. This division was made up of 500 soldiers of *Panzer-regiment 6* deployed as infantry, elements of *Infanterie-Regiment 234,* a 2 cm anti-aircraft machine-gun platoon, the *II. Bataillon/Flak-Regiment 11,* and four StuG. III assault guns of *Sturmgeschütz-Abteilung 202.*[159]

9 JANUARY 1942

Kampfgruppe 'Munzel' arrived at the northern foreground of Kirejkowo with the four assault guns. On the way, they had trouble with the deep snow and because of this elements of the *Kampfgruppe* were not deployable that day.[160]

Due to the snow and road conditions, deployment of the assault guns and tanks was only possible on those sections of the road that had been cleared and on the ridge of hills along the roads after thorough reconnaissance. Since the tactics of the *Kampfgruppe* had to be based on the few tanks and assault guns available to it, their deployment had to be adjusted to suit the circumstances. Moreover, the Soviet troops tended to avoid hills unless they were fighting to take settlements and – as had become obvious from battles fought east of and around the River Oka – gave preference to narrow valleys and gullies during reconnaissance missions and attacks. The reason for this was that the hills emerging from there were formidable anti-tank obstacles due to their covering of snow and their slippery slopes.[161]

10 JANUARY 1942

With the support of four tanks of *Panzer-Regiment 6* and four assault guns of *Sturmgeschütz-Abteilung 202*, part of the infantry of *Kampfgruppe 'Munzel'* repulsed Soviet troops that had penetrated into the western part of Kirejkowo the previous night. Before long, the settlement was attacked by Soviet cavalry from north, west and south. The four tanks and four assault guns of the *Kampfgruppe* launched a counter-thrust and dispersed a stronger cavalry formation.[162]

Panzerjäger-Abteilung 112 submitted a report of their experience that day in which it touched upon their cooperation with the assault guns of *Sturmgeschütz-Abteilung 202:*

157 NARA T314, R1314 (*LIII. Armeekorps*), F000187.

158 The lieutenant-colonel was the commander of *Panzer-Regiment 6.*

159 NARA T314, R1313 (*LIII. Armeekorps*), F000628.

160 NARA T314, R1313 (*LIII. Armeekorps*), F000634.

161 NARA T314, R1318 (*LIII. Armeekorps*), F000022-23.

162 NARA T314, R1313 (*LIII. Armeekorps*), F000640.

Advance detachment was especially advantageous with the following order of battle:

- *two companies of tank destroyers;*
- *two companies of infantry necessarily carried on trucks;*
- *a pioneer company (motorized);*
- *a heavy machine-gun section, necessarily carried on trucks;*
- *three 8.8 cm anti-aircraft guns;*
- *four 2 cm anti-aircraft machine guns;*
- *three assault guns.*

[...]

In another instance the light anti-tank guns of the Abteilung destroyed two light tanks with Pz. Gr. 40 ammunition at 200 m distance. A third was hit and the fleeing tank was destroyed by the assault guns.[163]

11 JANUARY 1942

Most of *Kampfgruppe 'Munzel'* was encircled by the Soviet cavalry groups in Kirejkowo. According to information as of the day, apart from the soldiers of *Panzer-Regiment 6* employed as infantry, there were at the disposal of the *Kampfgruppe* four tanks of the regiment, 11 tanks (some of them were not in a full combat-ready condition) of an armoured company of *Panzer-Regiment 39,* the *II. Bataillon* plus *13.* and *14. Kompanien/ Infanterie-Regiment 234,* a 2 cm anti-aircraft machine-gun platoon of the *II. Bataillon/Flak-Regiment 11,* and four assault guns of *Sturmgeschütz-Abteilung 202.*[164]

The tanks and assault guns of the *Kampfgruppe*, having spent the night outside the settlement of Gorjana, launched an attack to relieve their encircled comrades. The AFVs had a successful morning but the Soviet cavalry continued to launch strong attacks against Kirejkowo.

In the early afternoon, the tanks and assault guns of *Kampfgruppe 'Munzel'* launched another attack from the south-western foreground of Posniakowo in a north-westerly direction in the course of which they shattered a Soviet grouping that had just launched an attack on Posniakowo. The Soviets retreated in panic with the German AFVs inflicting serious losses on them.[165]

Around noon *Kampfgruppe 'Munzel'* was subordinated to the newly arrived *56. Infanterie-Division,* together with four assault guns of *Sturmgeschütz-Abteilung 202.*[166]

163 NARA T314, R1315 (*LIII. Armeekorps*), F000295.
164 NARA T314, R1314 (*LIII. Armeekorps*), F000547.
165 NARA T314, R1313 (*LIII. Armeekorps*), F000646.
166 NARA T314, R1313 (*LIII. Armeekorps*), F000648.

On this same day, the German assault guns shattered a Soviet artillery battery during their surprise advance 5 km south of Oserno, in the area of Oserenskij.[167]

From the four assault guns subordinated to them, two were to be handed over by the staff of the *112. Infanterie-Division* before noon.[168]

At around 1200 hours, an assault-gun platoon arrived under the command of *Leutnant* Meier in the sector of the *296. Infanterie-Division.* The platoon was subordinated to the staff of *Artillerie-Regiment 296,* which ordered the StuG. III assault guns to Leonowo to reinforce the weak defences there. This proved to be useful because at around 1500 hours, Soviet units launched an attack on the settlement.[169] However, with the support of the assault guns, the Germans carried out a counter-thrust in the sector that dispersed the Soviets.[170]

12 JANUARY 1942

In the sector of *296. Infanterie-Division,* on the western and north-western perimeter of Posniakowo, the *III. Bataillon/ Infanterie-Regiment (mot.) 'Grossdeutschland'* was ready to carry out an attack in a north-westerly direction, with the aim of destroying the Soviet units in the foreground of the settlement. The attack was launched at 1230 hours. The infantry's attack was supported very efficiently by the assault guns[171] and the aircraft of the *Luftwaffe.* Thus the German attack reached the southern foreground of Shelesniza by nightfall and the Soviets suffered yet more serious losses.[172]

13 JANUARY 1942

In the sector of the *296. Infanterie-Division* the German infantry, with the support of the assault guns, cleared the settlement of Gryn of the fragments of Soviet units.[173] However, the road conditions prevented the assault guns from penetrating into the settlement [174] so they provided only artillery support.

15 JANUARY 1942

During the afternoon, three assault guns of *Sturmgeschütze-Abteilung 202* plus a rifle platoon were ordered from Bolchow to Krapiwna where they were to provide

---

167 NARA T314, R1313 (*LIII. Armeekorps*), F000652. The parent unit of the assault guns attacking the artillery battery is unfortunately not mentioned in the source. We should not exclude the possibility, that in this case the war diary of the corps mentions the StuG. III assault guns of *Infanterie-Regiment (mot.) „Grossdeutschland"*, instead of those of *Sturmgeschütz-Abteilung 202.* However, the motorized infantry regiment's own assault guns are missing from *LIII. Armeekorps' order of battle being in effect* on 11 January 1942.

168 NARA T315, R1269 (*112. Infanterie-Division*), F000901.

169 NARA T315, R1954 (*296. Infanterie-Division*), F001012.

170 NARA T314, R1314 (*LIII. Armeekorps*), F001232.

171 The parent unit of the supporting assault guns is also unclear, but they were probably the combat vehicles of *Sturmgeschütz-Abteilung 202.*

172 NARA T314, R1313 (*LIII. Armeekorps*), F000654.

173 NARA T314, R1314 (*LIII. Armeekorps*), F001221.

174 NARA T315, R1954 (*296. Infanterie-Division*), F001016.

support for blocking force *'Von Mühlen'* that was deployed on the western flank of the *LIII. Armeekorps.* The blocking force was comprised of elements of *Pionier-Bataillon 45* and *Machinengewehr-Bataillon 5.*[175]

16 JANUARY 1942

In the sector of the *56. Infanterie-Division, Infanterie-Regiment 234* took Leonowskij, a settlement 2.5 km west of Posniakowo, in a violent urban fight with the support of the assault guns of *Sturmgeschütz-Abteilung 202.* Besides the heavy casualties sustained, Soviets lost a 76.2 mm gun, six anti-tank guns, nine heavy machine guns, four light machine guns, five light mortars, one heavy mortar, one anti-aircraft gun, six submachine guns, one periscope binoculars, 29 rifles, and four field kitchens.[176]

The soldiers of the German infantry regiment, together with the assault guns, pursued the enemy retreating westwards. During the day *Infanterie-Regiment 234* occupied Blinowo and Shelesinskij, and the assault guns penetrated in Oserenskij.[177]

18 JANUARY 1942

According to the information as of 0000 hours, elements of *Sturmgeschütz-Abteilung 202* fought as part of the *LIII. Armeekorps'* order of battle with following subordinations:

- four assault guns subordinated to the *56. Infanterie-Division,*
- two assault guns subordinated to the *112. Infanterie-Division,*
- two assault guns subordinated to the *296. Infanterie-Division,*
- battalion staff under direct command of the *LIII. Armeekorps.*[178]

On that day *Kampfgruppe 'Erdmannsdorf'* was raised from the blocking formation *'Mühlen'* strengthened by reinforcements. The *Kampfgruppe* consisted of *Infanterie-Regiment 171*, the *III. Bataillon /Artillerie-Regiment 156, Pionier-Bataillon 45, Machinengewehr-Bataillon 5*, the *I. Bataillon/Infanterie-Regiment 192,* a rifle platoon and three assault guns of *Infanterie-Regiment (mot.) 'Grossdeutschland'* and two assault guns of *Sturmgeschütz-Abteilung 202.* The main task of the *Kampfgruppe* was to prevent Soviet units from advancing southwards from the Gorodnitschewo–Krapiwna–Wesnini line.[179]

---

175 NARA T314, R1313 (*LIII. Armeekorps*), F000664.

176 NARA T314, R1313 (*LIII. Armeekorps*), F000668.

177 NARA T314, R1313 (*LIII. Armeekorps*), F000670.

178 NARA T315, R1479 (*167. Infanterie-Division*), F000598-600.

179 NARA T314, R1313 (*LIII. Armeekorps*), F000680.

19 JANUARY 1942

Assault guns of *Sturmgeschütz-Abteilung 202* deployed, together with some tanks, in the sector of the *56. Infanterie-Division* to provide support for the infantry, took and totally destroyed the villages of Simanowkij and Oserenskij. In the battle the Soviets suffered significant casualties. Besides that the Germans destroyed a T–34 tank, two machine guns and a heavy mortar.[180]

On that day the *112. Infanterie-Division* handed over the two assault guns that had fought in its sector to the *LIII. Armeekorps.*[181]

20 JANUARY 1942

In the sector of *Kampfgruppe 'Erdmannsdorf'*, the Soviet units, with the support of five tanks, launched an attack on Petuchowka, defended by the *III. Bataillon/Infanterie-Regiment 171.* The German infantry retreated in a southerly and south-easterly direction. With the support of the assault guns, a counter-thrust was soon launched but it failed to take back the village. By nightfall three Soviet battalions were defending the village.[182]

21 JANUARY 1942

Kampfgruppe 'Oven' was raised from elements of the *56. Infanterie-Division,* most of *Infanterie-Regiment (mot.) 'Grossdeutschland',* the *II. Bataillon/Schützen-Regiment 33, Pionier-Bataillon 45, Maschinengewehr-Bataillon 5, Aufklärungs-Abteilung 120,* most of *Artillerie-Abteilung 400,* the *II. Kompanie/Panzerjäger-Abteilung 529* and two assault guns of *Sturmgeschütz-Abteilung 202.*[183]

22 JANUARY 1942

Two assault guns of *Sturmgeschütz-Abteilung 202* stationed at Peredel, were ordered to Iwanowka as a standby reserve.[184]

23 JANUARY 1942

In the sector of *Gruppe 'Krischer',* made up of elements of the *296.* and *56. Infanterie-Divisionen,* the German infantry, with the support of the assault guns of *Sturmgeschütz-Abteilung 202,* pushed back the three-company-strong Soviet force that had clung to a gully in the western foreground of Iwanowka the previous evening. The Germans destroyed five smaller guns and two ant-tank guns in the battle.[185]

---

180 NARA T314, R1313 (*LIII. Armeekorps*), F000684.

181 NARA T315, R1269 (*112. Infanterie-Division*), F000912.

182 NARA T314, R1313 (*LIII. Armeekorps*), F000688.

183 NARA T314, R1313 (*LIII. Armeekorps*), F000696.

184 NARA T315, R1954 (*296. Infanterie-Division*), F001029.

185 NARA T314, R1313 (*LIII. Armeekorps*), F000704, and also T315, R1954 (*296. Infanterie-Division*), F001033.

In the sector of *Kampfgruppe 'Oven'* Soviet forces penetrated into the northern part of Ploskoje, but the *I. Bataillon/ Infanterie-Regiment 339,* with the support of the assault guns of *Sturmgeschütz-Abteilung 202,* forced them back.[186]

The staff of *Gruppe 'Krischer'* informed the corps at 1005 hours, that they had dispatched two assault guns towards Bolchow but one of them had broken down in the district of Gorschetschnij due to engine failure. Temporarily, the group was not able to dispatch another combat vehicle to substitute for the one that had fallen out because their other two assault guns were fighting on the north-western flank of the group and the two assault guns of *Kampfgruppe 'Munzel'* were in action west of Iwanowka.[187]

24 JANUARY 1942

The assault guns of *Sturmgeschütz-Abteilung 202* participated in more counter-thrusts.

At around 0745 hours in the zone of the *296. Infanterie-Division,* in the sector of *Infanterie-Regiment 521,* the Soviets penetrated into the settlement of Tscheremoschka. Their success was aided by the fact that the German minefield established north of the settlement could not be put into operation.

Sturmgeschütz-Abteilung 202 and *Panzerjäger-Abteilung 296* were deployed to restore the original situation. Soldiers of the tank destroyer unit had to clamber onto the assault guns.

At around 0900 hours the division commander, *Generalleutnant* Friedrich Krischer, ordered the assault guns to engage the Soviets attacking between Tscheremoschka and Dolbinskije Wys, but the enemy assault was successfully contained without the intervention of the StuG. IIIs.[188]

In the morning the Germans launched a counter-thrust with the support of the assault guns and drove the Soviet troops out of the main combat line. At around 1530 hours the assault guns were put into divisional reserve in the area of Grynskije Dwory.[189]

Around noon, in the sector of *Kampfgruppe 'Oven',* the Soviets attacked Wjasowaja from a north-westerly direction with a company-strength force. The Germans forced the attackers to retreat and inflicted heavy losses on them carrying out counter-thrusts supported by assault guns.[190]

---

186 NARA T314, R1313 (*LIII. Armeekorps*), F000706.

187 NARA T314, R1314 (*LIII. Armeekorps*), F000787.

188 NARA T315, R1954 (*296. Infanterie-Division*), F001035.

189 NARA T315, R1954 (*296. Infanterie-Division*), F001037

190 NARA T314, R1314 (*LIII. Armeekorps*), F001168.

25 JANUARY 1942

In the sector of *Kampfgruppe 'Krischer'* the Soviets penetrated into Tscheremoschka and Iwanowka again with a battalion-strength force at 0430 hours. With the support of two assault guns of *Sturmgeschütz-Abteilung 202*, the German *Infanterie-Regiment 192* launched counter-thrusts during the morning which succeeded in driving out the attackers and eliminating the penetrations.[191]

27 JANUARY 1942

On the front line of *Gruppe 'Krischer'*, at around 0630 hours in the sector of the *296. Infanterie-Division,* Soviet troops broke through the German defences north of Tscheremoschka. Quarter of an hour later *Infanterie-Regiment 519* was ordered to dispatch the two assault guns located with them to *Infanterie-Regiment 521.*

At around 0800 hours the Soviets launched another attack. This time the assault guns stationed at Iwanowka and the *1. Kompanie/Panzerjäger-Abteilung 296* were also ordered to the penetration. Finally, with the aid of the assault guns that had arrived from Grynskije Dwory, the German infantry successfully repelled the Soviets in the area of Tscheremoschka sometime after 0900 hours.[192]

29 JANUARY 1942

Soviets launched an attack with a force of two-battalions strength from Medwedki and Betowo on Wjasowaja, the front line of *Kampfgruppe 'Oven'.* Their attempt was halted by German artillery. The Germans commenced a counter-thrust with the support of the assault guns, inflicting serious losses and pushing back the attackers to their jump-off positions[193]

According to their report on their actual combat strength, *Sturmgeschütz-Abteilung 202* had the following at its disposal:[194]

- authorised strength: 24 officers, 564 NCOs and enlisted men;
- actual strength: 17 officers, 313 NCOs and enlisted men (including 122 NCOs and enlisted men permanently unfit for service due to illness, suffering frostbite or wounded);
- authorized weapons strength: 31 machine guns, 66 submachine guns, 251 pistols, 323 rifles;
- actual weapons strength: 21 machine guns, 41 submachine guns, 175 pistols, 279 rifles;
- authorized assault-gun strength: 21;

191 NARA T314, R1313 (*LIII. Armeekorps*), F000712.

192 NARA T315, R1954 (*296. Infanterie-Division*), F001041.

193 NARA T314, R1313 (*LIII. Armeekorps*), F000726.

194 NARA T314, R1314 (*LIII. Armeekorps*), F000924, as well as T314, R1314 (*LIII. Armeekorps*), F000951-952.

- actual assault-gun strength: 15 (seven combat-ready; five under long-term repairs, partly in the hinterland; three written off as total losses and reported as transferred to the hinterland;
- authorized strength motor cars: 27;
- actual strength motor cars: 21 (six conditionally serviceable, 15 unserviceable);
- authorized strength trucks: 68;
- actual strength trucks: 60 (18 conditionally serviceable, 42 unserviceable);
- authorized strength recovery vehicles: 21 (18×1-ton; 3×18-ton);
- actual strength recovery vehicles: 11 (9×1-ton; 2×18-ton; from which 8×1-ton and 1×18-ton unserviceable).

From the figures above, it seems that the unit was only conditionally combat-ready. However, on the basis of the actual assault gun and vehicle strength it proved to be out of action.

30 JANUARY 1942

With its own forces, *Kampfgruppe 'Oven'* (*10. Kompanie/ Infanterie-Regiment 339* together with the assault guns of *Sturmgeschütz-Abteilung 202* led by the platoon commander of the *2. Batterie*, *Leutnant* Helmut Weirich) advanced from the area of Wasiljewskoje in a westerly direction during an attack and in Shujewka ran into, and dispersed, a Soviet battalion preparing to attack. The German assault squad inflicted serious losses on the Soviets silencing an anti-tank gun and two infantry howitzers and capturing five machine guns, one light mortar and 40 rifles. Following this, the German advance reached Jatschnyj.[195]

31 JANUARY 1942

On the front line of *Kampfgruppe 'Oven'* the *II. Bataillon/ Infanterie-Regiment 331* and elements of the *III. Bataillon/ Infanterie-Regiment 339* advanced from the district Stolbtscheje in a westerly direction and, with the support of assault guns, took the village of Jatschnyj in a very short battle, destroying the 100-man-strong formation there and advancing towards Jatschoje. Here, in ferocious urban fighting lasting for almost two hours, they drove the Soviets from the settlement. The Germans burnt down both settlements. According to their own reports, the Soviets lost more than 200 men, a 122 mm howitzer, a 76.2 mm gun, one 76.2 mm and one 45 mm anti-tank gun, 10 machine guns, 10 light machine guns, six medium mortars, four light mortars and several submachine guns. The Germans sustained insignificant losses.[196]

---

195 NARA T314, R1313 (*LIII. Armeekorps*), F000730, as well as T314, R1314 (*LIII. Armeekorps*), F001141.

196 NARA T314, R1313 (*LIII. Armeekorps*), F000734, 000736.

2 FEBRUARY 1942

At around 1545 hours on the front line of *Gruppe 'Krischer'*, in the sector of *296. Infanterie-Division,* the Soviets broke into the area of Dolbinskije Wys but the significantly weakened *III. Bataillon/Infanterie-Regiment 521* were able to hold the settlement. Finally, with the help of the assault guns of *Sturmgeschütz-Abteilung 202* they were able to mop up the area around the locality.[197]

3 FEBRUARY 1942

In the sector of *Kampfgruppe 'Oven'*, the assault guns cleared the western foreground of Wjasowaja during an attack. In the course of the mission they took 18 soldiers of the Soviet 387 Rifle Division as prisoners, captured two light machine guns and destroyed a 76 mm gun.[198]

In the sector of *Kampfgruppe 'Krischer'*, a Soviet formation of around 150 soldiers was pushed back by a counter-thrust launched by German infantry supported by the assault guns of *Sturmgeschütz-Abteilung 202,* 2 km west of Dolbino.[199]

10 FEBRUARY 1942

Leutnant Josef Brandner, an officer of the *3. Batterie/Sturmgeschütz-Abteilung 202,* was wounded[200] when he was shot in the neck by a Soviet sniper.

11 FEBRUARY 1942

At daybreak the *LIII. Armeekorps* ordered *Sturmgeschütz-Abteilung 202* by telegram to dispatch every combat-ready assault gun from Bolchow by the shortest possible route to the staff of the *25. Infanterie-Division (mot.)* in the area of Teltsche.[201]

The staff of the *296. Infanterie-Division* issued orders at 2030 hours to *Infanterie-Regiment 192* to launch an attack at 0900 hours the following day towards Leninskoje and seize the settlement. To this end, besides an armoured company, two assault guns from *Sturmgeschütz-Abteilung 202* were attached to them.[202]

12 FEBRUARY 1942

At 0900 hours *Infanterie-Regiment 192,* reinforced with tanks and assault guns, launched its attack to take Leninskoje. The snow-bound, narrow, forest tracks and the extensive Soviet minefields and wooden road blocks significantly slowed the Germans. Detecting and neutralizing the wooden box mines laid by the Soviets gave them a lot of trouble. Despite this, the reinforced infantry division had taken

---

197 NARA T315, R1954 (*296. Infanterie-Division*), F001059.
198 NARA T314, R1313 (*LIII. Armeekorps*), F000750.
199 NARA T314, R1314 (*LIII. Armeekorps*), F001114.
200 NARA T313, R108 (*Panzerarmeeoberkommando 2*), F7352745.
201 NARA T314, R1313 (*LIII. Armeekorps*), F000776.
202 NARA T315, R1954 (*296. Infanterie-Division*), F001073.

two Soviet defensive positions and was within 1 km of Leninskoje by 1150 hours. In the afternoon, at around 1700 hours, two German infantry battalions launched an outflanking attack. At around 1830 hours the German tanks overran the last timber roadblocks and at around 2030 hours the settlement fell into the German hands. The StuG. III assault guns, together with the tanks, temporarily occupied Leninskoje.[203]

13 FEBRUARY 1942

Infanterie-Regiment 339, subordinated to *Kampfgruppe 'Oven'*, took Schwanowo where an assault gun of *Sturmgeschütz-Abteilung 202* destroyed a Soviet AFV.[204]

14 FEBRUARY 1942

Elements of *Kampfgruppe 'Oven'* occupied Jagodnaja (5 km south-east of Afonasowa) during violent urban fighting. They took three Soviet AFVs by surprise and blew them up. After cleaning up the surrounding woodland, *Infanterie-Regiment 339* captured Popow (4 km north-west of Schwanowo). Following that, the *II. Bataillon* of the infantry regiment with two assault guns of *Sturmgeschütz-Abteilung 202* pursued two Soviet tanks as they retreated in the direction of Afonasowa. The assault guns knocked out one of the tanks and damaged the other and in the area of Afonasowa they disabled more Soviet heavy weapons.[205]

16 FEBRUARY 1942

During the early part of the morning forces of the Soviet 3 Army, with the support of several modern tanks and bombers, launched an attack on the northern flank of the *25. Infanterie-Division (mot.)* in the area of Sinkowo.

Sturmgeschütz-Abteilung 202 was ordered to send an additional assault gun to the division under attack.[206] A StuG. III, returned from repairs, was transferred to the commander of *Kradschützen-Bataillon 25*, 14 km east of Bolchow without delay.[207] Apart from the assault gun, the division received the four 4.7 cm self-propelled anti-tank guns of *1. Kompanie/Panzerjäger-Abteilung 529.*[208]

17 FEBRUARY 1942

Leutnant Helmut Weirich of *Sturmgeschütz-Abteilung 202,* a platoon leader of the *2. Batterie*, knocked out four Soviet tanks in the day's fighting in the sector

---

203 NARA T315, R1954 (*296. Infanterie-Division*), F001075.
204 NARA T314, R1314 (*LIII. Armeekorps*), F001059.
205 NARA T314, R1314 (*LIII. Armeekorps*), F001058.
206 NARA T314, R1313 (*LIII. Armeekorps*), F000796.
207 NARA T314, R1314 (*LIII. Armeekorps*), F000429.
208 NARA T314, R1314 (*LIII. Armeekorps*), F000430.

of the *25. Infanterie-Division (mot.),* in the area of Kriwzowa.[209] Those tanks – according to German reconnaissance data – belonged to the newly formed Soviet 79 Tank Brigade.[210]

18 FEBRUARY 1942

In the morning, following a ferocious artillery preparation against the front line of the *25. Infanterie-Division (mot.),* the Soviet units launched an attack with armour and air support on the positions of the *III. Bataillon / Infanterie-Regiment 35 (mot.)* and *Kradschützen-Bataillon 25* in the area of Kriwzowa. Although eight Soviet tanks penetrated their defences, the Germans didn't give up their positions. The Soviet tanks that had broken through were heading towards Hill 203.5 when they were knocked out sometime after 1030 hours[211] by an assault gun of *Sturmgeschütz-Abteilung 202* (*Leutnant* Weirich); another two were destroyed by German field artillery (presumably by direct fire).[212]

The fate of another two Soviet tanks unfolds in the daily report of *Oberleutnant* Kaiser, commander of the *6. Kompanie/Panzer-Regiment 39*[213]:

It was known to me that significant armoured forces breached the sector there and that they were moving here and there behind the positions of the motorcycle rifle-infantry. Two heavy tanks (32-ton [214]) were stuck in the deep snow in the sector of the motorcycle rifle-infantry, north of Chmelewaja, in a narrow valley. The infantry's attempts to close on and destroy them failed because the two tanks provided covering fire for each other. I decided to hunt down the two tanks mentioned above with a Panzer III so I brought it forward in the narrow valley to within 400 m of them. Unfortunately none of the ammunition carried by the Panzer-Kampfwg. III was able to knock out the tanks. When I myself received fire from the tanks, I withdrew the Panzer III, and brought forward a Panzer IV that had fallen out because of its fuel supply. Two Rotkopfgranate hit its[the Soviet tank] *hull setting it ablaze.*

I hunted it down the second tank, of which only the muzzle of the 76.2 mm barrel could be seen and which was continuously firing at me, the following way:

---

209 NARA T314, R1314 (*LIII. Armeekorps*), F000399.

210 NARA T315, R812 (*25. Infanterie-Division [mot.]*), F000962. The 79 Tank Brigade had 20 T-34 and 26 T-60 tanks on 1 February 1942. *See* http://www.tankfront.ru/ussr/tbr/tbr079.html However, the 80 Tank Brigade was also deployed soon in this sector, raised on 21 January 1942, from 26 Valentine tanks of British-American origin and 20 Soviet T-60 tanks. *See* http://www.tankfront.ru/ussr/tbr/tbr080.html

211 NARA T315, R812 (*25. Infanterie-Division [mot.]*), F001001.

212 NARA T314, R1314 (*LIII. Armeekorps*), F001034.

213 In the morning of that day the company had three combat ready tanks plus the assault gun of *Leutnant* Weirich attached to them. *See* NARA T315, R812 (*25. Infanterie-Division [mot.]*), F001001.

214 It is also evident from the other part of the report, that those were T-34 tanks. The type was called 25-ton, 30-ton and 32-ton by the Germans until mid-1942. Finally it was included in the AFV identification aids as 26-ton medium tank.

I struggled forward on foot towards the tank, and at 50 m I moved sideways while the Panzer-Kampfwg. IV. remained in the position from which I had knocked out the first tank.. Making use of the curved trajectory, I used hand signals to indicate the direction in which the change in deflection was to be made. I disabled this tank with the fourth round – by a hit on the barrel. The crew got out of the tank and we took them as prisoners.

Just then four more (32-ton) tanks attacked the sector and the company, under the command of Leutnant Weirich, knocked them out with the aid of an assault gun. So on that day we destroyed six enemy tanks (32-ton T–34s).

Ammunition expenditure: 19×7,5 cm Pz. Gr. 38; 80×5 cm Pz. Gr. 38; 24×5 cm Pz. Gr. 40.[215]

Despite the events described in the armoured company's report – according to which the assault gun only provided aid in knocking out the Soviet tanks – verification of the report confirmed that four Soviet tanks had been destroyed by *Leutnant* Weirich while only two had been destroyed by the armoured company during the day's fighting.[216] In relation to this, the staff of the *17. Panzer-Division* recommended the officer's name to be mentioned to the corps.[217]

Another assault-gun commander of *Sturmgeschütz-Abteilung 202, Oberwachtmeister* Schirmer also put up a good fight that day. At around 1330 hours the Soviet troops attacked from the area of Fetischtschewo in a southerly direction. The *1. Kompanie/ Infanterie-Regiment 35 (mot.)* launched a counter-thrust with the efficient support from Schirmer's assault gun, and by doing that, they could not only prevent the Soviets from taking a significant hill, but they also pushed them back into Fetischtschewo.[218]

The new commander of the *LIII. Armeekorps, Generalleutnant* Heinrich Clößner,[219] expressed his gratitude by telegram to the *25. Infanterie-Division (mot.)* for their firmness during the three days of battle and at the same time praised the assault guns of *Sturmgeschütz-Abteilung 202* among the supporting forces.[220]

19 FEBRUARY 1942

The *LIII. Armeekorps* reported that its forces had won a defensive victory and that during the previous four days they had knocked out a total of 46 Soviet tanks (mostly T–34s). Among other things, the corps highlighted the heroic firmness shown during the fighting by two soldiers (*Leutnant* Weirich and *Oberwachtmeister* Schirmer) of *Sturmgeschütz-Abteilung 202.*[221]

215 NARA T314, R1315 (*LIII. Armeekorps*), F000269.

216 NARA T314, R1314 (*LIII. Armeekorps*), F000399.

217 NARA T314, R1314 (*LIII. Armeekorps*), F000908. Finally it didn't happen.

218 NARA T315, R812 (*25. Infanterie-Division [mot.]*), F000983.

219 The General-Lieutenant assumed command of the corps on 15 January 1942.

220 NARA T314, R1314 (*LIII. Armeekorps*), F000409.

221 NARA T314, R1313 (*LIII. Armeekorps*), F000806.

Schirmer and his assault gun received a mission as early as 0330 hours because the Soviets had broken through the positions of the *1. Kompanie/Infanterie-Regiment 35. (mot.)* in the district of Fetischtschewo. However, with the support of Schirmer's StuG. III, a German counter-thrust was launched and by 0500 hours the original situation was restored.[222]

At around 1100 hours in the south-eastern area of Kriwzowa, south of Fetischtschewo, the NCO knocked out two of 13 attacking Soviet tanks and seriously damaged a third.[223] The first of these three tanks was successfully knocked out by Schirmer when, at around 1035 hours, the Soviets launched an attack from Fetischtschewo. The tanks reached the German positions where only walls of tightly packed snow provided cover for them. After knocking out the first tank, at around 1100 hours, the Germans repulsed the assault of the Soviet rifle infantry before the tanks rolled back to the settlement.

At 1130 hours the Soviets launch another attack from the area of Fetischtschewo. At this time, Schirmer destroyed one more tank, and damaged another. Finally the Germans repelled this attempt, too.[224]

Sturmgeschütz-Abteilung 202 reported to the corps that the seventh combat-ready assault gun that had been promised would be ready for dispatch only by 21 February due to technical problems. The technical officer of the assault gun unit prepared a detailed report giving reasons for this delay:

Refitting the engine of the sixth assault gun was delayed due to different technical problems. The engine intended for the assault gun was not compatible with the series in which the assault gun had been produced. The engine was shipped without a clutch so the workshop had no other choice but to dismount the used clutch and fit it to the new engine. On 14 February 1942 we reported to the Abteilung about the failure of the workshop's generator without which it was not possible to perform counter-balancing on the turning lathe. Nor could I obtain spare parts – despite an immediate discussion with the V. [vehicle] *division of the LIII. Armeekorps and a discussion with the workshops in Bolchow and Orel. The drive shaft was repaired by arduous, manual work just as in the manufacture of the few screws used. I tried to make up for lost time in the same way as we did for the seventh assault gun – with night work – but due to a partial dropping out of the work force this was successful only to a certain extent. Two specialist engine-fitters from Maybach worked for 68 hours with only a four hours' rest. As a consequence, one of them had to cease work*

222 NARA T315, R812 (*25. Infanterie-Division [mot.]*), F000984.

223 NARA T315, R812 (*25. Infanterie-Division [mot.]*), F000985. In the corps' daily report it is also included, that „*an assault gun* [*Oberwachtmeister* Schirmer] *knocked out three enemy tanks*". *See* NARA T314, R1314 (*LIII. Armeekorps*), F0001031. However, in the course of the verifying process, the amount was reduced to two tanks, obviously because the damaged tank was able to return behind the Soviet lines.

224 NARA T315, R812 (*25. Infanterie-Division [mot.]*), F000985.

due to indisposition. Despite all the efforts of the repair detachment, the assault gun could not be repaired by the day previously fixed by Major Mainzinger and Oberinspector Hobusch.[225]

20 FEBRUARY 1942

The corps informed the staff of the *56. Infanterie-Division* that *Sturmgeschütz-Abteilung 202* would receive the repaired assault gun that would be ready for dispatch at 1300 hours. However, the StuG. III had, for reasons of supply, to be subordinated by the division to *Infanterie-Regiment (mot.) 'Grossdeutschland'* which was equipped with this kind of armoured fighting vehicle.[226]

21 FEBRUARY 1942

In the morning, the corps assembled the combat-ready tanks of *17. Panzer-Division,* the assault guns of *Sturmgeschütz-Abteilung 202* and some infantry to attack and take Fetischtschewo. Around noon, *Infanterie-Regiment 339* launched its attack – with the *II. Bataillon/Infanterie-Regiment 331,* two companies of *Pionier-Bataillon 25* and the *I. Bataillon/Schützen-Regiment 40* under its command – from the area of Boresnika in an easterly direction. The *II. Bataillon/Infanterie-Regiment 331* successfully penetrated into the southern part of Fetischtschewo.[227]

In the day's fighting *Leutnant* Weirich distinguished himself again by knocking out five more Soviet tanks.[228] The courage of the assault artillery lieutenant was emphasized by *Generalmajor* Rudolf-Eduard Licht, commander of the *17. Panzer-Division* in his telephone call to the staff of the corps that day and, at the same time, he recommended Weirich for the Knight's Cross of the Iron Cross.[229]

22 FEBRUARY 1942

Leutnant Weirich knocked out his 14 Soviet tank in the fighting that had been in progress since 17 February.[230] The lieutenant's assault gun was temporarily out of action due to damage to the clutch which had presumably been hit by an anti-tank round.[231]

---

225 NARA T314, R1314 (*LIII. Armeekorps*), F000737.

226 NARA T314, R1314 (*LIII. Armeekorps*), F000402.

227 NARA T314, R1313 (*LIII. Armeekorps*), F000814.

228 NARA T314, R1314 (*LIII. Armeekorps*), F000399. As to the tanks knocked out by the lieutenant, it is misleading, that in its daily report of 21 February 1942, the corps states that including the five knockouts scored by him on that day, Weirich knocked out his 9 Soviet tank during the battle along the Oka River. *See* NARA T314, R1314 (*LIII. Armeekorps*), F001019. However, according to the corps' detailed summary those were the 9-13 tanks knocked out by the lieutenant. *See* Appendix for details of knockouts.

229 NARA T314, R1315 (*LIII. Armeekorps*), F000271. According to the available information, in the end, Weirich was not given the award. But instead he received the certificate of recognition of the Supreme Commander of the German Army on 8 March 1942.

230 NARA T314, R1314 (*LIII. Armeekorps*), F000399.

231 NARA T314, R1314 (*LIII. Armeekorps*), F000725.

According to the war diary of the *25. Infanterie-Division (mot.),* a few minutes after 0800 hours the Soviets launched an attack from the direction of Fetischtschewo towards Lubny with armoured support. Three tanks and one assault gun of the German armoured group – that had just arrived – were fielded against them and knocked out two Soviet tanks.[232]

In the sector of the corps, a total of 59 knocked-out Soviet tanks were confirmed between 16 and 22 February. The two assault guns of *Sturmgeschütz-Abteilung 202* scored 16 kills. With this achievement, their tally was just one tank less than the 'top scoring' *6. Kompanie/Panzer-Regiment 39* which scored 17 knockouts.[233] The 'third placed competitor' was *Panzerjäger-Abteilung 25* of the *25. Infanterie-Division (mot.)* with 11 knocked-out enemy tanks.[234]

The commander of *Sturmgeschütz-Abteilung 202, Major* Karl Evers, made an account of the subordinate relations of his assault guns:

1. The *Kampfgruppe* of *Leutnant* Wahl operated in the sector of *296. Infanterie-Division* with four assault guns. Two were at the disposal of the division's staff and two provided cover on the line of *Aufklärungs-Abteilung 156.* Their supply base was in Peredel.
2. *Leutnant* Weirich and *Oberwachtmeister* Schirmer fought with one assault gun each in the sector of the *17. Panzer-Division*, in the area of Asarowo. Their supply base was in Beli-Kolodes.
3. *Oberwachtmeister* Osterhage with his assault gun was deployed in the sector of the *56. Infanterie-Division* in the area of Melechowo. His supply base was in Jagodnaja.

Major Karl Evers also gave his recommendations considering the distribution of the assault guns in the future:

The Kampfgruppe of Leutnant Wahl (296. Infanterie-Division) and the two independent assault guns (one of them is out of action) are subordinated – in terms provision – to the divisions. Ammunition and fuel is transported by the [*Sturmgeschütz-*] *Abteilung itself in advance upon request.*

An independent assault gun (56. Infanterie-Division) is subordinated in terms of provision to I. R. GD [*Infanterie-Regiment (mot.) 'Grossdeutschland'*].

A Kampfgruppe incorporates at least two, or as far as is possible, three combat-

232 NARA T315, R812 (*25. Infanterie-Division [mot.]*), F000987. If Weirich knocked out his 14 Soviet tank during this battle, is it possible, that the attack was launched earlier or the assault gun of the lieutenant was put out of action later, or was he successful with a disabled assault gun by chance?

233 If the corps made mistakes in totalizing the figures as to the knocked out AFVs, and *Oberwachtmeister* Schirmer indeed knocked out three tanks on 19 February 1942, then the two assault guns of *Sturmgeschütz-Abteilung 202* knocked out exactly as much Soviet combat vehicles as the eight tanks of the 6. company of *Panzer-Regiment 39*. It is worth to note, that the armoured company knocked out another two AFVs on 23 and an additional two on 26 February 1942. *See* NARA T314, R1314 (*LIII. Armeekorps*), F001005.

234 NARA T314, R1314 (*LIII. Armeekorps*), F000399.

ready assault guns in the event that one of them has to withdraw. Since the Abteilung has only six combat-ready assault guns after Leutnant Weirich's gun dropped out on 22 February and the corps is planning to leave the Kampfgruppe of Leutnant Wahl with four assault guns at the 296. Infanterie-Division, the Abteilung can set up only one more Kampfgruppe with the remaining two deployable assault guns. For this reason the Abteilung recommends transferring the independent assault gun from 56. Infanterie-Division and attaching it to the 17. Panzer-Division where there is already an independent assault gun (Oberwachtmeister Schirmer). In this way another Kampfgruppe could be set up under the command of Leutnant Weirich.

Regarding the at least two additional assault guns obtained after receiving and mounting the spare engines claimed in Smolensk, and which are already in transit from there, the Abteilung recommends that they should be attached as a third Kampfgruppe to the 56. Infanterie-Division.

Should the assault guns of I. R. GD be deployed again, the Abteilung suggests the additional assault guns that have been made ready (but not more than two) should be subordinated/attached to the I. R. GD which would mean temporarily giving up the idea of setting up a third Kampfgruppe of Sturmgeschütz-Abteilung 202.[235]

24 FEBRUARY 1942

A platoon leader of the *3. Batterie/Sturmgeschütz-Abteilung 202, Leutnant der Reserve* Randzio was wounded.[236]

26 FEBRUARY 1942

The corps informed the staff of *25. Infanterie-Division (mot.)* that the following day they would receive the two assault guns of *Sturmgeschütz-Abteilung 202* that had undergone repairs that same day and that they had been dispatched to Teltsche. The two assault guns were to be employed in one *Kampfgruppe* if possible.[237]

28 FEBRUARY 1942

In the morning, the *167. Infanterie-Division* asked the *LIII. Armeekorps* to reinforce the *Sturmgeschütz-Abteilung 202* due to the possibility of enemy tanks providing support for the expected Soviet attack.[238]

As an answer to that, the corps attached only one assault gun. It arrived, following its repair that day,[239] in the early afternoon.[240]

---

235 NARA T314, R1314 (*LIII. Armeekorps*), F000726.

236 NARA T313, R108 (*Panzerarmeeoberkommando 2*), F7352756.

237 NARA T314, R1314 (*LIII. Armeekorps*), F000385.

238 NARA T315, R1477 (*167. Infanterie-Division*), F001053.

239 NARA T315, R1479 (*167. Infanterie-Division*), F000644.

240 NARA T315, R1477 (*167. Infanterie-Division*), F001056.

At 2210 hours *Infanterie-Regiment 520*, which was part of the *296. Infanterie-Division's* order of battle, reported to the staff of the *167. Infanterie-Division* that the assault gun had arrived in Ruka.[241]

6 MARCH 1942

The corps ordered *Gruppe 'Krischer'* to dispatch one of the assault guns of *Sturmgeschütz-Abteilung 202* to Jagodnaja, to the command post of *Kampfgruppe 'Oven'*. The assault gun had been subordinated to this battle group but for reasons of supply it came under command of *Infanterie-Regiment (mot.) 'Grossdeutschland'*.[242]

7 MARCH 1942

The *2. Panzerarmee* sent an experience report to the *LIII. Armeekorps* so that its subordinate units could offer their opinion if they wished to do so. In relation to the assault guns[243] the report mentioned the following:

Infantry attacking on open ground with assault guns along roads and villages gives the best promise of success.

[...]

Timing of attack: in daylight the time of attack should be varied.

[...]

Assault guns: best weapon for infantry attack! Before missions, roads must be dug free [of snow]. For example, with the help of a construction battalion one-and-a-half km of road was cleared of deep snow and the mission achieved great success.

Arrive only at the time the attack starts: each mission must be planned and the ground inspected in advance! Infantry should order a light machine gun to each assault gun with plentiful ammunition and a two-man crew from the pioneer platoon of the infantry as far as possible...and they should be trained in mine detection.

It is useful and effective to employ the assault guns (three in one direction of attack worked well, but at least two are necessary) together with at least one self-propelled 2 cm Flak cannon to efficiently cover the vulnerable sides of the assault guns. On more extensive shrubby or woody terrain, assault guns are unsuccessful without such defence. Assault guns have no revolving turrets, they can fire only forward, so they must not be used as tanks. It must be ensured that all threats to their flanks is eliminated.[244]

---

241 NARA T315, R1477 (*167. Infanterie-Division*), F001057.

242 NARA T314, R1314 (*LIII. Armeekorps*), F000361.

243 Although the name of *Sturmgeschütz-Abteilung 202* is not mentioned in the report, in the first three months of 1941 there were no other assault artillery unit in the *2. Panzerarmee* order of battle, except for the assault guns of the *16. Kompanie/ Infanterie-Regiment (mot.) „Grossdeutschland"*.

244 NARA T314, R1315 (*LIII. Armeekorps*), F000206-208.

8 MARCH 1942

At 2300 hours the Soviets launched an attack on Leninskoje from an easterly direction after thorough, and ferocious, mortar and artillery preparation. They also managed to break through the line of the German advance guard. With the support of the *Sturmgeschütz-Abteilung 202*'s assault guns located in the settlement, a German counter-thrust was launched and by 0130 hours next day the original situation was restored.[245]

11 MARCH 1942

The *LIII. Armeekorps* subordinated two self-propelled 4.7 cm anti-tank guns of *1. Kompanie/ Panzerjäger-Abteilung 529* to *Sturmgeschütz-Abteilung 202* in terms of supply and registration but the corps retained the power to make decisions regarding their deployment.[246]

12 MARCH 1942

Two assault guns of *3. Batterie/Sturmgeschütz-Abteilung 202* provided support for two counter-thrusts in the area of Kriwzowa to repel Soviet forces that had broken into the German defences. Being short of ammunition, the assault guns opened fire only at close range in the hope of a higher probability of hitting their targets. The two StuG. IIIs knocked out a Soviet T–34 tank and an anti-tank gun in these actions. However, the Soviet tank was able to knock out one of the assault guns.[247]

13 MARCH 1942

At around 0400 hours in the sector of the *296. Infanterie-Division,* between strongpoints Nr. 2 and 3, the Soviets established an undermined wooden obstacle on the road by means of which they separated two bunkers from each other. The Germans tried to clear it by deploying an assault squad but they encountered fierce resistance. The Germans then deployed a *Kampfgruppe* – made up of infantry, pioneers and two assault guns – that managed to disperse the entrenched Soviet detachment and remove the undermined road block thereby restoring the connection between the bunkers.[248]

The corps instructed *Sturmgeschütz-Abteilung 202* to deploy one more assault gun in the sector of the *56. Infanterie-Division* as a response to an emerging tactical situation.[249]

---

245 NARA T315, R1954 (*296. Infanterie-Division*), F001103.

246 NARA T314, R1314 (*LIII. Armeekorps*), F000332.

247 Alfons, Fischer: Tagebuch eines Wolfurters zwischen 1939 und 1946. In: Heimat Wolfurt. Heft 10. p. 28.

248 NARA T315, R1954 (*296. Infanterie-Division*), F001107.

249 NARA T314, R1314 (*LIII. Armeekorps*), F000327.

15 MARCH 1942

In the sector of the *56. Infanterie-Division*, an attack of limited aims was planned to take place in the area of Nogaja. With the support of two assault guns of *Sturmgeschütz-Abteilung 202*, two companies dashed forward through a forest towards defensive strongpoints Nr. 2 and Nr. 3, cleaning up the Soviet troops. [250]

According to the actual order of battle that day, *Sturmgeschütz-Abteilung 202* was the only remaining assault artillery formation in the *2. Panzerarmee.*[251]

16 MARCH 1942

At 1100 hours in the sector of *296. Infanterie-Division*, an assault was launched to retake defensive strongpoint Nr. 2 in the Leninskoje area. The Soviet security forces were successfully driven back but the supporting assault guns of *Sturmgeschütz-Abteilung 202* could not gain access to the cleared road due to difficulties presented by the terrain. Thus the assault, which was without artillery support , was stopped by the Soviet artillery fire.[252]

17 MARCH 1942

The *56. Infanterie-Division* submitted an experience report to the corps in relation to the winter battles. The following things were highlighted in the document:

> *To carry out a successful attack against enemy strongpoints, it is of decisive importance to support infantry with tanks or assault guns in case the deep snow hinders their mobility and friendly heavy weapons are not able to follow the attack.*[253]

18 MARCH 1942

In the sector of the *296. Infanterie-Division* in Leninskoje area, the Germans launched another assault to try to re-establish contact with a formation to their left.

A Soviet attack delayed the launch of the German assault to 1400 hours. A platoon of pioneers from *10. Kompanie/ Infanterie-Regiment 520,* one tank and two StuG. III assault guns of *Sturmgeschütz-Abteilung 202*, with the fire support of heavy mortars and heavy machine guns, threw back the Soviet advance guard to the west of Leninskoje and took one their bunkers which was then blown up. The German force was unable to push any further forward because the Soviets defended with determination and the effective use of snipers placed in trees. The assault guns suffered minor damage to their sighting telescopes but this was nevertheless sufficient to disable them. Moreover, *6. Kompanie / Infanterie-Regiment 234* – the neighbour on their left – attacked in another direction than that which

250 NARA T314, R1313 (*LIII. Armeekorps*), F000898, 000900.

251 NARA T314, R1314 (*LIII. Armeekorps*), F000579.

252 NARA T315, R1954 (*296. Infanterie-Division*), F001113.

253 NARA T314, R1315 (*LIII. Armeekorps*), F000198.

was previously planned. The two German attacking parties were therefore unable to join forces and this put an end to the German assault.[254]

20 MARCH 1942

The *167. Infanterie-Division* prepared to withdraw its forces to the 'Baschkino' blocking position. In course of this – the 13 day of the operational move – it was planned that the single assault gun attached to the division would to be subordinated to *Infanterie-Regiment 331* and sent to Borisowka area.[255] The assault gun concealed the withdrawal of the troops by making itself frequently visible to the Soviet troops.[256]

On the same day the actual strength of *Sturmgeschütz-Abteilung 202* comprised a total of eleven StuG. III assault guns and 23 machine guns distributed as follows:

- four machine guns in the staff battery
- four assault guns and eight machine guns in *1. Batterie*
- four assault guns and seven machine guns in *2. Batterie*
- three assault guns and four machine guns in *3. Batterie.* [257]

21 MARCH 1942

The corps placed an additional assault gun under the command of the *296. Infanterie-Division* with immediate effect. *Sturmgeschütz-Abteilung 202* had to dispatch the assault gun to Peredel area, if road conditions allowed.[258]

22 MARCH 1942

The *LIII. Armeekorps* outlined the plans of an attack of limited aims on a bridgehead held by the Soviets in the Siwkowo–Tolkatschewo sector. The intention was to use forces of the *25. Infanterie-Division (mot.)* and the *112. Infanterie-Division,* and these would have been supported by a tank company subordinated to the corps and the assault guns of *Sturmgeschütz-Abteilung 202.*[259]

In the sector of the *296. Infanterie-Division* an assault gun of the assault artillery unit arrived at Peredel area in the afternoon.[260]

23 MARCH 1942

Sturmgeschütz-Abteilung 202 received orders to start to pull back to the 'Baschkino' blocking position the following day and carried out tasks connected with this.

254 NARA T315, R1954 (*296. Infanterie-Division*), F001116 and F001118, and also NARA T314, R1322 (*LIII. Armeekorps*), F000370.

255 NARA T315, R1479 (*167. Infanterie-Division*), F000686.

256 NARA T315, R1479 (*167. Infanterie-Division*), F000694.

257 NARA T314, R1314 (*LIII. Armeekorps*), F000581.

258 NARA T314, R1314 (*LIII. Armeekorps*), F000267.

259 NARA T314, R1314 (*LIII. Armeekorps*), F000261.

260 NARA T315, R1954 (*296. Infanterie-Division*), F001120.

24 MARCH 1942

The assault guns of the assault artillery unit covered the retreat of the troops with their demonstrative movements to make the Soviets believe that the positions were still held by the Germans.[261]

The *LIII. Armeekorps* submitted an experience report to the staff of the *2. Panzerarmee* with respect to anti-tank weapons. In connection with StuG. III assault guns the following conclusions were drawn:

> *The assault guns proved to be the best anti-tank weapons against light and medium (even T–34) tanks. To some extent, they were quite effective even against heavy tanks.*[262]

26 MARCH 1942

During the morning hours, as preparation for the planned attack of limited aims, the *LIII. Armeekorps* decided that two assault guns should be detached from the *56. Infanterie-Division* and subordinated to the *112. Infanterie-Division* on 28 March.[263]

27 MARCH 1942

At 1015 hours, the commander of the *LIII. Armeekorps, Generalleutnant* Clößner, had a discussion with *Generalleutnant* Friedrich Mieth, commander of the *112. Infanterie-Division.* The division commander brought up the subject of the assault guns of *Sturmgeschütz-Abteilung 202: 'I have only two of them, and they have to be repaired first, although two platoons were promised to me.'* The corps commander replied: '*As it is well-known, a platoon comprises two guns. The guns will be repaired here, soon, so they are truly at your disposal. I told you then that I would see if I could put two or three platoons at your disposal.'*[264]

28 MARCH 1942

At 1340 hours, in the sector of *296. Infanterie-Division, Infanterie-Regiment 519* received two assault guns that were transferred to Grynskije Dwory area due to the increased concentration of Soviet forces in vicinity of Gryn. In the afternoon the Germans indeed discovered one of the Soviet's readiness positions east of the settlement. The German counter-thrust, launched with the support of the assault guns, was thrown back by the Soviets. In the difficult terrain the StuG. IIIs were unable to provide effective support.[265]

261 NARA T314, R1315 (*LIII. Armeekorps*), F000362.

262 NARA T314, R1315 (*LIII. Armeekorps*), F000215. For the results of the test gunnery of the StuG. III against the T–34 and KV–2 tank conducted in the sector of the *9. Armee* see Appendix 5.

263 NARA T314, R1314 (*LIII. Armeekorps*), F000251.

264 NARA T314, R1315 (*LIII. Armeekorps*), F000182.

265 NARA T315, R1954 (*296. Infanterie-Division*), F001126.

29 MARCH 1942

The *112. Infanterie-Division* reported its revised conception on the subject of the attack on the bridgehead in the Siwkowo–Bolwanowka sector to the staff of the *LIII. Armeekorps*. In the course of the attack, which was planned for launch at dawn on 31 March, two assault gun platoons (theoretically four StuG. IIIs) of *Sturmgeschütz-Abteilung 202* were to be attached to the *Kampfgruppe* based on *Infanterie-Regiment 258*, together with one-and-a-half companies with flame-throwers from *Pionier-Bataillon 112.*[266] Organized into assault squads, the latter's main task was to eliminate Soviet fortified defensive positions and dug-in Soviet tanks used as strongpoints.[267]

31 MARCH 1942

After days of preliminary planning, the reinforced units of the *112. Infanterie-Division* began their attack on the Soviet bridgehead in the area around Siwkowo and Tolkatschewo at 0400 hours. By 0700 hours the Germans had reached the west bank of River Oka. After crossing the river, they pursued the retreating Soviet troops on the opposite bank. Later, the division went on the defensive: the main combat line ran along the western bank with the advance guard on the eastern side. In the course of the elimination of the Soviet bridgehead, the Germans reported 550 Soviets killed and 577 prisoners taken.[268]

In the sector of the *167. Infanterie-Division* an assault gun of *Sturmgeschütz-Abteilung 202* was ordered back to Utkino.[269]

The *LIII. Armeekorps* ordered the *112. Infanterie-Division* to release the assault gun of *Sturmgeschütz-Abteilung 202* – previously received from *25. Infanterie-Division (mot.)* – for reassignment to the *25. Infanterie-Division (mot.)* the following day.[270]

3 APRIL 1942

At 1145 hours, the *LIII. Armeekorps* issued orders to the staff of the *167. Infanterie-Division* to dispatch the only assault gun subordinated to them to Bolchow for maintenance.[271] In the end, the assault gun set off towards the town at 1900 hours.[272]

However, the *296. Infanterie-Division* was informed by the corps at 1330 hours, that *Sturmgeschütz-Abteilung 202* would dispatch an assault gun to the division next day.[273]

---

266 NARA T314, R1314 (*LIII. Armeekorps*), F000664. According to the version as of 25 March 1942, even the battle group of *25. Infanterie-Division (mot.)* would have received an assault gun platoon. See NARA T314, R1314 (*LIII. Armeekorps*), F000673.

267 NARA T315, R812 (*25. Infanterie-Division [mot.]*), F001032.

268 NARA T314, R1315 (*LIII. Armeekorps*), F000005.

269 NARA T315, R1477 (*167. Infanterie-Division*), F001132.

270 NARA T314, R1314 (*LIII. Armeekorps*), F000233.

271 NARA T315, R1477 (*167. Infanterie-Division*), F001141.

272 NARA T314, R1322 (*LIII. Armeekorps*), F000535.

273 NARA T314, R1319 (*LIII. Armeekorps*), F000374.

In the sector of the *112. Infanterie-Division*, it was planned to order two assault guns of the *2. Batterie/ Sturmgeschütz-Abteilung 202* in Paltschikowo to the sector of *Infanterie-Regiment 110*. This plan ran into difficulties because having crossed the bridge in the area of Staraja Melniza, the assault guns were unable to climb the icy slopes on the far side.[274]

4 APRIL 1942

In the morning, in the sector of *112. Infanterie-Division*, two assault guns of *Sturmgeschütz-Abteilung 202* arrived for the division in the area of Mentelowo.[275]

In the afternoon, at 1245 hours in the sector of *296. Infanterie-Division*, elements of two reinforced companies (*6.* and *10. Kompanie)* of *Infanterie-Regiment 519* launched an attack with limited aims on Mitrochij. The plan was worked out by the acting regimental commander, *Major* Alfred Druffner, on his own initiative.

The infantry was supported by part of the divisional artillery, an assault gun of *Sturmgeschütz-Abteilung 202* and a self-propelled 4.7 cm anti-tank gun. The two AFVs attacked from the direction of Star-Wyselky.

The Germans overran one of the 76.2 mm Soviet artillery batteries south of Mitrochij, took the artillerymen as prisoners, destroyed the guns and knocked out four more anti-tank guns in the settlement. Following that, the attack group was withdrawn to the Star-Wyselky area.[276]

According to a German report, the action was successful: the Soviets lost 80–100 dead, 23 POWs, four 76.2 mm guns and eight machine guns. In addition to this many small arms were captured. The assault gun that participated in the attack destroyed an anti-tank gun, scoring a direct hit.[277]

5 APRIL 1942

At 1630 hours, in the sector of *112. Infanterie-Division*, the ammunition depot of *Sturmgeschütz-Abteilung 202,* established in Paltschikowo, was set on fire by the weapons of two Soviet aircraft. In the ensuing explosions four houses were destroyed in the settlement.[278] The ammunition depot itself was in one of those buildings.[279]

The corps ordered its subordinate divisions to place the available assault guns and tanks in the positions corresponding to the probable focal points of the expected Soviet attack. The main reason for this was that the extremely muddy terrain restricted movement and so hindered the regrouping of armoured vehicles.

274 NARA T315, R1276 (*112. Infanterie-Division*), F000318.
275 NARA T314, R1322 (*LIII. Armeekorps*), F000533.
276 NARA T315, R1959 (*296. Infanterie-Division*), F000260.
277 NARA T314, R1322 (*LIII. Armeekorps*), F000530.
278 NARA T314, R1322 (*LIII. Armeekorps*), F000527.
279 NARA T315, R1276 (*112. Infanterie-Division*), F000320.

Troops were to deploy their armoured vehicles in preparation for counter-thrusts on ground higher than the sea of mud – so called 'islands.'[280]

6 APRIL 1942

The assault guns of *Sturmgeschütz-Abteilung 202* reported to the staff of the *112. Infanterie-Division* at 0815 hours to inform them that they had arrived in the area of Wys Marinskije.[281]

7 APRIL 1942

In the sector of the *296. Infanterie-Division* Soviet troops commenced an attack with about 800 soldiers at 1520 hours from the direction of Romanowka. The attempt was halted by the Germans at about 1700 hours, then elements of *Infanterie-Regiment 519* that had been attacked by the Soviets launched a counter-thrust from the direction of Annina towards Romanowka with the support of tanks, the assault guns of *Sturmgeschütz-Abteilung 202* and the divisional artillery. The Soviets retreated in the area of Romanowka in a panic.[282]

9 APRIL 1942

In the sector of the *296. Infanterie-Division,* north of Peredel, an assault detachment made up from two assault guns of *Sturmgeschütz-Abteilung 202*[283] and an infantry tank-destroyer squad eliminated a T–34 tank together with its crew at 1630 hours south of the so-called Graveyard Hill.[284] The assault guns fired at the Soviet tank several times but the hits were ineffective. Following that, one of the StuG. IIIs managed to fire into the fighting compartment through the driver's open hatch, scoring a devastating direct hit.[285] *25. Infanterie-Division (mot.)* received orders from the corps to dispatch the two assault guns of *Sturmgeschütz-Abteilung 202* attached to them to Bolchow the next morning where they were to remain at the corps' disposal.[286]

10 APRIL 1942

Three-and-a-half kilometres south-west of Saizewo, elements of the *296. Infanterie-Division* carried out a successful attack with the support of an armoured company and the assault guns of *Sturmgeschütz-Abteilung 202* taking a significant hill and shattering a Soviet concentration of around 1,000 soldiers. According German reports, 350 Red Army soldiers were killed and 44 taken prisoner. They also lost

280 NARA T314, R1319 (*LIII. Armeekorps*), F000368.

281 NARA T315, R1276 (*112. Infanterie-Division*), F000324.

282 NARA T314, R1322 (*LIII. Armeekorps*), F000519.

283 The two assault guns were attached to *Infanterie-Regiment 520* on that day. *See* NARA T315, R1959 (*296. Infanterie-Division*), F000861.

284 NARA T314, R1322 (*LIII. Armeekorps*), F000513.

285 NARA T315, R1959 (*296. Infanterie-Division*), F000270-272.

286 NARA T314, R1319 (*LIII. Armeekorps*), F000347.

seven anti-tank guns and 20 light machine guns with other equipment captured. The Germans sustained 27 casualties with 10 dead and 17 wounded. Two German tanks got stuck in the mud and had to be blown up.

The army commander called the attention of the corps headquarters to the fact that, since no tank or assault gun replacements could be expected in the near future, armoured fighting vehicles should be blown up only if their situation was truly irrecoverable but, at the same time, they should be used only behind friendly lines where recovery could more easily be accomplished.[287]

11 APRIL 1942

The *56. Infanterie-Division* received two repaired assault guns from *Sturmgeschütz-Abteilung 202,* that were put on standby for action in the area of Jagodnaja.[288]

13 APRIL 1942

In the sector of the *296. Infanterie-Division,* two assault guns of *Sturmgeschütz-Abteilung 202* and two self-propelled 4.7 cm anti-tank guns of *Panzerjäger-Abteilung 529* were in the regimental reserve of *Infanterie-Regiment 520.*[289]

17 APRIL 1942

The *LIII. Armeekorps* informed its subordinate divisions by telegram that from 21 April the commander of *Sturmgeschütz-Abteilung 202, Major* Karl Evers, would be temporarily the commanding officer of Bolchow. To carry out his mission, the staff of *Infanterie-Regiment 256* was placed under the major's command.[290]

18 APRIL 1942

The 1 (operations) staff officer of the *112. Infanterie-Division* gave orders to the commander of *Sturmgeschütz-Abteilung 202* to transfer the assault guns assigned to the division from Subkowo to Wys Marinskije area.[291]

21 APRIL 1942

The *112. Infanterie-Division* ordered *Sturmgeschütz-Abteilung 202* to relocate next morning with those elements that had been subordinated to the division from the area of Wys Marinskije to the settlement of Klutschnikowskije Wys, because the assault guns were heavily exposed to Soviet artillery fire in their current positions. One of the buildings used by the assault artillery unit had been demolished by a direct hit by that time.[292]

---

287 NARA T313, R108 (*Panzerarmeeoberkommando 2*), F7352863-864.

288 NARA T314, R1322 (*LIII. Armeekorps*), F000506.

289 NARA T315, R1959 (*296. Infanterie-Division*), F000849.

290 NARA T314, R1319 (*LIII. Armeekorps*), F000323.

291 NARA T315, R1276 (*112. Infanterie-Division*), F000340.

292 NARA T315, R1276 (*112. Infanterie-Division*), F000346.

1 MAY 1942

An assault gun platoon (led by *Leutnant* Wahl) from *Sturmgeschütz-Abteilung 202,* subordinated to the *296. Infanterie-Division,* together with the *1. Kompanie* (with self-propelled 4.7 cm anti-tank guns) of *Panzerjäger-Abteilung 529* stood by for action in the sector of *Infanterie-Regiment* 520.[293]

5 MAY 1942

The assault artillery unit had a total of 10 combat-ready StuG. III assault guns.[294]

6 MAY 1942

While subordinated to the *112. Infanterie-Division,* a *Kampfgruppe* of the *2. Batterie / Sturmgeschütz-Abteilung 202* operated with two StuG. III assault guns and 15 soldiers.[295]

13 MAY !942

In the early morning hours in the sector of *296. Infanterie-Division,* an assault group (two companies with two assault guns of *Sturmgeschütz-Abteilung 202*) of *Infanterie-Regiment 520,* under the command of *Oberleutnant der Reserve* Heinz Martin, holder of the Knight's Cross of the Iron Cross, took the north-eastern part of Peredel and broke through the enemy position held by the Soviet 1,178 Rifle Regiment after bitter house-to-house fighting. Elements of the Soviet force left behind 50 dead and 55 rifles as they fled toward the east (partly on trucks). The Germans captured eight prisoners, then blew up the Soviet strongpoints and set the remaining intact houses on fire.[296] The aim of the assault was to obtain more detailed reconnaissance information about the Soviet troops fighting in the area.[297]

14 MAY 1942

In a telephone conversation with the staff of the *2. Panzerarmee,* the chief of staff of the *LIII. Armeekorps, Oberst i.G.* Max Bork, reported in relation to the failed attempt against Mitrochij that, according to his original recommendation, the forces of the *296. Infanterie-Division* assigned with the task should have received only one or two tanks and (from *Sturmgeschütz-Abteilung 202* in all certainty) one assault gun for the mission. In comparison to that, the division commander, *Generalleutnant* Mieth, obtained a whole armoured company with seven tanks. However, in the course of the attack five of them ran into a Soviet minefield and, having sustained serious damage, had to be blown up.[298]

---

293 NARA T315, R1959 (*296. Infanterie-Division*), F000826.

294 NARA T314, R1320 (*LIII. Armeekorps*), F000376.

295 NARA T314, R1320 (*LIII. Armeekorps*), F000386.

296 NARA T314, R1322 (*LIII. Armeekorps*), F000438.

297 NARA T315, R1959 (*296. Infanterie-Division*), F000286.

298 NARA T314, R1318 (*LIII. Armeekorps*), F000172.

On the same day the corps instructed its subordinate divisions to hold the front line in the event of an attempted Soviet breakthrough. In preparation they were to organize their anti-tank force in depth with tank destroyer squads and a mobile anti-tank reserve (tanks, assault guns or self-propelled anti-tank guns) and emplace the assault guns in such a way that they could support immediate counter-thrusts against local incursions.[299]

25 MAY 1942

The *LIII. Armeekorps* ordered its subordinate divisions by telegram to dispatch the assault guns of *Sturmgeschütz-Abteilung 202* subordinated to the *56., 112.* and *296. Infanterie-Divisionen* to their parent unit at Bolchow for general overhaul. They were to arrive there on 28 May. At the same time, the commander of the assault artillery unit received orders to make the assault guns fully combat-ready as soon as possible, and report the number of fighting vehicles ready for combat regularly to the corps.[300]

27 MAY 1942

The *112. Infanterie-Division* ordered the *2. Batterie* (*Leutnant* Spannagel) of *Sturmgeschütz-Abteilung 202,* which at that point was attached to *Infanterie-Regiment 258*, to move off with the assault guns to Bolchow for general overhaul.[301]

On that day *56. Infanterie-Division* also received orders from the corps to dispatch the four StuG. IIIs under its command to Bolchow. However, the division pressed the corps for permission for one of the assault guns to remain in order to assist in an important attack with the forces of *Infanterie-Regiment 192* the following day.[302]

28 MAY 1942

At 0300 hours, elements of *Infanterie-Regiment 192* carried out an attack on Soviet bunkers and advanced positions near the German front line 2 km north-west of Kirejkowo. Besides three artillery batteries and a heavy infantry gun-platoon, the attempt was also supported by an assault gun of *Sturmgeschütz-Abteilung 202.* The Soviets had already retreated into the depths of a nearby forest during devastating fire lasting five minutes. Two assault squads entered the bunkers where, besides 12 dead, they found four soldiers from the 5 Company of the Soviet 1,168 rifle regiment, whom they took as prisoners. Finally, the three bunkers were blown up by the Germans.[303]

---

299 NARA T314, R1319 (*LIII. Armeekorps*), F000220.

300 NARA T314, R1319 (*LIII. Armeekorps*), F000197.

301 NARA T315, R1276 (*112. Infanterie-Division*), F000392, and also T315, R1277 (*112. Infanterie-Division*), F000050.

302 NARA T315, R969 (*56. Infanterie-Division*), F000153.

303 NARA T315, R969 (*56. Infanterie-Division*), F000153.

Following that, the assault guns of *Sturmgeschütz-Abteilung 202* were relieved from their assignment with to the *56. Infanterie-Division.*[304]

1 JUNE 1943

Sturmgeschütz-Abteilung 202 had 10 combat-ready StuG. III assault guns.[305]

4 JUNE 1942

The staff of *Sturmgeschütz-Abteilung 202* ordered the assault gun subordinated to the *112. Infanterie-Division* back to Bolchow for maintenance without notifying the corps. In response to this the division contacted the corps which confirmed the order relating to the withdrawal of the assault gun.[306]

11 JUNE 1942

Sturmgeschütz-Abteilung 202, with 10 deployable assault guns, was the only assault-gun formation under command of *2. Panzerarmee.*[307]

14 JUNE 1942

At 0200 hours, on the right flank of the *56. Infanterie-Division*, a Soviet artillery preparation began (eight batteries firing 1,200 rounds). The shelling of the German front line in the area of Shelesinskij lasted 76 minutes.

At 0330 hours, 150 Soviet soldiers commenced an attack from the eastern foreground of Ukolizy. The main attack was launched 15 minutes later: elements of the Soviet 149 and 346 Rifle Divisions (a total of 450 men) attacked with support provided by 13 tanks (four T–34s, nine T–60s) of the 68 Tank Brigade, flame throwers[308] and three aircraft.

Shelesinskij was defended by two platoons of *Infanterie-Regiment 192* in co-operation with advanced artillery observers from the *6.* and *12. Batterie /Artillerie-Regiment 156* respectively. At around 1530 hours the Germans ordered two additional platoons that were standing in reserve to move towards Shelesinskij. At 0428 hours the division requested assault guns from the corps. Two hours later an assault gun platoon was ready to march.[309]

At 0500 hours, having fought off three German anti-tank guns, three Soviet tanks penetrated into the area of Shelesinskij.[310] It was rather difficult for the Germans to get close to the Soviet tanks because they covered each other's movements.[311]

304 NARA T314, R1322 (*LIII. Armeekorps*), F000404.
305 NARA T314, R1320 (*LIII. Armeekorps*), F000374.
306 NARA T315, R1276 (*112. Infanterie-Division*), F000408.
307 NARA T314, R1320 (*LIII. Armeekorps*), F000361.
308 NARA T315, R970 (*56. Infanterie-Division*), F000137.
309 NARA T315, R969 (*56. Infanterie-Division*), F000127.
310 NARA T315, R970 (*56. Infanterie-Division*), F000137.
311 NARA T315, R970 (*56. Infanterie-Division*), F000163.

Nevertheless, a tank destroyer squad of the German infantry disabled one of the T–34s by damaging its track in a close combat. But the damage to one of the tanks didn't stop the advance of the others: at 0520 hours they reached the southern outskirts of the settlement. Following the tanks, Soviet riflemen occupied Shelesinskij in a quarter of an hour.

At 0600 hours the *56. Infanterie-Division* requested air support and an additional assault gun platoon from the corps. The division assembled its own rifle infantry and pioneer reserves. Twenty minutes later the Soviets pressed forward with 60 men and three T–34 tanks in the direction of Hill 268.9. After another ten minutes, the bulk of the Soviet forces continued their attack from Shelesinskij in an easterly direction, taking the German front line between the settlement and defensive strongpoint Nr. 153 (established 300 m west of Blinow) by 0700 hours. Forty-five minutes later, seven Soviet aircraft attacked the German troops in the area.

At 0905 hours, the first two assault guns of *Sturmgeschütz-Abteilung 202* arrived in Gorschetschnij south-east of Shelesinskij. Having received the reserves and the other two assault guns, the Germans commenced their counter-thrust at 1400 hours. On the right flank of the improvised *Kampfgruppe* was a company of the *II. Bataillon / Infanterie-Regiment 234 with the 3. Kompanie/ Infanterie-Regiment 192* in the middle and the *1. Kompanie/ Pionier-Bataillon 156* with the four StuG. III assault guns on the left flank. Artillery support was provided by a whole artillery battalion and eight batteries of various calibre. The attack was escorted by a group of German fighter aircraft and artillery reconnaissance aircraft.[312]

The counter-thrust was launched at 1400 hours from the sector of Gorschetschnij–Blinow in a westerly/north-westerly direction. After 48 minutes the Germans concentrated their artillery fire on the area of Shelesinskij because the resistance of the Soviet rifle infantry was at its stiffest there.

One of the German assault guns penetrated into the settlement, followed by German infantry. Shelesinskij fell into German hands once again at 1553 hours and by 1900 hours the sector, previously lost to the enemy, had been retaken. By then only three assault guns were combat-ready.[313] However, both sides suffered heavy losses during the violent fighting:

- Soviet troops: 50-55 dead, 15 prisoners (one of them was shot and killed by the Germans during an escape attempt), two 76.2 mm and two 45 mm anti-tank guns, one 76.2 mm infantry howitzer, one machine gun, one light machine gun and 15 rifles;
- German troops: 34 dead, 92 wounded, six missing in action.[314]

312 NARA T315, R969 (*56. Infanterie-Division*), F000123.

313 NARA T315, R970 (*56. Infanterie-Division*), F000143.

314 NARA T314, R1322 (*LIII. Armeekorps*), F000358-360.

The Germans knocked out three T–34s and four T–60 AFVs of the Soviet 68 Tank Brigade in the engagement. Five of them were destroyed by one of the assault guns from the *2. Batterie/ Sturmgeschütz-Abteilung 202,* the commander of which, *Oberwachtmeister* Heinrich Osterhage, was killed during the fighting around Shelesinskij.[315] The NCO's name was recorded in the Roll of Honour of the German Army *(Ehrenblatt des Heeres).* In addition, five enlisted assault artillerymen of the unit were wounded.[316] Of the tanks knocked out, one T–34 and one T–60 were retrieved by the Soviets. Thirty metres from the new front line the Germans blew up an knocked-out T–34 and T–60 to prevent the Soviets from towing them away and repairing them.

The experience report made after the engagement highlighted the role of the assault guns requested by the division:

The assault guns were requested without having been able to prepare their own defensive equipment properly. Screaming for assault guns makes the infantry develop an inferiority complex. They already have that. Assault guns are the corps' equipment for focal points. Therefore, infantry must be educated and trained in cooperation with other arms to fight off enemy attacks accompanied by tanks by themselves, employing their own equipment.[317]

In the sector of the *296. Infanterie-Division* at around 2200 hours, two assault guns of *Sturmgeschütz-Abteilung 202* were on their way from Gorjana toward Gorschetschnij.

15 JUNE 1942

At 0200 hours in the sector of *Sturmgeschütz-Abteilung 202*, the Germans towed back a damaged StuG. III from the front line.[318]

16 JUNE 1942

1025 hours: the four StuG. III assault guns received from *Sturmgeschütz-Abteilung 202* in the sector of the *56. Infanterie-Division*[319] were ordered to return to Bolchow.[320] The two assault gun platoons were finally detached from the division two days later.[321]

315 NARA T314, R1318 (*LIII. Armeekorps*), F000236.

316 NARA T315, R970 (*56. Infanterie-Division*), F000148.

317 NARA T314, R1322 (*LIII. Armeekorps*), F000349.

318 NARA T315, R1960 (*296. Infanterie-Division*), F000647.

319 NARA T315, R969 (*56. Infanterie-Division*), F000119.

320 NARA T314, R1318 (*LIII. Armeekorps*), F000240.

321 NARA T315, R969 (*56. Infanterie-Division*), F000115.

27 JUNE 1942

Following an order of the *Oberkommando des Heeres* (*OKH*/Supreme High Command of the German Army), *Heeresgruppe Mitte* ordered the staff of the *2. Panzerarmee* by telegram, that in the future, the number of assault guns should be indicated separately in the weekly reports on serviceable armoured fighting vehicles which were submitted and filed every Wednesday evening.[322]

30 JUNE 1942

During the day, the *56. Infanterie-Division* made a report regarding the German armoured fighting vehicles that had been disabled or left behind in its sector; this included a heavily damaged StuG. III assault gun of *Sturmgeschütz-Abteilung 202* in the area of Melechowo.[323]

4 JULY 1942

In the evening, the *296. Infanterie-Division* expected an imminent attack to be launched by the Soviet troops on its right flank and therefore requested assault guns from the corps.[324]

In relation to that, at 2300 hours *LIII. Armeekorps* ordered its subordinate units to dispatch four assault guns in the early hours of the next morning to the area of Tschikriak where they would be put at the corps' disposal.[325]

5 JULY 1942

On the front line of the *296. Infanterie-Division*, Soviet troops opened fire using artillery and multiple rocket launchers; significant air support was also deployed.

The focal point of their attack was east of Palenka, on the left flank of *Infanterie-Regiment 521*, where the Soviets commenced their assault at 0650 hours with about 60-80 tanks[326] from the direction of Bobriki. About 40 of these tanks broke through the German defences, pressing forward to the eastern foreground of Schpilewa and the northern area of Blisnowskij. Rifle infantry followed them slowly and were few in number.[327]

At 0405 hours, the four assault guns from *Sturmgeschütz-Abteilung 202* arrived at the command post of *Artillerie-Regiment 296* from the direction of Tschikriak. They were immediately switched from the direct control of the corps and subordinated

---

322 NARA T313, R123 (*Panzerarmeeoberkommando 2*), F7369515-516.

323 NARA T314, R1322 (*LIII. Armeekorps*), F000750.

324 NARA T315, R1959 (*296. Infanterie-Division*), F000306.

325 NARA T314, R1318 (*LIII. Armeekorps*), F000278.

326 According to the data obtained by the German reconnaissance, the Soviet 50, 51, 103 and 192 Tank Brigades were deployed in this sector. The first three of them belonged to the 3 Tank Corps, and the fourth was an independent tank brigade. All the four fought under the command of the Soviet 61 Army at that time. The 50 and 51 Tank Brigade had KV-1, T-34 and T-60s, the 103 Tank Brigade had KV-1, T-60 and Mk-2 Matildas, the 192 Tank Brigade had M3 Lee and M3 Stuart tanks at that time.

327 NARA T314, R1322 (*LIII. Armeekorps*), F000324.

to *296. Infanterie-Division.*[328] Following that, the division placed the assault guns and the four towed 76.2 mm captured Soviet anti-tank guns, received from the corps as reinforcement, under the command of *Infanterie-Regiment 521.*[329]

In the sector of the division, the Soviet troops took Blisnowskij at around 0800 hours. With its last reserves, and deploying the four StuG. III assault guns it had received earlier that morning, *Infanterie-Regiment 521* managed to seal off Soviet tank penetrations in a southerly direction at 0720 hours and retook the settlement by 0900 hours.[330]

During the attack the remaining Soviet tanks – a significant number had been lost in the German minefields – became stuck in the depression at Palenka so that only between eight and ten tanks were able to reach Blisnowskij and Blisnowo across Kabala. In Kabala an additional two or three Soviet tanks were disabled. In the battle the Germans knocked out a total of 16 Soviet tanks (five of them were disabled by the regiment's 5 cm anti-tank guns, four by the 76.2 mm captured anti-tank guns of the anti-tank battalion, four were destroyed by the infantry in close combat and three by an artillery battery with direct fire). Apart from these, the assault guns of *Sturmgeschütz-Abteilung 202* also knocked out or repulsed several Soviet tanks.[331]

Later, at 1130 hours, the *I. Bataillon /Infanterie-Regiment 521* and the *1. Kompanie/ Infanterie-Regiment 519* commenced a counter-thrust with the four assault guns during which they retook Kabala and threw the Soviet troops back in an easterly direction, blocking the penetration immediately to the west of the Blisnowo–Kabala road. Oddly enough, when the StuG. III assault guns appeared, the Soviet tanks retreated in a north-easterly direction, towards Palenka.[332]

At around 2000 hours elements of the *III. Bataillon/ Infanterie-Regiment 521* (i.e. the reinforced *11. Kompanie*), initially with the support of the assault guns of *Sturmgeschütz-Abteilung 202* attached to the *112. Infanterie-Division,* successfully occupied the German main combat line despite vicious fire from the Soviet troops.[333]

During the day the *II. Bataillon/ Panzer-Regiment 39* was subordinated to the division to resume fighting against Soviet tanks.

At 0645 hours, the *LIII. Armeekorps* attached three more assault guns from *Sturmgeschütz-Abteilung 202* to the sector of the *112. Infanterie-Division* but these were to be deployed only with the permission of the corps' staff.

The combat vehicles moved off from Bolchow to the area of Klutschnikowskije Wys at around 0700 hours. At the same time the 1 (operations) staff officer ordered the assault guns to prepare for their mission under the command of *Infanterie-*

328 NARA T314, R1318 (*LIII. Armeekorps*), F000282.

329 NARA T315, R1959 (*296. Infanterie-Division*), F000308.

330 NARA T314, R1318 (*LIII. Armeekorps*), F000284.

331 NARA T315, R1961 (*296. Infanterie-Division*), F000926.

332 NARA T315, R1959 (*296. Infanterie-Division*), F000310.

333 NARA T315, R1961 (*296. Infanterie-Division*), F000925.

Regiment 258 on the western outskirts of Baschkino where they were to cover the left flank of the division due to the Soviet breakthrough west of Baschkino. The officer asked them to make no delay.[334]

3. Kompanie/ I. Bataillon/ Infanterie-Regiment 258 launched an attack together with the assault guns of *Sturmgeschütz-Abteilung 202* and together they managed to take back Hill 244.4 at around 0930 hours.

At 1130 hours the battalion was assigned the task of holding the sector between Werch-Dolzy and Baschkino with a force consisting of a penal platoon, one platoon from the *14. Kompanie/ Infanterie-Regiment 258* and the assault guns of *Sturmgeschütz-Abteilung 202.*[335]

At 1325 hours, as the attack progressed at a rapid pace, a German assault squad managed to reach Hill 230, 500m north-east of Baschkino. The battalion received orders to take the hill and then the former German positions to the north with the *2. Kompanie/ Pionier-Bataillon 112.* That was achieved at around 1400 hours. Here the Germans took 160 prisoners and captured a few machine guns and mortars. The Soviets retreated toward Proletarskij with two tanks providing cover for them. Having completed their mission the assault guns, together with *2.Kompanie/ Pionier-Bataillon 112,* they waited in a gully south-west of Werch-Dolzy in combat readiness.

At 1645 hours the assault guns received orders to advance across Hill 238.7 to a small forest on the north-western outskirts of Baschkino where the *5. Kompanie/ Infanterie-Regiment 256* had been driven back and were in a critical situation following another Soviet attack on Baschkino (launched at 1445 hours). Following artillery preparation, the infantry company and the assault guns were to take back the former German positions.[336]

Elements of the *II. Bataillon / Infanterie-Regiment 256,* with the support of the assault guns from *Sturmgeschütz-Abteilung 202,* commenced another attack at around 1900 hours from the direction of Baschkino with the aim of clearing the Soviet troops from the former German main combat line running north and north-west of the settlement. Initially the Germans made a good progress, then from the western slope of Hill 230 they received a violent flanking artillery fire. After advancing 200m, the assault guns were forced to change direction by the ferocious enemy fire.[337] Apart from this, the area was heavily bombarded by Soviet rocket launchers while Soviet aircraft carried out bombing and ground attacks.[338]

In the face of this heavy resistance, the German attempt failed. Moreover, three Soviet '42-ton' tanks (probably KV-1s) appeared. The German assault guns were

---

334 NARA T315, R1276 (*112. Infanterie-Division*), F000460.

335 NARA T315, R1277 (*112. Infanterie-Division*), F001025.

336 NARA T315, R1277 (*112. Infanterie-Division*), F001025.

337 NARA T315, R1961 (*296. Infanterie-Division*), F000925.

338 NARA T314, R1322 (*LIII. Armeekorps*), F000734.

forced to engage them leaving the infantry without support. Consequently, the infantry company and the assault guns retreated to the northern perimeter of a small forest in the north-western part of Baschkino where they prepared for defence.[339]

At 2130 hours, the *112. Infanterie-Division* reported to the corps that the preconditions for the counter-attack to be launched in the area of Baschkino were to fight down the three KV-1 heavy tanks that had been clearly identified by the assault guns and to provide anti-aircraft defence for the area.[340]

In the early afternoon additional assault guns arrived at the division together with an anti-aircraft artillery group consisting of an 8.8 cm gun and a 2 cm cannon.[341] The 8.8 cm anti-aircraft gun proved its effectiveness against the Soviet tanks as well against their aircraft.

6 JULY 1942

At 0400 hours in the sector of the *296. Infanterie-Division*, Soviet troops penetrated into the defences from the direction of Schesterka and reached the road between Bolchow and Anina. Here the Germans launched a counter-thrust with the support of the assault guns of *Sturmgeschütz-Abteilung 202*.[342]

On that day, in the sector of *296. Infanterie-Division*, it was not only the four StuG. III assault guns of *Sturmgeschütz-Abteilung 202* that fought while subordinated to *Infanterie-Regiment 521*, but also the improvised anti-tank detachment of the assault artillery unit with four captured 76.2 mm anti-tank guns.[343]

In the line of the *112. Infanterie-Division*, in the area of Baschkino, the situation was still undecided. Therefore at 1100 hours an additional two assault guns were dispatched from *Sturmgeschütz-Abteilung 202* to the division from the corps-reserve in Bolchow.[344] They were received instead of the tanks of an armoured company *(2./ Panzer-Regiment 39)* that had been promised to the division the previous afternoon but had been ordered somewhere else.[345]

The assault guns arrived at the *I. Bataillon/ Infanterie-Regiment 258*, which had been assigned the task of recapturing the former German positions on the sides of the gully at Baschkino. However, due to the absence of tanks, the regiment refused to carry out the task. Thus, in accordance with the decision of the division, they had to take back the German main combat line west of the gully. That attack, however,

---

339 NARA T315, R1277 (*112. Infanterie-Division*), F001026.

340 NARA T315, R1277 (*112. Infanterie-Division*), F001039.

341 NARA T314, R1322 (*LIII. Armeekorps*), F000735, as well as T315, R1277 (*112. Infanterie-Division*), F000961.

342 NARA T313, R108 (*Panzerarmeeoberkommando 2*), F7353261.

343 NARA T315, R1961 (*296. Infanterie-Division*), F000928. The TD detachment had only 35 shells/gun. The formation, alarmed and drawn forward the previous day, lost six wounded, a gun and two towing vehicles on the way due to the attack of Soviet ground attack-aircraft and bombers. The AT-guns took up firing positions in the area of Plina, behind the infantry positions on 5 July, in the evening. *See* Alfons, Fischer: Tagebuch eines Wolfurters zwischen 1939 und 1946. In: Heimat Wolfurt. Heft 10. p. 30.

344 NARA T314, R1318 (*LIII. Armeekorps*), F000292.

345 NARA T315, R1277 (*112. Infanterie-Division*), F000997.

was cancelled because the StuG. III assault guns, dispersed over a total of six sites, were ordered to Baschkino by the division, where they were subordinated to the *II. Bataillon / Infanterie-Regiment 256.* The commander of the assault gun battery was to report his arrival.[346]

On the march, one of the assault guns was disabled by a Soviet artillery hit and this was reported to *Infanterie-Regiment 258* by the battery commander.

The *II. Bataillon /Infanterie-Regiment 256* received orders at 1810 hours that their attack was called off and that, after adopting defensive positions, they should dispatch the assault guns to the area of Klutschnikowskije Wis, where they would be at the disposal of the division.

At around 1900 hours the *LIII. Armeekorps* ordered the division by telegram to dispatch the two assault guns received in the afternoon for the counter-thrust, back to Bolchow where they would be available for the corps.[347]

But it seems the assault guns had still not used up enough fuel during their marches to and fro since, at 2310 hours, they were dispatched again, this time to Shukowskije Wys area.[348] According to another telegram sent by the division that day, the assault gun platoon under the command of *Leutnant* Maier were to be put on standby for action at this settlement.[349]

The corps reprimanded its subordinate divisions for leaving the assault guns which had been assigned to them with the body of troops (regiments, battalions) so that they could employ them for minor tasks. That was forbidden by the corps. It commanded the divisions to attach the assault guns to units only for the duration of their missions as this would allow regular maintenance to be carried out while they were subordinated directly to the division. In this way, assault guns would be deployable and divisional commanders could use them in focal points.[350]

7 JULY 1942

At 0440 hours three assault guns of *Sturmgeschütz-Abteilung 202,* subordinated to *112. Infanterie-Division,* arrived from Baschkino in the area of Shukowskije Wys under the command of *Oberleutnant* Dr. Georg Meyer. Following their repeated attempts in the early morning hours, the Soviets launched another attack at 0845 hours and managed to penetrate into the northern part of Baschkino. The commander of the *II. Bataillon /Infanterie-Regiment 256* defending there, *Major* Heinrich Knüppel, assembled all of his available reserves (including the equipment of his battalion staff) and launched a counter-thrust. The battalion received the assault guns, ordered

346 NARA T315, R1277 (*112. Infanterie-Division*), F000997.

347 NARA T315, R1277 (*112. Infanterie-Division*), F001008.

348 NARA T315, R1277 (*112. Infanterie-Division*), F000998.

349 NARA T315, R1277 (*112. Infanterie-Division*), F001006.

350 NARA T314, R1319 (*LIII. Armeekorps*), F000590.

back immediately from the area of Shukowskije Wys to Baschkino, and also the *1. Kompanie/ Feldersatz-Bataillon 112.* In cooperation with the assault guns, Knüppel's soldiers drove the Soviets (about 500 soldiers) out of Baschkino before the field reserve company arrived. During the battle the Soviets lost 250 dead, 65 prisoners, seven machine guns, six mortars and several automatic rifles and submachine guns.

By 1155 hours the Germans had cleared the enemy from the settlement. Of the three assault guns deployed, only one remained combat-ready. Another was disabled due to a broken cardan shaft in front of Baschkino and the third became bogged down in the northern part of the settlement.[351]

At 1745 hours another two assault guns arrived from *Sturmgeschütz-Abteilung 202* to the *II. Bataillon / Infanterie-Regiment 256.* Therefore, three combat-ready StuG. IIIs were at the disposal of *Major* Knüppel.

The assault guns proved their worth when, at around 2000 hours, the Soviets launched yet another attack on Baschkino with the support of tanks. However the attempt was halted in a hour by the concentrated fire of the assault guns and heavy anti-tank guns placed in positions in the area of the settlement. The Soviets retreated.[352]

At around 1230 hours in the sector of the *296. Infanterie-Division,* in the zone of *Infanterie-Regiment 521*, a Soviet attack was commenced with the support of about 40 tanks towards Blisnowskij and Blisnowo. The anti-tank detachment of *Sturmgeschütz-Abteilung 202* destroyed five of the Soviet tanks with its four captured 76.2 mm anti-tank guns in the area of Blisnowskij. However they ran out of ammunition and the detachment was forced to withdraw.[353] A soldier of the detachment gave a dramatic account of the events in his diary:

Ceaseless and ferocious artillery fire. At around 10 o'clock I observed 25 T–34s and a few trucks in a readiness position in a narrow valley one kilometre in front of us. The aim of their attack was unknown. At 11 o'clock the artillery fire shifted to the rear and the attack was launched on the forward positions. At around 12 o'clock, on the left, five T–34s broke through between us and a 21 cm mortar battery. The infantry drew back. Eight T–34 s were standing 150 metres from our positions. We managed to knock out three of them, but after that our gun was hit twice. Of our seven men, two were killed in action, one died at the first aid station and four were wounded. We escaped through an orchard.

[…]

In ten minutes, the Russian tanks blew up our three anti-tank guns and the 21 cm mortar that had previously disposed of a T–34 with direct fire. I was informed at the

351 NARA T315, R1277 (*112. Infanterie-Division*), F000970

352 NARA T315, R1277 (*112. Infanterie-Division*), F000971.

353 NARA T315, R1961 (*296. Infanterie-Division*), F000930.

hospital that the T–34 had intended to run our gun down, got stuck on it, and was knocked out during our counter-thrust. Of the 28 men in our detachment, 22 had been killed or wounded in three days and all our equipment was lost.[354]

A platoon commander from the *1. Batterie* of *Sturmgeschütz-Abteilung 202, Leutnant* Benno Schindowski distinguished himself in the fighting between July 5–7, and for this he received a certificate of recognition from the Supreme Commander of the *Heer.*[355]

8 JULY 1942

At midnight, *Sturmgeschütz-Abteilung 202* received orders from the corps to dispatch two of its assault guns the following day at 0100 hours from Bolchow to Tschikriak, to the staff of the *II. Bataillon / Panzer-Regiment 39,* to which they were attached. Moreover, the formation had to fetch two 7.5 cm towed anti-tank guns (with 20 shells each) from which they had to set up two anti-tank-gun platoons manned by their own personnel.[356]

In the sector of the *112. Infanterie-Division,* the commander of the *II. Bataillon/ Infanterie-Regiment 256, Major* Knüppel, received orders at 0400 hours to withdraw the six StuG. III assault guns of *Sturmgeschütz-Abteilung 202* subordinated to him into the area of Shukowskije Wys, because a German dive-bomber attack was expected in the sector where they were operating.[357]

9 JULY 1942

In the sector of the *296. Infanterie-Division,* the Soviet troops broke into Star. Wyselky. *Infanterie-Regiment 519,* defending the settlement, launched a counter-thrust together with two assault guns from the direction of Now. Derewnja, but failed.[358]

In the sector of the division, the *III. Bataillon / Infanterie-Regiment 119 (mot.)*[359] had to relieve the *III. Bataillon/ Infanterie-Regiment 521,* but having relieved them, the zone held by the battalion was taken into the sector of the *112. Infanterie-Division.* At the same time, the two assault guns of *Sturmgeschütz-Abteilung 202* were left subordinated to the battalion.[360] Because of that, the number of the assault guns from *Sturmgeschütz-Abteilung 202* increased to six in the sector of *112. Infanterie-Division.*

---

354 Alfons, Fischer: Tagebuch eines Wolfurters zwischen 1939 und 1946. In: *Heimat Wolfurt.* Heft 10. pp. 31-32.

355 Dörr, Manfred: *Die Inhaber der Anerkennungsurkunde des Oberbefehlshabers des Heeres 1941-1945.* Osnabrück, 1993. 123. o.

356 NARA T314, R1319 (*LIII. Armeekorps*), F000579.

357 NARA T315, R1277 (*112. Infanterie-Division*), F000952.

358 NARA T315, R1959 (*296. Infanterie-Division*), F000326.

359 The battalion belonged to the *25. Infanterie-Division (mot.)* 's order of battle.

360 NARA T314, R1319 (*LIII. Armeekorps*), F000569.

In the sector of the *112. Infanterie-Division* the assault guns of the assault artillery unit assigned to the division received orders at 0735 hours to reconnoitre the terrain in support of a mission to be carried out toward Merkulowo. At 1400 hours orders were received from the corps according to which the assault guns should march to the area of Merkulowo across Uschakow with the staff and two companies of the *III. Bataillon / Infanterie-Regiment 119 (mot.)*. In the evening four assault guns of *Sturmgeschütz-Abteilung 202* were in divisional reserve while another two were at Klutschnikowskije Wys. At 2030 hours they received orders to be ready to march.[361]

According to a report made by the corps, *Sturmgeschütz-Abteilung 202* hadn't lost any StuG. III assault guns destroyed during the fighting of 5–9 July 1942. The armoured troops providing support for the corps had to write off only one Panzer III and one Panzer IV as a total losses.[362]

10 JULY 1942

In the sector of the *112. Infanterie-Division* the assault guns were dispatched at 0410 hours from *Infanterie-Regiment 258* to the *II. Bataillon / Infanterie-Regiment 256*, but at 1030 hours they were ordered back to Shukowskije Wys.[363]

At 1740 hours the *56. Infanterie-Division* requested two assault guns from the corps as divisional reserve in the area of Nogaja. The request was refused due to the fact that, temporarily, there were no serviceable StuG. IIIs in the corps' own reserve.[364]

11 JULY 1942

The *LIII. Armeekorps* ordered the staff of the *112. Infanterie-Division* to relieve the two assault guns of *Sturmgeschütz-Abteilung 202* from assignment with them and dispatch them immediately to the *56. Infanterie-Division* in the area of Sereditchi.[365] At 0910 hours the division forwarded the orders to *Infanterie-Regiment 258*, where the armoured fighting vehicles were located.[366]

The *56. Infanterie-Division* was informed about receiving the two assault guns by the corps commander himself at 0805 hours.[367] Before that, at around 0500 hours, the division had been informed about the dispatch of a third assault gun that had just been repaired.[368]

361 NARA T315, R1277 (*112. Infanterie-Division*), F000933-934 and F000938.

362 NARA T313, R108 (*Panzerarmeeoberkommando 2*), F7353286.

363 NARA T315, R1277 (*112. Infanterie-Division*), F000922.

364 NARA T315, R969 (*56. Infanterie-Division*), F000179.

365 NARA T314, R1319 (*LIII. Armeekorps*), F000555

366 NARA T315, R1277 (*112. Infanterie-Division*), F000905.

367 NARA T315, R969 (*56. Infanterie-Division*), F000166.

368 NARA T315, R969 (*56. Infanterie-Division*), F000168.

In the sector of the *56. Infanterie-Division* an assault gun of *Sturmgeschütz-Abteilung 202* took up position in the zone of action of *Infanterie-Regiment 192* behind strongpoint 184/b according to a report submitted at 1400hours. [369]

Next day, in the early morning hours, an additional assault gun was placed under the command of the regiment in the southern part of Kirejkowo.[370]

12 JULY 1942

Four other assault guns from *Sturmgeschütz-Abteilung 202* were in the divisional reserve of the *112. Infanterie-Division* together with the reconnaissance armoured car company of *Kradschützen-Bataillon 25* and two anti-aircraft artillery groups.[371]

In the sector of the *56. Infanterie-Division* one of the assault guns subordinated to *Infanterie-Regiment 192* was ordered to move from its position at Point 259.5 south of Kirejkowo to the valley of a nearby stream.[372]

13 JULY 1942

In the sector of the *112. Infanterie-Division,* the assault guns of *Sturmgeschütz-Abteilung 202* subordinated to the *III. Bataillon* of *Infanterie-Regiment 119* were ordered to report to their battery commander at the settlement of Shukowskije Wys at dusk.[373]

In the sector of the division, a total of 161 knocked-out Soviet tanks were reported between 5 and 13 July 1942, nine of them disabled by a German tank destroyer squad. Unfortunately, sources do not contain the exact number of AFVs knocked out by the assault guns. Most of the kills, besides the ones by *Sturmgeschütz-Abteilung 202,* were distributed between elements of *Panzer-Regiment 35* and the *II. Bataillon/Flak-Regiment 11.*[374] The situation was similar on the front line of the *296. Infanterie-Division* which was operating in the sector of *Infanterie-Regiment 521* in relation to the total of the 85 Soviet tanks knocked out.[375]

15 JULY 1942

The commander in chief of the *2. Panzerarmee, Generaloberst* Rudolf Schmidt, expressed his gratitude in his daily order to the troops of the *LIII. Armeekorps* for the following achievement:

369 NARA T315, R970 (*56. Infanterie-Division*), F000476.

370 NARA T315, R970 (*56. Infanterie-Division*), F000484.

371 NARA T315, R1277 (*112. Infanterie-Division*), F000892.

372 NARA T315, R970 (*56. Infanterie-Division*), F000487.

373 NARA T315, R1277 (*112. Infanterie-Division*), F000884.

374 *See* NARA T314, R1320 (*LIII. Armeekorps*), F000839.

375 NARA T315, R1961 (*296. Infanterie-Division*), F000937-939.

Between 5 and 8 July 1942, the Russians tried to break through the north flank (LIII. Armeekorps and XXXXVII. Panzerkorps) of the Armee with numerically superior troops and masses of tanks that had previously not been used here to reach the Orel–Brjansk line and by means of that to halt the successful offensive of the German forces south of there. It is owing to the merit of the troops and the skill of the commanders that the Russian's plan failed. Suffering terribly bloody losses of 446 destroyed tanks and 161 aircraft that were shattered to pieces, he had to give up his plans. [...][376]

16 JULY 1942

The *56.* and the *112. Infanterie-Divisionen* received orders from the corps to dispatch the assault guns of *Sturmgeschütz-Abteilung 202* assigned to them to Bolchow on 19 July. The assault gun unit was ordered to conduct repairs in such a way that four of them would always be combat-ready.[377]

17 JULY 1942

Sturmgeschütz-Abteilung 202, with a total of 10 serviceable StuG. III assault guns,[378] was still the only assault artillery unit of the *2. Panzerarmee.*

19 JULY 1942

In the sector of *112. Infanterie-Division* the assault guns of *Sturmgeschütz-Abteilung 202* subordinated to *Infanterie-Regiment 258,* stationed in Shukowskije Wys area, set off at 2000 hours to the assault artillery formation at Bolchow.[379]

27 JULY 1942

Sturmgeschütz-Abteilung 202 received orders from the *LIII. Armeekorps* to raise an infantry company from its personnel to partly relieve the forces of the *56. Infanterie-Division* which would then be free to participate in the planned attack.[380]

28 JULY 1942

The *56. Infanterie-Division* reported the order of battle of its troops to the corps. They requested six assault guns of *Sturmgeschütz-Abteilung 202* for the right flank of the division, *Infanterie-Regiment 192.*[381]

---

376 NARA T315, R1277 (*112. Infanterie-Division*), F000843.

377 NARA T314, R1319 (*LIII. Armeekorps*), F000546.

378 NARA T314, R1320 (*LIII. Armeekorps*), F000344.

379 NARA T315, R1277 (*112. Infanterie-Division*), F000784.

380 NARA T314, R1318 (*LIII. Armeekorps*), F000354.

381 NARA T314, R1323 (*LIII. Armeekorps*), F000142.

29 JULY 1942

The assault artillery unit now had a total of 10 assault guns. Five of these were combat-ready; two were undergoing short-term repairs and three of them were in need of longer-term repairs. Another StuG. III assault gun had to be written off as a total loss.[382]

30 JULY 1942

The *2. Panzerarmee* informed the staff of the *LIII. Armeekorps* that one of the batteries of *Sturmgeschütz-Abteilung 600* would not be subordinated to the corps but would remain with its parent unit. Instead, *Sturmgeschütz-Abteilung 202* would receive six new assault guns as replacements.[383]

In the sector of the *26. Infanterie-Division* three assault guns of the assault artillery unit were attached to *Infanterie-Regiment 520.*[384]

31 JULY 1942

At 1745 hours, *Sturmgeschütz-Abteilung 202* received orders that the infantry company raised from the *3. Batterie* – named 'Handrik' after its commander[385]– should arrive in Jagodnaja by 1300 hours next day. Its commander was to report to the command post of *Infanterie-Regiment 171* in the sector of the *56. Infanterie-Division.* The next morning these orders were modified: the company would now set off from Bolchow on 1 August, at 2100 hours.[386]

4 AUGUST 1942

Sturmgeschütz-Abteilung 202 had 13 assault guns at this point in time, all of them combat-ready. Two of them were from the newly arrived StuG. IIIs and a third was expected to arrive two days later.[387]

5 AUGUST 1942

The assault artillery unit received orders from the staff of the *LIII. Armeekorps* to dispatch six assault guns to *Abschnittstab z. b. V. 2* [388] and four to *56. Infanterie-Division* on the night of 6/ 7 August. On the paper recording the orders it was put down in pencil that the first of these assault guns would be led by *Oberleutnant* Meier and the latter by *Hauptmann* Buhr. However, there was a problem – only

---

382 NARA T314, R1320 (*LIII. Armeekorps*), F000580.

383 NARA T314, R1318 (*LIII. Armeekorps*), F000796.

384 NARA T314, R1320 (*LIII. Armeekorps*), F000330.

385 The commander of the *3. Batterie/ Sturmgeschütz-Abteilung 202 was Hauptmann* Hans Handrik.

386 NARA T315, R969 (*56. Infanterie-Division*), F000189.

387 NARA T313, R123 (*Panzerarmeeoberkommando 2*), F7369569.

388 That was the codename of the *26. Infanterie-Division* at that time. The division requested an additional nine assault guns from the corps on 30 July 1942 to support *Infanterie-Regiments 77* and *520. See* NARA T314, R1323 (*LIII. Armeekorps*), F000129.

four StuG. IIIs assault guns were fully deployable and an additional three partly serviceable and ready to move off.[389]

6 AUGUST 1942

At 1200 hours *Major* Evers, commander of *Sturmgeschütz-Abteilung 202* reported to the staff of the *26. Infanterie-Division.* The *1. Batterie* of the assault artillery unit (with six assault guns) was placed under the command of the division. Four of the six assault guns were subordinated to *Infanterie-Regiment 77,* two of them to *Infanterie-Regiment 520.*[390]

7 AUGUST 1942

Assigned with the task of providing artillery support, the four assault guns of *Sturmgeschütz-Abteilung 202,* together with the anti-aircraft artillery group *'Rahn',* arrived at the readiness positions of the *56. Infanterie-Division* as it prepared to attack.[391]

As the *296. Infanterie-Division* prepared its attack , *Infanterie-Regiment 521* made a recommendation to take Bobriki and the nearby Hill 234.4. The plan was to deploy two reinforced infantry companies supported by two pioneer platoons and three or four assault guns against the hill. The pioneer platoons were to have mine detector and flamethrower squads at their service.[392]

10 AUGUST 1942

The staff of *Sturmgeschütz-Abteilung 202,* acting as the Bolchow traffic-control staff, cooperated with *Pionier-Bataillon 92* in relieving the guard at the bridge established over Nugr River.[393]

11 AUGUST 1942

Sturmgeschütz-Abteilung 202 had nine combat-ready assault guns.[394]

In the sector of the *26. Infanterie-Division* the troops took up their jump-off positions by 0230 hours. One of the assault guns of *Sturmgeschütz-Abteilung 202* had become disabled on the way there leaving only three StuG. IIIs under the command of *Infanterie-Regiment 77.*[395] The German assault commenced at 0400 hours in the direction of Shelesniza.

---

389 NARA T315, R970 (*56. Infanterie-Division*), F000798.

390 NARA T315, R821 (*26. Infanterie-Division*), Ia Kriegstagebuch vom 06. 08. 1942.

391 NARA T314, R1322 (*LIII. Armeekorps*), F000645.

392 NARA T315, R1959 (*296. Infanterie-Division*), F000950.

393 NARA T314, R1323 (*LIII. Armeekorps*), F000008.

394 NARA T313, R123 (*Panzerarmeeoberkommando 2*), F7369573.

395 NARA T315, R821 (*26. Infanterie-Division*), Ia Kriegstagebuch vom 11. 08. 1942.

The *III. Bataillon* /*Infanterie-Regiment 77* reached Hill 254.7 at 0440 hours with the support of the three assault guns. At first the resistance of the Soviet infantry was weak but one of the three assault guns struck a mine and was rendered unserviceable.[396]

At 0455 hours the corps gave notice that another assault gun had been dispatched to the *1. Batterie* of *Sturmgeschütz-Abteilung 202.*[397]

Soviet resistance stiffened on the south-western perimeter of Shelesniza. By 0700 hours all the assault guns providing support for the regiments of the *26. Infanterie-Division* had been disabled.[398] The war-correspondent working for the division covered the events:

After an artillery preparation lasting fifteen minutes, the decisive moment came for our infantry: jumping out of the trenches, jumping into the uncertainty of war toward an obscure and unknown fate. Assault guns are jumping off to support them. They will provide significant relief – it is well known that the Bolshevists are terrified of assault guns. Unfortunately that part of the plan failed to materialize. The assault guns struck mines, and were disabled.[399]

It was reported to the corps at 0810 hours that all of the six assault guns of *Sturmgeschütz-Abteilung 202* subordinated to the *26. Infanterie-Division* were now unserviceable due to mine damage and hits by anti-tank gun shells.[400] Two of the StuG. IIIs, having struck mines, had to be written off as total losses.[401]

The assault gun losses sustained in the minefields were all the more irritating because during its previous combat involvements the *26. Infanterie-Division* had worked out an efficient method for cooperating with the assault guns to breach mine barrages:

To help assault guns through minefields and anti-tank ditches, co-operation between the pioneers and the assault guns must be made clear. A tried and tested method is to tie a wood sledge behind the [assault gun battalion's] [halftrack] ammunition trailer loaded with fagots and pioneer's' equipment.

[...]

Equipment of a [pioneer] platoon accompanying assault guns is as follows:

field clothing with assault equipment (two hand grenades, 90 cartridges per soldier), three light machine guns, one anti-tank rifle, four incendiary bottles; two smoke candles

396 NARA T315, R821 (*26. Infanterie-Division*), Ia Kriegstagebuch vom 11. 08. 1942.

397 NARA T315, R821 (*26. Infanterie-Division*), Ia Kriegstagebuch vom 11. 08. 1942.

398 NARA T315, R821 (*26. Infanterie-Division*), Ia Kriegstagebuch vom 11. 08. 1942.

399 NARA T315, R822 (*26. Infanterie-Division*), F000764.

400 NARA T314, R1318 (*LIII. Armeekorps*), F000368.

401 NARA T313 R123 (*Panzerarmeeoberkommando 2*), F7369571.

per light machine gun, plus 5×3 kg and 3×5 kg explosive charges; four soldiers with jabbing sticks, nine with long-shafted spades; six cylindrical charges and 50 kg explosives in reserve, as well as concussion fuses and detonating cords; on the ammunition trailer of the assault artillery, fagots, five spades, five jabbing sticks, 10 ropes, five picks and three (3 m) assault ladders.[402]

In the sector of the *56. Infanterie-Division, Infanterie-Regiment 192* reported at 0610 hours that, south of Point 257.4, the Soviets had put up violent resistance from the cover a forest there. The attack of the German regiment was slow due to extensive blocks and minefields despite the support provided by four assault guns of *Sturmgeschütz-Abteilung 202.* The StuG. IIIs soon became bogged down in mud on their way to a position to the east of Point 257.4. To facilitate the recovery of the armoured fighting vehicles the infantry built a corduroy road.[403] Despite this difficulty the German infantry regiment took Ukolizy at around 1500 hours.[404]

12 AUGUST 1942

In the sector if the *56. Infanterie-Division* at around 1400 hours the *I. Bataillon/ Infanterie-Regiment 171* occupied Kosowka. After that, the infantry battalion was given the task of taking Tschuchlow with the soldiers of *3. Batterie / Sturmgeschütz-Abteilung 202* deployed as infantry and an assault pioneer company before proceeding northwards to re-establish contact with the right flank of the *134. Infanterie-Division* and the left flank of *Infanterie-Regiment 192.*[405]

At 1945 hours, *Infanterie-Regiment 234* received orders to prepare for defence north-east of Sorokino. For that purpose, four assault guns of *Sturmgeschütz-Abteilung 202,* two anti-tank gun platoons and an anti-aircraft artillery group with two 8.8 cm cannons and four 2 cm autocannons were assigned to the regiment.[406] Thus on 12 August 1942, four assault guns of the assault artillery unit were in the sector of the *56. Infanterie-Division,* three were fighting in the sector of the *26. Infanterie-Division* and five were undergoing short-term repairs.[407]

13 AUGUST 1942

In the sector of the *56. Infanterie-Division,* the attack of the *II. Bataillon/ Infanterie-Regiment 234* – launched at daybreak and with the support of the four assault guns from *Sturmgeschütz-Abteilung 202* – reached and occupied the designated

402 NARA T315, R822 (*26. Infanterie-Division*), F000059-61.
403 NARA T315, R969 (*56. Infanterie-Division*), F000281.
404 NARA T315, R970 (*56. Infanterie-Division*), F000879.
405 NARA T314, R1318 (*LIII. Armeekorps*), F000380.
406 NARA T315, R969 (*56. Infanterie-Division*), F000293.
407 NARA T313, R123 (*Panzerarmeeoberkommando 2*), F7369571.

main combat line at 0545 hours amidst sporadic mortar fire from the Soviets. The Soviets were still offering some resistance east of Debri, in the forested area 1.5 km north-north-east of Point 234.7. An attack was commenced against this resistance at 1900 hours with the support of two assault guns but it was repelled by the Soviet troops.[408] In the course of the battle, fought partly after nightfall, the two assault guns were disabled.[409]

14 AUGUST 1942

In the sector of the *56. Infanterie-Division,* the reinforced *II. Bataillon / Infanterie-Regiment 234* launched an attack at 1230 hours with *10. Kompanie*, two platoons from the *2. Kompanie / Pionier-Bataillon 156* and two StuG. III assault guns. Their objective was to occupy a forest clearing 750 m north-east of the eastern route out of Mysin.[410]

At around 1600 hours, the reinforced infantry battalion broke through from a westerly direction. At 1745 hours they reached the perimeter of the forest 1.5 km south-west of Oserenskij where one of the supporting assault guns of *Sturmgeschütz-Abteilung 202* destroyed a Soviet medium tank[411] and a reconnaissance armoured car.[412]

At 2030 hours, the infantry regiments of the division were given their task for the following day: to carry out an attack on Soviet positions in the area of Ewgeniew, Kumowo and Muschkan. For that purpose *Infanterie-Regiment 192* and *Infanterie-Regiment 171* received two assault guns each as well as other support.[413]

The *296. Infanterie-Division* received two of *Sturmgeschütz-Abteilung 202's* assault guns stationed at Schpilewa[414] and the *1. Kompanie/ Kradschützen-Bataillon 25* (armoured reconnaissance) from 1400 hours. The armoured cars, however, arrived next morning at 0630 hours and the assault guns only in the evening.[415]

The *3. Batterie/ Sturmgeschütz-Abteilung 202* (*Kompanie 'Handrik'*) had been fighting as infantry and were in the corps' reserve that day but measures were taken to return them to their parent unit.[416]

The *1. Batterie* of the assault artillery unit, subordinated to the *26. Infanterie-Division,* received orders at 0405 hours to stand by for action with its three combat-ready assault guns at the divisional command post.[417]

---

408 NARA T315, R970 (*56. Infanterie-Division*), F000971.

409 NARA T315, R970 (*56. Infanterie-Division*), F000975.

410 NARA T315, R970 (*56. Infanterie-Division*), F001005.

411 On that day in this sector two Soviet soldiers changed sides from the 50 Tank Brigade of the 3 Tank Corps. Based on that, the German StuG. III probably knocked out the AFVs of that brigade.

412 NARA T314, R1322 (*LIII. Armeekorps*), F000608, as well as NARA T315, R970 (*56. Infanterie-Division*), F001005.

413 NARA T315, R969 (*56. Infanterie-Division*), F000313.

414 NARA T315, R1959 (*296. Infanterie-Division*), F000603.

415 NARA T315, R1959 (*296. Infanterie-Division*), F000348-350.

416 NARA T315, R1959 (*296. Infanterie-Division*), F000607.

417 NARA T315, R821 (*26. Infanterie-Division*), Ia Kriegstagebuch vom 14. 08. 1942.

15 AUGUST 1942

At 0230 hours the *3. Batterie / Sturmgeschütz-Abteilung 202* was relieved from assignment with the *56. Infanterie-Division* and moved off.[418] The cars of the battery started towards the area of Rschewka at 0530 hours accompanied by an assault pioneer company.[419]

17 AUGUST 1942

Two assault guns of *Sturmgeschütz-Abteilung 202* were assigned to the *296. Infanterie-Division* and three combat vehicles were stationed in the sector of the *26. Infanterie-Division.*[420] Including these, the assault artillery unit had a total of nine StuG. IIIs in operational condition.[421]

18 AUGUST 1942

In the course of the attack of the *26. Infanterie-Division,* the *II. Bataillon / Infanterie-Regiment 78* (*Major der Reserve* Dr. Heinz Roth) with two assault guns of *Sturmgeschütz-Abteilung 202* (*Oberleutnant* Meyer) broke through the significantly reinforced and resolutely defended Soviet bunker-line in the area of Oserna and Goskowa at the first attempt (at around 0600 hours) and reached its attack objective for the day long before the other units of the division. Moreover, having made a rapid progress, the infantry battalion, reinforced with StuG. IIIs, was able to take and hold a very important hill east of Point 240.7.[422]

Soviet losses were immense: they had lost 250 dead, 233 prisoners and soldiers who had changed sides, as well as two tanks[423]. The Germans occupied, demolished by shelling or blew up 83 bunkers and firing positions. The assault guns of *Sturmgeschütz-Abteilung 202* destroyed an additional tank, six guns (including two anti-tank guns) and three trucks during the fighting.[424]

In the sector of the *56. Infanterie-Division* the Soviet troops penetrated into the area of Smetskije Wys at 0615 hours. The *II. Bataillon/ Infanterie-Regiment 171* launched a counter-thrust with the assault guns of *Sturmgeschütz-Abteilung 202* subordinated to the division and forced the attackers out of the settlement.

At 0725 hours *Infanterie-Regiment 234* received orders to commence an attack towards the Äskulap road with those assault guns and with at least one company. In the end the StuG. IIIs launched an attack at 1130 hours from Smetskije Wys with the regiment's bicycle company and the *5. Kompanie/ Infanterie-Regiment 171.* The *Kampfgruppe* soon

---

418 NARA T315, R970 (*56. Infanterie-Division*), F001023.

419 NARA T314, R1321 (*LIII. Armeekorps*), F000869.

420 NARA T315, R1959 (*296. Infanterie-Division*), F000596.

421 NARA T313, R123 (*Panzerarmeeoberkommando 2*), F7369573.

422 NARA T314, R1322 (*LIII. Armeekorps*), F000590-591.

423 One of the tanks was disabled by an over-calibre HEAT shell, the other one was set afire by a hit from an infantry gun.

424 NARA T315, R822 (*26. Infanterie-Division*), F000515-516.

broke down the weak resistance put up by the Soviets, and by 1155 hours, it approached to within 1 km of the Pesotchnaja stream from an easterly direction.[425] However, on the muddy, almost impassable road the assault guns were unable to accomplish their assigned task which was to reach Point 250.4. They turned and started back on the road they had driven on before.[426] The StuG. IIIs accompanied by infantry support arrived back at around 2215 hours.[427] Soon after that, at 2300 hours, the two assault guns were ordered to Smetskaja, where they were put into divisional reserve.[428]

At around 1600 hours, in the sector of *Infanterie-Regiment 192,* Soviet troops launched an attack on Kumowo with a force of at least battalion strength, three tanks and significant fire support from artillery, mortars and multiple rocket launchers. Having sustained serious losses, the Soviets were halted by the Germans at around 1730 hours. The German infantry regiment requested the attachment of two assault guns for one day, so that they could 'hunt down' the three Soviet tanks thought to be the shattered unit's last armoured fighting vehicles because the anti-tank and anti-aircraft guns had proven too clumsy for the task.[429]

19 AUGUST 1942

Sturmgeschütz-Abteilung 202 had a total of 18 assault guns after receiving six replacement StuG. IIIs. Of the assault guns in operational condition, four were under the command of the *56. Infanterie-Division,* two were subordinated to the *296. Infanterie-Division,* one was under the command of the *26. Infanterie-Division,* and one was located at Bolchow. Ten assault guns were undergoing short-term repairs at the Bolchow repair section.[430]

20 AUGUST 1942

At 1135 hours the *56. Infanterie-Division* issued orders to *Infanterie-Regiment 234* to assemble all four assault guns of *Sturmgeschütz-Abteilung 202* that were in the area of Smetskaja as divisional reserves.[431]

21 AUGUST 1942

The *56. Infanterie-Regiment* informed the commander of the assault guns stationed at Smetskaja, *Leutnant* Viede, that they had been attached to *Infanterie-Regiment 234* again, and ordered him to put the combat-ready StuG. IIIs into a state of readiness.[432] At 1748 hours *Hauptmann* Buhr reported that three assault guns

425 NARA T315, R969 (*56. Infanterie-Division*), F000338.
426 NARA T315, R970 (*56. Infanterie-Division*), F001074.
427 NARA T315, R970 (*56. Infanterie-Division*), F001090.
428 NARA T315, R970 (*56. Infanterie-Division*), F001093.
429 NARA T315, R970 (*56. Infanterie-Division*), F001074.
430 NARA T313, R123 (*Panzerarmeeoberkommando 2*), F7369576.
431 NARA T315, R969 (*56. Infanterie-Division*), F000348.
432 NARA T315, R969 (*56. Infanterie-Division*), F000350.

had just set off for the division and the fourth would follow in 30 minutes. The four assault guns arrived at *Infanterie-Regiment 234* at 1805 hours. Two of them were put into action with the *II. Bataillon* of the regiment after just 10 minutes.[433]

At 1940 hours, *Infanterie-Regiment 234* reported that the situation in the area of Smetskije Wys was calm again and retained two of the StuG. IIIs while the other two were sent back to Smetskaja.[434]

22 AUGUST 1942

Sturmgeschütz-Abteilung 202 received orders from the corps at around 0730 hours to dispatch its three combat-ready assault guns immediately from Bolchow. These were put under the command of *26. Infanterie-Division.*[435] Since, the *1. Batterie* of the assault artillery unit, which was subordinated to the division, had only two StuG. IIIs serviceable these were attached to the hard-pressed *Infanterie-Regiment 77* at 0750 hours.[436]

In the sector of the *296. Infanterie-Division,* the *9.* and *10. Kompanie*/ *Infanterie-Regiment 519*, together with two assault guns from the assault artillery unit (under the command of *Leutnant* Wahl), were ordered to Posdnjakowo by the command of the corps and arrived there at 1230 hours.[437]

In the sector of the *56. Infanterie-Division*, *Hauptmann* Buhr received orders at 0622 hours to send the two assault guns that were in reserve in the area of Smetskaja to *Infanterie-Regiment 234* where Soviet troops had broken through in the sector of the *7. Kompanie* not long before.[438] At 0825 hours the regiment reported to the division that the Soviet tanks had been unable to break through the line of the *7. Kompanie* but were standing in front of the German main combat line and were under fire from the German assault guns.[439]

At around 1250 hours three Soviet KV-1 heavy tanks dashed into Smetskije Wys. In the fighting that ensued one StuG. III was disabled.[440] At around 1330 hours the Germans evacuated the settlement but the assault guns remained in the vicinity to continue fighting. By then the Germans (possibly with their assault guns) had knocked out five Soviet tanks among the houses of Smetskije Wys.[441] After about a quarter of an hour the Germans counted as much as 30 Soviet tanks[442] in the settlement. Shortly after 1400 hours they launched an attack towards the west. Soon, German dive-bombers commenced an attack on the Soviet tanks that destroyed or disabled most

433 NARA T315, R971 (*56. Infanterie-Division*), F000012.
434 NARA T315, R969 (*56. Infanterie-Division*), F000352.
435 NARA T314, R1318 (*LIII. Armeekorps*), F000412.
436 NARA T315, R821 (*26. Infanterie-Division*), Ia Kriegstagebuch vom 22. 08. 1942.
437 NARA T315, R1959 (*296. Infanterie-Division*), F000356.
438 NARA T315, R969 (*56. Infanterie-Division*), F000354.
439 NARA T315, R969 (*56. Infanterie-Division*), F000356.
440 NARA T315, R969 (*56. Infanterie-Division*), F000361.
441 NARA T315, R969 (*56. Infanterie-Division*), F000362.
442 These were probably the elements of the 30 tank brigade of the Soviet 3 Tank Army.

of them.[443] By 1900 hours the Germans had reported an additional six Soviet tanks knocked out in the area of Smetskije Wys.[444] It is not impossible that the assault guns of *Sturmgeschütz-Abteilung 202* fighting there had played a significant part in this action.

23 AUGUST 1942

In the sector of the *56. Infanterie-Division* a Soviet KV-1 heavy tank crossed the bridge at around 0645 hours in the area of Smetskije Wys and came to a halt facing the command post of the *II. Bataillon/ Infanterie-Regiment 234.* Hits by the assault guns and heavy anti-tank guns were ineffective against it.[445]

At 1005 hours *Hauptmann* Buhr, the commander of the *3. Batterie / Sturmgeschütz-Abteilung 202* reported to the division that a Soviet KV-1 had run three assault guns down in the area of Hill 200.4. Two of them had to be written off as total losses, the third was towed to Smetskaja for repair.[446]

24 AUGUST 1942

Sturmgeschütz-Abteilung 197 was also subordinated to the *LIII. Armeekorps.* According to figures as of 26 August, the unit had 17 assault guns available.[447]

25 AUGUST 1942

In the sector of the *296. Infanterie-Division,* the two assault guns of *Sturmgeschütz-Abteilung 202* located at the hospital were subordinated to the *I. Bataillon/ Infanterie-Regiment 521* and ordered to proceed to Posdnjakowo.[448]

26 AUGUST 1942

The two assault guns assigned to *Infanterie-Regiment 520* in the sector of the *296. Infanterie-Division* were brought forward under the command of *Leutnant* Wahl at 0300 hours. The regiment carried out an attack at 0415 hours on a Soviet troop concentration located in a depression in the terrain in the area of Gromosdowo as they prepared to attack. By that time Germans had encircled the Soviets from east, west and north. Two assault guns of *Sturmgeschütz-Abteilung 202* jumped off with a part of company '*Kiesewetter*'[449] from a southerly direction. Although the Soviet troops launched a violent fire strike on German positions at around 0500 hours, the German attack ended successfully at 0530 hours. The Soviet concentration was then totally destroyed by the Germans. During the battle 127 Soviets were taken

---

443 NARA T315, R969 (*56. Infanterie-Division*), F000571.

444 NARA T315, R971 (*56. Infanterie-Division*), F000024.

445 NARA T315, R969 (*56. Infanterie-Division*), F000367.

446 NARA T315, R969 (*56. Infanterie-Division*), F000374.

447 NARA T314, R1318 (*LIII. Armeekorps*), F000423 and F000426.

448 NARA T315, R1959 (*296. Infanterie-Division*), F000365.

449 The improvised company was formed from the personnel of the supply columns of *Infanterie-Regiment 520, who hadn't been involved in fighting yet.*

prisoner while an additional two officers had previously changed sides. The Soviets also suffered significant casualties; in front of certain German machine-gun nests there lay the heaped bodies of perhaps 40 dead Soviet soldiers. In addition, the Germans knocked out two Soviet KV-1 heavy tanks as they encroached on friendly positions while a third was forced to withdraw having sustained serious damage.[450]

At 0800 hours the two assault guns were relieved from their assignment to the *296. Infanterie-Division* and attached to the *26. Infanterie-Division* by orders of the corps. However, the division received two other assault guns from *Sturmgeschütz-Abteilung 202.*[451] The assault guns remained in divisional reserve with the *5. Kompaniel Infanterie-Regiment 520.*[452]

The two regrouped assault guns arrived at the divisional command post in the sector of the *26. Infanterie-Division* at 1145 hours. They were put under the command of *Infanterie-Regiment 78* and ordered to report to the regimental command post.[453]

At this point in time , *Sturmgeschütz-Abteilung 202* had a total of 16 assault guns, two of the unit's StuG. IIIs having been written off during the previous days as total losses. Two assault guns were in need of short-term repairs while another two underwent long-term repairs. Two of the combat-ready StuG. IIIs[454] operated in the sector of the *56. Infanterie-Division,* six of them were in the zone of action of the *296. Infanterie-Division.*[455]

27 AUGUST 1942

At 0500 hours, one of the StuG. III assault guns of *Sturmgeschütz-Abteilung 202* was hit and damaged by a heavy anti-tank gun of *Schnelle-Abteilung 296*[456] belonging to the *296. Infanterie-Division* 600 m south-west of Leonowo while it was about the same distance behind the German main combat line. The division's report of the incident read as follows:

By orders of Leutnant Wahl an assault gun, in agreement with Infanterie-Regiment 520, changed position during a Russian attack supported by tanks and thus came into view of Leutnant Laurer's heavy anti-tank gun platoon which were in readiness position. The assault gun took up a position so that it could await the Russian armoured

---

450 NARA T315, R1961 (*296. Infanterie-Division*), F000877.

451 NARA T315, R1959 (*296. Infanterie-Division*), F000365.

452 NARA T315, R1959 (*296. Infanterie-Division*), F000557.

453 NARA T315, R821 (*26. Infanterie-Division*), Ia Kriegstagebuch vom 26. 08. 1942.

454 One of the two StuG. IIIs had limited mobility. *See* NARA T315, R971 (*56. Infanterie-Division*), F000185.

455 NARA T313, R123 (*Panzerarmeeoberkommando 2*), F7369581.

456 The *Schnelle Abteilung* (in 1942) was a divisional unit of battalion strength, raised by amalgamating elements of *Aufklärungs-Abteilung* and *Panzerjäger-Abteilung*. It usually had two bicycle-squadrons for reconnaissance purposes, two towed AT-gun companies against AFVs and a motorized heavy weapons company to provide fire support. During attack the advance detachment of the *Infanterie-Division was made up of them*, and in defence they were often deployed as ready reserves where reinforcements were needed.

fighting vehicles in case the Russian tanks broke through. When a Soviet 7.62 cm gun opened fire, Leutnant Laurer came out of his shelter to look around. Coming out, he thought he noticed a Russian tank and shouted: 'Tank!' Hearing this, one of the anti-tank guns (gun commander Unteroffizier Gittling) of his platoon on his right took a firing position and opened fire. After the 5 shot Leutnant Laurer realized, that it was a German assault gun. At the first hit the commander of the assault gun thought he was receiving Soviet fire, so he withdrew behind the sloping ground. Nevertheless, he took a second and third hit inside 30 seconds.

Crew casualties:

1. *Oberwachtmeister Woltaschewski, commander of the assault gun, was seriously wounded in his left arm and left shoulder, lost his left eye, shrapnel lodged in his mouth and jaw.*
2. *Unteroffizier Greiner, the driver of the fighting vehicle, his right arm was penetrated, wound to the right side of his throat with muscle involvement, pieces of shrapnel lodged in his left arm.*
3. *Another crew member was slightly wounded and remained with the troops.*

Damage to the assault gun: the running gear was torn away, penetration of the superstructure, hit to the radio equipment. The gun can be towed away. Firing occurred in clear visibility, at a distance of 800 m.[457]

In his comment to the corps *Major* Evers, commander of *Sturmgeschütz-Abteilung 202*, described the division's report as correct but added:

The report fails to mention the important fact that Oberleutnant Schäfer and Leutnant Laurer had been informed exactly about the presence of the assault gun, the latter being briefed personally by Leutnant Wahl. On the other hand, during the interrogation of the heavy anti-tank gun crew it became evident that they hadn't been briefed on the presence of the assault gun by their own superiors.[458]

The staff of the *26. Infanterie-Division* ordered its units, after more than a month, to sum up their combat experiences gained during the fighting of August 1942. The observations concerning the assault guns were as follows:

[At Infanterie-Regiment 39]

Cooperation with the assault guns was excellent. In attack we attached an assault squad to each assault gun. In each and every mission at least two assault guns were committed

457 NARA T314, R1323 (*LIII. Armeekorps*), F000227.

458 NARA T314, R1323 (*LIII. Armeekorps*), F000226.

to fight down a target. In defence, deployment was a little further back from the first line and concealed so that they could destroy enemy tanks that had broken through the main line of combat and to expose enemy infantry to the powerful psychological impact caused by the dash of the assault guns. Before each and every deployment of the assault guns, a detailed area reconnaissance was carried out by the relevant assault gun commanders and the commanders in charge of the zone of action.[459]

[...]

[At Infanterie-Regiment 77]

Cooperation with the assault guns and tanks was good and successful in attack. We employed them in a way that they 'fired' the infantry 'forward' from behind (especially by shelling bunkers and heavy weapons), then pushed their way forward. As for tanks – this statement relates only to the case when enemy heavy tanks were not present.[460] *[...]*

[At Infanterie-Regiment 78]

Cooperation with the assault guns was always good. The assault guns arrived as requested. We experienced skilfulness and fighting spirit from their commanders.[461] *[...]*

[At Aufklärungs-Abteilung 26]

Cooperation with the assault guns attached to the Abteilung was successful. Their commander is in our command post. The assault guns are in positions behind slopes. Sorties supporting infantry or fighting down tanks are kept on a short leash so the mobility of the weapon can be exploited at different sites due to their fast actions. Don't let them go forward with the infantry, but let them 'fire the infantry forward', otherwise the whole preventive fire will lie on our own lines![462] *[...]*

31 AUGUST 1942

At 1930 hours the *56. Infanterie-Regiment* received orders from the corps to send two assault guns of *2. Batterie / Sturmgeschütz-Abteilung 202* to Bolchow.[463] The assault guns deployed in the line of the *II. Batterie/ Infanterie-Regiment 192* were dispatched at 2100 hours towards Uljanowo.

1 SEPTEMBER 1942

The *296. Infanterie-Division* received an additional three assault guns which brought the number of StuG. IIIs subordinated to the division back six. These were kept in readiness in the area of Posdnjakowo.[464]

459 NARA T315, R822 (*26. Infanterie-Division*), F000120.
460 NARA T315, R822 (*26. Infanterie-Division*), F000130.
461 NARA T315, R822 (*26. Infanterie-Division*), F000140.
462 NARA T315, R822 (*26. Infanterie-Division*), F000150.
463 NARA T315, R969 (*56. Infanterie-Division*), F000418.
464 NARA T315, R1959 (*296. Infanterie-Division*), F000373.

The staff of the *56. Infanterie-Division* delivered orders to *Hauptmann* Buhr at 1015 hours by a motorcycle despatch rider instructing him to send the two assault guns relieved from assignment with the division to Bolchow.[465]

2 SEPTEMBER 1942

Seven of the 16 assault guns of *Sturmgeschütz-Abteilung 202* were undergoing short-term repairs. Of the StuG. IIIs that were operational, five remained in the sector of the *296. Infanterie-Division,* two were under the command of *26. Infanterie-Division* while another two were held as a corps reserve.[466]

5 SEPTEMBER 1942

Elements of *Sturmgeschütz-Abteilungen 202* and *197* provided support to the elements of the *26. Infanterie-Division.* Two assault guns from *Sturmgeschütz-Abteilung 202* were in readiness behind *3. Kompanie/ Infanterie-Regiment 510,* three StuG. IIIs of *Sturmgeschütz-Abteilung 197* operated in the sector of the regiment's *10. Kompanie* while an additional three StuG. IIIs were in position behind *6. Kompanie/Infanterie-Regiment 119.* The parent unit of the three assault guns held in divisional reserve cannot be detected from the sources available.[467]

9 SEPTEMBER 1942

The corps informed its subordinate divisions that *Sturmgeschütz-Abteilung 202* would be detached from the corps with its transfer starting on the morning of 12 September at earliest. To facilitate this transfer, the assault guns subordinated to the divisions were to be dispatched to Bolchow the next day at 1100 hours. The staff and a battery of *Sturmgeschütz-Abteilung 197,* subordinated to the corps on 10 September, took over the quarters of the departing assault artillery unit.[468]

On the same day, the corps published an order issued by the Supreme High Command of the German Army (*OKH*) which regulated reports concerning knocked-out enemy AFVs. According to this order, AFVs could only be reported as 'destroyed' if this happened behind the German main combat line, or were clearly set on fire by hits in front of the main combat line. All other AFVs were to be reported as 'knocked-out'. The designation of the unit that had scored the 'kills' was also to be included in the reporting.[469] This order applied to the whole of the eastern theatre of war.

---

465 NARA T315, R969 (*56. Infanterie-Division*), F000420.

466 NARA T313, R123 (*Panzerarmeeoberkommando 2*), F7369586.

467 NARA T314, R1320 (*LIII. Armeekorps*), F000546.

468 NARA T314, R1319 (*LIII. Armeekorps*), F000493.

469 NARA T314, R1319 (*LIII. Armeekorps*), F000498.

Sturmgeschütz-Abteilung 202 had 14 assault guns operational on that day with one undergoing short-term repairs. In the previous days one StuG. III had to be written off as a total loss.[470]

11 SEPTEMBER 1942

In his daily order the commander of the *LIII. Armeekorps, General der Infanterie* Clößner, said farewell to *Sturmgeschütz-Abteilung 202* as they were relieved from assignment to the corps:

> *To Sturmgeschütz-Abteilung 202:*
>
> *Sturmgeschütz-Abteilung 202 took its share in all major battles fought by the LIII. Armeekorps with proven fighting spirit from November 1941: In the defensive winter battle of Teploje in which the first commander of the Abteilung, Major Dr. Marder died a hero; in the battle of Shelesinskij, in the defensive victory at the end of July against strong enemy combat vehicles; and in the offensive and defensive battles in August during which elements of the corps smashed an enemy tank army. During this time the Abteilung became part of the LIII. Armeekorps' experience of war.*
>
> *On this day of your departure from my corps, I express my appreciation and gratitude to the valiant Sturmgeschütz-Abteilung 202 for its effective support in ever so many battles. Every infantryman in my corps will carry gratitude in his heart for the support provided, often at the last moment, by the fearless soldiers of the Sturmgeschütz-Abteilung and above all, like myself, they will think of the assault artillerymen who gave their lives for Germany during those missions.*
>
> *As for the future, my best wishes go with the Abteilung. I am sure, their missions will be just as successful in the future.*

On the same day, divisions of the *LIII. Armeekorps* were supported by the forces of *Sturmgeschütz-Abteilung 197* as follows: the *296. Infanterie-Division* was supported by the *2. Batterie* with five assault guns; the *25. Infanterie-Division (mot.)* by the *3. Batterie* with seven assault guns (including two mounted with long-barrelled guns). The staff and the *1. Batterie* with five assault guns were in divisional reserve in Bolchow. The newly arrived *Abteilung* took over not just the quarters of *Sturmgeschütz-Abteilung 202,* but also the stock of artillery ammunition that it left behind.[471]

12 SEPTEMBER 1942

The transfer of *Sturmgeschütz-Abteilung 202* from Orel into the sector of the *3. Panzerarmee* had begun.

---

470 NARA T313, R123 (*Panzerarmeeoberkommando 2*), F7369592.

471 NARA T314, R1320 (*LIII. Armeekorps*), F000533.

14 SEPTEMBER 1942

The first transfer of the staff and the *1. Batterie* of the assault artillery unit arrived in the area of *XX. Armeekorps.*[472]

15 SEPTEMBER 1942

The transfer of the personnel and equipment of *Sturmgeschütz-Abteilung 202*, with a total of 15 StuG. III assault guns, to the sector of the *XX. Armeekorps* was completed.[473]

16 SEPTEMBER 1942

The corps formulated a plan codenamed *'Blücher'.* The intention was to carry out a breakthrough manoeuvre from the bridgehead established at Alferowo towards Dubna and to destroy the Soviet forces that would be encircled by the combined forces of the corps and neighbouring German units. According to the plan of attack – which was to be launched on 19 October – the whole assault artillery unit would be subordinated to the *31. Infanterie-Division.*[474] The assault guns were to move forward during the German artillery preparation so that the noise of the explosions would conceal the approach of the StuG. IIIs.[475]

17 SEPTEMBER 1942

The 15 available assault guns[476] of *Sturmgeschütz-Abteilung 202* were assigned to the *31. Infanterie-Division.*

20 SEPTEMBER 1942

Sturmgeschütz-Abteilung 202 received three new StuG. IIIs. Including these, the unit now had 18 assault guns, 14 of which were combat-ready and subordinated to the *31. Infanterie-Division.*[477]

21 SEPTEMBER 1942

Fourteen of the assault artillery unit's 18 assault guns were operational while four were undergoing short-term repairs.[478]

472 NARA T314, R654 (*XX. Armeekorps*), F000600.
473 NARA T314, R653 (*XX. Armeekorps*), F000671.
474 NARA T314, R653 (*XX. Armeekorps*), F000962.
475 NARA T314, R653 (*XX. Armeekorps*), F000964.
476 NARA T314, R654 (*XX. Armeekorps*), F000585.
477 NARA T314, R654 (*XX. Armeekorps*), F000573.
478 NARA T314, R654 (*XX. Armeekorps*), F000570.

22 SEPTEMBER 1942

Sturmgeschütz-Abteilung 202, now under the direct command of the *XX. Armeekorps,* was held in the corps reserve in the area of Wlassowo. In the meantime, '*Blücher*' had been cancelled and the corps made preparations for defence along the Worja River.[479] The unit now had 16 StuG. IIIs serviceable with one in need of short-term repairs and one undergoing long-term repairs.[480]

24 SEPTEMBER 1942

Of the 18 assault guns of the assault artillery unit, 17 were operational.[481]

28 SEPTEMBER 1942

German reconnaissance verified significant motor-vehicle traffic in the direction of Belyj Kamen. Since this was suspected to be an enemy troop concentration, *Sturmgeschütz-Abteilung 202* (without its *3. Batterie*[482]), which was in the sector of the *183. Infanterie-Division* together with *3. Kompanie/Panzerjäger-Abteilung 31* and the *2. Kompanie/Panzerjäger-Abteilung 219,* were ordered to be ready to march at two hours' notice.[483]

30 SEPTEMBER 1942

An area reconnaissance was conducted by *Sturmgeschütz-Abteilung 202* in support of an action to be carried out towards Temkino village and Kordjukowo.[484] On that day 11 of the 12 assault guns available to the unit were operational.[485] It seems that between the 25 and 29 September 1942, *Sturmgeschütz-Abteilung 202* had to handover six of its 18 StuG. III assault guns.

1 OCTOBER 1942

The *1. Batterie / Sturmgeschütz-Abteilung 202* was put under the command of the staff of the *255. Infanterie-Division* and was in readiness in the area of Wjasischtschi.[486] The *2. Batterie* was stationed in Wlassowo with 11 operational assault guns operational and one in short-term repair.[487] The staff and the *2. Batterie* of the assault artillery unit was in the area of the *XX. Armeekorps* but in the reserve of the *3. Panzerarmee.* At this point in time the intention was to increase the number of StuG. III assault guns to 20 in the near future.[488]

---

479 NARA T314, R653 (*XX. Armeekorps*), F000675 and F000977.
480 NARA T314, R654 (*XX. Armeekorps*), F000564.
481 NARA T314, R654 (*XX. Armeekorps*), F000556.
482 NARA T315, R1548 (*183. Infanterie-Division*), F000071.
483 NARA T314, R653 (*XX. Armeekorps*), F000677.
484 NARA T315, R1548 (*183. Infanterie-Division*), F000077.
485 NARA T314, R654 (*XX. Armeekorps*), F000529.
486 NARA T314, R653 (*XX. Armeekorps*), F000677.
487 NARA T314, R654 (*XX. Armeekorps*), F000526.
488 NARA T313, R264 (*Panzerarmeeoberkommando 3*), F8535202.

2 OCTOBER

The assault artillery unit still had only 12 guns, including one in short-term repair.[489]

3 OCTOBER 1942

Four new StuG. IIIs arrived at *Sturmgeschütz-Abteilung 202.*[490]

5 OCTOBER 1942

Of the 16 assault guns available only 11 were operational but on the same day a new StuG. III arrived.[491]

6 OCTOBER 1942

Of the 17 available assault guns of the assault artillery unit, 14 were combat-ready.[492]

7 OCTOBER 1942

Sturmgeschütz-Abteilung 202 (without its *3. Batterie*) was stationed in the area of Stepaniki with 15 combat-ready assault guns. An additional combat-ready assault gun was in the area of Wjasma. Of the StuG. IIIs in need of repair, seven were located in Wjasma, two in Smolensk and one in Minsk.[493] From these figures it emerges that the strength of the unit had increased by nine assault guns (which were most likely to have been undergoing repairs) on that day.

8 OCTOBER 1942

Of the 26 assault guns of the assault artillery unit, 15 were combat-ready, 11 were undergoing short-term repairs.[494]

13 OCTOBER 1942

By order of *Heeresgruppe Mitte*, *Sturmgeschütz-Abteilung 202* (without *3. Batterie*) left its quarters behind *183. Infanterie-Division* where it was held in the direct reserve of the *3. Panzerarmee.*[495]

The next day, the assault artillery unit were to assemble in Wjasma where it would form a direct reserve for *Heeresgruppe Mitte.* The assault guns, together with nine 7.5 cm self-propelled anti-tank guns from the *Panzerjäger-Abteilung*[496] would be placed such that they could be quickly regrouped towards the west by either

489 NARA T314, R654 (*XX. Armeekorps*), F000522.
490 NARA T314, R654 (*XX. Armeekorps*), F000518.
491 NARA T314, R654 (*XX. Armeekorps*), F000508.
492 NARA T314, R654 (*XX. Armeekorps*), F000504.
493 NARA T314, R654 (*XX. Armeekorps*), F000499.
494 NARA T314, R654 (*XX. Armeekorps*), F000495.
495 NARA T315, R1548 (*183. Infanterie-Division*), F000215.
496 These tank destroyers were built from captured and modified French Lorraine prime movers.

road or rail.[497] The assault guns and the tank destroyers would be deployed north of Dukowschtschina if required.[498]

The *3. Batterie* was ordered to Wjasma by the staff of the *4. Armee* where it was reassigned to *Sturmgeschütz-Abteilung 202.*[499] However before setting off, the battery had to handover four of its StuG. IIIs (without crew) to *Sturmgeschütz-Abteilung 197.*[500]

On the same day, the assault artillery unit had 15 combat-ready assault guns, four were undergoing short-term repairs; another four were undergoing long-term repairs.[501] According to these figures, another three StuG. IIIs must have been withdrawn from the unit between 9 and 12 October 1942. It is highly possible that these were the assault guns transferred to *Sturmgeschütz-Abteilung 197* implying that the *3. Batterie* had handed over only three of its assault guns.

14 OCTOBER 1942

Sturmgeschütz-Abteilung 202 marched off from the area of the *XX. Armeekorps.*[502] Having arrived in Wjasma, the unit had to be in readiness to march at two hours' notice if such an order was issued.[503] The *3. Batterie* was loaded for transfer to Wjasma at Spas Demensk at 0700 hours next morning.[504]

20 OCTOBER 1942

The *3. Batterie* of the assault artillery unit arrived in Wjasma from the sector of the *4. Armee.*[505]

1 NOVEMBER 1942

A new combat table of organization and equipment was published in Germany for the assault gun units according to which, besides the 10 assault guns issued to each battery[506], the battalion commander should also receive a StuG. III Despite that, many units kept their original organizational structure – with batteries containing seven assault guns each – except for the fact that the battalion commander received an additional StuG. III From that point onwards each commander had a total of 22 assault guns at his disposal.[507] *Sturmgeschütz-Abteilung 202* continued fighting

497 NARA T313, R264 (*Panzerarmeeoberkommando 3*), F8535140.
498 NARA T313, R265 (*Panzerarmeeoberkommando 3*), F8535761.
499 NARA T313, R264 (*Panzerarmeeoberkommando 3*), F8534861.
500 NARA T313, R264 (*Panzerarmeeoberkommando 3*), F8535140.
501 NARA T314, R654 (*XX. Armeekorps*), F000474.
502 NARA T314, R653 (*XX. Armeekorps*), F000681.
503 NARA T313, R264 (*Panzerarmeeoberkommando 3*), F8534867.
504 NARA T313, R264 (*Panzerarmeeoberkommando 3*), F8535249.
505 NARA T313, R264 (*Panzerarmeeoberkommando 3*), F8534444.
506 Each assault gun platoon had three StuG. IIIs, the tenth was the AFV of the battery commander.
507 Spielberger, Walter J.: *Sturmgeschütze. Entwicklung und Fertigung der sPak.* Stuttgart, 1997. Third edition. p. 237.

according to that order of battle until March 1943, and switched over to the organizational structure of 31 assault guns.

4 NOVEMBER 1942

Sturmgeschütz-Abteilung 202 was in the reserve of *3. Panzerarmee* together with the tanks of *Panzerabteilung 18* and a self-propelled anti-tank gun company from *Panzerjäger-Abteilung 616.* As ordered, all the three units had to be in readiness to march at three hours' notice.[508]

6 NOVEMBER 1942

The assault guns of *Sturmgeschütz-Abteilung 202* were put in readiness to march so that they would be deployable from the following day by receiving four hours' notice.[509]

17 NOVEMBER 1942

All the vehicles, guns and armoured combat vehicles in the whole area of the *3. Panzerarmee* were painted white in compliance with the principles of winter camouflage. In accordance with this order, the StuG. III assault guns of the *Sturmgeschütz-Abteilung* were also painted white.[510]

26 NOVEMBER 1942

The assault artillery unit and the *1. Kompanie / Panzerjäger-Abteilung 616* (with nine 7.5 cm self-propelled anti-tank guns) were subordinated to the *XXXIX. Panzerkorps* in the sector of the *9. Armee,* and ordered to the area of Ssytschewka at dawn next day.[511]

508 NARA T313, R264 (*Panzerarmeeoberkommando 3*), F8534886.

509 NARA T313, R265 (*Panzerarmeeoberkommando 3*), F8536010.

510 NARA T313, R265 (*Panzerarmeeoberkommando 3*), F8536085.

511 NARA T313, R264 (*Panzerarmeeoberkommando 3*), F8534921.

CHAPTER 3

In the sector of the German 9. *Armee* in the area of Rschew

1942

Operational Background:

On 25 November 1942, the Soviet Western Front launched an offensive from the east with the forces of the Kalinin Front attacking from west to eliminate a bulge in the front line held by the German 9. Armee and the troops of the 3. Panzerarmee south-south-west of Rschew. The operation, codenamed 'Mars', was to destroy the German grouping there because they were still dangerously close to Moscow. The German units – supported by Sturmgeschütz-Abteilung 202 – collided with elements of the Soviet Western Front.

27 NOVEMBER 1942

At 0530 hours *Sturmgeschütz-Abteilung 202* set off on a march conducted on tracks and road wheels from Wjasma into the sector of the *9. Armee.*[512]

The acting commander of the assault artillery unit, *Hauptmann* Hans Handrik,[513] arrived at the command post of the *78. Infanterie-Division* at 0950 hours[514] and reported that his assault guns would arrive later – presumably in the evening – because of the snowstorm and snowdrifts. *Sturmgeschütz-Abteilung 202* had a total of 21 short-barrelled StuG. III assault guns but only one allowance of ammunition at their disposal.[515] The command post was established in Krjukowo.[516]

At around 1100 hours, the assault artillery unit was in march in the area of Nowo-Dugino.[517] In its report to the *78. Infanterie-Division*, submitted at 1530 hours, the assault artillery unit gave voice to its hope that they would arrive by 1900 hours. The division planned to assign one battery each to *Kampfgruppen 'Bömers'*,

512 NARA T313, R264 (*Panzerarmeeoberkommando 3*), F8534610, as well as T314, R933 (*XXXIX. Panzerkorps*), F000071.

513 The assigned commander of the unit, *Oberstleutnant* Karl Evers was probably reassigned to duty somewhere else. Due to that, the commander of the 3. battery, *Hauptmann* Handrik assumed command of *Sturmgeschütz-Abteilung 202* in November 1942, as an acting commander (*Führer*).

514 NARA T315, R1102 (*78. Infanterie-Division*), F000082.

515 NARA T314, R933 (*XXXIX. Panzerkorps*), F000005.

516 NARA T315, R1102 (*78. Infanterie-Division*), F000082.

517 NARA T314, R933 (*XXXIX. Panzerkorps*), F000006.

'*Kaether*' and '*Kohler*'[518] the intention being to deploy the later of these units in the area of Lopotok.[519]

After 2100 hours the corps recorded that *Sturmgeschütz-Abteilung 202* had arrived at Lopotok with one of its batteries (seven assault guns). One of the batteries of the unit was reserved for *Panzergrenadier-Regiment 13*[520] at Brannoje, and the other for *Kampfgruppe* '*Kaether*'[521] in the area of Blaguscha.[522]

The front line of the *78. Infanterie-Division* had been attacked for two days by the Soviet 26 Guards and 331 Rifle Division, the 148 and the 150 Rifle Brigades, as well as the 11 and the 17 Tank Brigade.[523] The division was ordered to hold its current positions. To provide support for that, *Sturmgeschütz-Abteilung 202* was assigned to them[524] together with the self-propelled anti-tank guns of the *1. Batterie/ Panzerjäger-Abteilung 616.*[525]

In the evening the assault artillery unit reported that they had only 16 combat-ready assault guns.[526] The march through the snowstorm must have taken its toll on the mechanical condition of the StuG. IIIs.

The assault guns that had been promised several times by *Heeresgruppe Mitte* and the *9. Armee* were eagerly awaited by the staff of the *XXXIX. Panzerkorps* because their 8.8 cm anti-aircraft artillery groups were unable to achieve permanent success against the superiority of the Soviet tanks.[527]

The German *9. Armee* informed its corps by telegram in the afternoon that Soviet troops had launched several successful night-time tank raids and more of such attacks should be expected. To repel these, the assault guns and tanks were to be placed in positions from which they could fire on the roads lengthwise. Rather than face the raiding tanks they were to engage them from prepared firing positions.[528]

Soviet troops penetrated the German defences north of Podossinowka on a narrow front. Through this gap the forces of the Soviet 2 Guards Cavalry Corps,

---

518 Battle Group '*Bömers*' comprised the staff of *Panzergrenadier-Regiment 13,* remainders of two grenadier battalions and a mountain pioneer battalion, half of an armoured infantry battalion, most of a field training battalion and an alarm (emergency) unit, Battle Group *'Kaether'* was made up of the staff of *Grenadier-Regiment 14*, remainders of two armoured infantry- and a grenadier-battalion, half of an armoured infantry battalion and *Schnelle Abteilung 178.*

519 NARA T314, R933 (*XXXIX. Panzerkorps*), F000007, and also T315, R1102 (*78. Infanterie-Division*), F000082.

520 The division belonged to the *5. Panzer-Division's* order of battle, but is was subordinated to the *78. Infanterie-Division* at that time.

521 *Oberstleutnant der Reserve* Ernst Kaether was the commander of *Grenadier-Regiment 14.*

522 NARA T314, R933 (*XXXIX. Panzerkorps*), F000009.

523 NARA T314, R933 (*XXXIX. Panzerkorps*), F000015.

524 According to certain sources when *Sturmgeschütz-Abteilung 202* was put under the command of the *78. Infanterie-Division*, it had reported as much as 500 Soviet tanks knocked out from September 1941. *See* Kurowski, Franz – Tornau, Gottfried: *Sturmgeschütze – Die Panzer der Infanterie.* Würzburg, 2008. p. 109. In our opinion, archival documents do not confirm that.

525 NARA T314, R933 (*XXXIX. Panzerkorps*), F000023.

526 NARA T315, R1101 (*78. Infanterie-Division*), F001225.

527 NARA T314, R933 (*XXXIX. Panzerkorps*), F000063.

528 NARA T314, R933 (*XXXIX. Panzerkorps*), F000027.

strengthened with tanks[529], reached and closed the railroad between Wjasma and Rschew in the area of Nikischkino Sovkhoz. With that, the Soviet troops gained access to the rear of the *9. Armee* –the main goal of their operation.[530]

28 NOVEMBER 1942

At 0339 hours the corps ordered the staff of the *78. Infanterie-Division* to dispatch *Schnelle Abteilung 129* to the area of Podossinowka to prevent Soviet troops from breaking through in a south-westerly direction. According to the division, that situation needed to be cleared up first since, as stated in its reports, at least 30 German tanks and more than that number of armoured personnel carriers were fighting there. The division intended to employ a battery of *Sturmgeschütz-Abteilung 202* with the personnel and equipment of the division's training school (training company) that had been assigned to *Kampfgruppe 'Kohler'* in a counter-thrust towards Sherebzowo.[531]

In the morning, the commander of the *78. Infanterie-Division, General der Infanterie* Paul Völckers, gave the following task to *Oberstleutnant* Dr. Walter Reissinger, commander of *Grenadier-Regiment 215:*

The enemy exerts pressure from the area of Arestowo towards Sherebzowo, Podossinowka and Mal. Kropotowo with significant forces. The enemy cavalry units have already broken through the railroad running west. Sherebzowo has been occupied by Schnelle Abteilung 178, and we have more units in Podossinowka, partly scattered ones and troop fragments. Our own forces are in Mal. Kropotowo, too. Oberstleutnant Reissinger will close the gap in the western perimeter of Sherebzowo, Podossinowka and the southern perimeter of Mal. Kropotowo and thereby block further breakthrough towards the railroad.[532]

The commander of *Grenadier-Regiment 215* arrived at Lopotok at 0830 hours – his regimental staff that had been sent there earlier. Here a training company *(Lehrkompanie)* deployed in a blocking position, a few scattered units, as well as the assault guns of *Sturmgeschütz-Abteilung 202* were put under their command. The German forces located here were soon alarmed as five Cossack cavalry battalions were trotting in closed formation from a north-westerly direction to break through between Lopotok and Podossinowka towards south-east. Suddenly every element of the German *Kampfgruppe*, including the StuG. III assault guns, fired on the attackers. Even a light field howitzer battery shelled the cavalry with direct fire;

529 On the operational map of the German *5. Panzer-Division* the German reconnaissance pinpointed the Soviet 100, 240 and 247 Tank Brigade. *See* Plato, Anton Detlev von: *Die Geschichte der 5. Panzerdivision 1938-1945*. Regensburg, 1978. p. 464.

530 Merker, Ludwig: *Das Buch der 78. Sturm Division.* Tübingen, 1965. p. 184 and p. 190.

531 NARA T314, R933 (*XXXIX. Panzerkorps*), F000339, and also NARA T315, R1102 (*78. Infanterie-Division*), F000086.

532 Merker, Ludwig: *Das Buch der 78. Sturm Division.* Tübingen, 1965. p. 191.

artillerymen who were free to do so grabbed carbines and joined the defence. Above the settlement a German Ju 88 bomber circled, adding to the fire with its on-board weapons and releasing bombs. In the concentrated fire the Soviet cavalry unit was almost totally destroyed. Only a few Cossacks managed to escape but they too were annihilated a few kilometres towards the east.

After repelling the Cossack assault, *Oberstleutnant* Reissinger went to Podossinowka to organize the defence with a reduced operational staff, the assault guns of *Sturmgeschütz-Abteilung 202,* a platoon of the *Lehrkompanie* and an ad hoc platoon formed from scattered units.

By the time the small *Kampfgruppe* arrived, the situation there was critical. The village was under constant Soviet artillery fire and in flames. The defending German forces had suffered heavy casualties and their ammunition was running out. Moreover, the locality was full of soldiers from scattered units of several service branches. The village was defended by a battalion of the *5. Panzer-Division,* the *II./Panzergrenadier-Regiment 13* supported by six combat-ready tanks and an anti-aircraft artillery squad.

Those forces were arranged into three small *Kampfgruppen* by *Oberstleutnant* Reissinger, so forming a continuous front line from Podossinowka to Mal. Kropotowo (the latter settlement being outside the line of defence). The German efforts were rewarded with success because, apart from artillery and mortar fire, the Soviet troops inexplicably called off their offensive operations.

Meanwhile in Lopotok, the *Lehrkompanie* was strengthened by the arrival of a tank company. The commander of the small *Kampfgruppe* reserved for intervention was *Hauptmann* Wilhelm Kohler, an officer from *Grenadier-Regiment 195.*

At 0740 hours, the *78. Infanterie-Division* reported that the German forces defending Podossinowka had been forced to evacuate the settlement and were retreating in a southerly or south-westerly direction where a fresh German battalion and an armoured battalion reinforced with armoured personnel carriers were fighting. The division sent a battery of *Sturmgeschütz-Abteilung 202* there to block the retreat.[533]

It soon became clear that elements of the *5. Panzer-Division* were still defending Podossinowka and they received categorical orders to continue their efforts. At the same time, an assault gun battery moving in the direction of Podossinowka ran into a Soviet cavalry regiment that had managed to get through the German strongpoints and was making rapid progress towards Ssidorowo. At 1015 hours *78. Infanterie-Division* reported to the corps that the assault guns had destroyed four companies of the cavalry regiment.[534]

Kampfgruppe 'Bömers' informed the staff of the *78. Infanterie-Division* at 1145 hours that a violent Soviet attack was underway at Chlepen and requested the support of assault guns. In response, an assault gun platoon was dispatched from

533 NARA T314, R933 (*XXXIX. Panzerkorps*), F000340.

534 NARA T314, R933 (*XXXIX. Panzerkorps*), F000341.

the battery assigned to *Kampfgruppe 'Kaether'* towards Star. Mursino. At 1200 hours *Schnelle Abteilung 178* reported to *Kampfgruppe 'Kaether'*, that its *2. Kompanie* was being hard-pressed by the Soviets and requested an immediate counter-thrust by the assault guns. After 1300 hours, Soviet tanks broke through the defences of the company but were unable to find them in a snowstorm.[535]

To aid *Schnelle Abteilung 178*, a company and an assault gun platoon were sent from *Kampfgruppe 'Reissinger'* to Sherebzowo at 1410 hours.[536]

At 1600 hours, according to a report by the division, two batteries of *Sturmgeschütz-Abteilung 202* were fighting in *Kampfgruppe 'Reissinger'*[537] and the third was assigned to *Kampfgruppe 'Kaether'* which was led by the commander of *Grenadier-Regiment 14*. The Soviet tanks broke through east of Sherebzowo at around 1500 hours, crushing the *2. Kompanie* of *Schnelle Abteilung 178*. Nevertheless, the Germans knocked out five tanks here.[538]

At 1740 hours the *78. Infanterie-Division* informed the corps that *Kampfgruppe 'Reissinger'*, having completed its task of re-establishing contact with the defenders of Mal. Kropotowo, had closed the gap in the front line that had been opened in the vicinity of the *5. Panzer-Division*. At that time, in defence around Sherebzowo were: *Schnelle Abteilung 178* in front of Podossinowka; the soldiers of the divisional training school in Podossinowka and north-west of there lay *I. Bataillon/Grenadier-Regiment 430*[539] with *Schnelle Abteilung 129*. Between Podossinowka and Mal. Kropotowo six tanks and an armoured infantry company from the armoured *Kampfgruppe 'Wuchenauer'* of the *9. Panzer-Division*, as well as three self-propelled anti-tank guns of *Panzerjäger-Abteilung 616* were in defence.

By the end of the day, in the area around Sherebzowo, the Germans had knocked out a total of eight Soviet T–34 tanks[540], destroyed 11 armoured fighting vehicles, immobilized one and captured another –and there were more knock outs yet to be confirmed.[541] *Sturmgeschütz-Abteilung 202* knocked out three Soviet tanks that day.[542] Of these, two were knocked out in the area around Taliza where the Germans knocked out a total of six Soviet tanks (two of these were disabled by the assault guns, another two by the anti-tanks guns of *Artillerie-Regiment 178* and two more by the infantry.[543]

535 NARA T315, R1102 (*78. Infanterie-Division*), F000089.

536 NARA T315, R1102 (*78. Infanterie-Division*), F000090.

537 The battle group was commanded by *Oberstleutnant* dr. Walter Reissinger, the commander of *Grenadier-Regiment 215*. On that day, besides the two battalions of *Sturmgeschütz-Abteilung 202*, the *I. Batterie/ Grenadier-Regiment 430*, *Schnelle Abteilung 129*, the armoured battle group of 9. *Panzer-Division 'Wuchenauer'* and the self-propelled AT-guns of the *2. Kompanie/ Panzerjäger-Abteilung 616* (without one of its platoons) were subordinated to him.

538 NARA T314, R933 (*XXXIX. Panzerkorps*), F000342.

539 The regiment originally belonged to the *129. Infanterie-Division's* order of battle.

540 NARA T314, R933 (*XXXIX. Panzerkorps*), F000342-343. None of them were knocked out by assault guns: four of them were disabled by AT-guns, three by AA-guns, and one by a patrol of TDs.

541 NARA T314, R933 (*XXXIX. Panzerkorps*), F000350.

542 NARA T314, R933 (*XXXIX. Panzerkorps*), F000761.

543 NARA T315, R1102 (*78. Infanterie-Division*), F000165.

Schnelle Abteilung 178 requested tanks or assault guns at 2245 hours to defend Sherebzowo because it had lost several of its heavy weapons that day, and another Soviet tank raid was in preparation. The division held out the prospect of dispatching two anti-aircraft artillery groups to them the following morning.[544]

At 2300 hours, the *78. Infanterie-Division* received orders from the *9. Armee* to provide the lead battalion of the *129. Infanterie-Division* with assault guns to enable them to clear the south-western foreground of Loshki of the Soviet troops that had penetrated the area.[545]

29 NOVEMBER 1942

In the early hours, the *XXXIX. Panzerkorps* received a telegram from the *9. Armee,* according to which fresh personnel had been dispatched two days earlier from Jüterbog to Ssytschewka. These were form the new *1. Batterie / Sturmgeschütz-Abteilung 202.* Following the arrival of the new personnel, the current personnel of the *1. Batterie* were to be dispatched, together with their small arms, to Jüterbog for reorganization. Furthermore, the personnel of the two groups were not to be allowed to mix. Before leaving, the 'old' personnel of *1. Batterie* were to be deloused and the procedure repeated on their arrival in Jüterbog.[546]

At 0015 hours an assault gun platoon was dispatched from *Kampfgruppe 'Reissinger'* for assignment to *Schnelle Abteilung 178* at Sherebzowo.[547]

At 1340 hours *Kampfgruppe 'Bömers'* requested assault gun support after Soviet troops launched an attack on Chlepen with 26 T–34 tanks and accompanying infantry riding on them. In just two minutes, an assault gun platoon left *Kampfgruppe 'Kaether'* and was *en route* to the settlement. However, at around 1500 hours Soviet tanks achieved a break through.[548]

Meanwhile, German reconnaissance had discovered that in the sector of the *78. Infanterie-Division* (Taliza and Sherebzowo) the Soviets had attacked with their 18, 25, 200 and 255 Tank Brigades.[549]

During the day's fighting, the assault guns of *Sturmgeschütz-Abteilung 202* knocked out 15 Soviet tanks (including six T–34, one KV-1 and six light tanks) all of which were confirmed.[550] An additional three kills were yet to be confirmed. In the evening, 15 of the 21 assault guns were operational, five StuG. IIIs needed

544 NARA T315, R1102 (*78. Infanterie-Division*), F000092.

545 NARA T314, R933 (*XXXIX. Panzerkorps*), F000344.

546 NARA T314, R934 (*XXXIX. Panzerkorps*), F000979.

547 NARA T315, R1102 (*78. Infanterie-Division*), F000094.

548 NARA T315, R1102 (*78. Infanterie-Division*), F000096.

549 NARA T314, R933 (*XXXIX. Panzerkorps*), F000266.

550 At least this score was reported by the *Arko* of the *XXXIX. Panzerkorps* on that day. However *Sturmgeschütz-Abteilung 202* represented only 11 knocked out Soviet AFVs in its summary of 5 December 1942. *See* NARA T314, R933 (*XXXIX. Panzerkorps*), F000761. It is highly possible that four of the 15 AFVs were knocked out by the self-propelled AT-guns of *Panzerjäger-Abteilung 616,* and not by the assault guns.

short-term repairs and one was undergoing longer-term repairs. By nightfall there was a total of only 212 shells left in the assault guns and on their ammunition trailers. Ammunition that had been issued but had not yet been received amounted to only 3,873 rounds.[551] Considering that the assault guns had fired 2,012 shells and 3,500 shells on 28 and 29 November respectively,[552] the quantity available for them was not at all sufficient.

30 NOVEMBER 1942

According to the morning report on 30 November, the complete *2. Batterie* and a platoon from *3. Batterie* of the assault artillery unit supported *Kampfgruppe 'Kaether'*[553] together with three anti-aircraft artillery groups of *leichte Flak-Abteilung 76*. The complete *1. Batterie* and most of the *3. Batterie* were given the task of providing support for *Kampfgruppe 'Reissinger'*[554] together with an anti-aircraft artillery group from *leichte Flak-Abteilung 76* and the self-propelled anti-tank guns of the *2. Kompanie/Panzerjäger Abteilung 616*.[555]

Kampfgruppe 'Kaether' reported to the division at 0735 hours that *Kampfgruppe 'Reissinger'* took the assault gun platoon[556] from *Schnelle Abteilung 178*, which, finding itself requiring support once more, requested its return at 0858 hours. However, no assault guns could be transferred to *Kampfgruppe 'Kaether'* temporarily which meant that it had to solve the problem faced by *Schnelle Abteilung 178* by itself.[557]

The staff of *Grenadier-Regiment 14* (i. e. *Kampfgruppe 'Kaether'*) informed *Schnelle Abteilung 178* at 0920 hours by radio that the assault gun platoon that had earlier been deployed on their left were no longer available as they were waiting in readiness the vicinity of Blaguscha in case they were needed in Sherebzowo.[558]

At 1027 hours, *Kampfgruppe 'Kohler'*, deployed on the left flank of *Kampfgruppe 'Reissinger'*, reported the forces at its disposal were: the *2. Kompanie/ Panzergrenadier-Regiment 13*; the *7. Kompanie/ Panzer-Regiment 33*; the *3.* and *4. Kompanien /*

551 NARA T314, R933 (*XXXIX. Panzerkorps*), F000268.

552 NARA T314, R933 (*XXXIX. Panzerkorps*), F000288.

553 On that day, *Kampfgruppe 'Kaether'* itself was made up of three smaller formations: *Gruppe 'Spindler'* (with the shattered remnants of the I*I.Bataillon* of *Grenadier-Regiment 14*, the regimental 13. and 14 companies and an alarm company), *Gruppe 'Bundenbender'* (with the staff of *Schnelle Abteilung 178* and its three and a half companies, the one and a half companies of *Feldausbildungs-Abteilung 178*, a merged company of the *5. Panzer-Division*, an infantry gun of the 9. company of *Panzergrenadier-Regiment 13* and supply elements of *Panzer-Pionierbataillon 89*), and *Gruppe 'Ziegenhorn'* (with the *1.Bataillon/ Panzer grenadier-Regiment* 14).

554 *Kampfgruppe 'Reissinger'* also comprised more elements on that day: *Gruppe 'Schneider'* (with the staff and a company of *Feldausbildungs-Abteilung 178*, the shattered remnants of the I*I.Bataillon Grenadier-Regiment 215*, the shattered remnants of the *1.Bataillon Grenadier-Regiment 14,* the training school of the *78. Infanterie-Division*, the elements of an armoured artillery observer battery and an alarm company), Group *'Wohlfart'* (with the forces of *Schnelle Abteilung 129*, and the *1.Bataillon* of *Grenadier-Regiment 430*) and Group „Kohler" (with the *2. Kompanie* of *Panzer-Regiment 33*, a mechanized infantry company of *Panzergrenadier-Regiment 10*) and a self-propelled infantry gun platoon of *schwere Infanteriegeschütz-Kompanie (Sfl.) 701*.

555 NARA T314, R934 (*XXXIX. Panzerkorps*), F000998.

556 NARA T315, R1102 (*78. Infanterie-Division*), F000099.

557 NARA T315, R1102 (*78. Infanterie-Division*), F000100.

558 NARA T315, R1102 (*78. Infanterie-Division*), F000178.

Panzergrenadier-Regiment 10; soldiers from the training school of *Infanterie-Division 78*, and the *1. Batterie* of *Sturmgeschütz-Abteilung 202*. The battery arrived with four StuG. III assault guns at 0900 hours. At 1115 hours an assault gun and a heavy machine gun section destroyed three 76.2 mm guns from well-concealed firing positions with a direct hit and harassed the Soviets with flanking fire and firing from behind.[559]

In the morning the Soviet troops commenced an attack with a rifle regiment and 40-50 tanks to take Mal. Kropotowo. Besides a few strongpoints, the Soviets overran the minor forces of the *5. Panzer-Division* defending here, and penetrated the village. The defenders knocked out three of the Soviet armoured combat vehicles attacking south of the strongpoint. Before noon the Soviets concentrated an additional one or two battalions, 14 T–34 and two T–60 tanks 800 m southwest of the settlement in a hollow.

By that time, the battle group of *Hauptmann* Kohler had grown stronger: the four assault guns of Sturmgeschütz-Abteilung 202 finally arrived at the group.

At around 1200 hours *Kampfgruppe 'Kohler'* launched an attack on its own initiative on Soviet forces assembling 800 m south-west of Mal. Kropotowo (one or two battalions of infantry soldiers and 16 AFVs). The assault gun battery, the amalgamated armoured *Kompanie 'Bichel'*, and a company from the division's training school outflanked the Soviets from the west, then overran them. Soviet losses, according to German reports, were the follows: 250-300 soldiers, 14 T–34 and two T–60 tanks, seven anti-tank guns, two anti-aircraft guns and 35-40 trucks.[560] In one of the Soviet tanks, operational maps were found with details of the attack. From the assault guns subordinated to *Kompanie 'Bichel'*, one StuG. III was lost with its crew.[561]

Exploiting their success, the *Kampfgruppe* continued its attack towards Mal. Kropotowo, and pursuing the Soviets as they withdrew eastwards, retook the settlement (partly in a fierce house-to-house-fighting) at around 1330 hours. During the mopping up, another 100-150 Soviet soldiers were killed. The German *Kampfgruppe* lost only one dead and five wounded. For his courageous determination and significant accomplishments the commander of the *Kampfgruppe* was awarded the Knight's Cross of the Iron Cross.[562]

After this, *Kampfgruppe 'Kohler'* established contact with the forces of the *5. Panzer-Division* attacking from the north and in doing so closed the gap opened by the Soviet breakthrough. With this, the Germans were able to cut the supply route to the enemy forces that had broken through earlier and were now fighting west of the Rschew–Ssytschewka railroad.[563]

---

559 NARA T315, R1102 (*78. Infanterie-Division*), F000221.

560 NARA T315, R1102 (*78. Infanterie-Division*), F000101.

561 NARA T315, R1102 (*78. Infanterie-Division*), F000221.

562 Merker, Ludwig: *Das Buch der 78. Sturm Division.* Tübingen, 1965. pp. 193-194.

563 NARA T315, R1102 (*78. Infanterie-Division*), F000102.

At 1730 hours the *78. Infanterie-Division* reported that they had detached two tanks and three assault guns and sent them as anti-tank reserves to Mal. Kropotowo to secure the contact that had been established with *5. Panzer-Division.*[564]

A total of 11 Soviet AFVs were reported as knocked out by the assault guns of *Sturmgeschütz-Abteilung 202* on 29 November 1942.[565]

According to German reconnaissance, units fighting under the command of *78. Infanterie-Division* faced the Soviet 26 Guards Division, the 247, 331, and 351 Rifle Divisions and the 148 and 150 Rifle Brigades. Behind the Soviet front line the 11, 17, 25, 240 and 255 Tank Brigades were suspected.[566]

1 DECEMBER 1942

At 0335 hours the *2. Batterie* of *Sturmgeschütz-Abteilung 202* was detached from *Kampfgruppe 'Kaether'* and sent to *Kampfgruppe 'Bömers'*, which was being hard pressed in the Podjablonka area.[567]

Sturmgeschütz-Abteilung 202 knocked out three Soviet AFVs and, by the end of the day, their ammunition stock had dropped to 3,902 shells. Of the 22 assault guns, 13 were operational, five were in need of short-term repairs, and four needed long-term repairs.[568]

2 DECEMBER 1942

The assault artillery unit reported only one knocked out Soviet AFV.[569]

3 DECEMBER 1942

In the evening, the *XXXIX. Panzerkorps* initially assigned two platoons (with four assault guns) of the *2. Batterie* to corps reserve[570] but then subordinated them to the *337. Infanterie-Division* in the Bobyschewo area (10 km east of Ssytschewka) because, according to reconnaissance, Soviet attacks were expected on the left flank of that division. The assault gun platoons were to deploy as mobile anti-tank reserves.[571]

During the day three assault guns of the *1. Batterie/ Sturmgeschütz-Abteilung 202* were combat-ready as were with five others from the *2. Batterie* and three of the *3. Batterie.*[572] By evening, 13 assault guns of the assault artillery unit were serviceable.[573]

564 NARA T315, R1102 (*78. Infanterie-Division*), F000181.
565 NARA T314, R933 (*XXXIX. Panzerkorps*), F000761.
566 NARA T314, R933 (*XXXIX. Panzerkorps*), F000230.
567 NARA T315, R1102 (*78. Infanterie-Division*), F000104.
568 NARA T314, R933 (*XXXIX. Panzerkorps*), F000624.
569 NARA T314, R933 (*XXXIX. Panzerkorps*), F000761.
570 NARA T315, R1102 (*78. Infanterie-Division*), F000109.
571 NARA T314, R933 (*XXXIX. Panzerkorps*), F000534 and F000537.
572 NARA T315, R1101 (*78. Infanterie-Division*), F001232.
573 NARA T314, R933 (*XXXIX. Panzerkorps*), F000595.

4 DECEMBER 1942

Soviet forces were mounting continuous attacks on Podossinowka in the sector of the *78. Infanterie Division.* These attacks, lasting from 0700 hours to 1430 hours, were conducted by 40-50 AFVs, two battalions of rifle infantry and significant artillery and mortar support. The Germans, partly with the support of two batteries of *Sturmgeschütz-Abteilung 202*, fended off the attacks and knocked out a total of 33 Soviet AFVs.[574]

On that day the assault artillery knocked out a confirmed total of 25 Soviet AFVs.[575] To achieve this, 250 shells were used. At the end of the day their stock of ammunition consisted of 3,282 shells. Of the assault guns 10 were combat-ready in the evening, eight were in need of short-term repairs (i.e. repairs expected to be completed within 14 days), and four in need of long-term repairs.[576]

Wachtmeister Fritz Amling, a platoon commander of the *3. Batterie*, distinguished himself during the day's fighting. In conjunction with another assault gun he engaged 20 Soviet AFVs, (a numerical disadvantage of 10 to 1) and in a short time knocked out 10 Soviet AFVs[577] with his assault gun. *Unteroffizier* Tantius, another soldier from *Sturmgeschütz-Abteilung 202*, was credited with knocking out a total of 15 AFVs in three days.[578]

On the same day, in the area of Sherebzowo and Podossinowka, in the barrage fire of the Soviet artillery and multiple-rocket launchers and the attacks of close-support aircraft, four StuG. IIIs of the assault artillery unit were disabled together with four anti-tank guns, five anti-aircraft guns and five tank destroyers from other German units.[579]

According to the report of the *78. Infanterie-Division* submitted at 2000 hours, *Sturmgeschütz-Abteilung 202* had six combat-ready StuG. IIIs in the sector of the division.[580] An additional three assault guns of the *2. Batterie* were in readiness in the sector of the *337. Infanterie-Division* in the area of Bobyschewo.[581]

5 DECEMBER 1942

At 0920 hours, *Schnelle Abteilung 178* reported to *Kampfgruppe 'Kaether'* that a significant Soviet attack had been launched on Sherebzowo with tank support, and for that reason they requested assault guns to be put on standby for action.[582]

574 NARA T314, R933 (*XXXIX. Panzerkorps*), F000502.

575 NARA T314, R933 (*XXXIX. Panzerkorps*), F000761. 10 of them were knocked out at Podossinowka at around noon. *See* NARA T315, R1102 (*78. Infanterie-Division*), F000198.

576 NARA T314, R933 (*XXXIX. Panzerkorps*), F000529.

577 In those days, *Wachtmeister* Amling knocked out a total of 16 tanks in 48 hours. *See* NARA T315, R1100 (*78. Infanterie-Division*), F000434.

578 NARA T314, R933 (*XXXIX. Panzerkorps*), F000429

579 NARA T314, R937 (*XXXIX. Panzerkorps*), F000209-210.

580 NARA T315, R1101 (*78. Infanterie-Division*), F001234.

581 NARA T314, R937 (*XXXIX. Panzerkorps*), F000208. The battery was subordinated to *337. Infanterie-Division* in terms of supply only on 27 December 1942. *See* NARA T314, R937 (*XXXIX. Panzerkorps*), F001006.

582 NARA T315, R1102 (*78. Infanterie-Division*), F000204.

A 1200 hours an assault gun platoon of *Sturmgeschütz-Abteilung 202* (with two StuG. IIIs, possibly from the *2. Batterie*) was ordered into the area of Shornowka, where it was subordinated to the *III. Bataillon/Grenadier-Regiment 313.* Twenty minutes later *Kampfgruppe 'Kaether'* received orders to dispatch one of its subordinated assault gun platoons to the division at the command post of *Kampfgruppe 'Bömers'* where another Soviet tank raid was expected.[583]

In the evening, the divisional reserve consisted of *Kampfgruppe 'Kaether'* (stationed in Lopotok), *Pionier-Bataillon 178* (without one of its companies and constructing positions at Ssidorowo), and the *2.* and *5. Kompanie / Panzergrenadier-Regiment 11* that were waiting in readiness in the area of Brannoje with an assault gun platoon of *Sturmgeschütz-Abteilung 202.*[584]

In the sector of the *78. Infanterie-Division* there were a total of nine assault guns operational from *Sturmgeschütz-Abteilung 202* (two of them were on march into the sector of the *337. Infanterie-Division*).[585]

On that day the assault gun unit reported that they had knocked out seven Soviet tanks. Including these, the assault guns had 61 confirmed AFV scores between 28 November and 5 of December 1942.[586]

6 DECEMBER 1942

At 0215 hours around 300 Soviet soldiers broke into the village of Sherebzowo which was defended by *Schnelle Abteilung 178,* a unit assembled from the reconnaissance and tank destroyer elements of the *78. Infanterie-Division.* The ensuing hand-grenade battle, fought after nightfall amongst buildings that had been demolished by shell-fire, led to indescribable confusion.

It was during this chaos that *Kampfgruppe 'Kohler'* intervened at 0600 hours with a counter-thrust launched by its 13 AFVs (including the StuG. III assault guns of *Sturmgeschütz-Abteilung 202*) and the infantry of the *Lehrkompanie.* The *Kampfgruppe* jumped off from a front line 300-400 m wide. Soldiers of *Schnelle Abteilung 178* joined the attack, which quickly gained ground and drove the Soviets out of the settlement. The German tanks and assault guns advanced an additional 1 km forward. Having noticed a readiness position, they attacked it and apart from knocking out three anti-tank guns, they also inflicted heavy casualties on the enemy. For some unknown reason, the platoon advancing on the left flank of the tank company continued to press on and due to that, lost two combat vehicles. Even the platoon commander's vehicle was knocked out. Only three men belonging to the second platoon of the *Lehrkompanie* accompanying the tanks survived.

583 NARA T315, R1102 (*78. Infanterie-Division*), F000114.

584 NARA T315, R1102 (*78. Infanterie-Division*), F000115.

585 NARA T315, R1101 (*78. Infanterie-Division*), F001235.

586 NARA T314, R933 (*XXXIX. Panzerkorps*), F000761.

Following that, the tanks and assault guns of *Kampfgruppe 'Kohler'* had to be put into action again because the Soviets launched another tank raid. The German AFVs, however, repelled this raid, knocking out six enemy tanks.[587]

At 1140 hours the acting commander of *Sturmgeschütz-Abteilung 202* received orders from the staff of the *78. Infanterie-Division* to dispatch two assault guns to Lopotok in order to cooperate with *Kampfgruppe 'Reissinger'*. The *Kampfgruppe* planned to move its subordinated StuG. IIIs forward to Sherebzowo.[588]

At 1211 hours the *337. Infanterie-Division* reported that the Soviets had broken through its front line with eight tanks between Romanowo and Burgowo. Two minutes later, *Sturmgeschütz-Abteilung 202* received additional orders from the staff of the *78. Infanterie-Division* to order two assault guns arriving from repairs to Shornowka instead of Lopotok. However, at 1330 hours the *337. Infanterie-Division* reported that part of the Soviet tank force that had broken through had been destroyed and the remainder had returned behind their own lines. Therefore the orders dispatching the assault gun platoon toward Shornowka were rescinded.[589] In the end, the two StuG. IIIs were sent to Sherebzowo at 1525 hours with a machine gun company where they joined with *Schnelle Abteilung 178* (subordinated to *Kampfgruppe 'Kaether'*).[590]

Meanwhile, at 1345 hours *Oberleutnant* Melzer received orders to dispatch two additional assault guns to Lopotok. Five minutes later the orders were modified by *Hauptmann* Handrik, acting commander of the assault gun unit, who sent the two StuG. IIIs to Krjukowo for repairs.[591]

According to the report submitted at 1930 hours there were seven combat-ready assault guns from *Sturmgeschütz-Abteilung 202* in the area of the *78. Infanterie-Division.*[592]

On that day the Quartermaster's department of the *XXXIX. Panzerkorps* reported the loss of one assault gun.[593]

7 DECEMBER 1942

Five assault guns of *Sturmgeschütz-Abteilung 202* were fighting attached to *Kampfgruppe 'Kaether'* and four were at *Kampfgruppe 'Reissinger'* in the evening.[594]

---

587 Merker, Ludwig: *Das Buch der 78. Sturm Division.* Tübingen, 1965. 198-199. o.

588 NARA T315, R1102 (*78. Infanterie-Division*), F000213.

589 NARA T315, R1102 (*78. Infanterie-Division*), F000117.

590 NARA T315, R1102 (*78. Infanterie-Division*), F000214.

591 NARA T315, R1102 (*78. Infanterie-Division*), F000213.

592 NARA T315, R1101 (*78. Infanterie-Division*), F001239.

593 NARA T314, R933 (*XXXIX. Panzerkorps*), F000438.

594 NARA T315, R1102 (*78. Infanterie-Division*), F000119.

8 DECEMBER 1942

Sturmgeschütz-Abteilung 202 had 30 winter-link track sets *(Winterketten).*[595]

In the evening, the assault gun unit still had nine combat-ready assault guns in the zone of action of the *78. Infanterie-Division.*[596]

9 DECEMBER 1942

In the evening, *Sturmgeschütz-Abteilung 202* reported 10 combat-ready assault guns in the sector of the *78. Infanterie-Division.*[597]

10 DECEMBER 1942

During the day, five assault guns of *Sturmgeschütz-Abteilung* were still subordinated to *Kampfgruppe 'Kaether'*. In *Kampfgruppe 'Reissinger'* there were only three StuG. IIIs operational.[598]

In the evening, *Sturmgeschütz-Abteilung 202* had only 12 assault guns serviceable in the sector of *78. Infanterie-Division.*[599]

11 DECEMBER 1942

After intensive artillery preparation Soviet forces launched an attack at 0820 hours along the Taliza–Sherebzowo–Podossinowka–Mal. Kropotowo sector, deploying two rifle divisions, one motorized rifle brigade and two or three tank brigades. The battalion of the *52. Infanterie-Division (I./Grenadier-Regiment 205)* defending here under the command of *Hauptmann* Dr. Otto Marxer put up fierce resistance but the Soviet rifle infantry and accompanying AFVs penetrated into Sherebzowo. The German defenders were dispersed or forced back to the artillery battery that was in position nearby.

At 0950 hours commander of *Kampfgruppe 'Kaether'* reported that Sherebzowo – apart from the eastern perimeter of the settlement – had fallen to the enemy and that the situation was grave. According to his statement, five StuG. IIIs had fought in Sherebzowo.[600]

At 1000 hours *Sturmgeschütz-Abteilung 202* received orders to send three assault guns to Ssidorowo to provide support for *Pionier-Bataillon 178.* From these forces *Kampfgruppe 'Kraft'* was raised, and this was subordinated to *Kampfgruppe 'Kaether'* to carry out a counter-thrust towards Sherebzowo. At around 1100 hours another 20 Soviet combat vehicles broke into the settlement.[601]

595 NARA T314, R937 (*XXXIX. Panzerkorps*), F000693.
596 NARA T315, R1101 (*78. Infanterie-Division*), F001241.
597 NARA T315, R1101 (*78. Infanterie-Division*), F001242.
598 NARA T315, R1102 (*78. Infanterie-Division*), F000121.
599 NARA T315, R1101 (*78. Infanterie-Division*), F001244.
600 NARA T315, R1102 (*78. Infanterie-Division*), F000238.
601 NARA T315, R1102 (*78. Infanterie-Division*), F000123.

Meanwhile, *Kampfgruppe 'Kaether'* had been subordinated to *Kampfgruppe 'Reissinger'* with the three assault guns. At 1227 hours, according to incoming reports to the staff of the *78. Infanterie-Division,* Podossinowka was under attack by an additional 20 Soviet tanks and rifle infantry and two of *Sturmgeschütz-Abteilung 202's* assault guns had been disabled. At 1250 hours the 20 Soviet AFVs penetrated into the settlement. At 1308 hours *Kampfgruppe 'Reissinger'* deployed the last reserves of the division, comprising *Schnelle Abteilung 178* and three StuG. III assault guns of *Sturmgeschütz-Abteilung 202,* in a counter-thrust towards Podossinowka.[602]

At 1230 hours the *78. Infanterie-Division* requested the corps' intervention to retrieve the *2. Batterie/ Sturmgeschütz-Abteilung 202* from the *337. Infanterie-Division,* on the plea that the assault guns might become 'battle-weary' there. However it was impossible to comply with the request because the left flank of the latter division was fighting and the assault guns were in action there. Moreover, the commander of the *337. Infanterie-Division, Generalmajor* Otto Schünemann, had requested yet another assault gun to be sent to Ssidorow sometime after 1000 hours.[603]

At 1250 hours, the *78. Infanterie-Division* reported to the corps that its own counter-attack had been launched east of Lopotok towards Sherebzowo. The pioneers of the division, *Pionier-Bataillon 178* reinforced with four guns of *Sturmgeschütz-Abteilung 202,* were given the task of executing a counter-thrust to retake Sherebzowo. The German attack commenced at 1200 hours with artillery support. The German pioneers reached the perimeter of the village without trouble but there they met very fierce Soviet resistance and had to retake or destroy each and every shelter and firing position one by one. German losses were constantly rising and *Major* Zeno Maria Kraft, commander of the pioneer battalion, was killed in action. The *I. Bataillon/ Grenadier-Regiment 205* also joined in the counter-thrust but were able to retake only the southern half of the settlement. *Hauptmann* Marxer was also killed in the course of the fighting. In the end, the settlement was occupied next day during another violent battle following the arrival of the reinforcement *Kampfgruppe* commanded by *Hauptmann* Kohler.[604]

The Soviet troops retreated from Sherebzowo in a north-westerly direction. However, two Soviet battalions launched an attack on Podossinowka with tank support. Five of their combat vehicles managed to break through the German defences, a serious situation for them because the German assault guns and fighting vehicles sent against the Soviet attack were running out of ammunition for their 7.5 cm guns.[605]

At 1320 hours, the acting commander of *Sturmgeschütz-Abteilung 202* reported to the staff of the *78. Infanterie-Division* that he had dispatched two repaired StuG. IIIs to Lopotok. The report was also forwarded to *Oberstleutnant* Reissinger.[606]

---

602 NARA T315, R1102 (*78. Infanterie-Division*), F000125.

603 NARA T315, R1102 (*78. Infanterie-Division*), F000239.

604 Merker, Ludwig: *Das Buch der 78. Sturm Division.* Tübingen, 1965. pp. 199-200.

605 NARA T314, R933 (*XXXIX. Panzerkorps*), F000703.

606 NARA T315, R1102 (*78. Infanterie-Division*), F000242.

At 1445 hours *Kampfgruppe 'Reissinger'* reported that another two of their assault guns had become disabled in Podossinowka.[607]

At around 1500 hours, the *78. Infanterie-Division* reported that the eastern and southern parts of Sherebzowo were in German hands and that although Podossinowka was encircled by Soviet armour, the German infantry held fast. By that time a total of 127 AFVs had been knocked out in the sector of the division,[608] most of them T–34 tanks. German reconnaissance units identified the Soviet 22 and 24 Tank Brigades among the attacking forces.[609]

In the course of the evaluation of captured documents and the interrogation of Soviet POWs, it became clear that the Soviets had deployed a total of three full-strength tank brigades, two rifle divisions and a motorized rifle brigade between Sherebzowo and Podossinowka in an area less than 4 km wide. By the end of the day a total of 137 Soviet tanks had been knocked out in the sector of the *78. Infanterie-Division,* including 110 tank kills scored in the zone of action of *Kampfgruppe 'Reissinger'.* The eight assault guns of *Sturmgeschütz-Abteilung 202* deployed there had between them 67 confirmed kills to their credit.[610]

In the sector of the division, two soldiers from *Sturmgeschütz-Abteilung 202* fought with distinction. A platoon leader of the *3. Batterie, Wachtmeister* Amling, knocked out 24 Soviet tanks and *Oberwachtmeister* Richard Schramm, assigned to a *Kampfgruppe* of the *5. Panzer-Division,*[611] knocked out 12 while in command of the assault gun named 'Alligator' (from the second platoon of *1. Batterie*[612]). Including these 12, Schramm had knocked out a total of 37 Soviet tanks in the course of 17 days.[613]

Amling's accomplishments in the defence of Podossinowka were recorded by war-correspondent Ernst Rinne in his article entitled 'The Tank killer'. The following quotation is taken from this source:

[...] The impacts are coming closer and closer, the black patches torn into the ground are becoming denser. The snow will be soon covered by black dust.

An hour is ticking away. Then another. The gun barrels are silent. Wachtmeister Amling, with a bandage wrapped around his hand, is peering at the dim twilight of

607 NARA T315, R1102 (*78. Infanterie-Division*), F000126.

608 NARA T312, R307 (*Armeeoberkommando 9*), F7873564.

609 NARA T314, R933 (*XXXIX. Panzerkorps*), F000704. The Soviet 22 Tank Brigade belonged to the 6 Tank Corps, and the 24 Tank Brigade to the 5 Tank Corps. The latter corps had to write off 17 KV-1, 20 T-34 and 11 T-70 tanks as total losses in the battle around Podossinowka on 11 December 1942. *See* http://www.tankfront.ru/ussr/tk/tk05.html (2 June 2015)

610 NARA T315, R1102 (*78. Infanterie-Division*), F000127.

611 *See* Scherzer, Veit - Farwick, Werner: *Die Ritterkreuzträger der Sturmartillerie 1939-45.* Band 2: Kranz-Z. Bayreuth, 2012. p. 215.

612 In our opinion *Sturmgeschütz-Abteilung 202* used intriguing tactical identification signs instead of the widely spread system using three numbers (number of the battery, the platoon and that of the vehicle). The assault guns were named after animals or imaginary creatures, not in a random way, but following a consistent system. We think, that the combat vehicles were named after aquatic animals in the *1. Batterie,* after aerial animals in the *2. Batterie,* and after terrestrial animals (mainly felines, especially Pantherinae) in the *3. Batterie* battery. It is highly possible, that the name was also used as a radio call sign.

613 NARA T312, R307 (*Armeeoberkommando 9*), F7873564.

the retreating night. Then, he catches sight of the dark, shapeless mass of the infantry, about one kilometre away, moving forward... 900 metres... 800 metres...it is only 500 now. The neighbouring assault gun opens fire then, its shrapnel shells reaping a bloody harvest. The grenadiers also hit the target. The attack halts.

The East-Prussian has not yet given an order to fire. He knows the reason why. He is saving ammunition, because... There they come...20-30 Soviet tanks. They are turning right, and riding toward P[odossinowka] *with such a dash that the assault gun just manages to hit the sides of those lagging behind. After several rounds, two giants come to a grinding halt in flames.*

Devastating fighting flares up in P[odossinowka]. *The plain echoes with the firing of the tanks, the distinct barking of the anti-tank guns, the bursting crack of the explosive mines. Then silence again. Whether the combat is... 'Tanks from behind!' The howl comes the from the grenadiers. The assault gun turns around, looking for a shelter and a sure target amongst the pine-grown terrain, aiming its gun barrel at the pack.*

Two against twenty. Daringly, Wachtmeister Amling is taking up the fight. Quick fire! Two T–34s are already burning in a sheet of flame. The others are tossing and turning wildly on the terrain, like a frightened flock that lost its bellwether. They don't fire a single shot. Then at once, the nearest tank is there, standing at 10 metres distance in front of the neighbouring assault gun. It gives full throttle again, goddam, and wants to run down the assault gun! Go ahead! Then it is turning away, the others follow. Shots, one after the other into the fleeing horde. Five are bagged, the rest disappear all of a sudden.

Stillness for a while. The assault guns take up their previous positions, just in time to receive the next wave. Having lost six armoured fighting vehicles they roll away towards P[odossinowka].

The third wave comes off as badly. By the time they could deploy, the East-Prussian knocks out five of the giants. They are standing one hundred metres away facing the assault gun like burning and smoking torches. This battle lasted only for five minutes.

A glance at the watch: half of the day has passed. Another glance at the ammunition: almost nothing left. Immediate supply is requested by radio, but the strongpoint has been encircled by [Soviet] tanks and a heavy defensive battle continues. The other assault gun decides to go back and load ammunition enough for both of them. Wachtmeister Amling is waiting. He is waiting for them in vain. The comrades will never return...

The Soviets are attacking again. Four T–34s are closing from left at full speed. The grenadiers are becoming anxious. Let them come! 300 metres, 200... Fire! One of them turns away, three tanks left. At the third shot the first one rears and comes to a stop burning. The second one is dashing away. A shot at the hatch of the turret and it starts smoking. The members of its crew are crawling out, the grenadiers deal with them. The third one is rattling back behind the hill in a big loop, venturing out in a little while, slowing down not far from the assault gun, which is tearing up its side and smashing it to pieces.

Amling has two shells left. He has no choice. He starts back, swerving past six heavy tanks, slipping away from them by the skin of his teeth. He reaches the [supply] strongpoint, draws ammunition…it's urgent. Together with another assault gun he slips out to defend P[odossinowka], still held by the infantry. He fights down two smaller tanks crossing his path. Go on!

Right of P[odossinowka] *he notices six or eight T–34s preparing to attack. Assault and fire! And another shot. The first is blazing. Bang! The assault gun is shaking. A hit! The forward steel plate is flying off right into the face of Amling, who collapses soaking wet with blood. However, the skull of the East-Prussian resisted the blow and the shock. The Wachtmeister pulls himself together, throws the plate down from the assault gun, and shouts: 'Reverse!' He wipes off the blood then lets the grenadiers bandage his wound behind a tree and bellows to the assault gun: 'Everything's all right!' By that time two heavy monsters got very close. He halts the first twenty metres from the barrel, then sends another round into its hide until, finally, it puffs out black clouds of smoke, which envelope it. He is dashing off in pursuit of the other one…it's trying to escape but it is stopped by our own tanks and set on fire by their combined fire.*

This is how the day ends. A black day for the Soviets. A bright and proud day to remember for Wachtmeister Amling.[614]

Unteroffizier Bruno Guskoswski, the gunner of his assault gun played a decisive part in Amling's success.

At 2250 hours the chief of staff of the *9. Armee, Generalmajor* Hans Krebs reported the result of the day's defensive battles to the *Führerhauptquartier* and also requested the award of the Knight's Cross of the Iron Cross to the following: the commander of the *78. Infanterie-Division, Generalleutnant* Paul Völckers; to *Hauptmann* Josef Fitz of the *19. Panzer-Division* and to *Wachtmeister* Amling from *Sturmgeschütz-Abteilung 202.* In less than 40 minutes he received a reply – Adolf Hitler had awarded the prestigious decoration to all three of them and they were informed of the decision later that night.[615]

12 DECEMBER 1942

At 0955 hours the German troops defending Krjukowo were brought into combat readiness. The command post of the *78. Infanterie-Division* and *Sturmgeschütz-Abteilung 202,* and the repair-and-maintenance section of the assault gun unit were also located there. To increase firepower, the StuG. IIIs undergoing repairs were towed into firing positions to cover an assigned field of fire in a northerly direction.[616]

In the sector of the *78. Infanterie-Division*, the Soviet troops made rapid progress towards Sherebzowo and Podossinowka with the support of as many as 70 tanks and managed to occupy certain parts of the settlements. Podossinowka was retaken by the Germans in the early afternoon but at Sherebzowo the Soviets nestled themselves

614 NARA T315, R1100 (*78. Infanterie-Division*), F000434-435.

615 NARA T312, R310 (*Armeeoberkommando 9*), F7877941.

616 NARA T315, R1102 (*78. Infanterie-Division*), F000130.

in the north-western part of the settlement. The Soviet AFVs that had broken through the German defences in the course of the day were hunted down by the German assault guns and the tanks of an armoured *Kampfgruppe* of the *2. Panzer-Division.*[617] The *II. Bataillon/ Panzer-Regiment 3,* together with two tank-riding pioneer companies of *Panzer-Pionier-Bataillon 38,* launched an attack to retake Podossinowka around noon. Most of the settlement was cleared by the Germans in the afternoon. During the fighting German tanks knocked out 40 Soviet AFVs (34 T–34s, three KV-1 and three T–60s).[618]

Meanwhile *Sturmgeschütz-Abteilung 202,* under the command of *Hauptmann* Handrik, had knocked out its 150 Soviet tank since the beginning of the fighting south-west of Kalinin on 27 November 1942.[619] At 1530 hours the assault artillery unit reported knocking out 21 Soviet AFVs in the day's battles.[620] In the sector of the *78. Infanterie-Division* German assault guns and tanks knocked out a total of 61 combat vehicles.[621]

The German losses were also severe. In a counter-thrust towards Podossinowka, *Kampfgruppe 'Buck',* for example, lost seven seriously and 13 slightly damaged. Four of its AFVs were also destroyed.[622]

In the day's fighting *Sturmgeschütz-Abteilung 202* had to write off one StuG. III Another five of its assault guns were seriously damaged while three received more minor damage. In the evening the unit had eight combat-ready StuG. IIIs.[623]

At 2200 hours the *XXXIX. Panzerkorps* ordered the staff of the *78. Infanterie-Division* by telegram to establish a mobile anti-tank reserve between Sherebzowo and Podossinowka from the assault guns of *Sturmgeschütz-Abteilung 202* and the tanks of the *2.* and *9. Panzer-Divisions.* They were given the task of preventing the Soviet tanks from achieving any further penetrations or breakthroughs.[624]

As recognition for their military achievement in the day's battles south-west of Kalinin, the *78. Infanterie-Division* and its supporting *Sturmgeschütz-Abteilung 202* (without its pennant number) were mentioned in the *Wehrmacht's* daily combat report.

13 DECEMBER 1942

At 0815 hours the staff of *Grenadier-Regiment 215* reported that Soviet rifle infantry and 12 tanks had launched an attack on Podossinowka, but had been repelled. At

617 NARA T314, R933 (*XXXIX. Panzerkorps*), F000654.

618 NARA T315, R93 (*2. Panzer-Division*), F000622.

619 NARA T314, R937 (*XXXIX. Panzerkorps*), F000064.

620 NARA T315, R1102 (*78. Infanterie-Division*), F000253.

621 The Soviet 5 Tank Corps had to write off four KV–1, 15 T–34 and four T–70 tanks as total losses during the fighting at Sherebzowo. *See* http://www.tankfront.ru/ussr/tk/tk05.html (2 June 2015) The Corps lost a total of 20 KV–1, 36 T–34, 22 T–70 and 52 T–60 tanks on 11 an 12 December 1942.

622 NARA T315, R1102 (*78. Infanterie-Division*), F000134, and T315, R93 (*2. Panzer-Division*), F000622.

623 NARA T315, R1101 (*78. Infanterie-Division*), F001245.

624 NARA T315, R1102 (*78. Infanterie-Division*), F000133.

that time two assault guns of *Sturmgeschütz-Abteilung 202* fought at Podossinowka and an additional two north-west of the settlement. In Sherebzowo another three StuG. IIIs were in action.[625] At 1905 hours the assault artillery unit reported the knock out of a total of 10 Soviet tanks[626] during the day's fighting. By then they had only five assault guns operational.[627]

In its daily report, *Heeresgruppe Mitte* recorded that a total of 1,568 Soviet AFVs had been destroyed in the sector of the *9. Armee* between 25 November and 13 December 1942. On the other hand, the total losses suffered by the Germans in that period were 66 tanks (including 34 long-barrelled ones) and 10 StuG. III assault guns.[628]

On the same day *Sturmgeschütz-Abteilung 202* lost one seriously and two slightly damaged assault guns. In the evening they had five StuG. IIIs still operational.[629]

The *78. Infanterie-Division* received orders to set up a mixed *Kampfgruppe* from assault guns, tanks and infantry to mop up Soviet forces that had infiltrated the main combat line up to the railroad.[630]

During the day, the *2. Batterie / Sturmgeschütz-Abteilung 667,* temporarily relieved from assignment with *102. Infanterie-Division* and attached to *9. Panzer-Division,* took part in repelling the Soviet attacks launched on Mal. Kropotowo and Podossinowka and in the course of the fighting knocked out 13 tanks (including six KV-1 and five T–34s).[631]

14 DECEMBER 1942

It was officially confirmed at 1100 hours that *Wachtmeister* Amling[632] had been awarded the Knight's Cross of the Iron Cross.[633]

On that day, *Sturmgeschütz-Abteilung 202* lost only one assault gun which required only short-term repair. In the evening it had four combat-ready StuG. IIIs in the sector of the *78. Infanterie-Division.*[634]

---

625 NARA T315, R1102 (*78. Infanterie-Division*), F000257.

626 The Soviet 5 Tank Corps had to write off two KV–1, seven T–34, five T–70 and 12 T–60 tanks as total losses in the area of the settlement. *See* http://www.tankfront.ru/ussr/tk/tk05.html (2 June 2015).

627 NARA T315, R1102 (*78. Infanterie-Division*), F000260.

628 NARA T313, R265 (*Panzerarmeeoberkommando 3*), F8536258-259.

629 NARA T315, R1101 (*78. Infanterie-Division*), F001246.

630 NARA T314, R933 (*XXXIX. Panzerkorps*), F000970.

631 NARA T315, R1236 (*102. Infanterie-Division*), F000375.

632 Amling was born in January 1916 in the east Prussian Preussisch Holland. He joined *Artillerie-Regiment 24* on 1 October 1937 as a volunteer. At the beginning of WWII he fought in the *3. Batterie/Artillerie-Regiment 168* in Poland and during the Western Campaign. He was transferred on 27 April 1941 to the assault artillery, and was re-trained at *Sturmgeschütz-Ersatz-Abteilung 200* stationed at Schweinfurt. In November 1941, he was assigned to the *3. Batterie/Sturmgeschütz-Abteilung 202.* In September 1943 he was transferred to *Sturmgeschütz-Ersatz-Abteilung 300* located in Neisse, where he was assigned with training tasks. He was withdrawn from front line duty. He died in March 1994 in Mainz. *See* Scherzer, Veit – Farwick, Werner: *Die Ritterkreuzträger der Sturmartillerie 1939-45.* Band 1: A-Krafft. Jena, 2010. 32-34. o.

633 NARA T315, R1102 (*78. Infanterie-Division*), F000263.

634 NARA T315, R1101 (*78. Infanterie-Division*), F001249.

The corps reported that, due to the increase in the number of the assault guns deployed, the expenditure of ammunition for the 7.5 cm KwK 34 tank gun was exceptionally high and mainly armour-piercing shells were requested from the depots of the *9. Armee.*[635]

15 DECEMBER 1942

The assault artillery unit knocked out three Soviet AFVs and lost only one assault gun which needed short-term repairs.[636] The StuG. IIIs used up 410 shells during the fighting. In the evening the total amount of ammunition available for the unit was 2,708 rounds. Of the 21 assault guns nine were operational, two required short-term repairs, nine were awaiting longer term repairs and one StuG. III had to be sent back to Germany for factory repair so that it could be made combat-ready again.[637]

The *XXXIX. Panzerkorps* reported that engineering personnel of *Sturmgeschütz-Abteilung 202* had, by working 18 hours daily, repaired 56 assault guns that had been damaged in combat during the period between 28 November and 15 December 1942. Of these, 39 StuG. IIIs (some of them heavily damaged) were made combat-ready in the field.[638]

One platoon from *Panzer-Berge-Kompanie 2* towed a total of four StuG. IIIs to repair shops between 2 and 31 December 1942.[639] The maintenance service of the corps repaired an additional 22 assault guns between 4 and 31 December 1942.[640]

On that day the *78. Infanterie-Division* issued a divisional order about its ensuing withdrawal. Its zone of action would been taken over by elements of the *2. Panzer-Division* and the *216. Infanterie-Division.* According to the plan, they were to be relieved on 17 December. However, there were to be no changes to the assignment of *Sturmgeschütz-Abteilung 202.*[641]

16 DECEMBER 1942

At 1050 hours, *Artillerie-Regiment 178* reported that the assault guns of *Sturmgeschütz-Abteilung 202* had possibly knocked out eight Soviet AFVs in the area of Podossinowka and Sherebzowo, in the zone of action of *Grenadier-Regiment 348*[642] (which was subordinated to *Kampfgruppe* '*Reissinger*'.[643]

In the evening, in the sector of *78. Infanterie-Division*, only five assault guns were operational because during the day's fighting two had been damaged and were undergoing short-term repairs.[644]

---

635 NARA T314, R937 (*XXXIX. Panzerkorps*), F000634.

636 NARA T315, R1101 (*78. Infanterie-Division*), F001251.

637 NARA T314, R933 (*XXXIX. Panzerkorps*), F000878.

638 NARA T314, R937 (*XXXIX. Panzerkorps*), F000013.

639 NARA T314, R937 (*XXXIX. Panzerkorps*), F000691.

640 NARA T314, R937 (*XXXIX. Panzerkorps*), F000692.

641 NARA T315, R93 (*2. Panzer-Division*), F000628.

642 The regiment was in the *216. Infanterie-Division's* order of battle, but was subordinated to the *78. Infanterie-Division.*

643 NARA T315, R1102 (*78. Infanterie-Division*), F000272.

644 NARA T315, R1101 (*78. Infanterie-Division*), F001252.

17 DECEMBER 1942

The assault gun artillery unit was assigned to the *2. Panzer-Division.*[645] Most of *Sturmgeschütz-Abteilung 202* was allocated to the *2. Panzer-Division* but four assault guns, and its *2. Batterie* (with another four AFVs) were subordinated to the *337. Infanterie-Division.*[646] In the sector of the *2. Panzer-Division*, the elements of the assault artillery unit stationed in the area of Lopotok were included in the division's communications network and, being subordinated to it, they received orders to cooperate with *Kampfgruppe 'Wuth'*[647].[648]

According to the summary report, from 26 November to 16 December 1942, the sector of the *78. Infanterie-Division* had been attacked by 10 tank brigades[649], 10 rifle divisions, four rifle brigades and two cavalry divisions. In the course of the fighting 440 Soviet combat vehicles were disabled with 431 of them destroyed.[650] The distribution of the kills was as follows:

- 176 AFVs by the assault guns of *Sturmgeschütz-Abteilung 202;*
- 99 AFVs by tanks;
- 51 AFVs by heavy anti-tank guns;
- 47 AFVs by the artillery;
- 27 AFVs by anti-aircraft -guns;
- 20 AFVs by self-propelled anti-tank guns;
- 11 AFVs by tank destroyer squads[651];
- 3-3 AFVs by light- and medium anti-tank guns;
- 2 AFVs by means of capture;
- 1 AFV by mines.[652]

10.5% of the destroyed combat vehicles were KV-1, 66% were T–34s, 23.5% were T–26s and T–60s.[653]

The experience report drafted by the *78. Infanterie-Division* summed up the fighting against the Soviet tanks as follows:

---

645 NARA T314, R937 (*XXXIX. Panzerkorps*), F000493.

646 NARA T314, R933 (*XXXIX. Panzerkorps*), F001192.

647 The battle group made up of *Grenadier-Regiment 348, Schnelle Abteilung 216*, elements of *Panzerjäger-Abteilung 137* and an artillery battalion. Those were supported by *Sturmgeschütz-Abteilung 202, II. Bataillon* of *Panzer-Regiment 3, and an additional* artillery battalion.

648 NARA T315, R93 (*2. Panzer-Division*), F000630.

649 These were the follows: the 24, 41 and 70 Tank Brigades of the 5. Tank Corps, the shattered remnants of the 22 and 200 Tank Brigade of the 6 Tank Corps, as well as the independent 9 Guard-, 11, 18, 20 and 25 Tank Brigade.

650 NARA T315, R1102 (*78. Infanterie-Division*), F000139.

651 Germans noticed during these battles, that the Soviets occasionally covered their tanks with fat, oil or wooden boards to hamper the attachment of the destructive German 3 kg HE anti-tank mines.

652 NARA T315, R1102 (*78. Infanterie-Division*), F000274.

653 NARA T315, R1102 (*78. Infanterie-Division*), F000307.

At the beginning of the attack the deployment of the [Soviet] *tanks was sporadic considering the number of them available. Significant tank formations were deployed only after successful breakthroughs. The tank units attacking the sector of the division were equipped exclusively by Russian made AFVs. The enemy tanks working independently or accompanying attacks were relatively unsuccessful and their deployment unsystematic due to insufficient training of the crews. When the first of these had been knocked out the others often began retreating. The fighting spirit of the tank crews is better than that of the infantry. The quality of the armour of the tanks is noticeably less than before. Despite previous experience, our light anti-tank guns are surprisingly effective against the T–34s and our assault guns (with 7,5 cm short-barrelled guns) are effective against the both T–34s and KV-1s even in case of disadvantageous hit ratios.*

[…]

Steady losses of heavy anti-tank guns deployed in the thick of the battle were inflicted by the enemy's artillery but placing our self-propelled anti-tank or assault guns (at least in platoon-strength) in concealed positions behind the threatened sector proved effective.

[…]

The assault guns with the 7.5 cm short-barrelled gun (long- barrelled ones were not available) proved to be the best anti-tank weapon but it is also an excellent weapon for providing support to counter-thrusts and counter-attacks. It is particularly advantageous that they are quickly re-deployable. Its frequent requisition for fuel and ammunition during combat is disadvantageous.' [654]

The staff of the German *9. Armee* added the following:

Ammunition:

The 7.5 cm hollow-charge shell must be used to fight against armoured fighting vehicles. It is sufficiently effective, although less so than the Panzergranate 39.

Assault guns:

The 'long' and 'short' assault guns are the best anti-tank weapons. Its low [aiming] elevation makes them easy to emplace in ambush positions.

The 'long' assault gun has an effective armour-piercing range of 1200 m and so has the potential to fight down enemy tanks beyond the range of the light and medium anti-tank weapons!

Regarding the priority of hollow-charge shells, the effectiveness of the 'short' assault gun is approximately the same as that of the 'long' assault gun. The effect on soft-shelled targets is the same with both versions.

Extremely important: even a single assault gun can effectively contain an enemy tank brigade! [655]

---

654 NARA T315, R1102 (*78. Infanterie-Division*), F000305, F000309, F000311.

655 NARA T312, R308 (*Armeeoberkommando 9*), F7875052.

19 DECEMBER 1942

The corps put *Sturmgeschütz-Abteilungen 202* and *667* under the direct command of *Arko 35* (the artillery command of the *XXXIX. Panzerkorps*). The eight combat-ready assault guns of *Sturmgeschütz-Abteilung 202* were divided equally between the sector of the *337. Infanterie-Division* and that of the *2. Panzer-Division.*[656]

21 DECEMBER 1942

The *216. Infanterie-Division* made preparations to relieve the *2. Panzer-Division* in its zone of action. In relation to that, the assault guns of *Sturmgeschütz-Abteilung 202* fighting in the sector of the armoured division, were ordered – together with the *II. Bataillon/ Panzer-Regiment 3* – to support *Grenadier-Regiment 348* which was subordinated to the infantry division.[657]

Due to the faltering fuel supply, the deployment of tanks and assault guns was limited because they had already used up most of their reserves.[658]

22 DECEMBER 1942

Part of the *1.* and *3. Batterie* of the assault artillery unit were operating in the sector of the *2. Panzer-Division* with four combat-ready assault guns. The *2. Batterie* fought under the command of the *337. Infanterie-Division* with an additional four operational StuG. IIIs.[659]

23 DECEMBER 1942

Another soldier from *Sturmgeschütz-Abteilung 202, Oberwachtmeister* Schramm,[660] was awarded the Knight's Cross of the Iron Cross.[661]

The staff of *Sturmgeschütz-Abteilung 202,* together with the five assault guns from the two batteries employed in the sector of the *2. Panzer-Division,* were put under the command of the *216. Infanterie-Division* and ordered to cooperate with the forces of *Grenadier-Regiment 348* to strengthen the defence of the sector between

---

656 NARA T314, R934 (*XXXIX. Panzerkorps*), F000794.

657 NARA T314, R933 (*XXXIX. Panzerkorps*), F001068.

658 NARA T315, R93 (*2. Panzer-Division*), F000663.

659 NARA T314, R933 (*XXXIX. Panzerkorps*), F001051.

660 Schramm was born in July 1913 in Langburkersdorf. He joined *4. Artillerie-Regiment* in March 1933. In October 1939 he was transferred to *schwere Artillerie-Abteilung (mot.) 711.* He was retrained as assault artilleryman from 12 May 1941 in Jüterbog. On 19 September he was assigned to the *1. Batterie/ Sturmgeschütz-Abteilung 202.* He was wounded in March 1943. Due to that, as it happened to most assault artillerymen convalescing for more than six weeks or in the hinterland, he was transferred to *Sturmgeschütz-Ersatz-Abteilung 300,* where, having recovered, he probably served as a trainer. In 1944, following an officer's training course, he was appointed lieutenant. In May 1944, he was reassigned to the *1. Batterie/ Sturmgeschütz-Brigade 202,* where he served as platoon leader or acting battery commander. In August 1944 he got out of his assault gun for reasons unknown, and was seriously wounded. He was transported to the rear, but his fate has not been cleared up to this day. It is highly possible, that he died of his wounds on 17 August 1944 north of Preekuln, in Latvia. *See* Scherzer, Veit - Farwick, Werner: *Die Ritterkreuzträger der Sturmartillerie 1939-45.* Band 2: Kranz-Z. Bayreuth, 2012. 214-216. o.

661 NARA T312, R307 (*Armeeoberkommando 9*), F7874349.

Sherebzowo and Podossinowka, as instructed by the order of the *XXXIX. Panzerkorps* by telegram[662] which was received at 1845 hours.[663]

24 DECEMBER 1942

Most of *Sturmgeschütz-Abteilung 202* (except for one battery) and *Panzerjäger-Abteilung 137* were subordinated to the *216. Infanterie-Division.*[664] Most of the assault artillery units (with the *2. Batterie* providing support to *Grenadier-Regiment 348*) had a total of four combat-ready assault guns, as did *3. Batterie* which was operating in the sector of the *337. Infanterie-Division.*[665]

On that day, with all due solemnity, decorations were awarded to those who had distinguished themselves in the fighting around Rschew and Ssytschewka. *Oberwachtmeister* Schramm and *Wachtmeister* Amling were decorated with the Knight's Cross of the Iron Cross. Christmas packages were also handed out with every man receiving 15 cigarettes, a bar of chocolate, some sweets and biscuits.[666]

25 DECEMBER 1942

By telegram to the corps, the *2. Panzer-Division* made a request for the commander of *Sturmgeschütz-Abteilung 202* to conduct reconnaissance next day in the area of the front line of the division's *Kampfgruppe 'Von Goerne'.*[667]

The battalion commander visited the new personnel of *1. Batterie.* The former personnel of the battery were bid farewell as they left for Germany.[668]

26 AND 27 DECEMBER 1942

The Soviet Air Force continuously attacked Wjasma. A total of 3,170 bombs were dropped. The railway-station and its vicinity were destroyed. Bombs also struck near to the quarters of the *1. Batterie / Sturmgeschütz-Abteilung 202* but they suffered no losses during the air raids.[669]

662 NARA T315, R93 (*2. Panzer-Division*), F000221.

663 NARA T314, R933 (*XXXIX. Panzerkorps*), F001017.

664 NARA T314, R937 (*XXXIX. Panzerkorps*), F000395.

665 NARA T314, R934 (*XXXIX. Panzerkorps*), F000139.

666 *Tagebuchaufzeichnungen vom 2. 12. 1942 bis 1. 2. 1944 von Kamerad Wachtmeister Georg Hiller.* In: *Der Sturmartillerist.* Heft 60. p. 1326.

667 NARA T315, R93 (*2. Panzer-Division*), F000223.

668 *Tagebuchaufzeichnungen vom 2. 12. 1942 bis 1. 2. 1944 von Kamerad Wachtmeister Georg Hiller.* In: *Der Sturmartillerist.* Heft 60. p. 1326. According to measure of 15 January 1943, the former *1. Batterie* would form the core personnel of *Sturmgeschütz-Abteilung 911* to be raised soon.

669 *Tagebuchaufzeichnungen vom 2. 12. 1942 bis 1. 2. 1944 von Kamerad Wachtmeister Georg Hiller.* In: *Der Sturmartillerist.* Heft 60. p. 1326.

30 DECEMBER 1942

The *9. Armee* made a request to *Heeresgruppe Mitte* to permit the new *1. Batterie*[670] of *Sturmgeschütz-Abteilung 202*, having arrived without AFVs, to take over the 13 still combat-ready assault guns from *Sturmgeschütz-Abteilung 189* (subordinated to the *78. Infanterie-Division*) as compensation for their lack of assault guns. According this plan, *Sturmgeschütz-Abteilung 189* would then be equipped with new assault guns.[671]

On the same day the new *1. Batterie* also received winter clothing, a sure sign of impending action.[672]

1943

Operational Background:

After the failure of the Soviet operation 'Mars', Sturmgeschütz-Abteilung 202 fought static battles south of Rschew until the end of January 1943.

1 JANUARY 1943

Sturmgeschütz-Abteilung 202 had a total of 10 assault guns with two of them undergoing repairs. Most of the unit was operating with four StuG. IIIs subordinated to the *337. Infanterie-Division,* just like the *2. Batterie* in the sector of the *216. Infanterie-Division.*[673]

At 1000 hours the new *1. Batterie* set off towards Lobodok south of Rschew where the personnel were housed in bunkers.[674]

3 JANUARY 1943

The *XXXIX. Panzerkorps* summarized the number of Soviet combat vehicles knocked out in the sector of the corps between 25 November and 17 December 1942 and submitted a report regarding this to the staff of the *9. Armee.* Following verification, the achievements of the most effective units were as follows:

---

670 The new *1. Batterie/ Sturmgeschütz-Abteilung 202* set off from Germany on 2 December 1942. On 17 December during their transport by railway to Wjasma, their train was attacked by enemy aircraft, but they suffered no losses. The battery was absorbed into the unit on 20 December. See *Tagebuchaufzeichnungen vom 2. 12. 1942 bis 1. 2. 1944 von Kamerad Wachtmeister Georg Hiller.* In: *Der Sturmartillerist.* Heft 60. pp. 1325-1326.

671 NARA T312, R307 (*Armeeoberkommando 9*), F7873707.

672 *Tagebuchaufzeichnungen vom 2. 12. 1942 bis 1. 2. 1944 von Kamerad Wachtmeister Georg Hiller.* In: *Der Sturmartillerist.* Heft 60. p. 1326.

673 NARA T314, R937 (*XXXIX. Panzerkorps*), F001418-1419.

674 *Tagebuchaufzeichnungen vom 2. 12. 1942 bis 1. 2. 1944 von Kamerad Wachtmeister Georg Hiller.* In: *Der Sturmartillerist.* Heft 60. p. 1326.

- *Sturmgeschütz-Abteilung 202* knocked out 195 AFVs,
- *Sturmgeschütz-Abteilung 667* (without *1. Batterie*) knocked out 109 AFVs,
- *III. Bataillon of Panzer-Regiment 33* knocked out 67 AFVs,
- *leichte Flak-Abteilung 76* knocked out 67 AFVs,
- *II. Bataillon of Panzer-Regiment 3* knocked out 48 AFVs.[675]

Of the total of the knock-outs scored by *Sturmgeschütz-Abteilung 202*,180 combat vehicles were fought down (10 KV-1s, 94 T–34s, 15 T–26s, as well as 61 T–60s and T–70s) by StuG. III assault guns in the sector of the *78. Infanterie-Division.* The assault artillery unit participated in those battles with only two of its batteries because its *1. Batterie* personnel had only arrived from Germany (without assault guns) at the end of December.[676]

According to their own figures, Soviet troops suffered a total loss of 1,366 AFVs during operation 'Mars' (also known as the Second Rschew–Ssytschewka offensive) with a tragic ending.[677] On this basis, during the course of this operation, more than 14% of the Soviet tank losses were inflicted by *Sturmgeschütz-Abteilung 202's* exclusively short-barrelled StuG. III assault guns.

4 JANUARY 1943

The *2. Batterie/ Sturmgeschütz-Abteilung 202* was detached from the *2. Panzer-Division.*[678] On that day, the unit had a total of 11 assault guns with two of them undergoing repairs. Of the combat-ready StuG. IIIs, four were operating while subordinated to the *216. Infanterie-Division,* one was assigned a special mission under the control of the *2. Panzer-Division,* and an additional four were attached to the *337. Infanterie-Division.*[679]

The *216. Infanterie-Division* prepared to launch an attack of limited aims to retake Sherebzowo and the hills north-east of the settlement. In relation to that, it emerged that the winter camouflage of the assault guns, AFVs and *Panzerjägers* (self-propelled anti-tank guns) subordinated to the division should be renewed.[680]

5 JANUARY 1943

The assault artillery unit had nine StuG. IIIs. Two of them were undergoing repairs.[681]

---

675 NARA T314, R938 (*XXXIX. Panzerkorps*), F000344.

676 NARA T314, R938 (*XXXIX. Panzerkorps*), F000338. The report was sent to the *216. Infanterie-Division* taking over the sector of the *78. Infanterie-Division* on 13 January 1943, by *Hauptmann* Martin Buhr, the new acting commander of *Sturmgeschütz-Abteilung 202.* The type designation 'T–27' in the original source is obviously a typing error. T–26 tanks were mentioned in a similar document earlier.

677 Gerasimova, Svetlana: *The Rzhev Slaughterhouse. The Red Army's Forgotten 15-Month Campaign against the Army Group Centre, 1942-1943.* Solihull, 2013. p. 121.

678 NARA T314, R937 (*XXXIX. Panzerkorps*), F001357.

679 NARA T314, R937 (*XXXIX. Panzerkorps*), F001364-1365.

680 NARA T314, R937 (*XXXIX. Panzerkorps*), F001355.

681 NARA T314, R937 (*XXXIX. Panzerkorps*), F001350-1351.

6 JANUARY 1943

Most of *Sturmgeschütz-Abteilung 202* was subordinated to *216. Infanterie-Division* in terms of supply. However *2. Batterie* was to be supplied by the supply units of the *337. Infanterie-Division.*[682]

On that day the corps informed the staff of the *102. Infanterie-Division* that *3. Batterie/ Sturmgeschütz-Abteilung 202* would be put under the command of the division as soon as the unit took over the assault guns of *Sturmgeschütz-Abteilung 189.*[683]

7 JANUARY 1943

Sturmgeschütz-Abteilung 202 was still comprised of only nine StuG. IIIs, two of which needed short-term repairs.[684]

8 JANUARY 1943

The *1. Batterie* of *Sturmgeschütz-Abteilung 202,* subordinated to the *216. Infanterie-Division,* had four assault guns serviceable while *2. Batterie* had three combat-ready StuG. IIIs in the sector of the *337. Infanterie-Division.* Maintenance work was performed on four assault guns on that day. Between 16 December 1942 and 8 January 1943, a total of six combat-ready StuG. IIIs arrived back in the echelon from the repair shop.[685]

In the central zone of action of the *337. Infanterie-Division*, the Germans experienced Soviet rifle-grenade fire (about 30 impacts) for the first time and noticed that the Soviet snipers used white paint on their rifles as camouflage.[686]

9 JANUARY 1943

Of the 11 assault guns of the assault gun unit only seven were operational.[687]

10 JANUARY 1943

The *1. Batterie/ Sturmgeschütz-Abteilung 202* with four combat-ready StuG. IIIs was subordinated to the *216. Infanterie-Division.* The *2. Batterie,* under the command of the *337. Infanterie-Division,* had three assault guns operational. One combat-ready StuG. III was with the staff of the *Abteilung.* An additional three were undergoing repairs.[688] On that day *1. Batterie* learned that the first long-barrelled assault guns intended for the unit had arrived.[689]

---

682 NARA T314, R938 (*XXXIX. Panzerkorps*), F000010.

683 NARA T315, R1236 (*102. Infanterie-Division*), F001235.

684 NARA T314, R937 (*XXXIX. Panzerkorps*), F001314-1315.

685 NARA T314, R937 (*XXXIX. Panzerkorps*), F001301-1302.

686 NARA T314, R937 (*XXXIX. Panzerkorps*), F001299.

687 NARA T314, R937 (*XXXIX. Panzerkorps*), F001287-1288.

688 NARA T314, R937 (*XXXIX. Panzerkorps*), F001270-1271.

689 *Tagebuchaufzeichnungen vom 2. 12. 1942 bis 1. 2. 1944 von Kamerad Wachtmeister Georg Hiller. In: Der Sturmartillerist.* Heft 60. p. 1326. o. The first long-barrelled StuG. III F assault guns were issued to the *Sturmgeschütz-Abteilung* of *Infanterie-Division (mot.) Grossdeutschland* with special order of battle in April 1942.

On the same day the *9. Armee* issued orders to the *XXXIX. Panzerkorps* and the *XXVII. Armeekorps* to prepare an attack with limited aims to stabilize the front line of the armoured corps so that the supplies could be delivered by day without Soviet interference. The attack was codenamed 'Sewastopol (505)' in the course of which 20 assault guns of *Sturmgeschütz-Abteilung 202* were planned to be sent into action together with 34 self-propelled anti-tank guns and 60 tanks to support elements of the *216.* and the *102. Infanterie-Divisions*.[690]

11 JANUARY 1943

In the sector of the *216. Infanterie-Division,* the commander of the *I. Bataillon/ Grenadier-Regiment 396* (with his command post in Bol. Kropotowo) received orders from the corps commander to establish contact with the *3. Batterie/ Sturmgeschütz-Abteilung 202* in order to organize anti-tank defences. Two captured T–34 tanks were also added into the anti-tank plan of fire.[691] On the previous day, the communication squad from *3. Batterie* reported to the command post of *Grenadier-Regiment 348*. Having relieved *3. Batterie/ Sturmgeschütz-Abteilung 667* from their assignment, there were only three self-propelled anti-tank guns of *Panzerjäger-Abteilung 561* left at their service as mobile anti-tank reserves.[692]

On that day *Sturmgeschütz-Abteilung 202* comprised a total of 11 short-barrelled StuG. IIIs, three of which still needed repairs.[693]

The command bunker of the *1. Batterie* received a direct hit by Soviet artillery. Two men were wounded: *Leutnant* Binder and *Kanonier* Otremba.[694]

12 JANUARY 1943

Sturmgeschütz-Abteilung 202 received its first long-barrelled StuG. III AFVs. Including these, the assault gun unit had a total of 13 short-barrelled and three long-barrelled assault guns on that day. Four of the short-barrelled StuG. IIIs were undergoing repairs.[695]

13 JANUARY 1943

The *3. Batterie /Sturmgeschütz-Abteilung 202* was subordinated to *102. Infanterie-Division* in terms of supply.[696]

At this point in time the staff of the assault gun unit, subordinated to the *216. Infanterie-Division,* had two short-barrelled and two long-barrelled assault guns

690 NARA T312, R308 (*Armeeoberkommando 9*), F7875006-007.

691 NARA T314, R937 (*XXXIX. Panzerkorps*), F001237.

692 NARA T314, R937 (*XXXIX. Panzerkorps*), F001238.

693 NARA T314, R937 (*XXXIX. Panzerkorps*), F001251-1252.

694 *Tagebuchaufzeichnungen vom 2. 12. 1942 bis 1. 2. 1944 von Kamerad Wachtmeister Georg Hiller.* In: *Der Sturmartillerist.* Heft 60. p. 1327.

695 NARA T314, R937 (*XXXIX. Panzerkorps*), F001232-1233.

696 NARA T314, R938 (*XXXIX. Panzerkorps*), F000017.

while its *1. Batterie* had four short-barrelled and one long-barrelled assault guns operational. The *2. Batterie,* assigned to the *337. Infanterie-Division,* had three short-barrelled and one long-barrelled combat-ready assault guns.[697] Two short-barrelled assault guns were undergoing short-term repairs while another two needed longer-term repairs.[698] Compared to the previous day there was one less AFV available but one more long-barrelled StuG. III with the staff; it is therefore possible that an AFV had been restored to combat readiness in a field repair shop.

14 JANUARY 1943

The staff of the assault gun unit subordinated to the *216. Infanterie-Division* had no combat-ready assault guns while *1. Batterie* had four short-barrelled and one long-barrelled StuG. IIIs serviceable. In the sector of the *337. Infanterie-Division,* the *2. Batterie* had three short-barrelled and one long-barrelled assault guns while the *3. Batterie,* under the command of the *102. Infanterie-Division,* had two short-barrelled and two long-barrelled combat vehicles operational. Four assault guns were undergoing repairs including one that required long-term repairs.[699]

A large-scale raid was planned, in the form of a memorandum, by the *102. Infanterie-Division.* This was to be carried out by seven battalions, 26–30 tanks, four self-propelled anti-tank guns and, besides the battery of *Sturmgeschütz-Abteilung 202* already subordinated to them, an additional battery would be put under their command (with a total of about 12–14 StuG. IIIs).[700]

15 JANUARY 1943

In the evening, the situation with regard to the combat-ready assault guns in the batteries of *Sturmgeschütz-Abteilung 202* was as follows:

- the staff of the assault gun unit subordinated to the *216. Infanterie-Division* had one long-barrelled assault gun, the *1. Batterie* had four short-barrelled and one long-barrelled assault guns;
- the *2. Batterie* in the sector of the *337. Infanterie-Division* possessed three short-barrelled and two long-barrelled assault guns;
- the *3. Batterie* subordinated to the *102. Infanterie-Division* had two short-barrelled StuG IIIs and two long-barrelled ones.

Maintenance personnel performed repairs on three short-barrelled StuG. IIIs and a captured T–34 tank.[701]

---

697 NARA T314, R937 (*XXXIX. Panzerkorps*), F001214.

698 NARA T314, R937 (*XXXIX. Panzerkorps*), F001215.

699 NARA T314, R938 (*XXXIX. Panzerkorps*), F000421-422.

700 NARA T315, R1236 (*102. Infanterie-Division*), F001167.

701 NARA T314, R938 (*XXXIX. Panzerkorps*), F000405-406.

16 JANUARY 1943

Sturmgeschütz-Abteilung 202 received two (temporarily out of action) T–34s for towing purposes from the Soviet combat vehicles captured in the fighting of November–December 1942.[702]

In the afternoon, by orders of the corps, the *3. Batterie/ Sturmgeschütz-Abteilung 202* was detached from the *102. Infanterie-Division* and put under the command of the *14. Infanterie-Division (mot.)*.[703]

In the evening the situation of the combat ready assault guns in the assault artillery unit was as follows:

- its staff, subordinated to the *216. Infanterie-Division,* had one long-barrelled assault gun and the *1. Batterie* had four short-barrelled and one long-barrelled StuG. IIIs;
- the *2. Batterie* in the sector of the *337. Infanterie-Division* possessed three short-barrelled and two long-barrelled assault guns;
- the *3. Batterie* under the command of the *14. Infanterie-Division (mot.)* had two short-barrelled and two long-barrelled StuG. IIIs.

The maintenance personnel performed repairs on three short-barrelled StuG. IIIs and two captured T–34 tanks.[704]

17 JANUARY 1943

In the evening, the situation regarding combat-ready assault guns was the same as during the previous day. However, the number of AFVs in need of repair increased to four short-barrelled and one long-barrelled assault guns and two captured combat vehicles.[705]

18 JANUARY 1943

No changes were reported in the assault gun strength of *Sturmgeschütz-Abteilung 202*.[706]

19 JANUARY 1943

In the evening the situation regarding combat-ready assault guns in the batteries of *Sturmgeschütz-Abteilung 202* was as follows:

702 NARA T314, R937 (*XXXIX. Panzerkorps*), F001166.

703 NARA T315, R1236 (*102. Infanterie-Division*), F000549.

704 NARA T314, R938 (*XXXIX. Panzerkorps*), F000393-394.

705 NARA T314, R938 (*XXXIX. Panzerkorps*), F000379-380.

706 NARA T314, R938 (*XXXIX. Panzerkorps*), F000363-364.

- the staff of the assault artillery unit subordinated to the *216. Infanterie-Division* had one long-barrelled assault gun while the *1. Batterie* had five short-barrelled StuG. IIIs and one long-barrelled one;
- in the sector of the *337. Infanterie-Division* the *2. Batterie* possessed three short-barrelled and two long-barrelled assault guns;
- the *3. Batterie*, attached to *14. Infanterie-Division (mot.)*, had one short-barrelled AFV and one long-barrelled one.

The maintenance service performed repairs on five short-barrelled StuG. IIIs, three of which were undergoing long-term repairs. Repairs to the two captured T–34 tanks were completed.[707]

20 JANUARY 1943

The staff and *1. Batterie* of the assault artillery unit were still subordinated to the *216. Infanterie-Division* in terms of supply; its *2. Batterie* was put under the command of the *337. Infanterie-Division,* and its *3. Batterie* was under control of the *14. Infanterie-Division (mot.).*[708]

The staff had one long-barrelled assault gun; the *1. Batterie* possessed five short-barrelled and two long-barrelled StuG. IIIs; the *2. Batterie* had two short-barrelled AFVs and one long-barrelled one operational. Maintenance personnel performed repairs on three short-barrelled StuG. IIIs.[709]

In the sector of the *14. Infanterie-Division (mot.)* one platoon of *3. Batterie* (with two assault guns) was put into readiness position south-east of Kriwoschtschekowo. The assault gun platoon was attached to *Kampfgruppe 'von Berken'* and was given the task of carrying out counter-thrusts and repelling attacks launched by Soviet armoured units. However, most of the battery took up its quarters south-east of Ssaburowo and came under the direct command of the divisional staff. The assault guns had to be prepared for their mission and, to that end, area reconnaissance was performed by the battery.[710]

21 JANUARY 1943

In the evening, the situation regarding the combat-ready assault guns in the batteries of *Sturmgeschütz-Abteilung 202* was as follows:

- the staff of the assault artillery unit subordinated to the *216. Infanterie-Division* had one long-barrelled assault gun while *1. Batterie* possessed five short-barrelled and two long-barrelled StuG. IIIs;

707 NARA T314, R938 (*XXXIX. Panzerkorps*), F000348-349.

708 NARA T314, R938 (*XXXIX. Panzerkorps*), F000026.

709 NARA T314, R938 (*XXXIX. Panzerkorps*), F000316-317.

710 NARA T315, R652 (*14. Infanterie-Division [mot.]*), F000663.

- in the sector of the *337. Infanterie-Division*, the *2. Batterie* had three short-barrelled and two long-barrelled assault guns;
- the *3. Batterie*, attached to the *14. Infanterie-Division (mot.)*, had one short-barrelled and two long-barrelled armoured StuG. IIIs.

The maintenance service performed repairs on three short-barrelled StuG. IIIs, two of which were undergoing long-term repairs.[711]

22 JANUARY 1943

No changes occurred in the number of combat-ready assault guns in the assault artillery unit, although four short-barrelled StuG. IIIs were in need of repairs.[712]

23 JANUARY 1943

In the evening the situation regarding combat-ready assault guns in the batteries of *Sturmgeschütz-Abteilung 202* was as follows:

- the staff of the assault artillery unit subordinated to the *216. Infanterie-Division* had one long-barrelled assault gun, *1. Batterie* possessed five short-barrelled and two long-barrelled StuG. IIIs;
- in the sector of the *337. Infanterie-Division*, the *2. Batterie* had three short-barrelled and two long-barrelled assault guns;
- the *3. Batterie*, attached to the *14. Infanterie-Division (mot.)*, had three short-barrelled and three long-barrelled StuG. IIIs.[713]

The maintenance service performed repairs on four short-barrelled StuG. IIIs of which two were undergoing long-term repairs.[714]

In the sector of the *14. Infanterie-Division (mot.)* two pioneer platoons began to construct covered winter shelters for the assault guns (*Boxen-Bunker für Sturmgeschütze*). Personnel of *3. Batterie/ Sturmgeschütz-Abteilung 202* not required for other tasks participated in this work.[715]

711 NARA T314, R938 (*XXXIX. Panzerkorps*), F000295-296.

712 NARA T314, R938 (*XXXIX. Panzerkorps*), F000282-283.

713 According to the strength report of *14. Infanterie-Division (mot.)* submitted at 1400 hours on that day, the *2. Batterie* (and not the *3.*) of the assault artillery unit was under its command, with only two short-barrelled and one long-barrelled assault gun. However, it is possible, that the mis-designation of the battery is only a typing error. *See* NARA T315, R652 (*14. Infanterie-Division [mot.]*), F000700.

714 NARA T314, R938 (*XXXIX. Panzerkorps*), F000270-271.

715 NARA T315, R652 (*14. Infanterie-Division [mot.]*), F000695.

24 JANUARY 1943

The maintenance service of *Sturmgeschütz-Abteilung 202,* stationed in Burzewo, was visited by the commander of the *9. Armee, Generaloberst* Walter Model, accompanied by the corps commander. The commander of the army promised to procure additional pre-heating devices for the company because, at that time, only one was installed at the unit. However, Model insisted that winter-proof shelters should be built for the assault guns and self-propelled anti-tank guns of *Panzerjäger-Abteilung 561.* To that end, the assault artillery unit required pioneers to carry out demolition tasks. The shelters for the combat vehicles were to be constructed in Krjukowo and as soon as they were ready, the unit would leave only one platoon in Lopotok ready for action. To ensure their continuous combat readiness, *Generaloberst* Model promised the allocation of five cubic metres of fuel.[716] In the evening, the staff of the assault artillery unit had one long-barrelled assault gun operational; its *1. Batterie* had three short-barrelled and two long-barrelled assault guns while the *3. Batterie* had two short-barrelled and three long-barrelled assault guns operational. An additional five short-barrelled StuG. IIIs were undergoing repairs, two of which required long-term repairs.[717]

25 JANUARY 1943

To carry out a planned attack on Podossinowka, in addition to the *1. Batterie/ Sturmgeschütz-Abteilung 202* that was already under their command, the *216. Infanterie-Division* requested the attachment of the *3. Batterie* which was at that time in reserve in Stanino and subordinated to *14. Infanterie-Division (mot.).* The corps commander granted his consent to that request. The division intended to deploy the *1. Batterie* from south-west and the *3. Batterie* from north-west.[718]

The number of combat-ready assault guns and those in need of repair remained the same as in the previous evening.[719]

26 JANUARY 1943

Starting at 0530 hours in the sector of the *216. Infanterie-Division*, two companies of *Grenadier-Regiment 396* (possibly with the assault guns of the *1. Batterie/ Sturmgeschütz-Abteilung 202*) carried out an attack 1.5 km north-north-west of Podossinowka with the limited aim of mopping up the so-called 'southern long trench' and taking the commanding hills in the area. However, since the clearing of the Soviet trench was halted several times, the corps commander, *General der Artillerie* Robert Martinek, who was present on the battlefield, ordered the *3. Batterie* of *Sturmgeschütz-Abteilung 202,* being in reserve in Stanino, to be deployed to support the grenadiers at around

716 NARA T314, R938 (*XXXIX. Panzerkorps*), F000240.

717 NARA T314, R938 (*XXXIX. Panzerkorps*), F000250-251.

718 NARA T314, R938 (*XXXIX. Panzerkorps*), F000224.

719 NARA T314, R938 (*XXXIX. Panzerkorps*), F000235-236.

0900 hours. Following that, elements of the *11. Kompanie* of the regiment also joined in the mopping up of the trench. At 0930 hours, the whole of the Soviet defensive position was in German hands. In view of this progress, *General der Artillerie* Robert Martinek retracted his previous order concerning the deployment of the *3. Batterie.*[720]

The attack pushed the German main combat line forwards by 1,200 m and prevented the Soviets from being able to observe the nearby railway. However, one StuG. III of the *1. Batterie* was burnt out in the attack.[721]

In the evening, in the sector of the *216. Infanterie-Division*, the staff of *Sturmgeschütz-Abteilung 202* had one long-barrelled assault gun operational; *1. Batterie* had two combat-ready long-barrelled assault guns and the *3. Batterie* one short-barrelled and two long-barrelled StuG. IIIs. The *2. Batterie*, attached to the *337. Infanterie-Division*, had three short-barrelled and two long-barrelled assault guns operational. Maintenance personnel performed repairs on 10 short-barrelled assault guns, two of them in need of long-term repairs.[722]

27 JANUARY 1943

In the evening the situation regarding combat-ready assault guns in the batteries of *Sturmgeschütz-Abteilung 202* was as follows:

- the staff of the assault artillery unit, subordinated to the *216. Infanterie-Division*, had one long-barrelled assault gun while *1. Batterie* had two short-barrelled and one long-barrelled StuG. IIIs and the *3. Batterie* two short-barrelled and one long-barrelled StuG. IIIs;
- in the sector of the *337. Infanterie-Division*, the *2. Batterie* had four short-barrelled and two long-barrelled assault guns.

The maintenance service meanwhile performed repairs on seven short-barrelled StuG. IIIs, two of which were undergoing long-term repairs. An additional three long-barrelled assault guns were in need of short-term repairs.[723]

28 JANUARY 1943

In the evening, the *3. Batterie / Sturmgeschütz-Abteilung 202* had three short-barrelled StuG. IIIs and one long-barrelled one operational. The combat-ready assault-gun strength of the other batteries was unchanged. Consequently, one less short-barrelled StuG. III was under repair.[724]

720 NARA T314, R938 (*XXXIX. Panzerkorps*), F000199.

721 *Tagebuchaufzeichnungen vom 2. 12. 1942 bis 1. 2. 1944 von Kamerad Wachtmeister Georg Hiller.* In: *Der Sturmartillerist.* Heft 60. 1327. o.

722 NARA T314, R938 (*XXXIX. Panzerkorps*), F000220-221.

723 NARA T314, R938 (*XXXIX. Panzerkorps*), F000523-524.

724 NARA T314, R938 (*XXXIX. Panzerkorps*), F000508-509.

30 JANUARY 1943

In the sector of the *216. Infanterie-Division* the assault squads of *Grenadier-Regiment 348* launched an attack at 0730 hours with the aim of recapturing Sherebzowo. This was the initial move of the attack with limited aims codenamed 'Sewastopol (505)' that had been planned twenty days before.

The raid was supported by the *1. Batterie/ Sturmgeschütz-Abteilung 202* 1 km west of Sherebzowo with locally directed assault gun fire. In a quarter of an hour every German assault squad was fighting on the northern perimeter of the settlement. The Soviets retreated to a fortified sector between Hill 198.8 and Hill 200, where they fought from previously established strongpoints and trenches. In the course of mopping up two bunkers in the north-east corner of Sherebzowo, the Germans sustained considerable losses. Having captured the north-eastern part of the settlement, a reserve company deployed as reinforcement was given the task, together with the *1. Batterie* and an assault gun platoon (with three StuG. IIIs) of *Sturmgeschütz-Abteilung 202,* of eliminating the Soviet trench system running in a south-easterly direction to the Soviet defensive strongpoint 700 m south-west of Hill 198.8. However, at around 0930 hours, drifting snow reduced visibility to 100 m and because of this the attack was called off. Despite this, one of the bunkers was taken with the support of the assault guns at 1500 hours.[725] During the fighting, the assault gun of *Stabswachtmeister* Schmoll advanced alone and the assault commander was killed.[726]

The *9. Armee* issued orders by telegram to the staff of the *XXXIX. Panzerkorps* to dispatch *Sturmgeschütz-Abteilung 202* in echelon by railway starting the following day to the sector of the *2. Armee.* The assault artillery unit was to be provided by four allotments (100 cubic metres) of fuel, two allotments of ammunition and 10 days' food rations.[727] The loading schedule was as follows:

- *2. Batterie* on 31 January 1943 from 1200 hours at Nowo Dugino railway station;
- *3. Batterie* on 1 February 1943, between 0900 and 1400 hours at Wjasma railway station;
- staff battery on 2 February 1943, between 0900 and 1400 hours, at Wjasma railway station;
- *1. Batterie* on 3 February 1943, between 0900 and 1400 hours at Wjasma railway station.[728]

---

725 NARA T314, R938 (*XXXIX. Panzerkorps*), F000449-452, as well as F000491.

726 *Tagebuchaufzeichnungen vom 2. 12. 1942 bis 1. 2. 1944 von Kamerad Wachtmeister Georg Hiller.* In: *Der Sturmartillerist.* Heft 60. p. 1327.

727 NARA T314, R938 (*XXXIX. Panzerkorps*), F000465.

728 NARA T314, R938 (*XXXIX. Panzerkorps*), F000468.

31 JANUARY 1943

The staff and the *1. Batterie / Sturmgeschütz-Abteilung 202* were detached from the *216. Infanterie-Division.*[729]

1 FEBRUARY 1943

The assault artillery unit was relieved from assignment with the *XXXIX. Panzerkorps.*[730]

3 FEBRUARY 1943

Most of *Sturmgeschütz-Abteilung 202* was detached from the other two divisions of the *XXXIX. Panzerkorps* in terms of supply.[731]

---

729 NARA T314, R938 (*XXXIX. Panzerkorps*), F000434.

730 NARA T314, R938 (*XXXIX. Panzerkorps*), F000793.

731 NARA T314, R938 (*XXXIX. Panzerkorps*), F000033.

CHAPTER 4

Divided

1943

The staff battery and the *1. Batterie/ Sturmgeschütz-Abteilung 202* in the sector of the German *2. Panzerarmee* south of Orel

Operational Background:

At the end of January 1943, the Soviets developed a plan to destroy Heeresgruppe Mitte involving more 'Fronts'. The offensive operation was commenced by the Brjansk Front on 12 February. The 13 and 48 Armies made an assault on positions held by the 2. Panzerarmee and strove to outflank Orel. The Soviets had advanced only 30 km by 24 February. The Germans reinforced their troops with forces withdrawn from the area of Rschew and Wjasma. The 16 Army of the Soviet Western Front launched an attack on 22 February north of Orel but its advance also ground to a halt after 13 km and it was forced to go on the defensive.

2 FEBRUARY 1943

The *1. Batterie/ Sturmgeschütz-Abteilung 202* was subordinated to the *LV. Armeekorps.*[732]

At 1500 hours the chief of staff of the corps, *Oberst i.G.* Werner Wagner, had a discussion with the 1 (operations) staff officer of the *299. Infanterie-Division* regarding the future of the assault gun battery that arrived with the *I. Bataillon /Panzergrenadier-Regiment 101*. According to the latter, '*the assault guns must avoid spending disproportionately long periods of time at any particular location. The Panzergrenadier-Bataillon has very few heavy weapons, therefore it needs assault guns as a support.*'[733]

3 FEBRUARY 1943

The *XXXV. Armeekorps*, subordinated to the *2. Panzerarmee,* received orders to move most of *Panzergrenadier- Regiment 101* attached to the *18. Panzer-Division,* an

732 NARA T314, R1376 (*LV. Armeekorps*), F001091.

733 NARA T314, R1376 (*LV. Armeekorps*), F001098.

artillery battery, two anti-aircraft artillery groups and an assault gun battery to the area of Chaustowo and Senowjewka where they would remain as an army reserve.[734]

On that day the train loaded with the assault gun battery remained at Ponyri railway station.[735] At 1035 hours the *LV. Armeekorps* issued orders to dispatch the assault guns – some of them in need of repair – to Gubkino, via Maloarchangelsk station. Its acting commander was to report to the corps. By direct order of the corps the assault guns were to be deployed together with the *I. Batterie/ Panzergrenadier-Regiment 101.*[736]

4 FEBRUARY 1943

The staff battery and *1. Batterie / Sturmgeschütz-Abteilung 202,* subordinated to *Kampfgruppe 'Källner',* arrived in the sector of the *2. Panzerarmee.*[737]

The assault gun battery attached to the *18. Panzer-Division* came under the command of the *LV. Armeekorps.* The corps had been given the task of holding its positions to prevent Soviet troops from advancing further towards Maloarchangelsk. In relation to that, the assault gun battery, together with a pioneer battalion, was to launch an attack to retake and hold Mokroje.[738]

In the evening the assault gun battery, subordinated to a *Kampfgruppe* made up of the *II. Bataillon/ Panzergrenadier-Regiment 101,* an artillery battery and an anti-aircraft artillery group, had to be drawn forward into the area of Droskowo.[739]

7 FEBRUARY 1943

The *18. Panzer-Division*, in conjunction with the *1. Batterie/ Sturmgeschütz-Abteilung 202* that had been attached to them, repelled Soviet attacks of battalion strength on Ponyri railway station and the western part of the town. The Germans knocked out a Soviet tank and reported 300 Soviet soldiers killed in action. In the evening the battery had two combat-ready assault guns.[740] The quarters of the battery were in the school of Machlostowo.[741]

8 FEBRUARY 1943

There were still two assault guns from *Sturmgeschütz-Abteilung 202* fighting while subordinated to the *18. Panzer-Division.* The other assault guns of the *1. Batterie* were stationed in the area of Smijewka (probably subordinated to

734 NARA T313, R153 (*Panzerarmeeoberkommando 2*), F7406927.

735 NARA T313, R172 (*Panzerarmeeoberkommando 2*), F7429562.

736 NARA T314, R1376 (*LV. Armeekorps*), F001124.

737 NARA T312, R1216 (*Armeeoberkommando 2*), F000096.

738 NARA T313, R153 (*Panzerarmeeoberkommando 2*), F7406928.

739 NARA T313, R153 (*Panzerarmeeoberkommando 2*), F7406931.

740 NARA T314, R1377 (*LV. Armeekorps*), F000410.

741 *Tagebuchaufzeichnungen vom 2. 12. 1942 bis 1. 2. 1944 von Kamerad Wachtmeister Georg Hiller.* In: *Der Sturmartillerist.* Heft 60. p. 1327.

the *45. Infanterie-Division*). The armoured division had a third StuG. III from *Sturmgeschütz-Abteilung 909*.[742]

10 FEBRUARY 1943

The *45. Infanterie-Division* 'lent' two of its subordinated assault guns to the *383. Infanterie-Division,* in whose zone of action Soviet troops broke into Gretschik. The Germans needed the StuG. IIIs to carry out a counter-thrust. The assault guns started from Nowo Sslobodka towards Chmelewaja.[743]

During the day, forces of the Soviet 399 Rifle Division penetrated the front line in the sector of the *45. Infanterie-Division* south of Topki. The German grenadiers pushed the Soviets back with the support of the assault guns, inflicting heavy losses on them. The Soviet infantry fled in panic as they were pursued by the StuG. IIIs. The Germans counted at least 450 Soviet dead and took 127 prisoners; they also captured 20 machine guns, 25 submachine guns and 25 anti-tank rifles.[744]

At 2110 hours the *45. Infanterie-Division* reported to the corps that they had seven assault guns operational. Two of them were on its left flank, three in the centre (without ammunition and fuel) and the remaining two had taken up positions at the interface with the *383. Infanterie-Division.* They were in need of minor repairs which were undertaken during the night. Thus the two lent StuG. IIIs were made combat-ready again by the early hours of the following day. Facing the right-hand neighbour of the *45. Infanterie-Division,* the Soviets were preparing to attack and it was therefore important that the assault guns could be quickly redeployed if necessary.[745]

12 FEBRUARY 1943

There were still two StuG. IIIs attached to the *18. Panzer-Division* from the assault artillery unit and an additional one from *Sturmgeschütz-Abteilung 909*.[746] Two of the three armoured fighting vehicles were operational while one was in need of short-term repairs.[747] The locksmiths' section in the workshop of *Sturmgeschütz-Abteilung 202* was burnt down.[748]

15 FEBRUARY 1943

In the evening, all three assault guns subordinated to *18. Panzer-Division* were combat-ready.[749] No significant engagement had taken place for days in the sector of the division.

742 NARA T314, R1377 (*LV. Armeekorps*), F000436.

743 NARA T314, R1376 (*LV. Armeekorps*), F001174.

744 NARA T314, R1376 (*LV. Armeekorps*), F001180-82.

745 NARA T314, R1376 (*LV. Armeekorps*), F001180.

746 NARA T314, R1377 (*LV. Armeekorps*), F000494.

747 NARA T314, R1377 (*LV. Armeekorps*), F000498.

748 *Tagebuchaufzeichnungen vom 2. 12. 1942 bis 1. 2. 1944 von Kamerad Wachtmeister Georg Hiller.* In: *Der Sturmartillerist.* Heft 60. p. 1327.

749 NARA T314, R1377 (*LV. Armeekorps*), F000541.

19 FEBRUARY 1943

An assault squad of the *18. Panzer-Division* launched an attack on a two-company-strong Soviet formation east of Hill 248.7 with the support of a StuG. III. The Soviets lost 30 dead, an anti-tank rifle, a machine gun and an anti-tank gun in a very short time. The latter was destroyed by a direct hit from the assault gun.[750]

In the evening the division reported three combat-ready assault guns plus one in need of short-term repairs (without the designation of the units).[751]

20 FEBRUARY 1943

Three combat-ready assault guns from the *1. Batterie / Sturmgeschütz-Abteilung 202* were subordinated to the *18. Panzer-Division*; two others were assigned to the *45. Infanterie-Division.* Besides those, two StuG. IIIs of the battery were undergoing short-term repairs while one was in need of long-term repairs.[752]

Between 6 and 20 February 1943, while the *1. Batterie* of the assault artillery unit was attached to the division, the sector of the *18. Panzer-Division* sustained 18 attacks of battalion strength, 23 attacks of company strength, as well as five armoured attacks. During these attacks 1,374 Soviet dead[753] and seven knocked-out combat vehicles (five T–34s, one KV-1 and a T–60) were counted.[754]

21 FEBRUARY 1943

At 0515 hours, by direct orders from the commander in chief of the *2. Panzerarmee,* all of the assault guns of *Sturmgeschütz-Abteilung 202* and *Sturmgeschütz-Abteilung 909* were to be dispatched to Orel with immediate effect.[755]

According to that order two-thirds of the *1. Batterie/ Sturmgeschütz-Abteilung 202* were detached from the *LV. Armeekorps* and put under the direct command of the *2. Panzerarmee.*[756] In relation to that, assault gun platoon *'Olchow'* was to move the next day to Protasowo having been relieved from assignment to the *18. Panzer-Division.*[757]

22 FEBRUARY 1943

In the sector of the *18. Panzer-Division* one StuG. III from assault gun platoon '*Olchow*' was disabled. Its recovery ran into difficulties due to the combat situation that had emerged in the course of the night and it seemed likely that the armoured

750 NARA T314, R1377 (*LV. Armeekorps*), F000585.

751 NARA T314, R1377 (*LV. Armeekorps*), F000580.

752 NARA T314, R1377 (*LV. Armeekorps*), F000591.

753 Besides the ones counted, the Germans supposed an additional 840 Soviet dead in the sector of the division.

754 NARA T314, R1377 (*LV. Armeekorps*), F000609.

755 NARA T314, R1376 (*LV. Armeekorps*), F001226.

756 NARA T314, R1377 (*LV. Armeekorps*), F000607.

757 NARA T314, R1377 (*LV. Armeekorps*), F000610.

fighting vehicle would have to be blown up.[758] Therefore the platoon had only one short-barrelled and one long-barrelled assault guns that were operational.[759]

23 FEBRUARY 1943

Assault gun platoon '*Olchow*' of the *1. Batterie /Sturmgeschütz-Abteilung 202* was detached from the *18. Panzer-Division.*[760] One disabled assault gun remained in Stepanowka along with two captured Soviet tanks.[761]

27 FEBRUARY 1943

At around 1000 hours the *2. Panzerarmee* received the order to dispatch the *1. Batterie/Sturmgeschütz-Abteilung 202* by railway to the area of Shisdra where it would be attached to *Korps Scheele.* This order countermanded a previous order received at 0045 hours, according to which the battery, together with *Pionier-Bataillon 750* was to be sent to Komaritschi and Derjugino, where it would have been subordinated to the *XXXXVII. Panzerkorps.*[762] The assault gun battery should have been deployed with *Jäger-Bataillon 11.*[763]

In the end, the *1. Batterie/ Sturmgeschütz-Abteilung* arrived at Derjugino railway station later that day and was ordered to the area of Bytschki, 2 km north-east of the settlement where it was held in the reserve of the *XXXXVII. Panzerkorps.* Someone should have been sent from the battery to the staff of the *707. Infanterie-Division* for further orders.[764]

28 FEBRUARY 1943

Kampfgruppe 'Kaellner' was set up to protect the southern flank of *2. Panzerarmee* (which was under threat by the enemy) and put under the command of the staff of the *XXXXVII. Panzerkorps.* The *Kampfgruppe* would have been made up of *Jäger-Bataillon 10* and *11*, the *Pionier-Bataillon 750,* three light gun artillery batteries, an armoured company of the *20. Panzer-Division, Jagdverband 'Huzel'* and *1. Batterie* of *Sturmgeschütz-Abteilung 202.*[765] Assault guns were later ordered to the *Kampfgruppe* from the elements of *Sturmgeschütz-Abteilung 909.*

Thus, the *1. Batterie/ Sturmgeschütz-Abteilung 202* came under the command of the *707. Infanterie-Division* during the day. At that point it had six combat-ready, short-barrelled assault guns plus one operational long-barrelled StuG. III[766]

---

758 NARA T314, R1377 (*LV. Armeekorps*), F000634.
759 NARA T314, R1377 (*LV. Armeekorps*), F000631.
760 NARA T314, R1377 (*LV. Armeekorps*), F000658.
761 NARA T314, R1376 (*LV. Armeekorps*), F001234.
762 NARA T313, R153 (*Panzerarmeeoberkommando 2*), F7407035.
763 NARA T313, R172 (*Panzerarmeeoberkommando 2*), F7429483.
764 NARA T314, R1127 (*XXXXVII. Panzerkorps*), F000295.
765 NARA T313, R153 (*Panzerarmeeoberkommando 2*), F7407041.
766 NARA T314, R1127 (*XXXXVII. Panzerkorps*), F000317.

According to the data provided by German reconnaissance, the front line of the *XXXXVII. Panzerkorps* was attacked by seven Soviet rifle divisions, four tank brigades, one breakthrough heavy tank regiment and two motorized rifle brigades.[767]

1 MARCH 1943

The *1. Batterie/ Sturmgeschütz-Abteilung 202* was subordinated to the staff of the *137. Infanterie-Division.* The division was informed of this by the chief of staff of the *XXXXVII. Panzerkorps* in the morning. He also added that the battery should be re-attached to the corps as soon as possible.[768]

At 0745 hours, Soviet troops broke through the German defences with 15-20 tanks in the southern foreground of Boguslowka. Two assault guns were immediately dispatched to the place.[769]

The commander of the corps, *General der Artillerie* Joachim Lemelsen, issued orders to the battery commander at 1155 hours to march to the division.

At 1205 hours, *Grenadier-Regiment 447* reported to the staff of the *137. Infanterie-Division* that the elements of *Grenadier-Regiment 747* subordinated to the division would not be able to hold on much longer unless the assault guns relieved them soon. Most of the assault guns set off 15 minutes later but, following the orders received from the 1 (operations) staff officer, they stopped at the church of Derjugino. The battery commander had to report to the command post of *Grenadier-Regiment 447.*[770]

Due to their limited cross-country ability, the assault guns were temporarily employed in the western part of Derjugino and because of that, they were unable to intervene against the Soviet armoured attack in the area of Boguslowka and Kilkono.[771]

A 1330 hours the division informed *Grenadier-Regiment 447* that there were six assault guns at the church but were unable to be brought forward one by one.[772]

Not long before 1600 hours the commander of the *1. Kompanie/ Pionier-Bataillon 137* reported that Boguslowka was being attacked continuously by Soviet troops and that his unit would be unable to contain them if assault guns didn't arrive immediately. In response, at 1605 hours, the 1 (operations) staff officer dispatched an assault gun platoon to Boguslowka with the order to return as soon as they destroyed the assaulting Soviets.[773]

At 1745 hours *Grenadier-Regiment 447* requested help again because the Soviets were attacking with two battalions supported by tanks. The 1 (operations) staff officer sent two more assault guns. However, at 1950 hours the division commander

767 NARA T313, R153 (*Panzerarmeeoberkommando 2*), F7407052.
768 NARA T315, R1429 (*137. Infanterie-Division*), F000722.
769 NARA T315, R1429 (*137. Infanterie-Division*), F000722.
770 NARA T315, R1429 (*137. Infanterie-Division*), F000721.
771 NARA T315, R1429 (*137. Infanterie-Division*), F000172.
772 NARA T315, R1429 (*137. Infanterie-Division*), F000723.
773 NARA T315, R1429 (*137. Infanterie-Division*), F000724.

issued orders to the regiment to inform the *1. Batterie / Sturmgeschütz-Abteilung 202* of their withdrawal.[774]

2 MARCH 1943

At around 0400 hours Soviet troops infiltrated into Derjugino. To counter this intrusion a strongpoint-like defence was improvised at the last moment near the cathedral by the hastily assembled, weak forces of the *137. Infanterie-Division* attached to the staff of *Grenadier-Regiment 447* together with the two assault guns of the *1. Batterie / Sturmgeschütz-Abteilung 202* sent at 0505 hours.[775] At around 1100 hours there were two Soviet battalions and eight to ten tanks fighting in the vicinity of the church. The settlement was also pounded by Soviet multiple rocket launchers.[776]

At around 1100 hours the division received additional reinforcement in the form of the *2. Batterie / Sturmgeschütz-Abteilung 909.*

At 1140 hours five Soviet tanks shelled Derjugino from south-east of Hill 221.3. At that time there was a Soviet tank attack at the cathedral. The staff of *137. Infanterie-Division* sent assault guns to both places. At 1715 hours *Grenadier-Regiment 447* reported to the staff of the division that the assault guns were fighting under the command of the regiment. By that time five Soviet tanks had been knocked out.[777] On that day the assault guns, anti-aircraft and anti-tank guns destroyed a total of eight Soviet tanks in the sector of the division.[778]

In the evening the *1. Batterie/ Sturmgeschütz-Abteilung 202* had five combat-ready assault guns and two in need of repairs. One StuG. III had to be written off as a total loss.[779]

3 MARCH 1943

At 1330 hours, the 1 (operations) staff officer of the *137. Infanterie-Division* issued orders to the commander of the *1. Batterie/ Sturmgeschütz-Abteilung 202* to entrain the assault guns at nightfall and transport them to the area of Komaritschi where they would be at the corps' disposal.[780] On the other hand, at 1420 hours he informed the staff of the *707. Infanterie-Division* that he would send assault guns against the Soviet tanks that had penetrated the right flank of the *137. Infanterie-Division* which, together with the reserves, would restore the original situation.[781]

---

774 NARA T315, R1429 (*137. Infanterie-Division*), F000725.

775 NARA T315, R1429 (*137. Infanterie-Division*), F000174.

776 NARA T315, R1429 (*137. Infanterie-Division*), F000743.

777 NARA T315, R1429 (*137. Infanterie-Division*), F000744.

778 NARA T315, R1429 (*137. Infanterie-Division*), F000746. Since there were two different assault gun batteries fighting under the command of the *137. Infanterie-Division*, it is impossible to determine the respective scores achieved by the batteries with no sources available.

779 NARA T314, R1127 (*XXXXVII. Panzerkorps*), F000381.

780 NARA T315, R1429 (*137. Infanterie-Division*), F000764.

781 NARA T315, R1429 (*137. Infanterie-Division*), F000765.

In the evening the StuG. IIIs of the assault gun battery were still in action and therefore it was impossible to find out, how many of them were still operational.[782]

4 MARCH 1943

In the evening, the *1. Batterie/ Sturmgeschütz-Abteilung 202* had four short-barrelled assault guns and one long-barrelled one operational.[783]

5 MARCH 1943

The *1. Batterie/ Sturmgeschütz-Abteilung 202* was tactically subordinated to the *707. Infanterie-Division* in the area of Litish. During the day the battery was regrouped by the divisional staff to the area of Pigarewo where they were to prepare for counter-thrusts against the right and left flanks of the division. It was emphasized in the divisional daily orders that: '*every counter-thrust of the assault guns must be accompanied by sufficient infantry to provide cover against enemy infantry*'.[784]

In the evening, the assault gun battery had still four short-barrelled StuG. IIIs and one long-barrelled one operational.[785]

6 MARCH 1943

The number of combat-ready assault guns of the assault gun battery subordinated to *707. Infanterie-Division* remained the same.[786]

8 MARCH 1943

The long-barrelled assault gun in the *1. Batterie* of *Sturmgeschütz-Abteilung 202* was temporarily in need of repairs. The four short-barrelled StuG. IIIs were still combat-ready.[787]

According to the war diary of an NCO in the *1. Batterie*, another assault gun attack was carried out on that day (possibly in the area of Paliki) during which the assault gun of *Leutnant* Linder was hit by an anti-tank gun. The driver, *Gefreiter* Friedrich, was killed and the other three members of the crew wounded. Another assault gun (commanded by *Leutnant* Petrik) was blown up due to a hit by an anti-tank gun. The commander of the assault gun was seriously wounded and his two crew members killed. The positions of the battery was also attacked by Soviet aircraft.[788]

---

782 NARA T314, R1127 (*XXXXVII. Panzerkorps*), F000401.

783 NARA T314, R1127 (*XXXXVII. Panzerkorps*), F000418.

784 NARA T315, R2247 (*707. Infanterie-Division*), F000571.

785 NARA T314, R1127 (*XXXXVII. Panzerkorps*), F000437.

786 NARA T314, R1127 (*XXXXVII. Panzerkorps*), F000466.

787 NARA T314, R1127 (*XXXXVII. Panzerkorps*), F000501.

788 *Tagebuchaufzeichnungen vom 2. 12. 1942 bis 1. 2. 1944 von Kamerad Wachtmeister Georg Hiller.* In: *Der Sturmartillerist.* Heft 60. p. 1328.

9 MARCH 1943

At 0500 hours, Soviet troops attacked the centre of the front line of the *707. Infanterie-Division* from the eastern foreground of Nowosselskij with rifle infantry and tanks. Having broken through the defences of the German division, 15 Soviet tanks turned towards Litish. The Soviet riflemen, closing up almost unnoticed in the thick fog, occupied the south-western and southern part of the settlement. In the noon hours, 10 Soviet tanks continued their drive and advanced up to Sapadnaja Poljana. Here they were finally halted when four of them were knocked out by the combined effort of the assault guns of the *1. Batterie/ Sturmgeschütz-Abteilung 202,* the divisional artillery and the *2. Kompanie / Panzerjäger-Abteilung 45*. However, it became obvious to the Germans that the Soviet armour had withstood the German gunfire quite well and they retreated in a southerly direction only after having been hit several times. German counter-thrusts, launched in the area of Litish and Kossinka, proved unsuccessful.

By nightfall only one short-barrelled assault gun was still combat-ready while another three short-barrelled StuG. IIIs and one long-barrelled StuG. III were in need of repair.[789]

10 MARCH 1943

At 1045 hours, the staffs of the *707.* and the *137. Infanterie-Divisionen* discussed the Soviet assault on Litish in which 15 tanks had carried infantry. Against them the Germans could only use an anti-aircraft gun and the three assault guns of the *1. Batterie / Sturmgeschütz-Abteilung 202*. At around 1600 hours, it turned out, that German dive-bombers had destroyed four Soviet combat vehicles while another two or three tanks had escaped southwards. However, apart from that, fighting for Litish continued.[790]

11 MARCH 1943

Fierce fighting continued for Litish. Finally, the *III. Bataillon/ Grenadier-Regiment 727* penetrated into the north-eastern part of the settlement with artillery and multiple rocket launcher support. In the sector of the *707. Infanterie-Division*, six Soviet tanks were knocked out three of which were destroyed by dive-bombers of the *Luftwaffe*.

In the evening the *1. Batterie/ Sturmgeschütz-Abteilung 202* had two combat-ready, short-barrelled assault guns.[791]

789 NARA T314, R1127 (*XXXXVII. Panzerkorps*), F000534.

790 NARA T315, R1429 (*137. Infanterie-Division*), F000863.

791 NARA T314, R1127 (*XXXXVII. Panzerkorps*), F000573.

12 MARCH 1943

In the sector of the *707. Infanterie-Division* the next German attack on Litish was halted by determined Soviet counter-thrusts. Although two Soviet tanks were knocked out by the Germans during the fighting, they were unable to recapture the north-western part of Litish despite the three penetrations achieved with the aid of remarkable artillery support.[792]

The *1. Batterie / Sturmgeschütz-Abteilung 202,* together with the *2.* (anti-tank) *Kompanie* of the divisional battalion of the *45. Infanterie-Division,* came under the command of *137. Infanterie-Division* at the end of the day after its staff assumed command in the sector of *707. Infanterie-Division.*[793]

In the evening the assault gun battery had three short-barrelled StuG. IIIs operational.[794]

13 MARCH 1943

According to the divisional orders issued by *137. Infanterie-Division*, the *1. Batterie / Sturmgeschütz-Abteilung 202* was subordinated to *Grenadier-Regiment 448* because of changes in the front line. The battery could only be deployed with the permission of the divisional staff.[795]

In the evening the assault gun battery had four short-barrelled and one long-barrelled StuG. IIIs operational.[796]

14 MARCH 1943

The *1. Batterie / Sturmgeschütz-Abteilung 202* was operating in the sector of the *137. Infanterie-Division,* subordinated to *Grenadier-Regiment 448.*[797] The division received orders by telegram that the *1. Batterie/ Sturmgeschütz-Abteilung 202* and the *2. Batterie/Sturmgeschütz-Abteilung 909,* both subordinated to the division, should report daily the numbers of assault guns operational, those in need of short or long-term repairs and the number written off.[798]

15 MARCH 1943

At 0200 hours the *III. Bataillon* of the *Grenadier-Regiment* and the *1. Kompanie* of *Divisions-Bataillon 137* launched an attack on the northern part of Litish '*with the support of all weapons*' (probably including those of *1. Batterie / Sturmgeschütz-Abteilung 202*). Having broken into the north-western half of the settlement, the

792 NARA T314, R1127 (*XXXXVII. Panzerkorps*), F000591.
793 NARA T315, R2247 (*707. Infanterie-Division*), F000558.
794 NARA T314, R1127 (*XXXXVII. Panzerkorps*), F000589.
795 NARA T315, R1429 (*137. Infanterie-Division*), F000907.
796 NARA T314, R1127 (*XXXXVII. Panzerkorps*), F000613.
797 NARA T315, R1429 (*137. Infanterie-Division*), F000182.
798 NARA T315, R1429 (*137. Infanterie-Division*), F000915.

German attack was stemmed by the Soviet positions established in the houses. The Soviets had a total of 10 tanks in Litish, partly dug in and camouflaged. Grenadiers destroyed two KV-1s and a T–34 using magnetic mines. Finally the Germans were forced back to their jump-off positions by a Soviet counter-thrust.[799]

In the evening the assault gun battery had only seven short-barrelled and one long-barrelled assault guns,[800] of which four short-barrelled guns and one long-barrelled gun were operational.[801]

16 MARCH 1943

In the evening, while attached to the *137. Infanterie-Division,* the *1. Batterie/ Sturmgeschütz-Abteilung 202* had six short-barrelled StuG. IIIs operational.[802]

17 MARCH 1943

At 0630 hours, in the sector of the *137. Infanterie-Division*, the Soviets launched an attack from Litish in a north-westerly direction with a force of battalion strength plus 19 tanks. At around 0800 hours the Germans held up the Soviet AFVs in an orchard and during the morning hours destroyed almost all of them. The division planned to attack from the orchard towards south-west, take back the former German positions and destroy the Soviet tanks that had been disabled during the fighting with elements of the division's *Bataillon 137,* the pioneer platoon of *Grenadier-Regiment 448* and the five assault guns of the *1. Batterie/ Sturmgeschütz-Abteilung 202.*[803]

Elements of *Grenadier-Regiment 448* reached and reoccupied the former defensive positions at 1640 hours and repulsed an attempted Soviet breakthrough leaving the combat area covered in burnt-out Soviet tanks.[804]

The assault gun battery had six short-barrelled StuG. IIIs operational in the evening.[805]

The corps issued orders calling for the subordinate tank, assault gun and self-propelled anti-tank gun units to pinpoint their positions more precisely using violet-blue smoke candles.[806]

20 MARCH 1943

The ammunition depot of the *1. Batterie/ Sturmgeschütz-Abteilung 202* was hit during a Soviet air raid.[807]

---

799 NARA T314, R1127 (*XXXXVII. Panzerkorps*), F000655.

800 NARA T314, R1127 (*XXXXVII. Panzerkorps*), F000668.

801 NARA T314, R1127 (*XXXXVII. Panzerkorps*), F000652.

802 NARA T315, R1429 (*137. Infanterie-Division*), F000934.

803 NARA T315, R1429 (*137. Infanterie-Division*), F000184.

804 NARA T315, R1429 (*137. Infanterie-Division*), F000185, F000952.

805 NARA T314, R1127 (*XXXXVII. Panzerkorps*), F000690.

806 NARA T315, R1429 (*137. Infanterie-Division*), F000973.

807 *Tagebuchaufzeichnungen vom 2. 12. 1942 bis 1. 2. 1944 von Kamerad Wachtmeister Georg Hiller.* In: *Der Sturmartillerist.* Heft 60. p. 1328.

21 MARCH 1943

An assault squad of the *137. Infanterie-Division* successfully carried out a mission with two assault guns from *1. Batterie / Sturmgeschütz-Abteilung 202* to destroy a disabled Soviet tank. The Germans took two prisoners in the action during which the Soviets suffered many casualties.[808]

22 MARCH 1943

The *137. Infanterie-Division* received orders from the staff of the *XXXXVII. Panzerkorps* to dispatch the *1. Batterie / Sturmgeschütz-Abteilung 202* into the sector of the *72. Infanterie-Division.*[809] The ammunition depot of the *1. Batterie* was hit again by a Soviet air raid.[810]

After 1800 hours the division ordered *Grenadier-Regiment 448* to march the battery – via Komaritschi and Apasha – to the area of Isbitschni, where they were to report to the staff of *Grenadier-Regiment 105.*[811]

According to the evening report submitted to the corps, five combat-ready, short-barrelled assault guns were subordinated to the *137. Infanterie-Division* at that time.[812]

23 MARCH 1943

The *1. Batterie / Sturmgeschütz-Abteilung 202* was detached from the *137. Infanterie-Division.*[813] The assault gun battery, together with the *1.* (self-propelled anti-tank gun) *Kompanie/ Panzerjäger-Abteilung 178,* was put under the command of the *72. Infanterie-Division,* and ordered to the area of Isbitschni.[814]

While moving in the direction of Komaritschi, *Unteroffizier* Klein's assault gun (*'Jaguar'*) struck a mine and blew up. The crew members were killed. During subsequent Soviet air raids, the battery suffered one more fatality and three crew members were wounded.[815]

In the evening, the assault gun battery had four short-barrelled StuG. IIIs operational while in the self-propelled anti-tank gun company there were nine combat-ready *Panzerjäger.*[816]

25 MARCH 1943

At 0700 hours Soviet troops launched an attack in three waves (each with 300-400 men and six tanks) on the right flank of the *72. Infanterie-Division.* The Germans

808 NARA T315, R1429 (*137. Infanterie-Division*), F000186.

809 NARA T315, R1429 (*137. Infanterie-Division*), F000187.

810 *Tagebuchaufzeichnungen vom 2. 12. 1942 bis 1. 2. 1944 von Kamerad Wachtmeister Georg Hiller.* In: *Der Sturmartillerist.* Heft 60. p. 1328.

811 NARA T315, R1429 (*137. Infanterie-Division*), F000188.

812 NARA T315, R1429 (*137. Infanterie-Division*), F001022.

813 NARA T315, R1429 (*137. Infanterie-Division*), F001045.

814 NARA T314, R1126 (*XXXXVII. Panzerkorps*), F000089.

815 *Tagebuchaufzeichnungen vom 2. 12. 1942 bis 1. 2. 1944 von Kamerad Wachtmeister Georg Hiller.* In: *Der Sturmartillerist.* Heft 60. p. 1328.

816 NARA T314, R1127 (*XXXXVII. Panzerkorps*), F000777.

repelled each attempt and knocked out four KV-1s, an additional heavy AFV was able to retreat while in flames.[817]

At 0940 hours, on the left flank of the division, 600-800 Soviet soldiers commenced an attack on Mal. Prudki and Ussoscha with the support of eight tanks. Following vicious close quarters combat the Germans were forced to evacuate Mal. Prudki.[818]

In the evening the *1. Batterie/ Sturmgeschütz-Abteilung 202* had four short-barrelled StuG. IIIs operational.[819]

The staff of the *72. Infanterie-Division* prepared to dispatch the assault gun battery to the staff of the *7. Infanterie-Division* (in the sector of *XXXXVI. Panzerkorps*) on the 28 March.[820]

27 MARCH 1943

The *XXXXVII. Panzerkorps* ordered the staff of the *72. Infanterie-Division* to withdraw the *1. Batterie/Sturmgeschütz-Abteilung 202* and send it to Apasha to be put under the direct command of the corps.[821]

The battery set off towards Apasha at around 1600 hours with its four combat-ready, short-barrelled StuG. IIIs.[822]

28 MARCH 1943

The *1. Batterie/Sturmgeschütz-Abteilung 202* was detached from the *XXXXVII. Panzerkorps.*[823] The battery received three new assault guns on that day.[824]

9 APRIL 1943

The staff battery and the *1. Batterie/ Sturmgeschütz-Abteilung 202* were dispatched by rail from the sector of the *2. Panzerarmee* into the sector of the *2. Armee.*[825]

10 APRIL 1943

The *1. Batterie/ Sturmgeschütz-Abteilung 202* received a new acting commander, *Leutnant* Seidel.[826]

---

817 NARA T314, R1127 (*XXXXVII. Panzerkorps*), F000806. In the sector of the *72. Infanterie-Division* a total of seven KV-1s and four T-34s were knocked out.

818 NARA T314, R1127 (*XXXXVII. Panzerkorps*), F000812.

819 NARA T314, R1127 (*XXXXVII. Panzerkorps*), F000812.

820 NARA T314, R1127 (*XXXXVII. Panzerkorps*), F000814.

821 NARA T314, R1127 (*XXXXVII. Panzerkorps*), F000823.

822 NARA T314, R1127 (*XXXXVII. Panzerkorps*), F000827.

823 NARA T314, R1127 (*XXXXVII. Panzerkorps*), F000840.

824 *Tagebuchaufzeichnungen vom 2. 12. 1942 bis 1. 2. 1944 von Kamerad Wachtmeister Georg Hiller.* In: *Der Sturmartillerist.* Heft 60. p. 1328.

825 NARA T313, R153 (*Panzerarmeeoberkommando 2*), F7407207.

826 *Tagebuchaufzeichnungen vom 2. 12. 1942 bis 1. 2. 1944 von Kamerad Wachtmeister Georg Hiller.* In: *Der Sturmartillerist.* Heft 60. p. 1329.

The *2.* and *3. Batterie/Sturmgeschütz-Abteilung 202* were in the sector of the *2. Armee,* in the area of Kursk and Ssumy

Operational Background:

On 24 January 1943, the Soviet Supreme Command commenced an attack on the German 2. Armee and the Hungarian III. Corps defending in the area of Voronezh and Kastornoye. The attacking Soviet forces consisted of the right flank and central section of the Voronezh Front and the left flank of the Brjansk Front. The objective of the Voronezh Front was to occupy the industrial area of Charkow by deploying its left flank against Charkow and its right flank (the 60 and the 38 Army) against Kursk and Obojan. The Soviet 60 Army retook Kursk on 8 February1943. The Soviet attack ground to a halt and from March to the end of July 1943, the Sturmgeschütz-Abteilung fought static battles in the area of Ssumy.

2 FEBRUARY 1943

The commander of the assault artillery unit still on the march received the following orders by telephone from the staff of the *2. Armee:*

The whole company, including Jäger-Bataillon 9, moves back along the railroad southwards to the area of Budanowka. There it joins forces with battalion 'Kursk' and together they hold up the enemy in mobile combat. We observed many enemy tanks. Leave the rear guard in Solotuchino for reconnaissance purposes. The arrival in Budanowka must be reported to here.[827]

4 FEBRUARY 1943

Most of *Sturmgeschütz-Abteilung 202* (that is of the *2.* and the *3. Batterie*) was subordinated to the *4. Panzer-Division* in the sector of the *2. Armee* and became part of the German forces securing Kursk.[828] At that time those elements of the unit had a total of six short-barrelled and four long-barrelled StuG. IIIs operational.

One of the assault gun batteries operating in the sector of the *4. Panzer-Division* together with *Jäger-Bataillon 9*[829] was assigned the task of securing the area of Bol. Shirowka from the direction of Fatesh.[830]

827 NARA T312, R1215 (*Armeeoberkommando 2*), Anlage 91b.

828 NARA T312, R1216 (*Armeeoberkommando 2*), F000101.

829 *Heeresgruppe Mitte* ordered *Jäger-Bataillon 9* and elements of *Sturmgeschütz-Abteilung 202* (probably an assault gun battery) to reinforce the German forces defending the area of Fatesh, to secure the *2. Panzerarmee* link with its right-hand-side neighbour next day, on 5 February.

830 NARA T312, R1216 (*Armeeoberkommando 2*), F000014.

The *Armee* command planned to support the *VII. Armeekorps* (which had been cut off by the Soviet forces) as it broke through towards Tim and the German front line by an attack that included assault guns assigned to a *Kampfgruppe* of the *4. Panzer-Division.* This attack would be launched the following morning from the direction of Kursk, that is to say from the west. The aim was to capture and hold the town with the German troops.[831] Within that operation, the mission of the assault guns (supported by infantry and artillery) was to clear the road to Tim, strengthen the fighting spirit of the German defenders in the town by getting a supply column to the settlement and carrying out minor attacks on the Soviet forces encircling the town. Having carried out their mission, the assault formation was to be withdrawn to the area of Kursk.[832]

6 FEBRUARY 1943

In the morning hours, a *Kampfgruppe* of the *4. Panzer-Division,* which included the assault guns of *Sturmgeschütz-Abteilung 202,* was withdrawn to defend Kursk because the combat mission towards Tim had failed. However, the command of the *2. Armee* had no plans to defend the town with the division that would be surely have been destroyed in the encirclement.[833]

7 FEBRUARY 1943

In the afternoon, the *4. Panzer-Division* received orders by telegram from the headquarters of the *2. Armee* to dispatch a reinforced battalion (*Kradschützen-Bataillon 34* or the *1. Bataillon/ Panzergrenadier-Regiment 12* equipped with APCs, strengthened if possible by a 10 cm field gun battery, tanks or an assault gun battery) on the night of 7/8 of February towards Obojan.[834] In the end, the division sent *Kampfgruppe 'Steuber'* which consisted of an armoured infantry battalion, a light artillery battery, two reconnaissance platoons and a battery of *Sturmgeschütz-Abteilung 202.*[835]

9 FEBRUARY 1943

In the morning, *Kampfgruppe 'Steuber'* arrived in Obojan. *Hauptmann* Steuber was given the task of defending the town with his forces positioned farther on. So far, the *Kampfgruppe* had not made contact with Soviet troops. From midnight, the *Kampfgruppe*, together with other forces of the *4. Panzer-Division*, came under the command of the *XIII. Armeekorps.*[836]

831 NARA T312, R1216 (*Armeeoberkommando 2*), F000013, as well as F000032.

832 NARA T312, R1216 (*Armeeoberkommando 2*), F000033.

833 NARA T312, R1216 (*Armeeoberkommando 2*), F000322.

834 NARA T312, R1216 (*Armeeoberkommando 2*), F000381.

835 NARA T312, R1216 (*Armeeoberkommando 2*), F000600.

836 NARA T312, R1216 (*Armeeoberkommando 2*), F000600, F000609-610, F000643.

The *VII. Armeekorps* requested, besides other materiel, the immediate delivery of the following types of ammunition from the staff of *2. Armee* for the forces defending Obojan:

- 80×7.5 cm HE shells for long-barrelled tank guns
- 20×7.5 cm HEAT shells for long-barrelled tank guns
- 120×7.5 cm HE shells for short-barrelled tank guns
- 40×7.5 cm HEAT shells for short-barrelled tank guns.[837]

Since the German *Kampfgruppe* defending Obojan was supported by one of the batteries of *Sturmgeschütz-Abteilung 202,* the required quantity of ammunition was intended for use by the StuG. IIIs.

10 FEBRUARY 1943

At 2010 hours the *VII. Armeekorps* reported to the staff of the *2. Armee* by telegram, that *Kampfgruppe 'Steuber'* had to get in touch with the staff of the *26. Infanterie-Division,* because it would be attached to that division further on.[838] The *Kampfgruppe* was supposed to carry out an attack with limited aims the next day towards Medwenskoje where it would destroy the Soviet forces found there and reconnoitre the situation as it emerged.[839]

Sturmgeschütz-Abteilung 202[840] took over the two assault guns left by *Sturmgeschütz-Abteilung 190* which had retreated with *Gruppe 'Cramer'* and had been practically destroyed.[841]

11 FEBRUARY 1943

From 0000 hours, *Kampfgruppe 'Steuber'*[842] came under the command of the *VII. Armeekorps.* Its task remained the same: to secure Obojan as an important strongpoint and conduct combat reconnaissance in the area of Korowino, Medwenskoje, Buschmino, Jakowlewka and Marino with the focal point of the attack being the highway between Kursk and Belgorod.[843]

---

837 NARA T312, R1216 (*Armeeoberkommando 2*), F000644.

838 NARA T312, R1216 (*Armeeoberkommando 2*), F000731.

839 NARA T312, R1216 (*Armeeoberkommando 2*), F000734.

840 In one of its reports of that date, the Artillery command of the *2. Armee* (*Arko 308*) only the staff and one battery of *Sturmgeschütz-Abteilung 202* mentioned as subordinated to the *4. Panzer-Division*, its other battery, operating in *Kampfgruppe 'Steuber'* is not. *See* NARA T312, R1216 (*Armeeoberkommando 2*), F000821.

841 NARA T312, R1216 (*Armeeoberkommando 2*), F000819. It is possible, that these assault guns were in *Sturmgeschütz-Abteilung 242* earlier. It might be this unit, that handed them over to *Sturmgeschütz-Abteilung* 190 after 24 January 1943. *See* NARA T312, R1215 (*Armeeoberkommando 2*), *Derzeitige Gliederung des Korps Cramer,* 24. 01. 1943.

842 Besides a battery from *Sturmgeschütz-Abteilung 202,* the battle group comprised the *I.* (armoured infantry) *Bataillon / Panzergrenadier-Regiment 12,* a light field howitzer battery, the reconnaissance armoured car platoons and eight 7.5 cm AT-guns of the 3. company of *Panzerjäger-Abteilung 257. See* NARA T314, R518 (*XIII. Armeekorps*), F000736.

843 NARA T312, R1216 (*Armeeoberkommando 2*), F000723.

On that day *Sturmgeschütz-Abteilung 202* was indirectly informed that, as soon as the tactical situation allowed, they should take over the assault guns of *Sturmgeschütz-Abteilung 190* [844] and all of its other vehicles and equipment and its ammunition assets.[845] At this point in time, the elements of *Sturmgeschütz-Abteilung 202* subordinated to the *4. Panzer-Division* had eight long-barrelled StuG. III assault guns.[846]

12 FEBRUARY 1943

Most of the *Kampfgruppe 'Steuber'* was reassigned to the *4. Panzer-Division* and ordered to be dispatched to that unit the following day. However, the battery of *Sturmgeschütz-Abteilung 202* that had been assigned to the *Kampfgruppe* was to be deployed in the sector of the *XIII. Armeekorps.*[847] The other battery – which was still under the command of the *4. Panzer-Division* – was in urgent need of ammunition.[848]

13 FEBRUARY 1943

The *26. Infanterie-Division* reported three combat-ready StuG. III assault guns subordinated to them.[849] It is possible that these were already part of *Sturmgeschütz-Abteilung 202.* On that day, including these three assault guns, the assault artillery unit possessed a total of 14 StuG. IIIs of which six or seven were combat ready. Meanwhile, in Obojan the remaining assault guns of *Sturmgeschütz-Abteilung 190* [850] awaited further orders.

In the afternoon, the *4. Panzer-Division* received orders from the staff of the *2. Armee* to send the *2. Batterie* and elements of the *3. Batterie/ Sturmgeschütz-Abteilung 202* to the area of Ssudscha following the arrival of the *1. Batterie/ Sturmgeschütz-Abteilung 904* which had been received as a relief.[851] That could have been in relation to the fact that *Kampfgruppe 'Steuber'* also received orders to withdraw the elements of the assault artillery unit attached to them and dispatch them to the area of Bolschoje Ssoldatskoje via Ssudscha by the command of the *XIII. Armeekorps.*[852]

---

844 This time the *Sturmgeschütz-Abteilung 190* had five assault guns attached to *VII. Armeekorps.* See NARA T314, R518 *(XIII. Armeekorps)*, F000736.

845 NARA T312, R1216 (*Armeeoberkommando 2*), F001038.

846 NARA T314, R518 (*XIII. Armeekorps*), F000736.

847 NARA T312, R1216 (*Armeeoberkommando 2*), F000999.

848 NARA T312, R1216 (*Armeeoberkommando 2*), F001032.

849 NARA T312, R1216 (*Armeeoberkommando 2*), F001065.

850 NARA T312, R1216 (*Armeeoberkommando 2*), F001154. According to an inventory, on 12 February 1943. there were a total of three StuG. IIIs in the remnants of *Sturmgeschütz-Abteilungen 190* and *242 subordinated to 26. Infanterie-Division. See* NARA T314, R357 (*VII. Armeekorps*), F001035.

851 NARA T312, R1216 (*Armeeoberkommando 2*), F001093.

852 NARA T312, R1216 (*Armeeoberkommando 2*), F001097.

17 FEBRUARY 1943

In the morning, the *4. Panzer-Division* dispatched the elements of *Sturmgeschütz-Abteilung 202* to the *2. Armee.*[853]

20 FEBRUARY 1943

According to information reported by the *68. Infanterie-Division,* Soviet troops recaptured the railway station at Pssel. Their further advance threatened the highway, which was so important for the Germans, in the area of the Beliza River. To enable them to cover the crossing from south, the *26. Infanterie-Division* sent a platoon from *Radfahr-Abteilung 26* and two StuG. III assault guns of *Sturmgeschütz-Abteilung 202* to the road bridge spanning the Beliza River.[854]

22 FEBRUARY 1943

The *26. Infanterie-Division* was subordinated to the *XIII. Armeekorps* from 2000 hours. The division received orders to dispatch the three assault guns of *Sturmgeschütz-Abteilung 202* operating in its sector to its parent unit in Ssudscha the next day.[855]

25 FEBRUARY 1943

The *2.* and the *3. Batterie*, together with the staff of *Sturmgeschütz-Abteilung 202*, had a total of 15 assault guns. Eight of these StuG. IIIs were operational (including the three under the command of the *57. Infanterie-Division*). Of the combat vehicles in need of repair, four were undergoing (short-term) repairs in Romny while maintenance personnel performed long-term repairs on another three in Konotop.[856]

26 FEBRUARY 1943

Wachtmeister Amling knocked out three Soviet tanks on the 26 February 1943 while subordinated to the *VII. Armeekorps* in the sector of the *75. Infanterie-Division* in the area of Ssimonowka (secured by *Ski-Bataillon 75*). Including these, he had a total of 43 confirmed kills.[857]

1 MARCH 1943

The *2. Batterie*/ *Sturmgeschütz-Abteilung 202* had three short-barrelled and three long-barrelled StuG. IIIs while the *3. Batterie* had one short-barrelled and five long-barrelled assault guns. The staff of the unit possessed an additional long-barrelled

853 NARA T314, R518 (*XIII. Armeekorps*), F000987.

854 NARA T315, R822 (*26. Infanterie-Division*), F001095.

855 NARA T315, R822 (*26. Infanterie-Division*), F001101.

856 NARA T314, R357 (*VII. Armeekorps*), F000968.

857 NARA T314, R357 (*VII. Armeekorps*), F000745.

StuG. III The assault artillery unit had a total of four short-barrelled and nine long-barrelled assault guns plus 15 machine guns.[858]

2 MARCH 1943

The two batteries of *Sturmgeschütz-Abteilung 202* sent a status report to the corps according to which its casualties during February 1943 were: one officer, two NCOs and four enlisted men dead and one officer, two NCOs and nine enlisted men wounded. One NCO became ill. During that period one NCO, seven enlisted men and an eastern European volunteer *(Hiwi)* arrived as replacements. Of their 13 assault guns five had been taken over from *Sturmgeschütz-Abteilung 190,* two from *Sturmgeschütz-Abteilung 667*, two from *Sturmgeschütz-Abteilung 189* and one from *Panzer-Verband 700.* The two batteries were at full strength in terms of personnel but, in view of the equipment and weapons available to them, their combat-readiness was down to 75%. Due to the fact that the staff battery was deployed far from the unit and the lack of a maintenance service and towing section, it is likely that the batteries' maintenance squads had been unable to conduct major repairs and, being without towing capacity, they were unable to recover bogged-down or damaged assault guns. In technical terms, it was mainly the engines of the assault guns that were in poor condition due to lack of maintenance and over-exertion during the course of the withdrawal. It was feared that on a longer march many of the assault guns would become unserviceable. The commander of *Sturmgeschütz-Abteilung 202, Hauptmann* Buhr, made it clear in a clause of his report: '*To achieve good, well-trained, experienced personnel and adequate fleet of vehicles, it would be very advantageous to equip the Abteilung with 22 new assault guns*'. According to the commander's evaluation, under the existing circumstances the assault artillery unit was only fit for carrying out limited offensive tasks.[859]

6 MARCH 1943

At 1825 hours the *VII. Armeekorps* informed the staff of *26. Infanterie-Division* that they would receive three long-barrelled StuG. IIIs the following day at 0500 hours, probably from *Sturmgeschütz-Abteilung 202.* This order might have been in connection with an expected Soviet tank attack in the direction of Sswerlikowschtschina.[860]

7 MARCH 1943

At around 0900 hours, the three long-barrelled assault guns promised by the *VII. Armeekorps* arrived under the command of *Oberleutnant* Hoffmann at the command post of the *26. Infanterie-Division.* From there the StuG. IIIs were sent to the

858 NARA T314, R357 (*VII. Armeekorps*), F000967, F001012.

859 NARA T314, R357 (*VII. Armeekorps*), F000916-917.

860 NARA T315, R822 (*26. Infanterie-Division*), F001139.

command post of *Füsilier-Regiment 39* in the area of Uspenowka, where they were to take up positions of readiness in the sector of the *III. Bataillon* of the regiment.[861]

The fog that had covered the area cleared at the approach of noon allowing the regiments of the *26. Infanterie-Division* to conduct intense reconnaissance to gain detailed information about the disposition of the Soviet tanks that had broken through the previous day prior to launching an attack to destroy them. At 1540 hours the regiments reported that all was quiet in their lines. Following that, the three assault guns received orders to relocate their command post together with the staff of *Füsilier-Regiment 39.*[862]

In the evening the two batteries of *Sturmgeschütz-Abteilung 202* had a total of 13 assault guns, including three short-barrelled and seven long-barrelled ones operational, and one short-barrelled and two long-barrelled StuG. IIIs, undergoing short-term repairs at the maintenance service.[863]

On that day the *2.* and *3. Batterie/ Sturmgeschütz-Abteilung 202* had a combined battle strength of 83 men.[864]

8 MARCH 1943

The *2. Batterie /Sturmgeschütz-Abteilung 202* had three short-barrelled and three long-barrelled assault guns operational while the *3. Batterie* had one short-barrelled and two long-barrelled combat-ready StuG. IIIs. In addition, the staff of the unit also had a combat-ready long-barrelled assault gun. An additional three combat-ready long-barrelled assault guns were stationed in the line of *26. Infanterie-Division.*[865]

10 MARCH 1943

In the sector of the *75. Infanterie-Division*, German grenadiers advancing towards Schablenoje riding on the top of the assault guns of *Sturmgeschütz-Abteilung 202* encountered a Soviet battalion retreating in the direction of Grebinikowka. They shattered the enemy unit. The Soviets lost 190 dead, 31 prisoners, one gun, one anti-tank cannon, one anti-tank rifle and a submachine-gun. The Germans also arrested 30 civilians suspected of being partisans. Two assault guns (one short-barrelled and one long-barrelled) of *Sturmgeschütz-Abteilung 202* were disabled during the fighting.[866]

12 MARCH 1943

In the morning, in the sector of the *26. Infanterie-Division*, Soviet troops launched an attack with the strength of two companies from a forest north-

861 NARA T315, R822 (*26. Infanterie-Division*), F001134-1136.

862 NARA T315, R822 (*26. Infanterie-Division*), F001136.

863 NARA T314, R357 (*VII. Armeekorps*), F000854.

864 Battle strength: nine officers, 25 NCOs, 49 enlisted men. *See* NARA T314, R357 (*VII. Armeekorps*), F001041.

865 NARA T314, R357 (*VII. Armeekorps*), F000957.

866 NARA T314, R357 (*VII. Armeekorps*), F000758.

east of Krassnokoje with the aim of retaking the settlement. The attempt was quickly smashed by the German infantry guns and artillery. *Grenadier-Regiment 78* received orders from the division at 1000 hours to carry out an attack the following day (supported by three assault guns and artillery) with the objective of mopping up the Soviet troops in the forest.[867]

At 1400 hours the regiment reported the plan of the attack which was timed for 0510 hours the next day. According to the plan, three assault groups would launch an attack on the so-called Korenewo forest: one of them south of the road, the second on the road, and the third north of the road. The limited aim of the attack was to occupy the crossing of the forest trail with the road to Korenewo. The three assault guns arrived at around 1600 hours at *Grenadier-Regiment 78* from *Füsilier-Regiment 39.*[868]

13 MARCH 1943

At 0510 hours, following a short artillery preparation, the attack was commenced. The *I. Bataillon /Grenadier-Regiment 78* in three assault groups, with the support of three long-barrelled assault guns of *Sturmgeschütz-Abteilung 202*, sent the Soviet forces fleeing after a short but violent battle. About 60 dead Soviet soldiers were left behind in the forest and the Germans captured significant amounts of weaponry. During the interrogation of Soviet prisoners of war it became clear that elements of the 687 Rifle Regiment of 141 Rifle Division had been driven out of the forest. Following the successful attack, the soldiers of the battalion established two securing positions in the forest and then started to develop them into defensive positions.[869]

On that day the total strength of the unit was 181 men plus six *Hiwi*s, of which 79 men made up the battle strength.[870]

14 MARCH 1943

At 2000 hours the *VII. Armeekorps* issued orders to the staff of the *26. Infanterie-Division* to put the three assault guns of *Sturmgeschütz-Abteilung 202* in the area of Obody (near the divisional command post) on standby for use by the corps staff.[871]

In the evening, of the 13 assault guns in *2. Batterie* and *3. Batterie/Sturmgeschütz-Abteilung 202*, two short-barrelled and seven long-barrelled StuG. IIIs were operational. Three of the long-barrelled StuG. IIIs were under the command of the *26. Infanterie-Division* while one short-barrelled and three long-barrelled StuG.

---

867 NARA T315, R822 (*26. Infanterie-Division*), F001146.

868 NARA T315, R822 (*26. Infanterie-Division*), F001148.

869 NARA T315, R822 (*26. Infanterie-Division*), F001150.

870 Strength: nine officers, an official, 39 NCOs, 132 enlisted men. Battle strength: eight officers, 24 NCOs, 47 enlisted men. Deficiencies: three officers, 10 NCOs, three enlisted men, 14 *Hiwis*. See NARA T314, R357 (*VII. Armeekorps*), F001039.

871 NARA T315, R822 (*26. Infanterie-Division*), F001154.

IIIs were subordinated to the *75. Infanterie-Division* and a long-barrelled StuG. III was stationed in Ssumy.[872]

15 MARCH 1943

At 1845 hours the three assault guns of *Sturmgeschütz-Abteilung 202* arrived at the command post of the *26. Infanterie-Division* in Obody where they remained on standby to support any missions determined by the corps.[873]

20 MARCH 1943

There were four long-barrelled and two short-barrelled assault guns in each of the two batteries of *Sturmgeschütz-Abteilung 202*. Of these, two short-barrelled and six long-barrelled StuG. IIIs were operational.[874] A long-barrelled assault gun (from the command staff) was in Ssumy. In the sector of the *26. Infanterie-Division*, the long-barrelled StuG. IIIs of *3. Batterie* were operating.[875]

21 MARCH 1943

The assault artillery unit had a total of 13 (four short-barrelled and nine long-barrelled) assault guns. Two short-barrelled and two long-barrelled StuG. IIIs were undergoing repairs.[876]

The strength of the assault artillery unit was 208 men and 20 *Hiwis*. The battle strength was 86 men.[877]

25 MARCH 1943

The staff of the *2. Armee* informed the headquarters of the *VII. Armeekorps* that the staff battery and *1. Batterie/ Sturmgeschütz-Abteilung 202* deployed in the sector of the *2. Panzerarmee* would be sent by rail to the *VII. Armeekorps* in the area of Woroshba where they would be subordinated to that corps.[878]

27 MARCH 1943

There were four long-barrelled and two short-barrelled assault guns in each of the two batteries of *Sturmgeschütz-Abteilung 202*. Of these, three short-barrelled and six long barrelled StuG. IIIs were operational.[879] An additional short-barrelled assault gun had been transported to Minsk (probably for overhaul); one long-

---

872 NARA T314, R357 (*VII. Armeekorps*), F000853.

873 NARA T315, R822 (*26. Infanterie-Division*), F001156.

874 NARA T314, R357 (*VII. Armeekorps*), F000851.

875 NARA T314, R357 (*VII. Armeekorps*), F000955.

876 NARA T314, R357 (*VII. Armeekorps*), F000852.

877 Strength: 10 officers, two officials, 41 NCOs, 156 enlisted men. Battle strength: nine officers, 25 NCOs, 52 enlisted men. Deficiencies: three officers, 11 NCOs, four enlisted men. *See* NARA T314, R357 (*VII. Armeekorps*), F001038.

878 NARA T314, R357 (*VII. Armeekorps*), F000860.

879 NARA T314, R357 (*VII. Armeekorps*), F000851.

barrelled StuG. III was in Ssumy. In the sector of *26. Infanterie-Division* two short-barrelled StuG. IIIs and one long-barrelled StuG. III from the assault artillery unit were operating.[880]

The strength of the assault artillery unit was 228 men plus 20 *Hiwis.* The battle strength was made up of 111 men.[881]

28 MARCH 1943

In the morning, the staff battery of the far-off assault artillery unit informed the other two batteries, via the staff of the *VII. Armeekorps,* that they still hadn't received orders to leave the sector of the *2. Panzerarmee* to return to the bulk of their unit. Meanwhile, however, the artillery command of the *2. Armee* instructed the staff of the *2. Panzerarmee* to issue the necessary orders.[882]

29 MARCH 1943

The three assault guns of *Sturmgeschütz-Abteilung 202* operating in the sector of the *26. Infanterie-Division* were ordered back to the area of Ssumy.[883]

30 MARCH 1943

The assault artillery unit was temporarily detached from the *VII. Armeekorps* and put under the direct command of the *2. Armee.*[884]

3 APRIL 1943

The chief of staff of the *2. Armee, Generalleutnant* Gustav Harteneck, visited *Sturmgeschütz-Abteilung 202* in Ssumy.[885]

9 APRIL 1943

At 1150 hours the *VII. Armeekorps* requested the staff of the *2. Armee* by telegram to temporarily attach the commanders of *Sturmgeschütz-Abteilung 202* and *Panzerjäger-Abteilungen 559* and *616* to them to conduct area reconnaissance.[886]

---

880 NARA T314, R357 (*VII. Armeekorps*), F000947.

881 Strength: 10 officers, two officials, 48 NCOs, 168 enlisted men. Battle strength: nine officers, 28 NCOs, 74 enlisted men. Deficiencies: two officers. *See* NARA T314, R357 (*VII. Armeekorps*), F001037.

882 NARA T314, R357 (*VII. Armeekorps*), F000859.

883 NARA T315, R822 (*26. Infanterie-Division*), F001180.

884 NARA T314, R357 (*VII. Armeekorps*), F000778.

885 NARA T314, R357 (*VII. Armeekorps*), F001052. According to certain sources due to the increasing number of partisan attacks the Germans were enforced to employ elements of *Sturmgeschütz-Abteilung 202* for security tasks. Thus some of the assault guns and assault gun platoons participated in some of the anti-partisan actions in the area. See Kurowski, Franz – Tornau, Gottfried: *Sturmgeschütze – Die Panzer der Infanterie.* Würzburg, 2008. p. 109.

886 NARA T314, R357 (*VII. Armeekorps*), F001057.

13 APRIL 1943

At 0835 hours the *75. Infanterie-Division* applied to the corps for one of the batteries of *Sturmgeschütz-Abteilung 202* due to a Soviet penetration. The request was forwarded to the staff of the *2. Armee* which approved the deployment of the assault guns in the area of Bol. Tschernetschina at 0852 hours.[887]At 1550 hours, the division reported that the Soviet penetration near the settlement had been eliminated by a successful counter-thrust.[888]

19 APRIL 1943

At 1530 hours the commander of *Sturmgeschütz-Abteilung 202* arrived at the command post of the *VII. Armeekorps* to discuss the preparations for the proposed attacks (codenamed *'Vitamin A'* and *'Vitamin B'*).[889]

26 APRIL 1943

Sturmgeschütz-Abteilung 202, together with *Panzerjäger-Abteilungen 559* and *616*, received orders by telegram from the corps to survey the line of the *68. Infanterie-Division* in terms of anti-tank defence.[890]

29 APRIL 1943

At 0100 hours the assault guns of the *1. Batterie/ Sturmgeschütz-Abteilung 202* were brought forward in a defile.

At 1300 hours, two companies of the *75. Infanterie-Division* launched an attack to seize Hill 210.6 in the area of Andrejewka with the support of four StuG. III assault guns and an 8.8 cm anti-aircraft artillery battery. The assault guns destroyed the Soviet positions, including three bunkers, using up 100 shells in the process. At around 1500 hours the Germans took the Hill. The Soviet troops suffered significant casualties: 50 dead and 30 prisoners. The Germans lost six wounded. For safety's sake, the assault guns remained in a state of readiness until 2000 hours.[891]

30 APRIL 1943

At 1600 hours orders were received from the staff of the *2. Armee* according to which *Sturmgeschütz-Abteilung 202*, together with *Panzerjäger-Abteilungen 559* and *616*, had again been put under the direct command of the *VII. Armeekorps*.[892]

887 NARA T314, R357 (*VII. Armeekorps*), F001059.

888 NARA T314, R357 (*VII. Armeekorps*), F001060.

889 NARA T314, R357 (*VII. Armeekorps*), F001064.

890 NARA T314, R357 (*VII. Armeekorps*), F001067.

891 NARA T315, R822 (*26. Infanterie-Division*), F001240, as well as *Tagebuchaufzeichnungen vom 2. 12. 1942 bis 1. 2. 1944 von Kamerad Wachtmeister Georg Hiller.* In: *Der Sturmartillerist.* Heft 60. p. 1329.

892 NARA T314, R357 (*VII. Armeekorps*), F001070.

2 MAY 1943

At 2125 hours, the 1 (operations) staff officer of the *26. Infanterie-Division, Major i.G.* Ernst Lassen, discussed the relocation of one battery of *Sturmgeschütz-Abteilung 202* to Grusskij with the equivalent officer of the *VII. Armeekorps, Major i.G.* Kurt von Tarbuk. The regiments of the division were to perform joint exercises to improve the effectiveness of their cooperation with the assault guns. In compliance with that, the corps issued orders at 2330 hours to one of the batteries of the assault artillery unit to relocate to the sector of the division the next day.[893]

3 MAY 1943

At 0650 hours, the commander of *Sturmgeschütz-Abteilung 202, Hauptmann* Buhr, reported to the staff of the *26. Infanterie-Division* that one of his batteries (*3.Batterie*) was stationed in Pawlowka 2 km west of Obody. The division could therefore order that battery to move to the area of Grusskij.[894]

4 MAY 1943

At 1205 hours the commander of the corps had the plan of the anti-tank defences revised, mainly in the area of Andrejewka. The *3. Batterie / Sturmgeschütz-Abteilung 202,* subordinated to the staff of the *26. Infanterie-Division* for the duration of the exercises, was notified that it might be deployed as an anti-tank reserve if required.[895]

6 MAY 1943

At 0845 hours the commander of *3. Batterie/ Sturmgeschütz-Abteilung 202* reported to the command post of the *26. Infanterie-Division.*[896] On that day one of the assault guns of *1. Batterie* was burnt out due to unknown reasons.[897]

At 2150 hours the *2. Armee* issued orders according to which the assault artillery unit was allotted to the army reserve.[898]

7 MAY 1943

At 0930 hours the commander of the assault artillery unit, *Hauptmann* Buhr, arrived at the command post of the *26. Infanterie-Division* to discuss details for the deployment of the assault guns.[899] A few minutes after 1000 hours, the assault

893 NARA T315, R822 (*26. Infanterie-Division*), F001247.

894 NARA T315, R822 (*26. Infanterie-Division*), F001248.

895 NARA T314, R357 (*VII. Armeekorps*), F001072.

896 NARA T315, R822 (*26. Infanterie-Division*), F001254.

897 *Tagebuchaufzeichnungen vom 2. 12. 1942 bis 1. 2. 1944 von Kamerad Wachtmeister Georg Hiller.* In: *Der Sturmartillerist.* Heft 60. p. 1329.

898 NARA T314, R357 (*VII. Armeekorps*), F001073.

899 NARA T315, R822 (*26. Infanterie-Division*), F001256.

artillery unit was informed by telegram that they would be detached from the *VII. Armeekorps* and assigned to the army reserve.[900]

9 MAY 1943

Early in the evening, *Sturmgeschütz-Abteilung 202* received orders to prepare for combat (without the battery already subordinated to the *26. Infanterie-Division*) against enemy armour in the sector of the *75. Infanterie-Division* and to provide support for German counter-thrusts.[901]

13 MAY 1943

The *3. Batterie / Sturmgeschütz-Abteilung 202* participated in exercises conducted by a battalion of *Füsilier-Regiment 39* to improve their cooperation with the infantry.[902]

16 MAY 1943

The *2. Armee* issued orders by telegram to *Sturmgeschütz-Abteilung 202* and *Panzerjäger-Abteilungen 559* and *616* to prepare for carrying out quick missions against Soviet armour on the whole of the front line of the *Armee*. For that reason, reconnaissance squads were sent out.[903]

17 MAY 1943

To discuss the details of missions conducted against Soviet tanks, the commander of the assault artillery unit was summoned to appear at the command post of the *VII. Armeekorps* at 1300 hours. There they also decided to survey, designate and re-establish a so-called *Panzer-Rollbahn* (freeway for armour). Two days later the relevant orders were issued.[904]

18 MAY 1943

At 1700 hours one battery of *Sturmgeschütz-Abteilung 202* was subordinated to the *75. Infanterie-Division* for training purposes.[905]

20 MAY 1943

At 1115 hours the corps expressed its opinion by telegram regarding the request from the staff of *26. Infanterie-Division* to receive assault guns for training purposes.[906]

900 NARA T314, R357 (*VII. Armeekorps*), F001074.
901 NARA T314, R357 (*VII. Armeekorps*), F001075.
902 NARA T315, R822 (*26. Infanterie-Division*), F001264.
903 NARA T314, R357 (*VII. Armeekorps*), F001078.
904 NARA T314, R357 (*VII. Armeekorps*), F001081.
905 NARA T314, R357 (*VII. Armeekorps*), F001080.
906 NARA T314, R357 (*VII. Armeekorps*), F001081.

22 MAY 1943

At 1120 hours, the commander of *Sturmgeschütz-Abteilung 202* began a lecture to the staff of the *26. Infanterie-Division* about the possibility of conducting missions by assault guns in the sector of the division.[907]

23 MAY 1943

From 1040 hours the commander of *Panzerjäger-Abteilung 26* informed the 1 (operations) staff officer of the division at the command post of the *26. Infanterie-Division* about the anti-tank plan of fire and the anti-tank reserves available in Ssumy. According to his report the division had a battalion of anti-aircraft artillery (with three heavy and five light batteries) and 32 combat-ready assault guns from *Sturmgeschütz-Abteilung 202* as an anti-tank reserve.[908]

25 MAY 1943

The battery from *Sturmgeschütz-Abteilung 202* that had been promised to the staff of the *75. Infanterie-Division* for training purposes could not be dispatched due to restrictions imposed by waterlogged the roads.[909]

26 MAY 1943

Once more, the *75. Infanterie-Division* requested the use of a battery of *Sturmgeschütz-Abteilung 202* for their training programme, asking the corps to put the battery under their command from the following day until the 5 June 1943.[910]

27 MAY 1943

At1100 hours, the *1. Batterie / Sturmgeschütz-Abteilung 202* set off towards Obottowin where it participated in an anti-tank training course. Two assault guns were ordered to a similar course run by the *88. Infanterie-Division* as demonstration aids.[911]

4 JUNE 1943

In the morning, the *75. Infanterie-Division* requested that the corps should extend the subordination of the assault gun battery to them until 6 June. The *VII. Armeekorps* complied with the division's request.[912]

---

907 NARA T315, R822 (*26. Infanterie-Division*), F001274.

908 NARA T315, R822 (*26. Infanterie-Division*), F001276.

909 NARA T314, R357 (*VII. Armeekorps*), F001084.

910 NARA T314, R357 (*VII. Armeekorps*), F001086.

911 *Tagebuchaufzeichnungen vom 2. 12. 1942 bis 1. 2. 1944 von Kamerad Wachtmeister Georg Hiller.* In: *Der Sturmartillerist.* Heft 60. p. 1329.

912 NARA T314, R357 (*VII. Armeekorps*), F001094.

6 JUNE 1943

The *68. Infanterie-Division* called upon the corps to provide *Sturmgeschütz-Abteilung 202's* towing vehicle to carry out a recovery operation; for training purposes the division wanted to haul away a disabled Soviet T–34 tank left behind in the area of Meshiritschi.[913]

21 JUNE 1943

The corps took measures to attach a battery of *Sturmgeschütz-Abteilung 202* to the *88. Infanterie-Division* for training purposes and in preparation for the attack codenamed *'Vitamin B'*. The battery would be dispatched on the 23 June to Grusskij.[914]

22 JUNE 1943

The *VII. Armeekorps* issued orders about the concept of an attack codenamed *'Vitamin B'*. The aim of the German corps was to break through the Soviet defences with the forces of the *75., 26.,* and *88. Infanterie-Divisionen* in the sector between Choten and Kondratjewka before destroying the Soviet forces in the area of Ssudscha. The more imminent aim of the attack was to establish a bridgehead across the Loknja River, north of Junakowka. *Sturmgeschütz-Abteilung 202,* subordinated to the *26. Infanterie-Division*, would be assembled in the area of Kekino and Grusskij six days before the scheduled attack.[915] In support of the attack, area reconnaissance was to be conducted as if only a mission of local significance (to straighten the main combat line) was to be carried out by a battalion-strength force supported by assault guns and self-propelled anti-tank guns. Commanders of the assault artillery unit and *Panzerjäger-Abteilung 616* were to be informed that the tasks to be carried out in the sector of the *68.* and *88. Infanterie-Divisionen* were intended to deceive the Soviets.[916]

The real task of *Sturmgeschütz-Abteilung 202* was to eliminate the Soviet trench system south of Alexejewka in cooperation with the infantry of the *26. Infanterie-Division* in an attack in a south-easterly direction and then occupy the area of Hill 221.7.[917] The attack was scheduled for the 1 August 1943.[918]

23 JUNE 1943

The 1 (operations) staff officer of the corps, *Major i.G.* Wolfgang Oldenburg, informed the staff of the *75. Infanterie-Division* that one of the batteries of

913 NARA T314, R357 (*VII. Armeekorps*), F001096.
914 NARA T314, R357 (*VII. Armeekorps*), F001108.
915 NARA T314, R362 (*VII. Armeekorps*), F000499-500.
916 NARA T314, R362 (*VII. Armeekorps*), F000505.
917 NARA T314, R362 (*VII. Armeekorps*), F000507.
918 NARA T314, R362 (*VII. Armeekorps*), F000514.

Sturmgeschütz-Abteilung 202 would be transferred to Grusskij and requested that the unit should be connected to the division's telephone network.[919]

25 JUNE 1943

Major i.G. Oldenburg had a meeting with the commanders of *Sturmgeschütz-Abteilung 202* and *Panzerjäger-Abteilung 616.* The reason for this was that the anti-tank obstacle system being constructed in the sector of the corps prevented the deployment of the two units according to the planned schedule. Thus, the two commanders had to survey the terrain between Choten and Konstantinowka again to select an alternative route of attack. The task was not to be carried out while wearing their own uniforms in an attempt to conceal their real intentions from the Soviets.[920]

30 JUNE 1943

At 2220 hours the commander of the *2. Batterie/ Sturmgeschütz-Abteilung 202* arrived at the command post of the *88. Infanterie-Division.* There he received orders to move his StuG. IIIs to the sector of *Grenadier-Regiment 246* between 1 and 5 July 1943, a move intended to make the Soviet reconnaissance believe that there was an armoured concentration there.[921] That action was taken to support the imminent German attack that was to be launched towards Kursk.

8 JULY 1943

The previously issued corps orders, including the plans of the attack codenamed *'Vitamin B'* were complemented by further means; besides others, the forces of the *327. Infanterie-Division* were to launch a deceptive attack in the general direction of Wiktorowka. To carry out the task, *Sturmgeschütz-Abteilung 202* and a part of *Panzerjäger-Abteilung 559* would be attached to the division.[922]

14 JULY 1943

There were seven short-barrelled and 24 long-barrelled combat-ready StuG. IIIs in *Sturmgeschütz-Abteilung 202.* Besides the assault guns, there were 40 anti-tank guns and a captured T–34 tank subordinated to the *VII. Armeekorps.*[923]

17 JULY 1943

The *VII. Armeekorps* issued new orders to outline the slightly revised plan for *'Vitamin B'* according to which *Sturmgeschütz-Abteilung 202* would support the forces of

---

919 NARA T314, R357 (*VII. Armeekorps*), F001110.

920 NARA T314, R357 (*VII. Armeekorps*), F001112.

921 NARA T315, R1154 (*88. Infanterie-Division*), F001429.

922 NARA T314, R362 (*VII. Armeekorps*), F000538.

923 NARA T314, R362 (*VII. Armeekorps*), F000700.

the *75. Infanterie-Division* along the road between Pissarewka and Junakowka, and north of it.[924]

31 JULY 1943

Of the assault guns of *Sturmgeschütz-Abteilung 202*, seven short-barrelled and 23 long-barrelled StuG. IIIs were operational.[925]

924 NARA T314, R362 (*VII. Armeekorps*), F000544.

925 NARA T314, R362 (*VII. Armeekorps*), F000718.

PART II

IN *HEERESGRUPPE SÜD*

CHAPTER 5

In the sector of the German *4. Panzerarmee* from Ssumy to the Dnieper river

1943

Operational background:

Sturmgeschütz-Abteilung 202, subordinated to 4. Panzerarmee, retreated from the area of Ssumy through the region of Kiev to Zhitomir while supporting the forces of the VII. Armeekorps during continuous counter-thrusts.

4 AUGUST 1943

At 1200 hours, the staff of the *4. Panzerarmee* assumed command of the sector of the *VII. Armeekorps.*[926]

In the evening of that day *Sturmgeschütz-Abteilung 202* had seven short-barrelled and 24 long-barrelled assault guns. The other 'armoured' unit of the corps, *Panzerjäger-Abteilung 616* possessed 17 combat-ready, self-propelled anti-tank guns.[927]

7 AUGUST 1943

One of the batteries of *Sturmgeschütz-Abteilung 202* was ordered to the area of Nish. Ssyrowatka.[928]

926 NARA T313, R379 (*Panzerarmeeoberkommando 4*), F8667451.

927 NARA T313, R379 (*Panzerarmeeoberkommando 4*), F8667455.

928 NARA T314, R362 (*VII. Armeekorps*), F000726.

10 AUGUST 1943

By now the whole of *Sturmgeschütz-Abteilung 202* was stationed in Nish. Ssyrowatka. The assault artillery unit had five short-barrelled and 25 long-barrelled StuG. IIIs operational.[929]

11 AUGUST 1943

Most of *Sturmgeschütz-Abteilung 202* (except for the battery deployed in the sector of the *68. Infanterie-Division*) was dispatched to the area of Mal. Wistery.[930] This also meant that the two batteries came under the command of the *XXXXVIII. Panzerkorps.*[931]

12 AUGUST 1943

At 0445 hours one of the batteries of *Sturmgeschütz-Abteilung 202* launched an attack with elements of the *7. Panzer-Division* in the sector of the *XXXXVIII. Panzerkorps* to retake the ravine and Point 180 in the area of Perwomaiskij. The Soviet troops put up fierce resistance. Despite this, the Germans managed to push them back to the eastern bank of the Boromlja River at around 1300 hours. Both sides suffered heavy losses during the fighting. Following this, the elements of *Sturmgeschütz-Abteilung 202* were reattached to the *VII. Armeekorps.*[932]

13 AUGUST 1943

At 0830 hours the *1. Batterie / Sturmgeschütz-Abteilung 202* carried out an attack under heavy artillery fire in the area of Werch-Ssyrowatka and lost two artillery guns during the fighting. One of them was *Wachtmeister* Stelzer's StuG. III which, having broken into their front line, was knocked out by the Soviets. The commander of the assault gun was killed and the other three crew members seriously wounded.[933]

14 AUGUST 1943

The *VII. Armeekorps* intended to launch an attack northwards in the sector of the *68. Infanterie-Division* (from the area of Gaponowka and Bratzkij) to eliminate a penetration by Soviet troops[934] with the assault guns of *Sturmgeschütz-Abteilung 202* and the self-propelled, anti-tank guns of *Panzerjäger-Abteilung 616.*[935]

929 NARA T313, R379 (*Panzerarmeeoberkommando 4*), F8667534.

930 NARA T314, R362 (*VII. Armeekorps*), F000730.

931 NARA T313, R379 (*Panzerarmeeoberkommando 4*), F8667555.

932 NARA T313, R379 (*Panzerarmeeoberkommando 4*), F8667568.

933 *Tagebuchaufzeichnungen vom 2. 12. 1942 bis 1. 2. 1944 von Kamerad Wachtmeister Georg Hiller.* In: *Der Sturmartillerist.* Heft 60. p. 1330.

934 The German intelligence – on the basis of, among others, captured documents – identified the 178 Tank Brigade and the 11 Motorized Rifle Brigade of the Soviet 10 Tank Corps. *See* NARA T313, R379 (*Panzerarmeeoberkommando 4*), F8667575.

935 NARA T314, R362 (*VII. Armeekorps*), F000736.

A battery from the assault artillery unit and an under-strength German battalion carried out a counter-thrust in the area of Gaponowka but ran into strong resistance by Soviet troops. Six Soviet AFVs were identified in the forest south of the settlement.[936]

The assault artillery unit destroyed a total of six tanks, 25 anti-tank guns, 23 machine guns, 11 artillery pieces, 20 trucks, two towing vehicles, 20 other vehicles and many mortars in the fighting between 12 and 14 August 1943.[937]

15 AUGUST 1943

The Germans knocked out four Soviet armoured fighting vehicles in the sector of the *68. Infanterie-Division,* in the area of Bratzkij.[938]

An assault gun from the *1. Batterie /Sturmgeschütz-Abteilung 202* ran out of ammunition and stopped 200 m before the German's own lines due to engine failure. Later it was successfully pulled into a narrow valley and from there a recovery vehicle towed it to the maintenance workshop after nightfall. The next day the assault gun was fitted with a new engine.[939]

At 2315 hours the two batteries of *Sturmgeschütz-Abteilung 202* together with the *II. Bataillon / Grenadier-Regiment 246* launched an attack in the southern sector of the *68. Infanterie-Division* to mop up the Soviet remnants in the forest in the area of Distr. Kerosinschtschina. However, the Germans only completed the task the following day.[940]

17 AUGUST 1943

According to the report of the *VII. Armeekorps,* submitted at 0600 hours, Soviet troops advanced with two tank corps and a total of four rifle divisions on the right flank of the German *68. Infanterie-Division* from the area of Schablenoje in a south-easterly direction towards Nish. Ssyrowatka.

The battered German grenadiers retreated behind the railway embankment south-east of Nish. Ssyrowatka from the attacking Soviet tanks and rifle troops. The *1.* and *3. Batterie/Sturmgeschütz-Abteilung 202* covered their withdrawal. The assault guns suffered significant losses: both assault gun commanders were rendered unfit for combat.[941]

---

936 NARA T313, R379 (*Panzerarmeeoberkommando 4*), F8667588.

937 NARA T314, R362 (*VII. Armeekorps*), F000737.

938 NARA T313, R379 (*Panzerarmeeoberkommando 4*), F8667598. Unfortunately there is no definite information as to the unit that knocked them out, but the battery of *Sturmgeschütz-Abteilung 202* fighting here was probably participated in repulsing the attack.

939 *Tagebuchaufzeichnungen vom 2. 12. 1942 bis 1. 2. 1944 von Kamerad Wachtmeister Georg Hiller.* In: *Der Sturmartillerist.* Heft 60. p. 1330.

940 NARA T314, R362 (*VII. Armeekorps*), F000739.

941 Scherzer, Veit – Farwick, Werner: *Die Ritterkreuzträger der Sturmartillerie 1939-45.* Band 1: A-Krafft. Jena, 2010. p. 119.

When part of the Soviet forces crossed the railway embankment in a westerly direction, the *VII. Armeekorps* deployed a reserve battalion and the assault guns of *Sturmgeschütz-Abteilung 202* to block their advance.[942]

At 0915 the corps reported that Hill 197.4 had been occupied by Soviet troops. A German battalion with a battery of *Sturmgeschütz-Abteilung 202* also launched a counter-thrust there.[943]

In the afternoon, Soviet troops reached Nish. Ssyrowatka. At this moment, *Major* Martin Buhr, the commander of the assault artillery unit, appeared on the scene. Having assumed command of his two assault gun batteries in combat, he launched a counter-thrust on his own initiative without the support of accompanying infantry. The assault guns dashed towards the Soviets, firing with all of their weapons. Unexpectedly, they ran into one of the assembly areas of Soviet armour. The assault guns shattered it and the Soviet attack ground to a halt. Having completed their task, the StuG. IIIs were called to the settlement's railway station at the southern corner of the embankment.[944]

The Germans brought the Soviet attack to a halt on the southern and eastern outskirts of Nish. Ssyrowatka only in the late afternoon. Seventy-nine knocked-out Soviet tanks were reported.[945] These knock-outs were distributed among the following units:

- *Sturmgeschütz-Abteilung 202:* 28 AFVs;
- *Panzerjäger-Abteilung 616:* 16 AFVs;
- *Panzerjäger-Abteilung 168:* eight AFVs;
- *schwere Flak-Abteilung 231:* 13 AFVs;
- artillery of the *68. Infanterie-Division:* 12 AFVs;
- anti-tank mines: 2 AFVs.[946]

The assault gun of the *2. Batterie/ Sturmgeschütz-Abteilung 202* named '*Adler*' (Eagle) disabled a T–34 tank of the 26 Tank Brigade of the 2 Tank Corps by practically running it down in a close-quarters combat in the area of Nish. Ssyrowatka.[947]

The Soviets also reached Nish. Ssyrowatka railway station in the afternoon and so fighting continued with the Soviet AFVs into the evening.

The assault guns of *1.* and *3. Batterie/Sturmgeschütz-Abteilung 202,* closing at high speed near the embankment, launched an attack and repelled the Soviet forces from the railway station. Soon afterwards, Soviet troops commenced another attack on

942 NARA T313, R372 (*Panzerarmeeoberkommando 4*), F8658906.

943 NARA T313, R372 (*Panzerarmeeoberkommando 4*), F8658906.

944 Scherzer, Veit – Farwick, Werner: *Die Ritterkreuzträger der Sturmartillerie 1939-45.* Band 1: A-Krafft. Jena, 2010. 120. o.

945 NARA T314, R362 (*VII. Armeekorps*), F000741,

946 NARA T313, R379 (*Panzerarmeeoberkommando 4*), F8667646.

947 *Tagebuchaufzeichnungen vom 2. 12. 1942 bis 1. 2. 1944 von Kamerad Wachtmeister Georg Hiller.* In: *Der Sturmartillerist.* Heft 60. 1330. o.

Nish. Ssyrowatka and recaptured the railway station. *Major* Buhr made rapid progress northwards along the embankment with the three assault guns still operational. They ran into a Soviet tank group and knocked out four of them but during the skirmish an assault gun was hit and disabled. The Soviet attack halted. At that time, *Major* Buhr's driver reported a fault in the clutch of their assault vehicle which made it no longer fit for combat. Under enemy fire, the commander took over the last combat-ready assault gun and continued fighting. Finally, the German infantry received orders to withdraw. The commander of *Sturmgeschütz-Abteilung 202* was given the task of covering the evacuation of the German positions with his only StuG. III – a task that was successfully completed. In the day's fighting, *Major* Buhr knocked out 14 Soviet tanks with his assault guns.[948] Including these, the Germans knocked out an additional 22 Soviet tanks in the sector of the *68. Infanterie-Division* (another 20 by the assault guns of *Sturmgeschütz-Abteilung 202*).[949]

Thus, on 17 August 1943, a total of 48 knock-outs were confirmed for *Sturmgeschütz-Abteilung 202.* In recognition of his achievements that day, *Major* Buhr [950] was awarded the Knight's Cross of the Iron Cross.

18 AUGUST 1943

In the evening *Sturmgeschütz-Abteilung 202* had only 13 combat-ready StuG. IIIs.[951]

26 AUGUST 1943

There were 20 assault guns operational in *Sturmgeschütz-Abteilung 202.*[952]

3 SEPTEMBER 1943

One of the batteries of *Sturmgeschütz-Abteilung 202* and a battalion of the *75. Infanterie-Division* were dispatched into the area of Buryn.[953] At the same time it was planned at the corps level to subordinate two-thirds of the assault artillery unit to the *88. Infanterie-Division.*[954]

948 Scherzer, Veit - Farwick, Werner: *Die Ritterkreuzträger der Sturmartillerie 1939-45.* Band 1: A-Krafft. Jena, 2010. 120. o. Including this, a total of 29 knocked out AFVs were confirmed for him.

949 NARA T314, R362 (*VII. Armeekorps*), F000743.

950 Buhr was born in April 1913 in Marienhafe bei Norden. He joined the *5. Artillerie-Regiment* in Fulda in April 1934. Having served in several artillery and artillery observer units, he was retrained as an assault artilleryman in Jüterbog in December 1941. Between February and April 1942 he was the acting commander of *Sturmgeschütz-Abteilung 428* as a captain. He was assigned to the *2. Batterie/Sturmgeschütz-Abteilung 202* in 22 May 1942, then he joined the staff battery in mid-November. He was assigned as the commander of *Sturmgeschütz-Abteilung 202* on 15 March 1943. He was promoted to *Major* on 1 May 1943. He was transferred to *Sturmgeschütz-Ersatz-Abteilung 500* on 5 September 1943, and was assigned as the commander of it. He underwent a regimental commander's training course in mid-December 1944, and fought as the commander of *Panzerartillerie-Regiment Müncheberg* from 6 March 1945. He served in the *Bundeswehr* from 1955 to 1971. He died in Karlstadt in August 1988. *See* Scherzer, Veit - Farwick, Werner: *Die Ritterkreuzträger der Sturmartillerie 1939-45.* Band 1: A-Krafft. Jena, 2010. pp. 117-120.

951 NARA T314, R362 (*VII. Armeekorps*), F000743.

952 NARA T313, R379 (*Panzerarmeeoberkommando 4*), F8667741.

953 NARA T314, R362 (*VII. Armeekorps*), F000759.

954 NARA T314, R362 (*VII. Armeekorps*), F000760.

4 SEPTEMBER 1943

In the morning, a battery of *Sturmgeschütz-Abteilung 202* together with 250 soldiers of *Grenadier-Regiment 196* moved in the direction of Grun but the rainy weather hindered their march.[955]

6 SEPTEMBER 1943

In the sector of the *88. Infanterie-Division* a German attack was launched at 1230 hours. It quickly reached the zone between the south-eastern foreground of Gaj. Wasiljewka and Hill 170.1. However the attack was brought to a halt by the fierce resistance of the Soviets and their own lack of air support.[956] It is likely that the newly appointed commander of *Sturmgeschütz-Abteilung 202, Hauptmann* Vollrad Kutscher, was killed during the attack on Wasiljewka having been shot in the head[957] (probably by a Soviet sniper) while in his assault gun. The officer had been in command for just a single day.[958]

At 2100 hours the *2. Batterie / Sturmgeschütz-Abteilung 202* set off from the area of Tschernetsche towards Bischewka. The *1.* and *3. Batterien* were to march to the area of Nedrigailoff in the sector of *68. Infanterie-Division* the next day, moving out at 0400 hours.[959]

7 SEPTEMBER 1943

In the evening, *Sturmgeschütz-Abteilung 202* had 11 combat-ready StuG. III assault guns.[960]

8 SEPTEMBER 1943

The supply column of the *1. Batterie/ Sturmgeschütz-Abteilung 202* was attacked by Soviet partisans 13 km east of Pryluki. They also had anti-tank guns. During the raid a German ammunition truck exploded and the battery's office car was captured by the Soviets. The German unit lost one dead and three wounded.[961]

---

955 NARA T314, R362 (*VII. Armeekorps*), F000761.

956 NARA T314, R362 (*VII. Armeekorps*), F000765.

957 *Tagebuchaufzeichnungen vom 2. 12. 1942 bis 1. 2. 1944 von Kamerad Wachtmeister Georg Hiller.* In: *Der Sturmartillerist.* Heft 60. p. 1331. For the place and date of the casualty *See*: http://www.volksbund.de/index.php?id=1775&tx_igverlustsuche_pi2[gid]=e638a9038a5189f0fd120275f1b1f7a9 (Visited: 22 March 2015.)

958 Due to the death of the captain, *Major* Buhr returned, to reassume command of *Sturmgeschütz-Abteilung 202. See Tagebuchaufzeichnungen vom 2. 12. 1942 bis 1. 2. 1944 von Kamerad Wachtmeister Georg Hiller.* In: *Der Sturmartillerist.* Heft 60. p. 1331.

959 NARA T314, R362 (*VII. Armeekorps*), F000061.

960 NARA T314, R362 (*VII. Armeekorps*), F000768.

961 *Tagebuchaufzeichnungen vom 2. 12. 1942 bis 1. 2. 1944 von Kamerad Wachtmeister Georg Hiller.* In: *Der Sturmartillerist.* Heft 60. p. 1331.

9 SEPTEMBER 1943

In the morning, *Sturmgeschütz-Abteilung 202* moved to the area of Jurjewka. The assault artillery unit launched an attack from the area of this settlement in a southerly direction during the day which, with the support of dive-bombers, significantly improved the situation of the grenadiers of the *75. Infanterie-Division* who had been engaged in a fierce battle.[962]

10 SEPTEMBER 1943

At 0400 hours, *Sturmgeschütz-Abteilung 202* launched an attack with the last reserves of the *75. Infanterie-Division* from the south-east, from Kartawyj, to push back the Soviet forces that had penetrated between Kusirew and Wladimirowka. The attack was successful and the Germans reached their former main combat line. Of the seven Soviet armoured fighting vehicles carrying rifle infantry on top of them during the attack, four were knocked out by the aircraft of the German *Luftwaffe*. The remainder were engaged by the StuG. IIIs of *Sturmgeschütz-Abteilung 202.*[963]

11 SEPTEMBER 1943

In its daily report, the *VII. Armeekorps* announced that *Sturmgeschütz-Abteilung 202* had run out of ammunition.[964]

12 SEPTEMBER 1943

A group of Soviet tanks moving alongside the Ssula River, having noticed the assault guns of *Sturmgeschütz-Abteilung 202,* decided to get out of their way.[965]

According to a corps order issued that day, *Sturmgeschütz-Abteilung 202* was at the disposal of the *VII. Armeekorps,* and had assembled in the area of Dolgopolowka.[966]

In the evening, the blocking force *(Sperrverband)* of *Oberstleutnant* Heinz Schlegel was set up and assigned task of blocking the crossings on the Ssula between Lochwiza and Perchopowka. The *1. Batterie/ Sturmgeschütz-Abteilung* was also assigned to this mission.[967]

13 SEPTEMBER 1943

In the morning the *3. Batterie/ Sturmgeschütz-Abteilung 202*[968], subordinated to *Sperrverband* Schlegel, together with the forces of *Pionier-Regimentsstab 685* and *Pionier-Bataillon 215*, advanced from the area of Jarmolinzy southwards to block

962 NARA T314, R362 (*VII. Armeekorps*), F000770.

963 NARA T314, R362 (*VII. Armeekorps*), F000772-773.

964 NARA T314, R362 (*VII. Armeekorps*), F000775.

965 NARA T313, R372 (*Panzerarmeeoberkommando 4*), F8659816.

966 NARA T314, R362 (*VII. Armeekorps*), F000123.

967 NARA T314, R362 (*VII. Armeekorps*), F000139.

968 Unfortunately no information has been found in the documents of the *VII. Armeekorps* about when and why was the *3. Batterie* subordinated to *Sperrverband 'Schlegel'* instead of the *1. Batterie.*

the route of the Soviet troops and cover the withdrawal of the corps to a new main combat line.[969]

14 SEPTEMBER 1943

The *VII. Armeekorps* issued orders concerning further battle plans. *Sperrverband* Schlegel (including the *3. Batterie/ Sturmgeschütz-Abteilung 202*) and *Aufklärungs-Abteilung 175* were to block, and if possible, push back the advancing Soviet troops in the area of Tscheberjaki. These forces were attached to the *82. Infanterie-Division* from 1800 hours that day, but they were to be withdrawn on the 15 September. However, most of the assault artillery unit was ordered to the area of Loknja where they were to be deployed in the focal point while subordinated to the *75. Infanterie-Division.* The *3. Batterie* was also to join the others as soon as possible.[970]

17 SEPTEMBER 1943

At 1024 hours the *82. Infanterie-Division* reported to the staff of the *VII. Armeekorps* that six Soviet tanks had broken through its main combat line at around 0730 hours (while it was still under construction) south of Totschenowschtschina. As consequence of this, the assault guns of *Sturmgeschütz-Abteilung 202* and the self-propelled, anti-tank guns of *Panzerjäger-Abteilung 616* had to hold the narrowed bridgehead in the area of Degtjary and Menjailowka until the retreating German troops had crossed to the western bank.[971]

At 1125 hours, having calmed down, the *82. Infanterie-Division* reported to the staff of the *VII. Armeekorps* that the assault guns had already knocked out six Soviet tanks.[972]

Most of *Sturmgeschütz-Abteilung 202* remained attached to the *75. Infanterie-Division* during that time.[973]

22 SEPTEMBER 1943

The *VII. Armeekorps* issued orders to defend the bridgehead in the area of Kiev. In relation to this, *Sturmgeschütz-Abteilung 202* was ordered to move into the area of Staraja Darniza on the morning of 24 September.[974]

25 SEPTEMBER 1943

The corps issued additional orders in the event of the need to evacuate the Kiev bridgehead, codenamed '*Heinrich III*'. In theory, only Adolf Hitler himself

969 NARA T314, R362 (*VII. Armeekorps*), F000778.
970 NARA T314, R362 (*VII. Armeekorps*), F000155.
971 NARA T314, R362 (*VII. Armeekorps*), F000214.
972 NARA T314, R362 (*VII. Armeekorps*), F000216.
973 NARA T314, R362 (*VII. Armeekorps*), F000218.
974 NARA T314, R362 (*VII. Armeekorps*), F000328.

could have ordered such a withdrawal. Were this to happen, the assault guns of *Sturmgeschütz-Abteilung 202* would be withdrawn to the west bank of the Dnieper. Following that, the assault artillery unit would be at disposal of the *VII. Armeekorps* in Protassoff. *Panzerjäger-Abteilung 616* and *Panzerjäger-Abteilung 731* were to proceed to Ssolomenka with their self-propelled anti-tank guns and each of the three units would send a liaison officer to the advanced corps command post.[975]

26 SEPTEMBER 1943

The *VII. Armeekorps* issued orders regarding the defence of the Kiev bridgehead. The bridgehead was defended by four divisions. The forces of *Sturmgeschütz-Abteilung 202* and the two *Panzerjäger-Abteilungen* in the corps reserve would be withdrawn behind the Dnieper after the evacuation had begun. Afterwards, the assault artillery unit would have prepared in the south-western part of Kiev to provide support for the four divisions defending the western bank of the river. Their deployment would be in the following order: firstly in the sector of the *76. Infanterie-Division* then in the sectors of the *68., 291.*, and, finally, in the zone of the *88. Infanterie-Division.*[976]

27 SEPTEMBER 1943

At 0400 hours, elements of *Sturmgeschütz-Abteilung 202* advanced to within 500 m of the Soviet perimeter. The StuG. III assault guns took up ambush positions to await the attack of reported Soviet tanks but they failed to appear. Meanwhile, the crew of one of the assault guns of the *1. Batterie* turned on music while artillery shells whistled over their heads.[977]

28 SEPTEMBER 1943

By morning, the Germans had evacuated the Kiev bridgehead – all troops and weaponry had been transferred to the west bank of the river. The last bridges over the Dnieper were blown up by the Germans at 0738 hours.[978]

12 OCTOBER 1943

One-and-a-half kilometres west of Ljutesh, the assault gun with chassis number '95015' (the combat vehicle '*Alligator*' of *Oberwachtmeister* Schramm) was set on fire by a Soviet artillery hit to its engine compartment. It exploded. One kilometre north-west of Ljutesh, the left-side track of the assault gun with chassis number

975 NARA T314, R362 (*VII. Armeekorps*), F000367.

976 NARA T314, R362 (*VII. Armeekorps*), F000477.

977 *Tagebuchaufzeichnungen vom 2. 12. 1942 bis 1. 2. 1944 von Kamerad Wachtmeister Georg Hiller.* In: *Der Sturmartillerist.* Heft 60. p. 1331.

978 NARA T313, R379 (*Panzerarmeeoberkommando 4*), F8668155.

'90866' was damaged and, since it was irreparable, it was blown up to prevent it being captured by the Soviets.[979]

An NCO from the *1. Batterie/ Sturmgeschütz-Abteilung 202* gave an account of the day's fighting in his diary:

At 5 o'clock in the morning we move to the command post of Infanterie-Regiment 188 [980] *and are given the task of removing the obstacles from the path of the attacking infantry. Our platoon leader, Oberwachtmeister Schramm, advanced ahead of us. The whole engagement took place in a forest under heavy artillery fire. A direct hit on the 'Alligator', the assault gun of Oberwachtmeister Schramm, set it on fire and it then it blew up. The crew managed to get out. I see* [Gefreiter] *Martin Heck fighting for his life; he must have got stuck. He was burning like a torch but unfortunately no one could help him. All of the crew members suffered severe burns. We fought on and repelled the enemy. We secured against armour by night.*[981]

13 OCTOBER 1943

At 0500 hours the assault guns of *Sturmgeschütz-Abteilung 202* took up ambush positions having received reports of approaching Soviet tanks. However, the Soviet troops launched their attack at around 0900 hours. According to the diary of the NCO from the *1. Batterie*:

The Russian attacks at 9 o'clock, and we have to set our shoulder to the wheel to remain in control of the situation. We inflicted heavy casualties on them. At 10 o'clock tanks are coming, seven in number. I knocked out the first one in no time, upon that the others abruptly swung right before the barrel of Wachtmeister Türgst's assault gun, who knocked out four of them. We received a hit from the tank I had knocked out before – on our rear, above the fuel tank. Shaking our heads, we were overjoyed at our good luck.[982]

14 OCTOBER 1943

The StuG. III with chassis number '95637' struck two mines south of Ljutesh. A track was damaged and so too were the driving wheel and two idler wheels. The assault gun was immobilized, but it was impossible to repair it due to the immense Soviet pressure.[983]

979 Laugier, Didier: *Sturmartillerie*. Tome I. Bayeux, 2011. p. 201.

980 Correctly: *Grenadier-Regiment 188* from *68. Infanterie-Division*.

981 *Tagebuchaufzeichnungen vom 2. 12. 1942 bis 1. 2. 1944 von Kamerad Wachtmeister Georg Hiller.* In: *Der Sturmartillerist.* Heft 60. p. 1332.

982 *Tagebuchaufzeichnungen vom 2. 12. 1942 bis 1. 2. 1944 von Kamerad Wachtmeister Georg Hiller.* In: *Der Sturmartillerist.* Heft 60. p. 1332.

983 Laugier, Didier: *Sturmartillerie*. Tome I. Bayeux, 2011. p. 201.

The NCO of the *1. Batterie*, quoted before, wrote the following into his diary:

At 5 o'clock in the morning we move forward again, since tanks were reported. We repulsed the attack of the Soviet infantry. At 4 o'clock in the afternoon we see four tanks: I knocked out one, two of them were disabled by Leutnant Heimbach, and one by Wachtmeister Türgst. At 5 o'clock in the evening, when it was dark, we moved back and when we stopped, I see a T–34 behind myself. They probably mistook us for a Russian outfit as they moved beside us, following a forest trail. I could hardly believe my eyes when I noticed another Russian tank behind me, obviously with the intention to join us. Wachtmeister Waldner overran the first one as did Leutnant Heimbach. I gave orders to the driver to drop backwards into the forest and, before the crew of the second tank could recover their wits, our AP-shell hit the Russian armoured combat vehicle from 3 metres. We nicked off from there like mad because the tank was in flames.[984]

15 OCTOBER 1943

At 0300 hours the assault guns in the *1. Batterie/Sturmgeschütz-Abteilung 202* clashed with seven Soviet tanks in the dark; two of them were knocked out by the assault gun of *Leutnant* Heimbach. One of the disabled Soviet tanks had his gun trained on *Wachtmeister* Hiller's StuG. when it received a hit. At 1000 hours the assault guns started moving back, but two of them remained there: *'Nilpferd'* (Hippopotamus), *Wachtmeister* Hiller's Assault gun, and *'Krake'* (Octopus) the assault gun under the command of *Unteroffizier* Prietsch. At 1200 hours they realized they were encircled by Soviet troops. *Wachtmeister* Hiller recorded the following in his diary:

We are anxious about the future because we hadn't eaten anything for two days by then, and we are thirsty. We have to be sparing of ammunition, and we are running out of fuel. [985]

16 OCTOBER 1943

The assault gun with the chassis number '91396' was knocked out by a Soviet anti-tank gun 1 km south-west of Ljutesh. The hit damaged its cardan shaft and right-side track. Recovery attempts failed due to the soft ground and the proximity of the Soviet troops.[986] This was probably *Wachtmeister* Hiller's assault gun *'Nilpferd'*. Having removed all of its usable parts, it was blown up by *Unteroffizier* Prietsch. Its crew reached its battery, stationed in Kiev the following evening after a wearisome and dangerous march on foot.[987]

---

984 *Tagebuchaufzeichnungen vom 2. 12. 1942 bis 1. 2. 1944 von Kamerad Wachtmeister Georg Hiller.* In: *Der Sturmartillerist.* Heft 60. p. 1332.

985 *Tagebuchaufzeichnungen vom 2. 12. 1942 bis 1. 2. 1944 von Kamerad Wachtmeister Georg Hiller.* In: *Der Sturmartillerist.* Heft 60. p. 1332.

986 Laugier, Didier: *Sturmartillerie.* Tome I. Bayeux, 2011. p. 201.

987 *Tagebuchaufzeichnungen vom 2. 12. 1942 bis 1. 2. 1944 von Kamerad Wachtmeister Georg Hiller.* In: *Der Sturmartillerist.* Heft 60. p. 1333.

17 OCTOBER 1943

Sturmgeschütz-Abteilung 202 together with the self-propelled anti-tank guns of *Panzerjäger-Abteilung 616* were given the task of providing support for *Grenadier-Regiment 246* in mopping up the road between Wyschgorod and Staryj Petrowzy towards north.[988] The StuG. III with the chassis number '92072' was hit in its engine compartment by a Soviet AP-shell west of Nowo Petrowzy, causing irreparable damage.[989]

18 OCTOBER 1943

Soviet troops penetrated into the northern part of Wyschgorod from Walki with infantry in battalion strength and nine tanks. The Germans blocked the attack. The assault guns of *Sturmgeschütz-Abteilung 202* and the self-propelled anti-tank guns of *Panzerjäger-Abteilung 606* launched a counter-attack. The Germans knocked out five Soviet tanks during the heavy, swaying battle, pushing the Soviets back in the direction of Walki and the Dnieper.[990] The StuG. III assault gun with chassis number '92083' was destroyed by the fire of a Soviet tank 1 km north of the temple in Wyschgorod. The German armoured fighting vehicle was left behind the Soviet lines.[991]

In the sector of the *VII. Armeekorps*, the Germans knocked out a total of 23 Soviet armoured fighting vehicles.[992]

19 OCTOBER 1943

One hundred metres from the temple in Wyschgorod, the assault gun with chassis number '92079' was hit by an armour-piercing shell. Having been hit in its left track, the StuG. III side slipped on the muddy slope and became immobilised. Because the Soviet troops retook their former positions, German recovery attempts failed and the combat vehicle was left behind.[993]

23 OCTOBER 1943

In the evening *Sturmgeschütz-Abteilung 202* had 12 assault guns operational.[994]

29 OCTOBER 1943

In the evening, *Sturmgeschütz-Abteilung 202* had 11 combat-ready StuG. III assault guns.[995]

---

988 NARA T314, R362 (*VII. Armeekorps*), F000819.

989 Laugier, Didier: *Sturmartillerie*. Tome I. Bayeux, 2011. p. 201.

990 NARA T313, R380 (*Panzerarmeeoberkommando 4*), F8668788 and F8668790.

991 Laugier, Didier: *Sturmartillerie*. Tome I. Bayeux, 2011. p. 201.

992 NARA T313, R380 (*Panzerarmeeoberkommando 4*), F8668791.

993 Laugier, Didier: *Sturmartillerie*. Tome I. Bayeux, 2011. p. 201.

994 NARA T313, R380 (*Panzerarmeeoberkommando 4*), F8668884.

995 NARA T313, R380 (*Panzerarmeeoberkommando 4*), F8668979.

2 NOVEMBER 1943

The *1. Batterie/ Sturmgeschütz-Abteilung 202* knocked out a Soviet Churchill II tank (probably north of Kiev, in the area of Saborje). The supply base of the battery was raided by Soviet ground-attack aircraft: an officer was killed and two other soldiers wounded.[996]

5 NOVEMBER 1943

Elements of the *1. Batterie/ Sturmgeschütz-Abteilung 202* moved back to Belgorodka, north of Kiev. *Wachtmeister* Waldner arrived wounded; his assault gun had received 12 hits by anti-tank guns. *Unteroffizier* Prietsch's assault gun, *'Tigerhai'* (Tiger Shark) was knocked out by a Soviet KV-1 heavy tank (probably south-west of Saborje), and *Leutnant* Heimbach was killed.[997]

6 NOVEMBER 1943

The office car of the *1. Batterie/ Sturmgeschütz-Abteilung 202* got stuck on the way to Wassilkow and was captured (for the second time) by Soviet troops.[998]

12 NOVEMBER 1943

The *VII. Armeekorps*, together with *Sturmgeschütz-Abteilung 202*, were subordinated to *Armeegruppe M* from 0000 hours.[999]

15 NOVEMBER 1943

Elements of *Sturmgeschütz-Abteilung 202* were deployed in the sector of the *7. Panzer-Division* from Skonorochi in a south-easterly direction to eliminate a Soviet penetration. Another group of assault guns which attacked northwards from Ssinguri at 1300 hours, encountered fierce Soviet resistance south of Zhitomir, in a wooded area. The Soviets knocked out two StuG. IIIs.[1000]

16 NOVEMBER 1943

Seven combat-ready assault guns of *Sturmgeschütz-Abteilung 202* were attached to the *68. Infanterie-Division.*[1001] Apart from these, four long-barrelled Panzer IIIs, 10 long-barrelled Panzer IVs, five Panthers and six Tiger tanks as well as seven 10.5

---

996 *Tagebuchaufzeichnungen vom 2. 12. 1942 bis 1. 2. 1944 von Kamerad Wachtmeister Georg Hiller.* In: *Der Sturmartillerist.* Heft 60. p. 1333.

997 *Tagebuchaufzeichnungen vom 2. 12. 1942 bis 1. 2. 1944 von Kamerad Wachtmeister Georg Hiller.* In: *Der Sturmartillerist.* Heft 60. p. 1334.

998 *Tagebuchaufzeichnungen vom 2. 12. 1942 bis 1. 2. 1944 von Kamerad Wachtmeister Georg Hiller.* In: *Der Sturmartillerist.* Heft 60. p. 1334.

999 NARA T313, R380 (*Panzerarmeeoberkommando 4*), F8669434.

1000 NARA T313, R380 (*Panzerarmeeoberkommando 4*), F8669476.

1001 NARA T313, R380 (*Panzerarmeeoberkommando 4*), F8669510.

cm Wespe self-propelled field howitzers of the *2. SS-Panzer-Division 'Das Reich'* fought in the sector of the *VII. Armeekorps.*[1002]

18 NOVEMBER 1943

The *1. Batterie/ Sturmgeschütz-Abteilung 202* received four new StuG. IIIs, previously cement-plastered for added protection.[1003]

21 NOVEMBER 1943

Sturmgeschütz-Abteilung 202 was ordered back from *Armeegruppe M* to the zone of action of the *VII. Armeekorps.*[1004] However, the *198. Infanterie-Division* reported to the corps during the day that *Sturmgeschütz-Abteilung 202* had not yet arrived in their sector. [1005]

27 NOVEMBER 1943

Divisions of the *VII. Armeekorps* received a map showing possible missions for *Sturmgeschütz-Abteilung 202.* In relation to this, the *75., 82.* and *198. Infanterie-Divisionen* received orders to strengthen the relevant bridges (so that the assault guns could carry out their missions) and to prepare quarters and the field-telephone network in the readiness positions.[1006]

28 NOVEMBER 1943

The *75. Infanterie-Division* submitted an experience report about the operations carried out during the summer to the staff of the *VII. Armeekorps.* In connection with their cooperation with the assault guns of *Sturmgeschütz-Abteilung 202,* we can read the following in their document:

> *...] Cooperation with the assault guns was excellent since the division had been fighting together for months with the same unit and crews. Where the assault guns were available in due time, each and every penetration could be eliminated. The presence of even a few assault guns raised the morale and fighting spirit of the troops. Fear of tanks disappeared where it came to the troops' attention that they had usable weapons against them.*
>
> *Experience showed that even a few (three of four) assault guns could have a decisive influence on the fighting spirit of a division.*

1002 NARA T314, R363 (*VII. Armeekorps*), F000066.

1003 *Tagebuchaufzeichnungen vom 2. 12. 1942 bis 1. 2. 1944 von Kamerad Wachtmeister Georg Hiller.* In: *Der Sturmartillerist.* Heft 60. p. 1334.

1004 NARA T313, R380 (*Panzerarmeeoberkommando 4*), F8669620.

1005 NARA T314, R363 (*VII. Armeekorps*), F000115.

1006 NARA T314, R363 (*VII. Armeekorps*), F000014.

The self-propelled anti-tank guns were sometimes considered as a supplement for assault guns, and during counter-thrusts they were deployed as support for the infantry, etc. In this respect, they didn't prove suitable since, due to their weak armour, they had to fall behind and were therefore slowing down the infantry instead of taking them along. On the other hand, they proved to be useful in artillery missions carried out in rear-guards, where they could put the enemy under fire at greater distances. [...] [1007]

1 DECEMBER 1943

At 1430 hours the *VII. Armeekorps* put one of the platoons (three assault guns) of *Sturmgeschütz-Abteilung 202* under the command of the staff of the *82. Infanterie-Division* and ordered it to move to the divisional command post in the area of Bendjugowka.[1008]

3 DECEMBER 1943

The *VII. Armeekorps* issued orders to *Sturmgeschütz-Abteilung 202*, which was stationed in the area of Ostrijki, to survey the terrain in the sectors of each division and be prepared to undertake missions. Besides this, the assault artillery unit were also instructed to prepare their winter readiness positions.

One assault gun platoon with three StuG. IIIs was still subordinated to the *82. Infanterie-Division.* These assault guns could be employed by the division to get its infantry used to working alongside the AFVs. The StuG. IIIs rolled over the grenadiers who were in foxholes so that they could gain experience of the armoured combat vehicles at close quarters. After further arrangements, the *75. Infanterie-Division* also received some assault guns for that purpose. The troops of the *198. Infanterie-Division* practised close cooperation with two assault guns. The next day, two more combat vehicles were ordered into the sector of the *88. Infanterie-Division* with similar training tasks.[1009]

5 DECEMBER 1943

The *VII. Armeekorps* made its own plan to retake the important railway junction, Fastoff. As part of the plan, codenamed '*Wintersonnenwende*' (Winter Solstice), *Sturmgeschütz-Abteilung 202,* subordinated to the *75. Infanterie-Division,* was to have supported the reinforced *Grenadier-Regiment 222.*[1010] The regiment was to have joined the attack of the *1. Panzerdivision.*

1007 NARA T314, R363 (*VII. Armeekorps*), F000204.

1008 NARA T314, R363 (*VII. Armeekorps*), F000018 and F000225.

1009 NARA T314, R363 (*VII. Armeekorps*), F000237.

1010 NARA T314, R363 (*VII. Armeekorps*), F000256-258.

10 DECEMBER 1943

In the evening there were 20 combat-ready long-barrelled (L/48) StuG. IIIs in *Sturmgeschütz-Abteilung 202.*[1011] At that time, there was another assault artillery unit under the command of the *VII. Armeekorps: Sturmgeschütz-Batterie 741,*[1012] with nine operational assault guns, was subordinated to the *18. Artillerie-Division* at this time.[1013]

14 DECEMBER 1943

In the morning, the assault of the *82. Infanterie-Division* carried out by company-strength forces on Point 190 was supported by the *3. Batterie/ Sturmgeschütz-Abteilung 202.* The Germans destroyed or captured the entire personnel and weaponry of the Soviet strongpoint established there. In the course of the battle they detonated 16 bunkers and an anti-tank gun and took 50 prisoners from the 4 Company of the 269 Rifle Regiment of the Soviet 136 Rifle Division. The Soviets lost 14 dead and the Germans only four wounded during the fighting.[1014]

17 DECEMBER 1943

The corps issued orders regarding preparations for winter warfare. Among other measures, each of the divisions was to establish 30 heated winter shelters for the assault guns and tanks in Mirowka, Rosalejewka, Grebenki and Pol. Polowezkoje.[1015]

18 DECEMBER 1943

Sturmgeschütz-Abteilung 202 had 21 combat-ready long-barrelled StuG. IIIs. *Sturmgeschütz-Batterie 741* possessed an additional 10 StuG. IIIs operational.[1016]

In the evening, the corps issued orders by telegram to the *82. Infanterie-Division* to return the assault gun platoon subordinated to them to *Sturmgeschütz-Abteilung 202.*[1017]

19 DECEMBER 1943

By the evening hours, the number of the combat-ready assault guns in *Sturmgeschütz-Abteilung 202* increased to 24; *Sturmgeschütz-Batterie 741* still had 10 combat-ready StuG. IIIs.[1018]

1011 Besides those, *Sturmgeschütz-Abteilung 202* also had one short-barrelled(L/24) and 13 long-barrelled (three L/43, 10 L/48) assault guns, although all of them were in need of repairs. From the eight Sd.Kfz. 252 armoured ammunition carrier halftracks of the unit four were serviceable on that day. *See* Laugier, Didier: Sturmartillerie. Tome I. Bayeux, 2011. 202. o.

1012 *Sturmgeschütz-Batterie 741* arrived in the southern foreground of Kiev in December 1943.

1013 NARA T313, R381 (*Panzerarmeeoberkommando 4*), F8670146.

1014 NARA T314, R363 (*VII. Armeekorps*), F000024 and F000349.

1015 NARA T314, R363 (*VII. Armeekorps*), F000408.

1016 NARA T314, R363 (*VII. Armeekorps*), F000411.

1017 NARA T314, R363 (*VII. Armeekorps*), F000413.

1018 NARA T314, R363 (*VII. Armeekorps*), F000422.

20 DECEMBER 1943

In the evening, the number of combat-ready StuG. IIIs in the assault gun units of the *VII. Armeekorps* was unchanged compared to the figures of the previous day.[1019]

21 DECEMBER 1943

From 1145 hours, the deputy of the chief of staff of the *VII. Armeekorps* participated in a discussion with the acting commander of *Sturmgeschütz-Abteilung 202, Hauptmann* Gerhard Essigke, about equipping the heated winter shelters for the assault guns and tanks. At the same time, the assault artillery unit received orders to dispatch one or two assault gun platoons into the sector of the *75. Infanterie-Division* in the area of Rosalejewka after Christmas to assist in the training of the grenadiers for close-quarter combat against AFVs, and to be ready to provide armoured support for forthcoming assaults.[1020]

22 DECEMBER 1943

Sturmgeschütz-Abteilung 202 still had 24StuG. IIIs and *Sturmgeschütz-Batterie 741* had 10 StuG. IIIs operational.[1021]

23 DECEMBER 1943

At 1620 hours *Sturmgeschütz-Abteilung 202* received orders to send six StuG. IIIs into the sector of the *75. Infanterie-Division* on 26 December at 0900 hours to support an intended assault.[1022]

25 DECEMBER 1943

At 1300 hours *Pionier-Bataillon 215,* directly under command of the *VII. Armeekorps* and reinforced with the *3. Batterie/Sturmgeschütz-Abteilung 202,* set off from the area of Biala Zerkwa to block the line of the Kamenka River between Potschuiki and Paripssy, and to conduct reconnaissance along the Unawa River between Romanowka and Losowiki. Most of the assault artillery unit (without one of its batteries) was ordered into the area of Wel. Polowezkoje to be at the disposal of the corps.[1023]

At 2225 hours the corps issued further orders to the *88. Infanterie-Division* to launch an attack the next day to take and hold the hills around Kaschljaki with most of *Sturmgeschütz-Abteilung 202* subordinated to them, plus a battalion in reserve with the assault guns. In the event of weak resistance the attack was to be continued to the eastern half of Romanowka.[1024]

1019 NARA T314, R363 (*VII. Armeekorps*), F000433.

1020 NARA T314, R363 (*VII. Armeekorps*), F000032-33.

1021 NARA T314, R363 (*VII. Armeekorps*), F000445.

1022 NARA T314, R363 (*VII. Armeekorps*), F000035.

1023 NARA T314, R363 (*VII. Armeekorps*), F000476.

1024 NARA T314, R363 (*VII. Armeekorps*), F000038.

26 DECEMBER 1943

At 1145 hours *Pionier-Bataillon 215* reported that Soviet troops had occupied Popelnja and, at around 1000 hours, had approached the bridge at Paripssy with four T–34s and shelled the settlement before turning back. Five minutes later the *Pionier-Bataillon* reported that the assault guns of *Sturmgeschütz-Abteilung 202* had scattered the Soviet troops attacking from the direction of Kaschljaki and had retaken the hills south of the settlement. At the time the report was submitted the assault guns were still fighting the Soviet forces on the railway embankment.[1025]

At 1430 hours *Pionier-Bataillon 215,* with the support of the assault guns attached to them, commenced a counter-thrust from the area of Nowosseliza toward Potschuiki. By 1600 hours the Germans had occupied the south-western part of the settlement but, following a Soviet flank attack at around 1700 hours, they had to give it up. According to the German report, 25 Soviet soldiers were killed and four machine guns were captured during the fighting. *Pionier-Bataillon 215* lost two dead and nine wounded, as well as one light machine gun. Three StuG. IIIs in the *3. Batterie/ Sturmgeschütz-Abteilung 202* were disabled due to gun damage.[1026]

27 DECEMBER 1943

The Soviet 72 Rifle Division attacked the sector of the *88. Infanterie-Division* between Koshanka and Strokoff. The indecisive Soviet raids were repulsed by counter-thrusts supported by the assault guns of *Sturmgeschütz-Abteilung 202.* The Soviet rifle infantry retreated in panic.

Between 1300 and 1430 hours, the division carried out another counter-thrust with the support of the assault guns towards Trylissy where they relieved the *II. Bataillon/ Sicherungs-Regiment 318* which had been encircled by the Soviets. According to the Germans the 797 Rifle Regiment of the Soviet 232 Rifle Division lost 150 dead, seven prisoners, 12 light machine guns, two anti-tank rifles, two heavy mortars and five submachine guns.[1027]

The *VII. Armeekorps* ordered the German division to defend its main combat line by offensive combat with the support of a battery of the assault artillery unit subordinated to them.[1028]

On the same day, *Pionier-Bataillon 215* reported to the corps that the Soviets had been attacking the area of Nowosseliza from 1000 hours with a battalion-strength force. Because the four combat-ready StuG. IIIs subordinated to the German *Pionier-Bataillon* had run out of ammunition the pioneers, left without the support of the assault guns, were forced to give up the settlement.[1029]

1025 NARA T314, R363 (*VII. Armeekorps*), F000040.

1026 NARA T314, R363 (*VII. Armeekorps*), F000532-533.

1027 NARA T313, R372 (*Panzerarmeeoberkommando 4*), F8670520.

1028 NARA T314, R363 (*VII. Armeekorps*), F000582.

1029 NARA T314, R363 (*VII. Armeekorps*), F000567, F000570-571.

In the evening, at the link-up of *88. Infanterie-Division*, *Kampfgruppe* Böhm was set up under the command of *Oberst* Dr. Böhm, deputy of *Artillerie-Kommandeur 124*. The *Kampfgruppe* was made up of the staff of *Artillerie-Regiment 617*, the alarm battery of *schwere Artillerie-Abteilung 625* deployed as infantry, the *I. Bataillon/Sicherungs-Regiment 177*, *Aufklärungs-Abteilung 175* and most of *Sturmgeschütz-Abteilung 202* (without its *3. Batterie*). This improvised formation was given the task of defending the line between Jachny and Strokoff with offensive combat by making use of the assault guns against a possible Soviet attack in a south-easterly direction. If the Soviets had crossed that zone of action, they would have been repulsed.[1030]

At 2245 hours, the corps issued orders to *Pionier-Bataillon 215* to return the *3. Batterie/Sturmgeschütz-Abteilung 202* subordinated to them to its parent unit next day.[1031]

28 DECEMBER 1943

At 0400 hours the *1. Batterie* of *Sturmgeschütz-Abteilung 202* arrived in the area of Truschki, from where they jumped-off two hours later without infantry support in front of the Soviet positions. At around 1100 hours three assault guns in the battery had to relieve four encircled StuG. IIIs of the *3. Batterie* at a penetration. On their way back, the assault guns unexpectedly ran into a Soviet rifle battalion, which they destroyed.[1032]

At 1315 hours the *VII. Armeekorps* issued orders by telegram to *Sturmgeschütz-Abteilung 202* to assemble its forces in the area of Ruda, and send an officer for further orders to the command post of the *88. Infanterie-Division.*[1033]

29/30 DECEMBER 1943

At 1735 hours, the *88. Infanterie-Division* received orders by radio from the corps to dispatch two batteries of *Sturmgeschütz-Abteilung 202* from the area of Truschki through Malaja Swirka and Gorodischtsche into the area of Wolodarka without delay. After sunrise the following day, the batteries were then to march in a north-westerly direction towards Antonow and report to the commander of *Grenadier-Regiment 417* at Tschorowka. This was because the regiment had been attacked around mid-day by a Soviet force with the strength of two regiments and 30 tanks which forced it out of the area of Skwira towards south-east.[1034] *Grenadier-Regiment 417,* having knocked out eight of the 30 Soviet tanks with

---

1030 NARA T314, R363 (*VII. Armeekorps*), F000583.

1031 NARA T314, R363 (*VII. Armeekorps*), F000044.

1032 *Tagebuchaufzeichnungen vom 2. 12. 1942 bis 1. 2. 1944 von Kamerad Wachtmeister Georg Hiller.* In: *Der Sturmartillerist.* Heft 60. p. 1335.

1033 NARA T314, R363 (*VII. Armeekorps*), F000602-603.

1034 NARA T314, R363 (*VII. Armeekorps*), F000048.

its own forces, had indicated at 1250 hours that they were still waiting for the arrival of the promised assault guns.[1035]

On that day the *1. Batterie/ Sturmgeschütz-Abteilung 202* made rapid progress on the highway from 0800 hours before encountering Soviet resistance. One of the assault guns was hit by an anti-tank gun but the StuG. IIIs knocked out a total of eight anti-tank guns. The damaged assault gun was successfully towed back to the command post of the *88. Infanterie-Division* where the battery took up quarters.[1036]

At 1845 hours, the *VII. Armeekorps* informed the acting commander of the *4. Panzerarmee, General der Panzertruppe* Erhard Raust, about the situation. The general noted that help would arrive in a few days saying: '*20 tanks are nothing for 10–15 assault guns*'.[1037]

Grenadier-Regiment 417 received orders at 2040 hours to prevent the Soviet advance towards Pustowarowka and Antonow and block the road to Wolodarka. However, in the event of strong Soviet pressure they would be allowed to retreat into the area of Pustowarowka. The regiment was informed only then that one of the batteries of *Sturmgeschütz-Abteilung 202* had been put under their command and had been dispatched to their sector.[1038]

In the evening *Sturmgeschütz-Abteilung 202* had a total of 15 combat-ready StuG. III assault guns.[1039]

30 DECEMBER 1943

According to a German report submitted at 0840 hours, Soviet troops had penetrated into Ruda and Matjuchi in the sector of *88. Infanterie-Division* with a regiment-strength force and 20 tanks. The StuG. III assault guns of *Sturmgeschütz-Abteilung 202* knocked out 11 Soviet AFVs in the area of Ruda despite thick fog during the day.[1040] The assault artillery unit was subordinated to the staff of the *198. Infanterie-Division* from 1630 hours that day.[1041]

The assault gun *'Krake'* (commanded by *Wachtmeister* Hiller) of the *1. Batterie* was disabled at around 0600 hours due to engine failure. The StuG. III was towed via Olschanka to Biala-Zerkow for repairs.[1042]

1035 NARA T314, R363 (*VII. Armeekorps*), F000047.

1036 *Tagebuchaufzeichnungen vom 2. 12. 1942 bis 1. 2. 1944 von Kamerad Wachtmeister Georg Hiller.* In: *Der Sturmartillerist.* Heft 60. p. 1335.

1037 NARA T314, R363 (*VII. Armeekorps*), F000048.

1038 NARA T314, R363 (*VII. Armeekorps*), F000049.

1039 NARA T314, R363 (*VII. Armeekorps*), F000605.

1040 NARA T314, R363 (*VII. Armeekorps*), F000049.

1041 NARA T314, R363 (*VII. Armeekorps*), F000050.

1042 *Tagebuchaufzeichnungen vom 2. 12. 1942 bis 1. 2. 1944 von Kamerad Wachtmeister Georg Hiller.* In: *Der Sturmartillerist.* Heft 60. p. 1335.

31 DECEMBER 1943

At 1915 hours the *VII. Armeekorps* issued orders to the forces of the *88.* and the *198. Infanterie-Divisionen* as well as to *Sturmgeschütz-Abteilung 202* to detach mobile reserves on the first day of the new year to eliminate Soviet penetrations in the front line. Further reinforcements were due to arrive: at 2010 hours the corps was informed of the orders issued by the *4. Panzerarmee* according to which *Sturmgeschütz-Abteilung 239* would be subordinated to the *VII. Armeekorps* next day.[1043]

In the evening *Sturmgeschütz-Abteilung 202* had 17 combat-ready assault guns.[1044]

1043 NARA T314, R363 (*VII. Armeekorps*), F000052.

1044 NARA T314, R363 (*VII. Armeekorps*), F000642.

CHAPTER 6

In the sector of the German *1. Panzerarmee* in the area of Korsun-Shevchenkovsky

Operational background:

The Soviet 1, 2, 3 and 4 Ukrainian Fronts launched an attack to establish bridgeheads on the western bank of the Dnieper River on 2 December 1943. As a result, two German corps defending along the Dnieper in the area of Korsun-Shevchenkovsky were in danger of encirclement. To destroy the two German corps, the 2 Ukrainian Front launched the Korsun-Shevchenkovsky Offensive on 24 January 1944 from the south-east. The 1 Ukrainian Front commenced its offensive north-west of the German salient on 26 January 1944 with a force that included the newly raised 6 Tank Army among others. Sturmgeschütz-Abteilung 202 was fighting in this sector.

1 JANUARY 1944

Sturmgeschütz-Abteilung 202 had a total of 34 StuG. III assault guns, of which 24 were operational.[1045]

Wachtmeister Hiller was on his way to the echelon of the *1. Batterie* with the repaired assault gun *'Krake'*, when at 0700 hours Soviet ground-attack aircraft swooped on the German armoured fighting vehicle as it drove on a roadway. Eight bombs struck the ground nearby, but they missed their target.[1046]

2 JANUARY 1944

At 2100 hours the staff of the *1. Panzerarmee* assumed command of the troops of the *VII. Armeekorps.*[1047]

3 JANUARY 1944

Heavy fighting continued in the sector of the *88. Infanterie-Division.* The Soviet troops launched seven attacks with regiment-strength forces, partly supported by armour, on Olschanka. The Germans repelled all of these attacks and during

1045 NARA T78, R269 (*General der Artillerie im OKH*), F6216845.

1046 *Tagebuchaufzeichnungen vom 2. 12. 1942 bis 1. 2. 1944 von Kamerad Wachtmeister Georg Hiller.* In: *Der Sturmartillerist.* Heft 60. p. 1335.

1047 NARA T313, R69 (*Panzerarmeeoberkommando 1*), F7305756.

ferocious urban fighting pushed the Soviet troops out of Olschanka.[1048] The diary of *Wachtmeister* Hiller gives the following account of the battle fought by the *1. Batterie*:

At 0330 hours in readiness position. Kanonier Fabenscher got under the assault gun. At 6 o'clock tanks were reported. The assault gun was towing away one of our recovery vehicles when it received anti-tank gun fire and had no choice but to intervene in the battle: I knocked out a T-34 and six anti-tank guns, then pulled the towing vehicle away. At 1300 hours I was combat-ready again. At 1500 hours a smaller-scale attack with two assault guns. We destroyed a company of Russian infantry. In the evening we changed position.[1049]

In these battles, *Grenadier-Regiment 417*[1050], *Sturmgeschütz-Abteilung 202*[1051] and *Pionier-Bataillon 188,* all of them subordinated to the division, distinguished themselves. According to German reports, the Soviets lost 220 dead, 50 prisoners, 42 anti-tank guns and seven knocked out T–34 tanks during the fighting.[1052] The commander of the *1. Panzerarmee, General der Panzertruppe* Hans Hube, expressed his gratitude and appreciation to the troops for their remarkable achievements by telegram on the same day.[1053]

In the evening *Sturmgeschütz-Abteilung 202* had 13 combat-ready StuG. III assault guns.[1054]

7 JANUARY 1944

In the sector of the *34. Infanterie-Division* Soviet troops attacked the German readiness positions and occupied Luka then, immediately south-west of Dybnizy, they made rapid progress eastwards but were brought to a halt when the Germans knocked out seven of their tanks. In the evening, a German counter-thrust supported by assault guns retook Luka.[1055] Besides *Sturmgeschütz-Abteilung 202,* the StuG. IIIs of *Sturmgeschütz-Abteilung 239* also participated in this attack. According to the combat history of the latter unit, Luka was reoccupied only the following day, on the morning of 8 January:

1048 NARA T313, R69 (*Panzerarmeeoberkommando 1*), F7305738.

1049 *Tagebuchaufzeichnungen vom 2. 12. 1942 bis 1. 2. 1944 von Kamerad Wachtmeister Georg Hiller.* In: *Der Sturmartillerist.* Heft 60. p. 1336.

1050 The regiment originally belonged to the *168. Infanterie-Division*'s order of battle.

1051 The assault artillery unit was still commanded by *Hauptmann* Essigke as acting commander.

1052 NARA T313, R69 (*Panzerarmeeoberkommando 1*), F7305723.

1053 NARA T313, R69 (*Panzerarmeeoberkommando 1*), F7305726.

1054 NARA T313, R69 (*Panzerarmeeoberkommando 1*), F7305723.

1055 NARA T313, R69 (*Panzerarmeeoberkommando 1*), F7305771.

Having overcome the difficulties caused by roads that were covered with ice, we were able to use the assault guns in the morning of 8 January and knocked out a T–34. During our attack in cooperation with Sturmgeschütz-Abteilung 202 we destroyed an assault gun with a 85 mm gun [a SU–85 self-propelled gun], *a KV-1 and two T–34s, occupied the settlement and relieved the Kampfgruppe encircled in Koschewatoje, thereby creating an adequate jump-off base for further operations.*[1056]

12 JANUARY 1944

In the evening, while subordinated to the *VII. Armeekorps, Sturmgeschütz-Abteilung 202* had 12, and *Sturmgeschütz-Abteilung 239* seven combat-ready StuG. III assault guns.[1057]

On the same day *Hauptmann* Brandner temporarily (until 15 January) assumed command of *Sturmgeschütz-Abteilung 239* because – due to illness, a mine explosion and other reasons – the unit had lost three commanders in the space of a few days.[1058]

14 JANUARY 1944

At 1100 hours, the *VII. Armeekorps* launched an attack in a south-westerly direction to close the gap opened up in the front line in the area of Belaja Zerkwa. The troops of the *34., 75.* and *83. Infanterie-Divisionen* broke through the defence of the surprized Soviet troops with assault gun-support.[1059]

Attacking through the area of Repki, the *34. Infanterie-Division* took Wotelewka then dashed onwards. At around 2000 hours they penetrated into Winograd. The Germans identified four Soviet artillery batteries and multiple rocket launchers in the settlement.

In a heavy fighting the *75. Infanterie-Division* occupied Beresowka where the Soviets had concentrated a significant number of anti-tank guns.

During the day's fighting the troops of the *VII. Armeekorps* destroyed 14 anti-tank guns, several anti-tank rifles and took 150 Soviet soldiers as prisoners. However, of the StuG. IIIs supporting the grenadiers, four were disabled (including one written off as a total loss).[1060]

15 JANUARY 1944

At 1100 hours, the attacking troops of the *75. Infanterie-Division* linked up with elements of the *17. Panzer-Division.* By so doing, the Germans closed the gap between the *VII. Armeekorps* and the *III. Panzerkorps.* Following that, the *VII. Armeekorps* continued its attack towards west by order of the *1. Panzerarmee.*[1061]

1056 *Der Sturmartillerist.* Heft 45. p. 982.

1057 NARA T313, R69 (*Panzerarmeeoberkommando 1*), F7306236.

1058 *Der Sturmartillerist.* Heft 45. p. 982.

1059 NARA T313, R69 (*Panzerarmeeoberkommando 1*), F7306285.

1060 NARA T313, R69 (*Panzerarmeeoberkommando 1*), F7306286.

1061 NARA T313, R69 (*Panzerarmeeoberkommando 1*), F7305794.

16 JANUARY 1944

At around 1200 hours the *34. Infanterie-Division* reached Poboika with a vigorous attack then, at around 1500 hours, occupied Nagornaja and Glinka following violent urban fighting to established a bridgehead on the western bank of the Burty stream.

The northern *Kampfgruppe* of the *75. Infanterie-Division* was fighting in the area of Konstantinowka; its southern *Kampfgruppe* was fighting in the area of Kuty. Elements of the Soviet 5 Guards Tank Corps advanced from a south-easterly direction towards Bagwa through Risino, cutting off the supply route of the German division.[1062]

In the evening, *Sturmgeschütz-Abteilung 202* possessed 12 assault guns while *Sturmgeschütz-Abteilung 239* had five combat-ready StuG. IIIs.[1063]

17 JANUARY 1944

In the sector of *34. Infanterie-Division*, the Soviets continuously attacked the positions of the German grenadiers between Glinka and Nagornaja with considerable rifle forces and 25 tanks. However, with the support of assault guns, the Germans smashed the attacks in front of their main combat line, knocking out all of the charging Soviet tanks.[1064]

A *Kampfgruppe* of the *75. Infanterie-Division* with the support of assault guns (from *Sturmgeschütz-Abteilung 202*) retook Ulschanowka from the Soviets, pushed the forces of the Red Army from Bagwa and, in the evening hours, continued its attack toward Rubannyj Most. According to German radio reconnaissance information, the Soviet 32, 136 and 167 Rifle Divisions had been encircled in the settlement but were preparing to break out.[1065]

In his diary, an NCO of the *1. Batterie/ Sturmgeschütz-Abteilung 202* recorded the following about the day's fighting:

At 6 o'clock attack towards Ulschanowka, which we took without any resistance, then we advanced towards Rubannyj Most. Following a two-hour battle, it is in our hands again. On to Bagwa. Violent flanking fire, we went there with three assault guns and successfully cleared the flank. Meanwhile the other assault guns in Bagwa got into difficulties because the Russians attacked from Rubannyj Most. The attack ended at 1400 hours. I knocked out four assault guns here.[1066]

1062 NARA T313, R69 (*Panzerarmeeoberkommando 1*), F7305798.

1063 NARA T313, R69 (*Panzerarmeeoberkommando 1*), F7305749.

1064 NARA T313, R69 (*Panzerarmeeoberkommando 1*), F7305800.

1065 NARA T313, R69 (*Panzerarmeeoberkommando 1*), F7305801.

1066 *Tagebuchaufzeichnungen vom 2. 12. 1942 bis 1. 2. 1944 von Kamerad Wachtmeister Georg Hiller.* In: *Der Sturmartillerist.* Heft 60. p. 1336.

18 JANUARY 1944

Soviet troops attacked along the whole front of the *VII. Armeekorps.* In the sector of the *82. Infanterie-Division* the Soviets retook Tinowka in a see-saw battle with the support of 18 tanks.

In the zone of action of the *34. Infanterie-Division,* the Soviets penetrated into the south-western part of Baschtetschki following four unsuccessful attempts during which they suffered significant losses.[1067]

On that day, the German troops reported 40 knocked out Soviet AFVs in the sector of the *VII. Armeekorps.*[1068]

The commander in chief of *Heeresgruppe Süd, Generalfeldmarschall* Erich von Manstein, gave thanks by telegram for the courage shown in the offensive battles of the previous days and expressed his appreciation to the *34.* and *75. Infanterie-Divisionen* as well as to the personnel of *Sturmgeschütz-Abteilung 202.*[1069]

19 JANUARY 1944

Soviet forces continued to attack in the zone of the *VII. Armeekorps* with their focal point lying between Tinowka and Baschtetschki. They reoccupied the southern half of Tinowka and almost the whole Baschtetschki. In the sector of the German corps, 10 Soviet tanks were knocked out on that day. In the evening, *Sturmgeschütz-Abteilung 202* had 11 combat-ready assault guns; *Sturmgeschütz-Abteilung 239* possessed three operational StuG. IIIs.[1070]

21 JANUARY 1944

At 2015 hours the *VII. Armeekorps* informed the staff of the *1. Panzerarmee* of its intention to launch an attack with half of the forces of the *82. Infanterie-Division,* two-thirds of *Sturmgeschütz-Abteilung 202,* the artillery and alarm units of *Kampfgruppe* Böhm and other smaller fragments in the south-eastern foreground of Winograd with the objective of destroying the Soviet troops encircled there.[1071]

In the evening *Sturmgeschütz-Abteilung 202* had 15 and *Sturmgeschütz-Abteilung 239* three combat-ready StuG. IIIs.[1072]

22 JANUARY 1944

The forces assigned to the attack were divided into three *Kampfgruppen.* The commander of one of these battle groups was *Hauptmann* Essigke, commander of *Sturmgeschütz-Abteilung 202.* Two batteries of the assault artillery unit (with a total

---

1067 NARA T313, R69 (*Panzerarmeeoberkommando 1*), F7305804.
1068 NARA T313, R69 (*Panzerarmeeoberkommando 1*), F7306305.
1069 NARA T313, R69 (*Panzerarmeeoberkommando 1*), F7305805.
1070 NARA T313, R69 (*Panzerarmeeoberkommando 1*), F7306305.
1071 NARA T313, R69 (*Panzerarmeeoberkommando 1*), F7306340.
1072 NARA T313, R69 (*Panzerarmeeoberkommando 1*), F7306341.

of nine combat-ready assault guns) as well as the *II. Bataillon/Grenadier-Regiment 158* were subordinated to him.[1073]

Gruppe Essigke attacked towards Dubowka from a south-westerly direction, but the operation was to be called off at nightfall because the settlement was defended by significant Soviet forces.[1074]

23 JANUARY 1944

Kampfgruppe of *Hauptmann* Essigke mopped up the hills south-west and north-west of Dubowka. In the evening there were still 15 combat-ready assault guns in *Sturmgeschütz-Abteilung 202,* and 5 StuG. IIIs operational in *Sturmgeschütz-Abteilung 239.*[1075]

24 JANUARY 1944

The assault gun battery of *Oberleutnant* Martin Zollenkopf was given the task of destroying an 800-man-strong, excellently equipped Soviet formation that had been observed by German reconnaissance in the area of Korsun, around a *kolkhoz* (collective farm). The assault guns jumped off in thick fog with visibility reduced to 40-50 metres and passed the *kolkhoz* they were looking for. However, the Soviets opened fire at the German armoured fighting vehicles which replied with high explosive shells. One of the Soviet anti-tank guns tried to knock out the assault guns but during the fighting the *kolkhoz* caught fire.

The battery commander dashed into one of the Soviet strongpoints. The assault gun of *Unteroffizier* Heimann accompanied him but got stuck in a perfectly concealed Soviet position and was unable to break free. The gun commander ordered the crew to leave the combat vehicle. Fortunately, the commander of a third assault gun saw what was happening and reported it by radio. Upon that, *Oberleutnant* Zollenkopf rushed to the spot with his assault gun, eliminated the strongpoint and freed the stuck assault gun. However, by that time Heimann's gunner, *Unteroffizier* Rinas, and his loader, *Kanonier* Hartz, had been killed and the assault gun commander had been wounded by a hit from an anti-tank rifle.[1076]

25 JANUARY 1944

In the evening *Sturmgeschütz-Abteilung 202* had 15 combat-ready assault guns; *Sturmgeschütz-Abteilung 239* possessed eight StuG. IIIs that were operational.[1077]

1073 NARA T313, R69 (*Panzerarmeeoberkommando 1*), F7306363.

1074 NARA T313, R69 (*Panzerarmeeoberkommando 1*), F7306368.

1075 NARA T313, R69 (*Panzerarmeeoberkommando 1*), F7306377.

1076 Kurowski, Franz – Tornau, Gottfried: *Sturmgeschütze – Die Panzer der Infanterie.* Würzburg, 2008. p. 235.

1077 NARA T313, R69 (*Panzerarmeeoberkommando 1*), F7306400.

26 JANUARY 1944

At 0630 hours, Soviet troops launched an attack with a mechanized corps and infantry of more than four rifle divisions from the area of Tinowka in the sector of the *VII. Armeekorps.* They broke through the southern flank of the *88. Infanterie-Division* south of Krutyje Gorby and attacked along the whole of the front line of the *198. Infanterie-Division* so that they could envelope the right flank of the corps. This forced the Germans to withdraw to the Dolg. Grenlja–Poradowka–Petrowskaja–Wotelewka line. In the heavy fighting that day, a total of 82 Soviet tanks were knocked out in the sector of the *VII. Armeekorps.*[1078] Of these, the assault guns of *Sturmgeschütz-Abteilung 202* knocked out 43 tanks including nine confirmed for the leader of the first platoon of the *1. Batterie, Leutnant der Reserve* Ahrend Höper.[1079] *Hauptmann* Josef Brandner, the commander of the *2. Batterie,* also distinguished himself in the day's combat and his name was included in the Roll of Honour Roll of the German Army *(Ehrenblatt des Heeres).*[1080]

In the evening, *Sturmgeschütz-Abteilung 239* was relieved from its assignment with the *VII. Armeekorps* and placed under command of the *XXXXII. Armeekorps.*[1081]

27 JANUARY 1944

Soviet troops continued their attack west of Winograd and penetrated into Tschessnowka with significant rifle forces and 15 AFVs. Late in the late evening they occupied Winograd, too. Their advance was halted by the Germans only on the southern perimeter of the Winograd–Sofijenko–Tscherwona line.

On that day 37 knocked-out Soviet tanks were reported in the focal point of the attack. Of these, 25 were confirmed for *Sturmgeschütz-Abteilung 202.* In all, the Germans knocked out a total of 109 Soviet AFVs on 26 and 27 January in the sector of the *34. Infanterie-Division,* in the area of Winograd. Sixty-eight of these were knocked out by the StuG. IIIs of *Sturmgeschütz-Abteilung 202*[1082] four of which were disabled by *Leutnant de Reserve* Höper of the *1. Batterie* within no more than three minutes.[1083] The officer also had an encounter with the Soviet tanks on the night of 27/28 January. A contemporary press report gave an account of the event:

At night, when the bolshevists tried to interfere with the withdrawal of the battalion with 10 tanks, he [Höper] *was all alone with his assault gun in the dead of the night facing heavy odds as he covered the retreat. Under the light of a star-shell he saw the gun barrels of ten Soviet tanks aimed at his assault gun. In spite of that he took up the*

1078 NARA T313, R69 (*Panzerarmeeoberkommando 1*), F7305829.

1079 Scherzer, Veit – Farwick, Werner: *Die Ritterkreuzträger der Sturmartillerie 1939-45.* Band 1 A-Krafft. Jena, 2010. p. 295.

1080 Scherzer, Veit – Farwick, Werner: *Die Ritterkreuzträger der Sturmartillerie 1939-45.* Band 2: Kranz-Z. Bayreuth, 2012. p. 382.

1081 NARA T313, R69 (*Panzerarmeeoberkommando 1*), F7306421.

1082 NARA T313, R69 (*Panzerarmeeoberkommando 1*), F7306440.

1083 Scherzer, Veit – Farwick, Werner: *Die Ritterkreuzträger der Sturmartillerie 1939-45.* Band 1 A-Krafft. Jena, 2010. p. 295.

fight and opened fire: he set one tanks on fire, immobilized two of them with his hits and, with the other assault guns that had arrived in the meantime, repulsed the attack with a counter-thrust.[1084]

30 JANUARY 1944

In the evening there were 15 combat ready StuG. III assault guns in *Sturmgeschütz-Abteilung 202.*[1085]

8 FEBRUARY 1944

The *34. Infanterie-Division*, while operating in the sector of *III. Panzerkorps*, destroyed 14 Soviet AFVs with its own anti-tank guns and the assault guns of *Sturmgeschütz-Abteilung 202* that had been subordinated to the division.[1086] It was probably on this day that *Wachtmeister* Albert Krämer knocked out six T–34 tanks for which he was awarded the German Cross in Gold *(Deutsches Kreuz in Gold)*. The other two assault guns of the unit knocked out an additional seven Soviet tanks.[1087]

17 FEBRUARY 1944

Sturmgeschütz-Abteilung 202 supported the troops of the *34. Infanterie-Division* in the area of Pawlowka which the Soviets attacked with rifle forces supported by artillery, mortars and multiple-rocket launchers. The enemy penetrations were eliminated by the assault guns joining forces with the grenadiers. By evening, the former main combat line had been retaken.[1088]

18 FEBRUARY 1944

In the sector of the *34. Infanterie-Division*, Soviet troops penetrated the German positions south and east of Tinowka but the Germans repelled them, again with the support of the assault guns of *Sturmgeschütz-Abteilung 202,* and inflicted heavy losses on them.[1089]

21 FEBRUARY 1944

With immediate effect, an order of the *Oberkommando des Heeres* came into force according to which each independent *Sturmgeschütz-Abteilung* would be renamed as a *Sturmgeschütz-Brigade* while keeping its designation number and TOE and without changing its existing subordination.[1090]

1084 Citing Scherzer, Veit - Farwick, Werner: *Die Ritterkreuzträger der Sturmartillerie 1939-45.* Band 1 A-Krafft. Jena, 2010. p. 295.

1085 NARA T313, R69 (*Panzerarmeeoberkommando 1*), F7306520.

1086 NARA T313, R69 (*Panzerarmeeoberkommando 1*), F7305870.

1087 Kurowski, Franz – Tornau, Gottfried: *Sturmgeschütze – Die Panzer der Infanterie.* Würzburg, 2008. 235. o.

1088 NARA T313, R69 (*Panzerarmeeoberkommando 1*), F7305900.

1089 NARA T313, R69 (*Panzerarmeeoberkommando 1*), F7305905.

1090 NARA T312, R64 (*Armeeoberkommando 8*), Ia Nr. 220/44 g. Kdos.

CHAPTER 7

In the sector of the *8. Armee* from Uman to the withdrawal

1944

Operational background:

The Soviet 2 Ukrainian Front launched the Uman-Botosan Operation on 5 March. By 10 March 1944, forces of the 2 and 5 Guards Tank Army in cooperation with the 52 Army, despite heavy fighting, retook Uman, a significant junction and supply depot. On 20 March, the 38 Army of the 1 Ukrainian Front also captured Vinnitsa.

4 MARCH 1944

At 0900 hours the *VII. Armeekorps,* together with *Sturmgeschütz-Brigade 202*, came under the command of the *8. Armee.*[1091]

5 MARCH 1944

At 0615 hours, following an artillery preparation lasting 45 minutes, Soviet troops launched an attack with the forces of three all-arms and two tank armies towards Nowo Archangelsk and Uman.

In the zone of action of the *VII. Armeekorps*, a critical situation emerged in the sectors of the *4. Gebirgs-Division* and the *198. Infanterie-Division.* In the area of the *4. Gebirgs-Division*, two Soviet rifle divisions and around 75 AFVs made an indentation in the main combat line; in the area of the *198. Infanterie-Division* four or five Soviet rifle divisions and around 80 tanks destroyed the German defences in the vicinity of Tschishowka and Schubennyj Staw. The whole artillery of the *198. Infanterie-Division* was forced into close quarters combat against the enemy AFVs and suffered heavy losses.

After 0700 hours the Soviets achieved breakthroughs in the sector of the corps, in the area of Barwinok, as well as in the north-western part

1091 NARA T312, R66 (*Armeeoberkommando 8*), F7585933. However, with *Sturmgeschütz-Abteilung 202,* the order to rename the unit to *Sturmgeschütz-Brigade 202* was dated as of 21 March 1944. Irrespective of that, we use the latter designation from now on.

of Rubannyj Most and on the right flank of the *34. Infanterie-Division.* The assault gun brigades of the *VII. Armeekorps* commenced counter-thrusts.[1092]

At around 1000 hours, in the sector of the *198. Infanterie-Division,* in the north-western part of Tscheremiskoje and through the route of the breakthrough west of there, significant rifle forces and 11 AFVs were pushed forwards by the Soviets. Again the StuG. IIIs were deployed to fight them down.[1093]

In the front line of the two German divisions, according to sub-totals, 13 tank kills were reported. Besides these, in the sector of the *VII. Armeekorps,* the anti-tank aircraft of the *Luftwaffe* knocked out an additional three AFVs.[1094]

6 MARCH 1944

Soon after 0800 hours, Soviet troops occupied the eastern perimeter of Buni with 15 tanks. Six of the AFVs then crossed a bridge that had not been duly destroyed by the retreating Germans. The *VII. Armeekorps* deployed three StuG. IIIs and a towed heavy anti-tank gun against them.[1095] It is possible, that the three assault guns operated under the command of *Leutnant der Reserve* Wolfgang Kühn.

Meanwhile, *Oberleutnant* Zollenkopf started off with the assault guns repaired in Uman to find the AFVs of *Leutnant* Kühn. He came across them at the moment when *Wachtmeister* Krämer was trying to blow up his assault gun because its track had been torn away. With the other assault guns providing cover, the damage was repaired and the assault gun made combat-ready.

In the afternoon, Soviet troops caught up with the German assault guns at a large village, where they had been slowed by German infantry retreating along the road. In the ensuing battle around the settlement the assault guns knocked out seven T–34 tanks and two anti-tank guns. A colonel regrouped the retreating the infantry that were pouring back on the road to launch a counter-thrust with the support of two assault guns.

Oberleutnant Zollenkopf then retreated to Uman with the assault guns where the destruction of military objectives had already begun – fuel supplies of vital importance to the assault guns had been destroyed and the bridge across the Umanka River had been blown up. The assault guns tried to wade through the river at a shallow point but, one after the other, five of them became stuck in the mud. In the end, all of them had to be blown up, including the assault gun of *Oberleutnant* Zollenkopf, the first of the assault guns to have become bogged

1092 NARA T312, R64 (*Armeeoberkommando 8*), Kriegstagebuch vom 5. 3. 1944. 07.45 Uhr.

1093 NARA T312, R64 (*Armeeoberkommando 8*), Kriegstagebuch vom 5. 3. 1944. 10.15 Uhr.

1094 NARA T312, R66 (*Armeeoberkommando 8*), F7585919-20. According to a summary of the following day, a total of 71 Soviet AFVs were knocked out by the Germans in the sector of the corps on 5 March 1944. *See* NARA T312, R66 (*Armeeoberkommando 8*), F7585903. Unfortunately, it is not clear from the sources, how many Soviet AFVs were knocked out by *Sturmgeschütz-Abteilung 202* on that day.

1095 NARA T312, R64 (*Armeeoberkommando 8*), Kriegstagebuch vom 6. 3. 1944. 10.15 Uhr.

down. Having reached the western bank, as the assault artillerymen ran from the approaching Soviet troops in drifting snow, the commander of the *3. Batterie* lost contact with his comrades. In an abandoned railway station he found a brand new assault gun on a rail car and assembled a crew from amongst the soldiers nearby. With this armoured fighting vehicle he found his battery and together they retreated to the Bug river.[1096]

10 MARCH 1944

The two assault gun brigades of the *VII. Armeekorps* submitted their status reports from which it was obvious that both units were coming to their end.

Sturmgeschütz-Brigade 261 had only two disabled long-barrelled StuG. III assault guns left. Its strength had been reduced to two officers and 60 NCOs and enlisted men. Of its vehicles, two cars were operational and an 18-ton towing vehicle partly usable. The unit assembled in Berschad 20 km west of Geiworon. From 5 March 1944, the brigade lost eight assault guns knocked out by the Soviets and 12 StuG. IIIs blown up by the crews.

Sturmgeschütz-Brigade 202 had just eight long-barrelled assault guns left but one of the StuG. IIIs had lost its gun. The unit's strength consisted of one officer, three officials and 40 NCOs and enlisted men. Of its vehicles, one truck, one overhead trolley and an 18-ton recovery vehicle were serviceable, the latter only conditionally. Most of the brigade assembled in the area of Geiworon but its deployable elements fought on under subordination to the *VII. Armeekorps.* Other elements, including two disabled StuG. III assault guns, were still on the march. From 5 March 1944, the assault artillery unit had lost 20 assault guns.[1097]

12 MARCH 1944

At 0300 hours a German *Kampfgruppe* led by the commander of *Grenadier-Regiment 245, Oberstleutnant* Josef Bregenzer, reached the village of Dshulinka with the support of *Sturmgeschütz-Brigade 202.* The riverside village and the nearby bridge over the Bug had been captured a little bit earlier by Soviet tanks and rifle infantry. The exhausted Germans, having been fighting continuously for 16 hours during the previous day,[1098] had no choice but to break through or die. *Oberstleutnant* Bregenzer personally directed the breakthrough standing on the top of an assault gun. The Germans managed to fight themselves over the Bug amidst severe urban fighting. During the battle they destroyed 15 Soviet tanks, a multiple-rocket launcher battery and several trucks, and inflicted heavy casualties on the Soviet rifle infantry. For his bravery, *Oberstleutnant*

1096 Kurowski, Franz – Tornau, Gottfried: *Sturmgeschütze – Die Panzer der Infanterie.* Würzburg, 2008. 236. o.

1097 NARA T312, R64 (*Armeeoberkommando 8*), Anlage zum Kriegstagebuch Nr. 105 am 10. 3. 1944.

1098 The forces of the German battle group, including the assault guns, knocked out a total of 24 Soviet AFVs during the defensive battle at the German bridgehead in the area of Dshulinka on 11 March 1944.

Bregenzer was awarded the Oak Leaves to his Knight's Cross of the Iron Cross a few days later.[1099]

In the early afternoon, Soviet troops attacked the flank of a German *Kampfgruppe* in the area of Mankowka with 100 soldiers from a westerly direction and destroyed it. A German counter-thrust towards the town was commenced from the direction of Bereski with three assault guns.[1100]

Mankowka was soon occupied by the Soviets who had by now also penetrated into Woitowka with a battalion-strength force. Elements of *Kampfgruppe 'Bregenzer'* launched an attack towards Woitowka with the support of assault guns.[1101] The StuG. IIIs, with scraped together infantry support, still held their positions south of Woitowka at around 2200 hours.[1102]

13 MARCH 1944

In the evening, in the sector of the retreating *VII. Armeekorps,* the *34. Infanterie-Division* occupied its new zone of action on the western part of the Berschad bridgehead–Balanowka–Obodowka Novaja line. However, at 0350 hours the next day, the Germans were ambushed in Balanowka by small arms and tank gunfire. Two StuG. III assault guns of *Sturmgeschütz-Brigade 202* were sent to deal with the situation.[1103]

17 MARCH 1944

In the morning, the forces of the *VII. Armeekorps* were in a battered condition. The staff of the corps had no connection with its right-hand-side neighbour nor with the forces of the *72.* and *82. Infanterie-Divisionen* subordinated to them. They were in command of just two weak *Kampfgruppen*: *Kampfgruppe 'Totenkopf'* of the *3. SS-Panzer-Division* with four weak battalions, one tank, three SS-assault guns and 12×2 cm anti-tank machine guns; and a *Kampfgruppe* made up of the remnants of the *34. Infanterie-Division* fighting in the area of Werbka with 440 soldiers, five light machine guns and a few 2 cm anti-tank machine guns.[1104]

In the sector of the *34. Infanterie-Division* the Soviet advance was successfully halted at Werbka after the Germans knocked out three of their tanks. *Hauptmann*

1099 NARA T312, R66 (*Armeeoberkommando 8*), F7585791.

1100 NARA T312, R66 (*Armeeoberkommando 8*), F7585792.

1101 NARA T312, R66 (*Armeeoberkommando 8*), F7585787.

1102 NARA T312, R64 (*Armeeoberkommando 8*), Kriegstagebuch vom 12. 3. 1944. 22.00 Uhr.

1103 NARA T312, R66 (*Armeeoberkommando 8*), F7585767.

1104 NARA T312, R66 (*Armeeoberkommando 8*), F7585705.

Josef Brandner,[1105] commander of the *2. Batterie/ Sturmgeschütz-Brigade 202,* recorded his 55 confirmed Soviet tank kill.[1106]

19 MARCH 1944

Sturmgeschütz-Brigade 261 had no assault guns left.[1107] The last two StuG. IIIs were destroyed or found their way to *Sturmgeschütz-Brigade 202.*

24 MARCH 1944

The *VII. Armeekorps* temporarily assumed command of deployable elements of *Sturmgeschütz-Brigade 228* located in Bakscha.[1108]

27 MARCH 1944

By this time *Sturmgeschütz-Abteilung 202* had no assault guns either. The last ones were probably taken over by *Sturmgeschütz-Brigade 203* which was also under the command of *VII. Armeekorps.*[1109]

28 MARCH 1944

Sturmgeschütz-Brigade 202, together with other battle-weary, independent artillery units were relieved from assignment to the *8. Armee* and dispatched to Stryj south of Lemberg. The assault artillery unit had to leave all of its equipment, assault guns and vehicles behind for the assault gun brigades still fighting under subordination to the *8. Armee.*[1110]

1105 Brandner was born in September 1915 in Hohnberg, Austria. He joined the Austrian army in 1936. In March 1938, he was taken over by the German *Wehrmacht*, where he began his service in *Artillerie-Regiment 102.* He participated in the Polish campaign, then in January 1940, he was transferred to *leichte Artillerie-Ersatz-Abteilung (mot.) 102*, from where he was sent to Jüterbog in February to undergo an artillery officers' training course. In July 1940 he was promoted to a lieutenant in reserve in July. On 21 August 1941, he was transferred to *III./Artillerie-Regiment 2* in Jüterbog, where he was retrained as assault artilleryman. On 10 September 1941. he got into the *3. Batterie/Sturmgeschütz-Abteilung 202.* In March 1942, he went off to *Sturmgeschütz-Ersatz-Abteilung 200* for a short while, then he was transferred to *Sturmgeschütz-Ersatz-Abteilung 300.* On 27 May 1942, he joined *Sturmgeschütz-Abteilung 202* again, as (first acting, then, from 15 November as assigned) commander of the *2. Batterie.* From 13 June 1942 he was first lieutenant in reserve, then, from 1 October he became a regular officer. He was recommended twice for the Knight's Cross of the Iron Cross, but he was awarded other decorations instead. He was promoted to captain in July 1943. On 16 September, he was awarded the German Cross in Gold, having knocked out a total of 45 Soviet tanks with its assault gun '*Phönix*', as commander of the *2. Batterie.* From 24 October to 10 December 1944 he underwent an assault gun brigade commanders' training course, the in mid-December he was assigned as commander of *Sturmgeschütz-Brigade 912.* During the battles fought by this unit (they knocked out a total of 600 Soviet AFVs while suffering 38 knocked-out assault guns in Courland) he was finally awarded the Knight's Cross of the Iron Cross, which he received on 17 March 1945. The number of his own knock-outs had increased to 66 by then. Taken by the Soviets, he was POW until November 1947. He died in June, 1996 in Vienna. *See* Scherzer, Veit – Farwick, Werner: *Die Ritterkreuzträger der Sturmartillerie 1939-45.* Band 1: A-Krafft. Jena, 2010. pp. 98-101.

1106 NARA T312, R66 (*Armeeoberkommando 8*), F7585696.

1107 NARA T312, R64 (*Armeeoberkommando 8*), Kriegsgliederung der 8. Armee. Stand vom 19. 3. 1944.

1108 NARA T312, R64 (*Armeeoberkommando 8*), Anlage zum Kriegstagebuch Nr. 132 am 24. 3. 1944.

1109 NARA T312, R64 (*Armeeoberkommando 8*), Kriegsgliederung der 8. Armee. Stand vom 27. 3. 1944.

1110 NARA T312, R64 (*Armeeoberkommando 8*), Anlage zum Kriegstagebuch Nr. 134 am 28. 3. 1944. However, according to German daily situation maps *Sturmgeschütz-Brigade 202* was subordinated to the *VII. Armeekorps* until 2 April 1944 and to *XXXX. Panzerkorps* until 20 April with two other assault gun brigades. *See* NARA T78, R136 (*Oberkommando des Heeres*), F6065350.

Reorganization of *Sturmgeschütz-Brigade 202* in Germany, April–June, 1944.

The remnants of the brigade were transported by rail via Ploesti and Nagyszeben across Hungary to Vienna and from there they were ordered to the area of Neisse in Upper-Silesia for reorganization.[1111]

In the course of its reorganization, *Sturmgeschütz-Brigade 202* was equipped in accordance with the new assault gun battery TOE (St.N. 446A) issued on 1 June 1944. An assault gun battery was now made up of the assault gun of the battery commander, three assault guns in the first and third platoons respectively, and three assault howitzers theoretically concentrated in the second platoon.[1112] Including the assault gun of the battalion commander, the brigade still had 31 assault guns, at least in theory.

1 JULY 1944

The brigade still had no assault guns but at least the 22 StuG. III assault guns and 9 StuH. 42 assault howitzers[1113] had been provisionally issued to the unit.[1114]

In the first half of July 1944, *Sturmgeschütz-Brigade 202* received its combat vehicles and completed 10 weeks of reorganization in the area of Ziegenhals and Langendorf in Upper-Silesia.[1115]

1111 Kurowski, Franz – Tornau, Gottfried: *Sturmgeschütze – Die Panzer der Infanterie.* Würzburg, 2008. p. 236.

1112 Spielberger, Walter J.: *Sturmgeschütze. Entwicklung und Fertigung der sPak.* Stuttgart, 1997. Third edition. p. 240. Based on available photos, we assume, that besides their individual names and the German military sign the identification symbols of their platoon was painted according to the digits of the number of the vehicle (among others, on the side armour plates). The markings were: circle, a rhombus standing on one of its points, column, triangle standing on its side and a *Balkenkreuz.* In the photograph taken in July 1944, in Ziegenhals we can see a column painted inside the rhombus standing on one of its points. The higher cross might be a symbol indicating that the vehicle is that of the battery commander.

1113 To carry out the original task of the assault artillery (to provide direct fire support subordinated to the infantry) more effectively the Germans developed the assault howitzer equipped with a 10.5 cm main armament in 1942, which carried a howitzer in its assault gun-like superstructure; it was effective mainly against personnel and field fortifications. With HEAT shells it was also effective against AFVs. The first Sturmhaubitze (abbreviated as StuH.) 42 was shown to Adolf Hitler on 2 October 1942. A total of 1,217 were built before the end of the war.

1114 NARA T78, R269 (*General der Artillerie im OKH*), F6217463.

1115 Kurowski, Franz – Tornau, Gottfried: *Sturmgeschütze – Die Panzer der Infanterie.* Würzburg, 2008. p. 214.

PART III

IN *HEERESGRUPPE NORD*

CHAPTER 8

In the sector of the German *16. Armee* in the Baltic area

1944

Operational background:

The reorganized Sturmgeschütz-Brigade 202 was operating in the northern part of the eastern theatre during the last months of the war. Its assault guns defended the southern and south-eastern foreground of Riga, then fought on Sworbe Peninsula and finally repelled the Soviet's repeated attacks in the area of Frauenburg and Preekuln during the so-called Battles for Courland (Kurlandschlachten).

14 JULY 1944

The unit entrained at Ziegenhals railway station and set off for its new deployment area in Finland. However the transports were stopped in Danzig as a result of the serious operational situation that had emerged in the area of Dünaburg and Vilnius and it was to these locations that the newly equipped assault gun brigade was deployed.

20 JULY 1944

At 1030 hours the German *16. Armee* informed the staff of the *XXXXII. Armeekorps* that the whole of *Sturmgeschütz-Brigade 202,* brought up to full strength, would soon be put under the command of the corps.[1116]

1116 NARA T314, R1021 (*XXXXIII. Armeekorps*), F000499.

As soon as the unit arrived by rail in the area of Dünaburg, the Soviets opened fire at the transport at a minor railway station – the struggle for Dünaburg had already begun by that time.

Soviet troops cut the railroad to Dünaburg forcing *Sturmgeschütz-Brigade 202* to detrain before it reached the town. That operation was commanded by *Oberleutnant* Zollenkopf. Securing tasks were carried out by three AFVs of the *1. Batterie* (commanded by *Leutnant* Gebhard). The other two assault gun commanders were *Wachtmeister* Scharf and *Unteroffizier* Leo Heimann.

The three assault guns took up firing positions on the eastern perimeter of the railway station, observing the wooded area nearby. As soon as the Soviets dashed out from the forest, the German assault gun battery opened fire, forcing them back among the trees. Having detrained successfully, the battery moved to the small Latvian town of Zakischky through an area controlled by partisans.[1117]

22 JULY 1944

At 1000 hours, forces of *Sturmgeschütz-Brigade 202* and *Sturmgeschütz-Brigade 184* – subordinated to the *XXXXIII Armeekorps* on that day – were put under the command of the divisions of the corps in batteries with their focal point in the sector of the *58. Infanterie-Division.*[1118] That division received the *2. Batterie / Sturmgeschütz-Brigade 202* and the *3. Batterie/ Sturmgeschütz-Brigade 184.*[1119]

23 JULY 1944

The *1. Batterie /Sturmgeschütz-Brigade 202* fought in the sector of *61. Infanterie-Division* in the area of Ponemunok where the Germans knocked out two Soviet T–34 tanks. The *3. Batterie* was put into action in the area of Weherinja.[1120]

At around 1800 hours, the *61. Infanterie-Division* received orders from the corps to dispatch the *3. Batterie/ Sturmgeschütz-Brigade 202* to the sector of the *225. Infanterie-Division*[1121] where it was put into action along the highway running southwards to prevent the Soviets from advancing towards Rakischki.

By the orders of the *16. Armee*, the staff of the *58. Infanterie-Division* was to dispatch the *1. Batterie*, and the staff of the *61. Infanterie-Division* the *2. Batterie/ Sturmgeschütz-Brigade 202*, to Zarasai immediately, to the sector of the *87. Infanterie-Division.*[1122]

At 2145 hours the *225. Infanterie-Division* reported that they had put four assault guns into action against five Soviet tanks that had broken through at Hill 128 in the sector of *Füsilier-Bataillon 58.* Ten minutes later the division reported

---

1117 Kurowski, Franz – Tornau, Gottfried: *Sturmgeschütze – Die Panzer der Infanterie.* Würzburg, 2008. p. 214.

1118 NARA T314, R1021 (*XXXXIII. Armeekorps*), F000503.

1119 NARA T314, R1022 (*XXXXIII. Armeekorps*), F000295.

1120 NARA T314, R1022 (*XXXXIII. Armeekorps*), F000301.

1121 NARA T314, R1021 (*XXXXIII. Armeekorps*), F000509.

1122 NARA T314, R1021 (*XXXXIII. Armeekorps*), F000768.

that they had already knocked out two of the five Soviet AFVs standing in the area of Skrobischki with the other three retreating into the forest in a south-easterly direction under attack by the grenadiers with anti-tank small arms.[1123]

24 JULY 1944

At 0330 hours the *1. Batterie/ Sturmgeschütz-Brigade 202* moved off in the direction of Zarasai, towards the front line of the *87. Infanterie-Division* which was assigned to *II. Armeekorps*. The *2. Batterie* (with three assault guns) followed the *1. Batterie* at 0830 hours.[1124]

The *3. Batterie* of the brigade was still subordinated to *225. Infanterie-Division.* In the sector of that division, a total of 14 Soviet AFVs were knocked out that day (these were probably from the 117 Tank Brigade of the 1 Tank Corps).[1125]

25 JULY 1944

At 0230 hours, the *II. Armeekorps* informed its subordinate units that the newly arrived *1. Batterie /Sturmgeschütz-Brigade 202* had been attached to the *132. Infanterie-Division.* The staff of the brigade together with its *2. Batterie* was held in corps reserve in the area of Sarassai. One of the officers of the assault artillery unit was sent to the command post of the *87. Infanterie-Division* for further orders.[1126]

The *1. Batterie /Sturmgeschütz-Brigade 202* (with nine combat-ready assault guns) arrived in the sector of *132. Infanterie-Division* at 1040 hours where it came under the command of *Grenadier-Regiment 436.*[1127]

During the day the *2. Batterie /Sturmgeschütz-Brigade 202* (with eight combat-ready assault guns) was relieved from assignment to *Grenadier-Regiment 173* in the sector of *87. Infanterie-Division* in the area of Azuoline[1128] and attached to the *215. Infanterie-Division.* That division had its own assault gun unit in its anti-tank battalion, namely *Sturmgeschütz-Abteilung 1215* (with four combat-ready assault guns).[1129]

26 JULY 1944

At 0300 hours, the staff of the *II. Armeekorps* subordinated the *1. Batterie/ Sturmgeschütz-Brigade 202* to *Kampfgruppe 'Wagner'*[1130]. The *2. Batterie* of the brigade (still with eight combat-ready assault guns) remained in the sector of the *215. Infanterie-Division.*[1131]

1123 NARA T314, R1021 (*XXXXIII. Armeekorps*), F000511.

1124 NARA T314, R1021 (*XXXXIII. Armeekorps*), F000513.

1125 NARA T314, R1022 (*XXXXIII. Armeekorps*), F000801.

1126 NARA T314, R161 (*II. Armeekorps*), F000102.

1127 NARA T314, R161 (*II. Armeekorps*), F000120.

1128 NARA T314, R161 (*II. Armeekorps*), F000132.

1129 NARA T314, R161 (*II. Armeekorps*), F000119.

1130 Battle group of *Generalleutnant* Herbert Wagner, commander of *132. Infanterie-Division*.

1131 NARA T314, R161 (*II. Armeekorps*), F000313.

In the sector of the *132. Infanterie-Division*, the *1. Batterie /Sturmgeschütz-Brigade 202* (with four combat-ready assault guns) was operating in the sector of *Grenadier-Regiment 437.*[1132]

27 JULY 1944

At 1410 hours the *225. Infanterie-Division* received orders from the staff of the *XXXXIII. Armeekorps* to dispatch the *3. Batterie/Sturmgeschütz-Brigade 202* and the *1. Batterie/ Sturmgeschütz-Brigade 184* to the sector of the *58. Infanterie-Division.*[1133]This was because the Soviets had launched an attack on the sector of that division with three rifle divisions and two tank brigades, and support from ground attack aircraft, in the area of Gindviliai and Skapiskis and had achieved a significant breakthrough.[1134]

At 1615 hours the staff, as well as the *1.* and *2. Batterie*[1135] of *Sturmgeschütz-Brigade 202* were ordered from the sector of the *II. Armeekorps* to the zone of action of the *58. Infanterie-Division* and subordinated to the *XXXXIII. Armeekorps.* The commander of the corps, *General der Infanterie* Ehrenfried Boege, planned to deploy them, together with a battalion, in the area of Lebedziai in order to push out the attacking Soviets from the Levuo valley.[1136]

28 JULY 1944

At 0940 hours the commander of *Sturmgeschütz-Brigade 202*, *Hauptmann* Essigke, reported to the commander of *XXXXIII. Armeekorps.*[1137]

The staff of the *58. Infanterie-Division* planned to defend their main combat line with an attack launched by the reinforced *Feldersatz-Bataillon 158,* supported by four Tiger tanks of *Panzer-Abteilung 502* plus an assault gun battery. As soon as the *2. Batterie/ Sturmgeschütz-Brigade 202* arrived, they would be put into action together with the *II. Bataillon/ Grenadier-Regiment 220.*[1138]

The *1. Batterie/ Sturmgeschütz-Brigade 202* set off at 1930 hours from the sector of the *132. Infanterie-Division* behind the line of the *58. Infanterie-Division.*[1139]

1132 NARA T314, R161 (*II. Armeekorps*), F000333.

1133 NARA T314, R1021 (*XXXXIII. Armeekorps*), F000523.

1134 NARA T314, R1021 (*XXXXIII. Armeekorps*), F000848.

1135 The 2. battery of *Sturmgeschütz-Brigade 202* had already been under command of the *290. Infanterie-Division.* It was ordered back from there to the *II. Armeekorps*, then under command of the *XXXXIII. Armeekorps. See* NARA T314, R161 (*II. Armeekorps*), F000388.

1136 NARA T314, R1021 (*XXXXIII. Armeekorps*), F000525.

1137 NARA T314, R1021 (*XXXXIII. Armeekorps*), F000527.

1138 NARA T314, R1022 (*XXXXIII. Armeekorps*), F000325.

1139 NARA T314, R161 (*II. Armeekorps*), F000423.

29 JULY 1944

Another battery of *Sturmgeschütz-Brigade 202* arrived in the sector of the *XXXXIII. Armeekorps.*[1140]

30 JULY 1944

One battery of *Sturmgeschütz-Brigade 202* was attached to *Gruppe 'Krappe'*, named after the commander of *61. Infanterie-Division, Generalleutnant* Günther Krappe.[1141]

1 AUGUST 1944

Sturmgeschütz-Brigade 202 had 19 StuG. III assault guns and eight StuH. 42 assault howitzers.[1142] Of those AFVs, 12 assault guns and six assault howitzers were operational.[1143]

6 AUGUST 1944

At 1130 hours *Sturmgeschütz-Brigade 202*, together with the forces of the *290. Infanterie-Division* and other independent field and anti-aircraft artillery units, were subordinated to the staff of *I. Armeekorps.*[1144]

About half an hour later Soviet troops launched a ferocious attack with armoured support on the whole sector of the *290. Infanterie-Division,* with the focal point in the area of Murino and Svirgeliskiai. The German counter-thrusts partly repulsed the attack during which they knocked out 19 tanks and captured one.

The minor Soviet penetration at Svirgeliskiai was eliminated only at around 1700 hours. With that, the former front line was in German hands again.[1145]

In the morning, *Leutnant* Kühn of the *3. Batterie/ Sturmgeschütz-Brigade 202* hurried to a Soviet penetration in the sector of *215. Infanterie-Division* with most of the assault gun brigade, leaving two assault guns behind under the command of *Oberwachtmeister* Schulz and *Wachtmeister* Scharf. The latter's assault gun was not in the most perfect condition – its steering brakes were clogged. The two crews were lazily sunbathing when a grenadier officer ran to them yelling: '*Tanks! Tanks!*'

The eight assault artillerymen quickly took their seats inside their assault guns and started off from the farm where they had been located to the nearby battalion command post. They were within a distance of about 500 m of the command post when the first of the T–34 tanks that had broken through the German defences appeared. The Soviet AFVs, with accompanying rifle infantry, were advancing toward the command post of the *Grenadier-Regiment.* It was Scharf who initially

1140 NARA T314, R1022 (*XXXXIII. Armeekorps*), F000336.

1141 NARA T314, R1022 (*XXXXIII. Armeekorps*), F000339.

1142 According this the unit might have written off three assault guns and an assault howitzer as a total loss in July 1944.

1143 NARA T78, R269 (*General der Artillerie im OKH*), F6217721.

1144 NARA T314, R1022 (*XXXXIII. Armeekorps*), F000377.

1145 NARA T314, R75 (*I. Armeekorps*), F000022.

noticed the first three T–34 tanks approaching from the left. Scharf's driver turned the assault gun towards them and the gunner set one of the T–34s on fire with his first shot. The second round ripped away the next tank's turret. The gunner then disabled the third T–34 with several more shots. Meanwhile, Schulz's assault gun knocked out a fourth T–34. However, more Soviet tanks dashed forward from the right. They penetrated into the nearby farm buildings, then one of them broke out at high speed. The tank aimed his gun at *Wachtmeister* Scharf's assault gun. The driver was fully aware that he had to turn the assault gun as quickly as possible but the steering brakes were clogged. He engaged the reverse gear and pulled the left-side brake lever. The assault gun turned inside its own length, then stopped. Realizing his driver's intentions, the gunner was already aiming at the Soviet tank by that time. He fired. The forth T–34 burst into flames.

As the StuG. III assault guns rolled forward, the crews noticed the gun barrel of a tank at the corner of one of the estate buildings. The assault guns fired shells into the building, setting it on fire. Flames ran up the walls and across the roof. The commander of the Soviet tank, which had taken up an ambush position inside the building, decided to try to reach nearby woodland at high speed. *Wachtmeister* Scharf's assault gun opened fire, delivering a strong blow to the side of the T–34 which burst into flames.

Meanwhile, *Oberwachtmeister* Schulz advanced to contain the approaching Soviet rifle infantry. Scharf's assault gun joined the attack and together they smashed the enemy infantry that had passed through the German defences with HE shells and machine-gun fire. Having completed their immediate task, they reported to the regimental command post where they were given the task of relieving a battalion of the regiment that had been encircled by the Soviets about 7 km away. After discussing a suitable course of action, they started off. However, they soon ran into additional Soviet tanks that had broken through the German lines. Two of these were knocked out by *Wachtmeister* Scharf; *Oberwachtmeister* Schulz scored four tank kills. Having knocked out his seventh AFV, *Unteroffizier* Wulf – the gunner of Scharf's assault gun – was wounded when his assault gun took a hit. Despite this, he remained at his post and knocked out one more Soviet tank before his commander ordered him to withdraw to the dressing station.[1146] With that, *Wachtmeister* Scharf's assault gun knocked out a total of eight Soviet tanks on that day[1147] inside – according to certain sources[1148] – five minutes. Summing these up, Scharf had by then scored 40 knock-outs.[1149]

1146 Kurowski, Franz – Tornau, Gottfried: *Sturmgeschütze – Die Panzer der Infanterie*. Würzburg, 2008. p. 215. *Unteroffizier* Wulf died of his wounds in a hospital in Riga after a short while.

1147 The tanks probably belonged to the Soviet 1 Tank Corps.

1148 Scherzer, Veit – Farwick, Werner: *Die Ritterkreuzträger der Sturmartillerie 1939-45*. Band 2: Kranz-Z. Bayreuth, 2012. p. 191.

1149 NARA T314, R75 (*I. Armeekorps*), F000026-27.

Although reduced in numbers, the crews of the two assault guns continued fighting. They refuelled and drew ammunition then reshuffled the crewing tasks: Othmar, the loader, took over from the wounded gunner and *Wachtmeister* Scharf performed both the command and loading duties. Once again they jumped off with their assault gun and successfully repelled Soviet forces that had broken through, therby restoring the former main combat line. Having completed this task, Scharf left his assault gun to report the situation at the battalion command post just as it came under concentrated Soviet artillery fire. The NCO was wounded and dropped to the ground. His two comrades leapt out from their assault gun to rescue him. They carried him back inside the combat vehicle and drove to the brigade command post in sixth gear.[1150]

However, according to another source, having run out of ammunition, *Wachtmeister* Scharf returned to the supply strongpoint, left the wounded gunner there and, having found a replacement, took on fuel and ammunition before re-joining the battle with his assault gun, which was still not in perfect condition. While providing effective support for the infantry, *Wachtmeister* Scharf was seriously wounded inside his assault gun and was then carried back to the dressing station.

In recognition of his achievement that day, *Wachtmeister* Scharf[1151] was awarded the Knight's Cross of the Iron Cross on 17 August 1944.[1152] The NCO also received the highest form of praise – being mentioned by name in the *Wehrmacht* daily report on the 9 August 1944.

7 AUGUST 1944

Within the sector of the *I. Armeekorps*, most of *Sturmgeschütz-Brigade 202* was operating in the zone of action of the *290. Infanterie-Division* while part of it was fighting in the sector of the *61. Infanterie-Division,* subordinated to *Grenadier-Regiment 390.*[1153]

In the sector of the *290. Infanterie-Division*, *Grenadier-Regiment 503* was cut off by Soviet troops east of Radviliskis, in the area of Kurmene, but with the support of '*unknown assault guns*' (probably those of *Sturmgeschütz-Brigade 202*), the grenadiers

---

1150 Kurowski, Franz – Tornau, Gottfried*: Sturmgeschütze – Die Panzer der Infanterie*. Würzburg, 2008. p. 215.

1151 Scharf was born in April 1920 in Lichtenstein, Saxony. He joined the German army in August, 1938. He served in more construction battalions, machine gun replacement companies and also in *Infanterie-Regiment 118*. He volunteered into the assault artillery in January 1941. He was retrained as an artilleryman in Jüterbog. On 10 February 1941, he was transferred to the *3. Batterie/Sturmgeschütz-Abteilung 204*, from where, following its re-designation on 1 March, he moved to *Sturmgeschütz-Ersatz-Abteilung 200*. He was transferred to the *3. Batterie/Sturmgeschütz-Abteilung 202* on 14 February 1942. Having been wounded on 6 August 1944, he joined *Sturmgeschütz-Ersatz-Abteilung 300* on 1 September. In November 1944, he was transferred to *Artillerieschule II* in Groß-born, then, in January 1945, he was assigned as cadet sergeant major to *Fähnrichs-Regiment 1* raised as an alarm unit. On 8 February, he was wounded again, and with that, the war was over for him. He died in July 2001 in Glauchau. *See* Scherzer, Veit - Farwick, Werner: *Die Ritterkreuzträger der Sturmartillerie 1939-45.* Band 2: Kranz-Z. Bayreuth, 2012. pp. 189-192.

1152 Scherzer, Veit - Farwick, Werner: *Die Ritterkreuzträger der Sturmartillerie 1939-45*. Band 2: Kranz-Z. Bayreuth, 2012. p. 191. According to this remarkable writing, *Wachtmeister* Scharf achieved this accomplishment on 8 August 1944. However, contemporary documents of the *I. Armeekorps* clearly show, that the correct date is 6 August 1944.

1153 NARA T314, R74 (*I. Armeekorps*), F000056.

successfully broke out having, it must be admitted, suffered heavy casualties in the course of the engagement.[1154]

8 AUGUST 1944

At 0100 hours, the *290. Infanterie-Division* reported to the *I. Armeekorps* that they strengthened the defence of *Kampfgruppe Meyer*[1155] with five assault guns and a grenadier company.[1156]

9 AUGUST 1944

In the sector of the *290. Infanterie-Division,* where three batteries of *Sturmgeschütz-Brigade 202* fought, the Germans eliminated a Soviet penetration in the area of Sniukiskiai and knocked out six Soviet tanks there.[1157]

During the day, the *3. Batterie/ Sturmgeschütz-Brigade 202* (with four assault guns) was dispatched from the division back to the sector of the *XXXXIII. Armeekorps* where it took up positions 800 m north of Zemaiu.[1158] At 2100 hours the assault gun battery, although still subordinated to the *XXXXIII. Armeekorps,* was added to the reserve of the *16. Armee* together with the forces of *Grenadier-Regiment 333,* with immediate effect.[1159]

10 AUGUST 1944

From 1800 hours the *XXXXIII. Armeekorps* took over the sector of the *290. Infanterie-Division* which it withdrew and placed at the disposal of the *16. Armee.* However, independent units fighting under the command of the *290. Infanterie-Division* remained in position. These including the staff and *1.* and *3. Batterie/ Sturmgeschütz-Brigade 202,* which were again put under the command of the *XXXXIII. Armeekorps.*[1160]

11 AUGUST 1944

Two batteries of *Sturmgeschütz-Brigade 202* were fighting in the sector of the *58. Infanterie-Division.* The Soviet 67 Guards Rifle Division attacked the positions of *Grenadier-Regiment 220* east of the Memele throughout the day with the support of AFVs, ground attack aircraft and multiple-rocket launchers. They achieved minor penetrations, most of which were eliminated by the Germans. During the battle, *Sturmgeschütz-Brigade 202* and the *leichte Flak-Abteilung* provided excellent support

---

1154 Bauer, Josef: *290. Infanterie-Division 1940-1945.* Selbstverlag Kameradenhilfswerk 290. Inf. Div., Delmenhorst, 1960. p. 396.

1155 It was a blocking squad based on an AA-artillery battle group.

1156 NARA T314, R73 (*I. Armeekorps*), F000599.

1157 NARA T314, R75 (*I. Armeekorps*), F000033.

1158 NARA T314, R74 (*I. Armeekorps*), F001093.

1159 NARA T314, R1021 (*XXXXIII. Armeekorps*), F000561, and also F000999.

1160 NARA T314, R73 (*I. Armeekorps*), F000970.

for the grenadiers: the Germans knocked out six SU–85 self-propelled guns, two T–34 and two T–34/85 tanks as well as 17 anti-tank guns.[1161]

During the day the *3. Batterie/ Sturmgeschütz-Brigade 202* (with six batteries) came under the command of the *81. Infanterie-Division.*[1162]

12 AUGUST 1944

The whole *Sturmgeschütz-Brigade 202* was under the direct command of the *XXXXIII. Armeekorps.*[1163]

At 1800 hours, the *2. Batterie/ Sturmgeschütz-Brigade 202* was ordered from the sector of the *58. Infanterie-Division* to the zone of action of *225. Infanterie-Division.*[1164]

In the late evening, the forces of the *225. Infanterie-Division* eliminated a Soviet penetration in the area of Zageri with assault gun support.[1165]

15 AUGUST 1944

At 1100 hours *Sturmgeschütz-Brigade 202* was ordered to the sector of the *I. Armeekorps* again with immediate effect.[1166]

At 1105 hours the corps chief of staff, *Oberst i.G.* Heinz von Ziegler und Klipphausen, promised the assault-artillery unit to the *81. Infanterie-Division.*[1167] At 1425 hours he issued orders to the commander of *Sturmgeschütz-Brigade 202, Hauptmann* Essigke, to bring forward his unit into the area of Kirpes. The brigade commander had to undertake the necessary measures at the command post of the *61. Infanterie-Division* because his assault guns were at that time subordinated that division. The *81. Infanterie-Division* had to wait an hour for the *1. Batterie* to arrive, and three for the another one – the rest came later. *Sturmgeschütz-Brigade 202* had a total of 19 combat-ready assault guns at that time.[1168]

During the day in the sector of the *61. Infanterie-Division,* in the course of a counter-thrust carried out in the south-western foreground of Skaistkalne, the three German assault guns providing support knocked out a total of three Soviet T–34 tanks.[1169]

At 1835 hours the brigade again came under the command of the *290. Infanterie-Division* the front line of which had been breached in the area of Breileni by Soviet troops attacking from the east and pushed back to the line of Muzeni–Meireni–Gerozini. In the sector of the division a total of 34 Soviet tanks were reported as knocked out.[1170]

1161 NARA T314, R1022 (*XXXXIII. Armeekorps*), F000394, and also T314, R1022 (*XXXXIII. Armeekorps*), F000732.

1162 NARA T314, R74 (*I. Armeekorps*), F001104.

1163 NARA T314, R1022 (*XXXXIII. Armeekorps*), F000134.

1164 NARA T314, R1021 (*XXXXIII. Armeekorps*), F000569.

1165 NARA T314, R1021 (*XXXXIII. Armeekorps*), F000571.

1166 NARA T314, R1021 (*XXXXIII. Armeekorps*), F000575.

1167 NARA T314, R73 (*I. Armeekorps*), F000680.

1168 NARA T314, R73 (*I. Armeekorps*), F000682.

1169 NARA T314, R74 (*I. Armeekorps*), F001123 and F001127.

1170 NARA T314, R75 (*I. Armeekorps*), F000050 and F000052. From these 34 knock-outs 22 were achieved by the assault guns of *Sturmgeschütz-Brigade 912. See* T314, R75 (*I. Armeekorps*), F000543.

The staff of the *290. Infanterie-Division* had to block a Soviet attack in the area of Jaunsaule with two batteries of *Sturmgeschütz-Brigade 202*; the *3. Batterie* was in action in the same area but in the sector of *215. Infanterie-Division.*[1171]

According to the corps' daily orders, one battery of *Sturmgeschütz-Brigade 202* remained in the sector of the *290. Infanterie-Division* while the staff and two batteries were under the command of the *215. Infanterie-Division.*[1172]

One of the assigned assault gun batteries arrived at around 2000 hours at Keri from where it was ordered to the command post of *Grenadier-Regiment 435.*[1173]

16 AUGUST 1944

At 1700 hours, the staff of the *XXXXIII. Armeekorps* was informed that the *I. Armeekorps* would order the staff and two batteries of *Sturmgeschütz-Brigade 202* back into the sector of the *225. Infanterie-Division,* in the area of Girupnieki, with a total of 10 assault guns.[1174]

In the evening, at 1930 hours, following orders received from the *16. Armee,* the *I. Armeekorps* issued orders to the staffs of the *215.* and *290. Infanterie-Divisionen* to pull out the *2. Batterie* (with seven assault guns) as well as a platoon of the *1. Batterie/Sturmgeschütz-Brigade 202* (with three assault guns) from the front line after nightfall and send them, under order by the staff of the brigade, into the sector of the *XXXXIII. Armeekorps* on an assigned route of march via Valle and Luikas.[1175]

However, those orders were soon revoked by the staff of the *16. Armee* at the request of the *I. Armeekorps* because of continuing Soviet attacks in the sector of the corps' *290. Infanterie-Division,* where *Sturmgeschütz-Brigade 912* had lost two batteries of assault guns (two of the assault guns were destroyed).[1176] The forces of *Sturmgeschütz-Brigade 202* were therefore badly needed in this sector.

In the zone of action of the *215. Infanterie-Division,* at around 1300 hours, six assault guns of *Sturmgeschütz-Brigade 202* were deployed in the defensive sector of *Grenadier-Regiment 435* against a Soviet penetration in the area of Vecamuiza.[1177] Nightly assaults were carried out by that regiment – launched from the German bridgehead south of Bauske – with the support of the assault guns with the objective of preventing the entrenchment of Soviet anti-tank guns.[1178]

1171 NARA T314, R73 (*I. Armeekorps*), F000683.

1172 NARA T314, R75 (*I. Armeekorps*), F000635.

1173 NARA T314, R73 (*I. Armeekorps*), F000684.

1174 NARA T314, R1021 (*XXXXIII. Armeekorps*), F000577, and also F001056-57.

1175 NARA T314, R75 (*I. Armeekorps*), F000637.

1176 NARA T314, R75 (*I. Armeekorps*), F000543, and also T314, R73 (*I. Armeekorps*), F000692.

1177 NARA T314, R75 (*I. Armeekorps*), F000279.

1178 Von den Kämpfen der 215. württembergisch-badischen Infanterie-Division. Ein Erinnerungsbuch. Bearb.: Walter Schelm/ Dr. Hans Mehrle, Hrsg. vom Kameradenhilfswerk und Trad. Verb. d. ehem. 215. Inf.Div., Stuttgart 1955. p. 258.

17 AUGUST 1944

During the previous three days, in their drive towards Riga, the eight rifle divisions of the Soviet 6 Guards Army and 43 Army had been unable to breach the defences of *I. Armeekorps.* In the sector of the German corps, 119 Soviet tanks and self-propelled guns were reported as knocked out during these three days. The forces of the *290.* and *81. Infanterie-Divisionen*, which had suffered heavy losses, were efficiently supported by the assault guns of *Sturmgeschütz-Brigade 202* among others.[1179]

18 AUGUST 1944

In accordance with directives received from the *16. Armee,* the *XXXXIII. Armeekorps* issued orders to its subordinate divisions to prepare for raising organic grenadier platoons to accompany the assault guns.[1180]

Temporarily, the order applied only to the *Sturmgeschütz-Abteilungen* established in the *Panzerjäger-Abteilungen* of the divisions. Nevertheless, those divisions which still didn't have a *Sturmgeschütz-Abteilung* of their own, could request assault guns for their 14-day training courses. The accompanying grenadier platoons were made up of five NCOs and 56 enlisted men (12 of them pioneers). Each three-vehicle assault gun platoon was given an accompanying grenadier section. An NCO (section commander), a pioneer and three grenadiers were assigned to the commander's assault gun and a squad leader, a pioneer, two machine-gunners (with a light machine gun) and a grenadier was assigned to the second and third assault guns in the platoon.[1181]

In the sector of the *215. Infanterie-Division*, Soviet assault groups occupied the local brickworks in the town of Bauske and the *II. Bataillon/ Grenadier-Regiment 380* was unable to retake its former positions despite repeated attempts. On this occasion the Soviet anti-tank guns provided too much resistance for the Germans to overcome. However, after nightfall, *5. Kompanie* managed to repel the Soviet troops from the brickworks.[1182]

19 AUGUST 1944

From the forces of the *XXXXIII. Armeekorps* and *X. Armeekorps*, *Gruppe 'Boege'* was set up and the *I. Armeekorps* promised to release *Sturmgeschütz-Brigade 202* to

1179 NARA T314, R74 (*I. Armeekorps*), F000153.

1180 NARA T314, R1021 (*XXXXIII. Armeekorps*), F000581.

1181 NARA T314, R1021 (*XXXXIII. Armeekorps*), F001066-67.

1182 Von den Kämpfen der 215. württembergisch-badischen Infanterie-Division. Ein Erinnerungsbuch. Bearb.: Walter Schelm/ Dr. Hans Mehrle, Hrsg. vom Kameradenhilfswerk und Trad. Verb. d. ehem. 215. Inf.Div., Stuttgart 1955. pp. 258-259.

them.[1183]However, the assault artillery battalion was still fighting in the bridgehead held in the area of Bauske, and could only be withdrawn from the front line and dispatched by midnight at the earliest.[1184]

At 0300 hours the Soviets[1185] launched an attack on the German bridgehead – following an artillery preparation lasting half an hour – with the fire support of several mortars and anti-tank guns. The defending *I. Bataillon/Grenadier-Regiment 380* was unable to prevent the Soviets from penetrating the western part of the bridgehead under the veil of night. Then, taking advantage of the descending fog, the Soviet forces penetrated the western half of the town via the peninsula at Bauske and advancing from there in a north-easterly direction they reached the bridge at the northern part of the town.

The Germans immediately launched a counter-attack with the support of the assault guns of *Sturmgeschütz-Brigade 202,* elements of *Füsilier-Bataillon 215* (along the north-western bank of the Memele River) and regimental units of *Grenadier-Regiment 380,* with the other parts of the *Füsilier-Bataillon 215,* on the Soviet forces that had broken into the town. Having crushed stubborn resistance, the Germans repelled the Soviets behind the Musa and Lielupe rivers by 0910 hours during vicious street-by-street and house-to-house fighting.

Around noon, the Soviets launched an attack on the eastern part of the bridgehead from three directions with the aim of eliminating the German troops that continued to offer resistance in a westerly direction.

The Germans regrouped their forces and at 1700 hours began a counter-thrust. By 2300 hours the *I. Bataillon/ Grenadier-Regiment 380* and the *II. Bataillon/ Grenadier-Regiment 435,* together with the assault guns of *Sturmgeschütz-Brigade 202* – and later joined by *Füsilier-Bataillon 215* – had retaken the part of the bridgehead previously lost and defended it against a renewed Soviet attempt to occupy it at 0300 hours.[1186]

According to certain sources, the assault guns knocked out a total of 21 tanks and self-propelled guns that day and therefore made a significant contribution to the narrowing down of the bridgehead.[1187] Thirteen Soviet armoured combat vehicles were knocked out by *Wachtmeister* Scharf.[1188] However, contemporary German and Soviet sources do not mention any Soviet AFVs in the bridgehead on that day. It is likely that the events described here actually happened a month later, on 15 September 1944 (cf. later in this work).

1183 NARA T314, R1021 (*XXXXIII. Armeekorps*), F000587. The *16. Armee* originally proposed that *Sturmgeschütz-Brigade 912* should be regrouped, since *Sturmgeschütz-Brigade 202* was in action. *See* NARA T314, R73 (*I. Armeekorps*), F000703.

1184 NARA T314, R75 (*I. Armeekorps*), F000544. The *I. Armeekorps* instructed the staff of the *290. Infanterie-Division* at 0355 hours to dispatch an assault gun battery (with at least five assault guns) toward Bauske. *See* NARA T314, R73 (*I. Armeekorps*), F000700.

1185 The attack was carried out by the 15 Independent Assault Battalion of the Soviet 43 Army, the 938 and 992 Rifle Regiment of the 306 Rifle Division, the 47 and 67 penal company, a total of 2,000 men.

1186 NARA T314, R74 (*I. Armeekorps*), F000690.

1187 *See* Kurowski, Franz – Tornau, Gottfried: *Sturmgeschütze – Die Panzer der Infanterie.* Würzburg, 2008. p. 216.

1188 Kern, Erich: *Generalfeldmarschall Schörner.* Rosenheim, n. d. 4. edition. p. 155.

The achievement of the German troops involved in retaking the bridgehead was praised two days later by the commander of the *16. Armee, General der Infanterie* Carl Hilpert.[1189]

The staff officer in charge of the anti-tank defence of the *I. Armeekorps* issued orders to the staff of the *215. Infanterie-Division* to dispatch the staff and two batteries of *Sturmgeschütz-Brigade 202* immediately, and then a third battery by midnight at the latest, to the sector of the *XXXXIII. Armeekorps,* in the area of Koknese. The brigade commander was to report to the corps' command post in the area of Dzeni for further briefing.[1190]

20 AUGUST 1944

Sturmgeschütz-Brigade 202 moved out from the sector of the *I. Armeekorps* to the zone of action of the *XXXXIII. Armeekorps.*[1191]

At 1400 hours, in the sector of the *329. Infanterie-Division, Major* Manfred Beutner assumed command of a *Kampfgruppe* made up of two battalions of the reinforced *Grenadier-Regiment 551,* a battalion of the *51. Infanterie-Division,* an additional subordinated battalion, a pioneer battalion and the *3. Batterie/ Sturmgeschütz-Brigade 202.* These forces attacked Soviet troops[1192] that had captured the town of Ergli the previous day from the west with the support of a German artillery corps and the ground-attack aircraft of *Schlachtgeschwader 2.*[1193] The commander of the *Kampfgruppe, Major* Beutner, later summed up the events when he wrote:

During the fighting that day we forced back the enemy one kilometre west of Ergli. Military operations ceased. Considering the rather peacetime behaviour of the [enemy] *troops, we concluded that, following six weeks of pursuit, the enemy considered a night attack impossible. At the forest facing us, several tanks, vehicles and infantry could be observed at a distance of 600-800 m. At 600-700 m an enemy battle group was assembling with tanks, heavy weapons and several vehicles carrying supplies for the troops after nightfall, almost as if it were peacetime. Combat vehicles were fuelled up; they loaded up with ammunition and soldiers were grouping around the field kitchens. A little farther off a battery was taking up a firing position to provide close support. Behind the formation being supplied there was a wooded area up to the Ogre River, obviously full of combat and supply vehicles. Since the enemy had ceased its military operations, our attack made good progress and we were given the task of taking Ergli. I decided to continue the attack after nightfall, following a short but devastating artillery preparation. Since the commander*

1189 NARA T314, R74 (*I. Armeekorps*), F000180.

1190 NARA T314, R75 (*I. Armeekorps*), F000647.

1191 NARA T314, R75 (*I. Armeekorps*), F000070.

1192 The town was retaken by the elements of the Soviet 5 Tank Corps, which possessed 45 serviceable tanks and self-propelled guns on 20 August 1944. *See* http://militera.lib.ru/memo/russian/eremenko_ai3/11.html (2. June 2015).

1193 Pape, Klaus: *329. Infanterie-Division. Cholm – Demjansk – Kurland.* Jena, 2007. p. 174.

of the assault gun battery[1194] *had notified me that he would support the attack with his assault guns before darkness set in, the other battalion commanders also gave their consent to continue the attack. I gave orders for the attack orally, on the spot. I began the attack with artillery fire, at around 2030 hours. Unfortunately it turned out that we had no signals communication with the artillery. Therefore I took appropriate emergency measures... and they worked well. The task was given to the artillery by radio from the assault gun battery to the command post of the Sturmgeschütz-Brigade, from which it was forwarded by an officer to the commander of the artillery corps. What happened next, was one of the most distinctive experiences of the war for every soldier.*

At nightfall, at 2045 hours, in that beautiful summer evening, by the silvery light of the rising moon, the immense fire strike of the artillery began. At the same time, the immaculately dressed officer of the assault gun battery opened fire at identified targets with all of his assault guns. Three or four tanks immediately caught fire. An ammunition truck was hit and exploded. In the light, provided by the continuous flashes of the exploding shells, more targets became visible. When the artillery shifted its fire to the wooded area farther back, and the enemy formation was still covered by smoke, the grenadiers of the battalions launched an attack along a 1.5 km front. During their advance, they were firing all of their small arms – rifles, automatic rifles, machine guns. Flares illuminated the battlefield as if by daylight. [...]

The enemy didn't put up any organized resistance. We cut off the withdrawal routes to Ergli, thereby making it possible for them to escape only westwards, across the Ogre River without any vehicles. The shock attack presented an awe-inspiring sight full of pride. The enemy fire was dying down. They left tanks, artillery pieces, anti-tank guns, mortars, motor vehicles and machine guns behind. Among the captured vehicles we found ones lost by the 23. Infanterie-Division. We resupplied the ammunition used up from a German ammunition dump found there. It was with the greatest pleasure that we came across a German food dump partly plundered by the Russians. While the two battalions attacked between the railway and the highway, as well as along the highway towards the bridge at Ergli, according to their assigned tasks, the third battalion with the assault gun battery received the mission of covering our northern flank and taking positions along the Ogre. Having made rapid progress, Grenadier-Regiment 551 reached the perimeter of Ergli at around midnight meeting no resistance whatsoever. On the way to Ergli there were several armoured fighting vehicles that had been destroyed by our dive bombers.[1195,1196]

The panic-stricken Soviet defenders immediately evacuated Ergli, which fell into German hands again. The forces of the *Kampfgruppe* exploited the confusion amongst the Soviets, and occupied a bridgehead east of the Ogre River. The Germans

1194 The commander of the *3. Batterie/Sturmgeschütz-Brigade 202* was *Oberleutnant* Martin Zollenkopf.

1195 It is highly possible that the air strike was carried out by the Fw 190 and Ju 87 ground attack aircraft of *Schlachtgeschwader 2.*

1196 Pape, Klaus: *329. Infanterie-Division. Cholm – Demjansk – Kurland.* Jena, 2007. pp. 174-175.

inflicted heavy casualties on the Soviet troops: they destroyed 34 tanks and assault guns and captured an additional 17 AFVs, 27 anti-tank guns, 12 pieces of 12 cm heavy mortars, several motor vehicles, small arms and quantities of ammunition. In the course of the fighting the Germans freed 60 seriously wounded comrades who were in captivity in the town. By reoccupying Ergli during the night raid, connection between the *X.* and *XXXXIII. Armeekorps* was restored. For this achievement, the commander of the German *Kampfgruppe* was awarded the Knight's Cross of the Iron Cross on the 30 September, 1944.[1197]

21 AUGUST 1944

At 1030 hours, the *2. Batterie/ Sturmgeschütz-Brigade 202* marched out from the area of Irsi to the sector of *389. Infanterie-Division* via Kapmaliesi and Bulvani, in the direction of Zalaci.[1198]

The *X. Armeekorps* prepared to deploy anti-tank guns and anti-tank weapons, including the assault guns[1199] subordinated to *Gruppe 'Wagner'*, in, and to the south of, the retaken settlement of Ergli [1200] as soon as possible in order to defend against a probable attack by Soviet armour.

The *3. Batterie /Sturmgeschütz-Brigade 202* under the command of *Oberleutnant* Zollenkopf was still supporting the grenadiers of the *329. Infanterie-Division* in the area of Ergli. In the fighting of the previous night, the assault artillerymen captured a total of 12 tanks and several trucks. Having retaken Ergli from elements of the Soviet 5 Tank Corps, another nine AFVs fell into German hands. The assault guns destroyed an additional two Soviet tanks. Later (probably on 22 August 1944), the assault gun battery again clashed with Soviet forces east of the settlement and scored another 16 AFV knock-outs.[1201]

Oberleutnant Zollenkopf's accomplishments in this action were recognized by the inclusion of his name in the Roll of Honour of the German Army *(Ehrenblatt des Heeres).*

23 AUGUST 1944

At 1900 hours, *1.* and *3. Batterie/ Sturmgeschütz-Brigade 202*[1202] were subordinated to the staff of the *389. Infanterie-Division* together with two 21 cm mortar battalions and one heavy field howitzer battalion of *Artillerie-Regiment z.b.V. 610.*[1203] The

1197 Pape, Klaus: *329. Infanterie-Division. Cholm – Demjansk – Kurland.* Jena, 2007. p. 176.

1198 NARA T314, R1021 (*XXXXIII. Armeekorps*), F000593.

1199 Including the AFVs of the 1. and 3. batteries of *Sturmgeschütz-Brigade 202.*

1200 NARA T314, R476 (*X. Armeekorps*), F000186.

1201 Kurowski, Franz – Tornau, Gottfried: *Sturmgeschütze – Die Panzer der Infanterie.* Würzburg, 2008. p. 216. For his merit, Zollenkopf was soon promoted to a captain, at the age of only 22.

1202 The two assault gun battery was detached from *Gruppe 'Wagner'* on 23 August 1944, after nightfall. *See* NARA T314, R476 (*X. Armeekorps*), F000156.

1203 NARA T314, R1021 (*XXXXIII. Armeekorps*), F000601.

commander of *Sturmgeschütz-Brigade 202, Hauptmann* Essigke, was to report to the divisional command post in Apali.[1204]

In the late afternoon, forces of the *389. Infanterie-Division* retook a group of houses north of Baltuzi. Following intense artillery and mortar-preparation, the Soviets launched another attack with the support of AFVs and reoccupied the buildings. Here, the assault guns subordinated to the German division, knocked out six Soviet tanks and a seventh was knocked out by a grenadier's *Panzerschreck* anti-tank rocket launcher.[1205]

At 2330 hours, the *X. Armeekorps* received orders from the *Höhere Artillerie-Kommandeur 315, Generalleutnant* Christian Usinger, that *Sturmgeschütz-Brigade 202* should take over the remaining assault guns of the *2. Batterie/ Sturmgeschütz-Brigade 909.* Following that, the battery was assigned to *Sturmgeschütz-Brigade 912* as its *4. Batterie.*[1206]

24 AUGUST 1944

At 0800 hours, the whole of *Sturmgeschütz-Brigade 202* was subordinated to the *389. Infanterie-Division.*[1207]

At 1945 hours the staff battery and the *1.* and *3. Batterie/Sturmgeschütz-Brigade 202* were ordered to the area of Irsi under the command of *Gruppe 'Boege'.*[1208] *Hauptmann* Essigke had to report to the command post of the *24. Infanterie-Division* at Irsi at 0430 hours next day.[1209] The *2. Batterie* of the assault gun unit remained under the command of *389. Infanterie-Division.*[1210]

25 AUGUST 1944

At 1600 hours, one battery of *Sturmgeschütz-Brigade 202* was sent from Irsi to the area of Berzini where Soviet armoured forces had broken through the defences of the *X. Armeekorps.* The German assault guns eliminated the penetration by 1745 hours then, in accordance with the orders received at 2130 hours, they came back under the command of *Gruppe 'Boege'* in the area of Irsi where they were placed in reserve.[1211]

27 AUGUST 1944

In the sector of the *389. Infanterie-Division,* the *2. Batterie / Sturmgeschütz-Brigade 202* provided support for an assault squad during their attempt to occupy a group

1204 NARA T314, R1021 (*XXXXIII. Armeekorps*), F001111.
1205 NARA T314, R1022 (*XXXXIII. Armeekorps*), F000460.
1206 NARA T314, R476 (*X. Armeekorps*), F000154.
1207 NARA T314, R1022 (*XXXXIII. Armeekorps*), F000140.
1208 NARA T314, R1021 (*XXXXIII. Armeekorps*), F000603.
1209 NARA T314, R1021 (*XXXXIII. Armeekorps*), F001119.
1210 NARA T314, R476 (*X. Armeekorps*), F000151.
1211 NARA T314, R1021 (*XXXXIII. Armeekorps*), F000605.

of houses north of Baltuzi, and the wooded area south of Jakteni. Following a short engagement, the Germans pushed back the Soviet troops in a south-easterly direction. The assault guns knocked out five Soviet tanks west of the church in Vietalva.[1212]

28 AUGUST 1944

In the morning, the *3. Batterie/ Sturmgeschütz-Brigade 202* and the *II. Bataillon/ Grenadier-Regiment 438,* were withdrawn from the sector of the *121. Infanterie-Division* and sent to the area of Irsi with instructions to arrive there by 1000 hours. *Gruppe 'Boege'* was then disbanded.[1213]

29 AUGUST 1944

At 1650 hours, *Sturmgeschütz-Brigade 202* was ordered to the area of Lielmani and Kalnaulini.[1214] Due to that, the *2. Batterie* of the brigade was also relieved from assignment with the *389. Infanterie-Division.*[1215]

30 AUGUST 1944

At 0800 hours, *Sturmgeschütz-Brigade 202* came under the direct command of the *XXXXIII. Armeekorps.*[1216]

The *XXXXIII. Armeekorps* reported to the staff of the *16. Armee* that the grenadier platoons of the *58.* and *205. Infanterie-Divisionen*, accompanying the assault guns, would be trained together with the AFVs of *Sturmgeschütz-Brigade 202.* In those two divisions the training began in Kalnaulini on 2 September.[1217]

1 SEPTEMBER 1944

Sturmgeschütz-Brigade 202 had a total of 18 StuG. III assault guns and seven StuH. 42 assault howitzers.[1218] Of these, 14 assault guns and four assault howitzers were combat-ready.[1219]

2 SEPTEMBER 1944

Sturmgeschütz-Brigade 202 received orders to survey the area then take up readiness positions between Bunduli and Stirnas due to a Soviet troop concentration that had been observed in the line of the *389. Infanterie-Division.*[1220]

1212 NARA T314, R1022 (*XXXXIII. Armeekorps*), F000478.

1213 NARA T314, R1021 (*XXXXIII. Armeekorps*), F000611.

1214 NARA T314, R1021 (*XXXXIII. Armeekorps*), F000613, as well as F001166.

1215 NARA T314, R1022 (*XXXXIII. Armeekorps*), F000488.

1216 NARA T314, R1022 (*XXXXIII. Armeekorps*), F000144.

1217 NARA T314, R1021 (*XXXXIII. Armeekorps*), F001172-73.

1218 According this source one assault gun and one assault howitzer of the unit were total losses in August 1944.

1219 NARA T78, R269 (*General der Artillerie im OKH*), F6217718.

1220 NARA T314, R1021 (*XXXXIII. Armeekorps*), F001200.

4 SEPTEMBER 1944

At 1700 hours, elements of the *225. Infanterie-Division* launched a successful attack with the support of three assault guns of *Sturmgeschütz-Brigade 202* south of Daudzeva where the Soviet forces had penetrated into the main combat line during the night. The Germans restored the original situation and took nine prisoners.[1221]

At 2015 hours, one battery of *Sturmgeschütz-Brigade 202,* together with the soldiers of *Grenadier-Regiment 209,* were ordered to the zone between Jaunbebri and Blankas (within the sector of the *389. Infanterie-Division*) where, on joining the *'Wenden'* position, they had to survey and establish a blocking position with a north-eastern front line.[1222]

10 SEPTEMBER 1944

The *389. Infanterie-Division* was planning an assault. To this end, at 1300 hours, it requested and received a battery of *Sturmgeschütz-Brigade 202* from the staff of the *XXXXIII. Armeekorps* which was initially adamant that this would not be the *2. Batterie.*[1223] However, the division explicitly required the *2. Batterie* on the grounds that it had become well acquainted with the assigned area around Silakalns during its previous missions.[1224] The corps then reluctantly agreed to subordinate the *2. Batterie* to them.

At 2030 hours, the corps retracted its permission for subordination of the *2. Batterie* to the *389. Infanterie-Division* because a significant attack was expected in the sector of the neighbouring *I. Armeekorps.* Therefore, the *2. Batterie/ Sturmgeschütz-Brigade 202* remained in the corps reserve.[1225]

11 SEPTEMBER 1944

At 2000 hours, the whole of *Sturmgeschütz-Brigade 202* was placed into the *XXXXIII. Armeekorps* reserve. The staff and two batteries of the brigade were stationed 2 km south-west of Friedrichstadt and 2 km north of Dulmani.[1226] They were supposed to move to their respective positions at 0500 hours the following day and to prepare to undertake a mission in the sector of the *58.* and *225. Infanterie-Divisionen.*[1227]

The *58. Infanterie-Division* received orders to bring the grenadier platoon accompanying the assault guns into combat readiness in case a joint mission should be carried out with *Sturmgeschütz-Brigade 202.*[1228]

1221 NARA T314, R1022 (*XXXXIII. Armeekorps*), F000509.
1222 NARA T314, R1021 (*XXXXIII. Armeekorps*), F000621.
1223 NARA T314, R1021 (*XXXXIII. Armeekorps*), F001244.
1224 NARA T314, R1021 (*XXXXIII. Armeekorps*), F001245.
1225 NARA T314, R1021 (*XXXXIII. Armeekorps*), F000631.
1226 NARA T314, R1021 (*XXXXIII. Armeekorps*), F001255.
1227 NARA T314, R1021 (*XXXXIII. Armeekorps*), F000633.
1228 NARA T314, R1021 (*XXXXIII. Armeekorps*), F001255.

14 SEPTEMBER 1944

At 1145 hours, the chief of staff of the *XXXXIII. Armeekorps, Oberst i.G.* Wilhelm Hetzel, ordered *Sturmgeschütz-Brigade 202* and the *I. Bataillon/Grenadier-Regiment 353* to the area of Blankas where they were to take up blocking positions defending the flanks of the corps.[1229]

This order was modified at 2250 hours, because the staff and the *1.* and *3. Batterie/Sturmgeschütz-Brigade 202*, with most of *Heeres-Pionier-Bataillon 671*, were immediately sent to the sector of the *I. Armeekorps* in the area of Bauske where the Soviets had breached the German defences.[1230]

At 2330 hours, the 1 (operations) staff officer of the *16. Armee, Oberstleutnant i.G.* Albert Bach, issued orders to the chief of staff of the *XXXXIII. Armeekorps, Oberst i.G.* Hetzel, to relieve *Sturmgeschütz-Brigade 202* (without one of its batteries), *Armee-Panzerjäger-Abteilung 751* (without its *3. Batterie*) and the *Heeres-Pionier-Bataillon 671* (minus one company) from assignment to the corps, and attach them to the *I. Armeekorps.* The latter corps was to establish an anti-tank blocking position from the reinforcement received in the Iecava–Buluzi–Groteni line.[1231]

15 SEPTEMBER 1944

In the morning, the *2. Batterie /Sturmgeschütz-Brigade 202,* which remained with its six assault guns[1232] in the sector of the *XXXXIII. Armeekorps,* was put under the command of the staff of the *389. Infanterie-Division* together with the soldiers of *Bau-Pionier-Bataillon 100,* and given the task of preventing Soviet tanks from breaking through between Vecbebri and Vilkares.[1233]

On the same day, the staff of the *16. Armee* issued orders relating to the statement that the penetration of Soviet armoured forces was no reason for pulling out the German divisions. According to these orders, if enemy armour opened a gap in the front line it had to be sealed by an immediate counter-thrust to trap them behind the German lines before hunting them down with the assault guns.[1234]

In the morning the staff and the *1.* and *3. Batterie/ Sturmgeschütz-Brigade 202* arrived in the sector of the *I. Armeekorps*[1235] and were subordinated to the *215. Infanterie-Division.*[1236] At 1155 hours the division informed the corps that the assault artillery unit and the pioneer battalion would be deployed in the area of Kverini.[1237]

1229 NARA T314, R1021 (*XXXXIII. Armeekorps*), F000635.

1230 NARA T314, R1021 (*XXXXIII. Armeekorps*), F000637.

1231 NARA T312, R627 (*Armeeoberkommando 16*), F8253630.

1232 NARA T314, R73 (*I. Armeekorps*), F001088.

1233 NARA T314, R1021 (*XXXXIII. Armeekorps*), F000639.

1234 NARA T312, R628 (*Armeeoberkommando 16*), F8254346.

1235 The commander of *Sturmgeschütz-Brigade 202* reported to the CP of the *I. Armeekorps* at 0830.

1236 NARA T314, R75 (*I. Armeekorps*), F000677.

1237 NARA T314, R73 (*I. Armeekorps*), F000794.

We can read the following in the history of the *215. Infanterie-Division* about situation in the late morning hours that day:

On the isthmus east of Bauske[1238] *Grenadier-Regiment 435 is fighting desperately with its back to the Memele River. Groups of tanks are attacking, the assault guns of Hauptmann Vogel, very few in numbers (Sturmgeschütz-Abteilung 215*[1239]*), are unable to overcome them. At the corner of a house, one of the assault guns runs into a T–34 dashing past the corner. The crew of the assault gun react to the situation with lightning speed, and at a half-metre distance, that is to say in a close-quarter combat, knocks out the T–34.*[1240]

The total of 12 combat ready assault guns of the two batteries of *Sturmgeschütz-Brigade 202* were ordered to the bridge at Buluzi where they established an anti-tank blocking position – in conjunction with the eight 8.8 cm and six 7.5 cm anti-tank guns of *Armee-Panzerjäger-Abteilung 751* and the soldiers of *Heeres-Pionier-Bataillon 671* – in the line of Grivaskogs–Buluzi–Zaki–Groteni.[1241]

It was probably on this day that the assault guns of *Sturmgeschütz-Brigade 202* knocked out a total of 21 tanks and self-propelled guns in the area of Bauske.[1242] *Wachtmeister* Scharf was credited with 13 confirmed tank knock outs.[1243] This indeed coincides with Soviet figures, since the rifle divisions of the Soviet 22 Guards Rifle Corps occupying Bauske on 14 September were supported by a total of five heavy tanks, 36 T–34 medium tanks and eight T–70 light tanks as well as 21 SU–85 medium and 10 ISU–122 heavy self-propelled guns.

16 SEPTEMBER 1944

At 0930 hours, the *2. Batterie / Sturmgeschütz-Brigade 202* was sent to the sector of the *58. Infanterie-Division* in the area of Krici because Soviet tanks were advancing towards Pepini and threatening the right flank of the division.[1244] The battery commander reported to the command post of the *58. Infanterie-Division* in Pendersadza.[1245]

At 1530 hours, the *58. Infanterie-Division* planned to deploy the arriving assault gun battery, reinforced by a pioneer company, towards Pepini where the Soviet attack had been launched.[1246]

1238 I. e.: in the foreground of Bauske between the Musa and the Memele rivers.

1239 Correctly: *Sturmgeschütz-Abteilung 1215*. This was the *215. Infanterie-Division's* own unit, a company of *Panzerjäger-Abteilung 215*.

1240 Von den Kämpfen der 215. württembergisch-badischen Infanterie-Division. Ein Erinnerungsbuch. Bearb.: Walter Schelm/ Dr. Hans Mehrle, Hrsg. vom Kameradenhilfswerk und Trad. Verb. d. ehem. 215. Inf.Div., Stuttgart 1955. p. 263.

1241 NARA T314, R75 (*I. Armeekorps*), F000677.

1242 *See* Kurowski, Franz – Tornau, Gottfried: *Sturmgeschütze – Die Panzer der Infanterie*. Würzburg, 2008. p. 216.

1243 Kern, Erich: *Generalfeldmarschall Schörner*. Rosenheim, n.d. 4. edition. p. 155.

1244 NARA T314, R1021 (*XXXXIII. Armeekorps*), F000641.

1245 NARA T314, R1021 (*XXXXIII. Armeekorps*), F001305.

1246 NARA T314, R1021 (*XXXXIII. Armeekorps*), F000643.

In the sector of the *I. Armeekorps*, most of *Sturmgeschütz-Brigade 202* was subordinated to the staff of the *205. Infanterie-Division* at 0215 hours with immediate effect.[1247]

At 2145 hours, the corps reported the anti-tank plan of fire in its sector to the staff of the *16. Armee.* According to that plan, the corps had the following anti-tank defences installed along its 30 km front line west of the Lielupe river:

- behind the front line, in the depth of the defence up to the anti-tank blocking position (to the line of the artillery positions of the divisions) nine 7.5 cm and twelve 76.2 mm anti-tank guns;
- from the anti-tank blocking position to the position behind, eight 8.8 anti-tank guns, 16 assault guns and two assault howitzers;
- in the line of the position behind, seven 8.8 cm anti-tank guns;
- at the rear of the position behind, three 7.5 cm anti-tank guns, 17 assault guns and four assault howitzers were standing by for action.[1248]

17 SEPTEMBER 1944

The Soviet 46 Guards Rifle Division launched an attack on the right flank of the *58. Infanterie-Division* with ground attack aircraft and armoured combat vehicles. The Soviets had almost completely enveloped the German division in the area of Vilcini when the *2. Batterie/ Sturmgeschütz-Brigade* and *Pionier-Bataillon 158* were deployed. These forces pushed the Soviet troops that had infiltrated the road between Vilcini and Maurini back to the forest west of Vilcini.[1249]

18 SEPTEMBER 1944

In the sector of the *58. Infanterie-Division* the Soviets attacked along the road between Riesti and Cuksteli on several occasions. At around 1300 hours their attack, launched with a force of battalion strength and three AFVs, achieved a significant penetration. Against it the German division put *Pionier-Bataillon 158,* the *II. Bataillon / Grenadier-Regiment 333* and an assault squad of *Grenadier-Regiment 220* into action with the support of assault guns. Only the *2. Batterie/ Sturmgeschütz-Brigade 202* was placed under the command of the division together with *Sturmgeschütz-Abteilung 1225.*[1250]

19 SEPTEMBER 1944

At 1045 hours, the *58. Infanterie-Division* received an additional battery of *Sturmgeschütz-Brigade 202* from the staff of the *215. Infanterie-Division* until its own *Sturmgeschütz-*

1247 NARA T314, R73 (*I. Armeekorps*), F000800.

1248 NARA T312, R627 (*Armeeoberkommando 16*), F8254006.

1249 NARA T314, R1022 (*XXXXIII. Armeekorps*), F000558.

1250 NARA T314, R1022 (*XXXXIII. Armeekorps*), F000566.

Abteilung 1158 arrived from Germany.[1251] In the sector of the division, in the area of Bruntani, the Germans knocked out three Soviet tanks, and damaged one that day.[1252]

In the evening, Soviet troops broke through the defences of the *XXXXIII. Armeekorps* at Majori. In response, the *58. Infanterie-Division* sent *Pionier-Bataillon 158* and five assault guns there (probably from the *2. Batterie / Sturmgeschütz-Brigade 202*). By 2100 hours the penetration had been eliminated by the Germans.[1253]

Between 16 and 19 September 1944, *Sturmgeschütz-Brigade 202* lost a total of 26 soldiers (one NCO killed in action, 21 enlisted men wounded and an additional four missing in action).[1254]

20 SEPTEMBER 1944

In the morning, the staff and the *1.* and *3. Batterie/ Sturmgeschütz-Brigade 202* were operating under the command of the *205. Infanterie-Division* while the *2. Batterie* was subordinated to *58. Infanterie-Division.*[1255]

21 SEPTEMBER 1944

At night, the *2. Batterie / Sturmgeschütz-Brigade 202* knocked out a Soviet tank in the sector of the *58. Infanterie-Division* (in the sector of *Grenadier-Regiment 220.*)[1256] The assault guns eliminated a Soviet penetration at Zivarti then destroyed another four Soviet tanks approaching the front line, east of Bruntani.[1257]

At 2200 hours, each element of *Sturmgeschütz-Brigade 202* fighting in the sector of the *XXXXIII. Armeekorps,* was put under the direct command of the staff of the corps.[1258]

25 SEPTEMBER 1944

At dawn, one of the assault guns of *Sturmgeschütz-Brigade 202* destroyed a Soviet anti-tank gun behind the Soviet front line.[1259]

At 0845 hours, three assault guns of the *2. Batterie/ Sturmgeschütz-Abteilung 202* were ordered to the sector of the *389. Infanterie-Division.*[1260] At 2100 hours, the *58. Infanterie-Division* received orders from the corps to dispatch the remainder of the battery to the sector of the *389. Infanterie-Division.*[1261]

1251 NARA T314, R1021 (*XXXXIII. Armeekorps*), F000657.
1252 NARA T312, R628 (*Armeeoberkommando 16*), F8254810.
1253 NARA T314, R1021 (*XXXXIII. Armeekorps*), F000659.
1254 NARA T312, R630 (*Armeeoberkommando 16*), F8256896.
1255 NARA T314, R1022 (*XXXXIII. Armeekorps*), F000146-47.
1256 NARA T314, R1022 (*XXXXIII. Armeekorps*), F000583.
1257 NARA T314, R1022 (*XXXXIII. Armeekorps*), F000584.
1258 NARA T314, R1021 (*XXXXIII. Armeekorps*), F000667.
1259 NARA T314, R1022 (*XXXXIII. Armeekorps*), F000602.
1260 NARA T314, R1021 (*XXXXIII. Armeekorps*), F000679.
1261 NARA T314, R1021 (*XXXXIII. Armeekorps*), F000681.

Meanwhile *Sturmgeschütz-Brigade 202* also received orders that its eight assault guns should be combat-ready from noon next day in the sector of *389. Infanterie-Division.*[1262]

26 SEPTEMBER 1944

At 1510 hours, the *2. Batterie/ Sturmgeschütz-Brigade 202* and the *1. Kompanie*[1263] of *Armee-Panzerjäger-Abteilung 751* were also subordinated to the *389. Infanterie-Division.* At 2100 hours, the remnants of the assault gun brigade, fighting in the sector of the *I. Armeekorps,* was placed under direct command of the *XXXXIII. Armeekorps.*[1264]

THE NIGHT OF 26/27 SEPTEMBER 1944

Two assault guns of the *2. Batterie/ Sturmgeschütz-Brigade 202* were attacked by Soviet aircraft and were disabled while on their way to the sector of the *389. Infanterie-Division.*[1265]

28 SEPTEMBER 1944

At around 1000 hours, elements of the *1. Batterie/ Sturmgeschütz-Brigade 202* arrived from the front sector of the *I. Armeekorps.*[1266]

30 SEPTEMBER 1944

At 1000 hours, *Füsilier-Bataillon 225,* which was in the corps reserve behind the left flank of the *389. Infanterie-Division,* and *Sturmgeschütz-Brigade 202* were brought into alarm readiness because the Soviets had launched an attack with armoured support in the area of Ozolmuiza on the front line of the *X. Armeekorps,* the left-hand-side neighbour of the *XXXXIII. Armeekorps.* However, the attack was halted by the neighbouring corps with its own forces and the state of alarm readiness was called off at around 1800 hours.[1267]

At around 2300 hours, the chief of staff of the *16. Armee, Generalmajor* Paul Reinhold Herrmann, suggested to the corps that, due to the imminent attack of the Soviets along the Düna River, it would be more favourable to draw the anti-tank weapons in reserve closer to the front line. From there they could get to where they were needed much sooner and they wouldn't be as exposed to attack by Soviet aircraft. The corps took the advice and immediately ordered *1.* and *3. Batterie/ Sturmgeschütz-Brigade 202* to draw forward along the river up to the area of Kegums.[1268]

1262 NARA T314, R1021 (*XXXXIII. Armeekorps*), F001474.

1263 The company had self-propelled 7.5 cm Pak 40 AT-guns mounted on *Raupenschlepper Ost* vehicles.

1264 NARA T314, R1021 (*XXXXIII. Armeekorps*), F000683.

1265 NARA T314, R1022 (*XXXXIII. Armeekorps*), F000610.

1266 NARA T314, R1021 (*XXXXIII. Armeekorps*), F000687, and also T314, R1022 (*XXXXIII. Armeekorps*), F000617.

1267 NARA T314, R1021 (*XXXXIII. Armeekorps*), F000691.

1268 NARA T314, R1021 (*XXXXIII. Armeekorps*), F000691.

1 OCTOBER 1944

Sturmgeschütz-Brigade 202 had a total of 22 StuG. III assault guns and five StuH. 42 assault howitzers.[1269] Of these, 14 assault guns and four assault howitzers were combat-ready.[1270]

The *3. Batterie* of the assault artillery unit was put into corps' reserve in the sector of the *58. Infanterie-Division* on that day.[1271]

3 OCTOBER 1944

The *XXXXIII. Armeekorps* outlined Operation 'Donner' in its corps orders, namely the withdrawal of the *18. Armee* and the left flank of the *16. Armee* in five phases to the blocking position established at Balkas as well as the eastern position at Riga. According to the plan, the withdrawal of *Sturmgeschütz-Brigade 202* in the corps reserve was a matter to be settled by the staff of the corps.[1272]

4 OCTOBER 1944

At 1315 hours, the staff of the *XXXXIII. Armeekorps* subordinated the *2. Batterie/ Sturmgeschütz-Abteilung 202* and *Armee-Panzerjäger-Abteilung 751* to the *389. Infanterie-Division* and put the other two assault gun batteries – on the north bank of the Düna River – under the direct command of the corps.[1273]

In relation to Operation 'Donner', the corps issued the following order:

1. Sturmgeschütz-Brigade 202

a. The 2. Batterie/ Sturmgeschütz-Brigade 202 remains subordinated to the 389. Infanterie-Division during the move.
b. The staff, the 1. and the 3. Batterie of the brigade will be assigned to the corps directly and will assemble on 5 October until 0800 hours and immediately south-east of Oger, north of the Düna. The brigade shall stay in this sector until the 389. Infanterie-Division withdraws to the Oger-position. Until then it will be ordered to the north-western area of Ikskile so that by the beginning the withdrawal from the Ikskile II position to the Riga eastern position, they could be placed in the area three or four kilometres west of Salaspils.
c. In the Riga eastern position, the brigade will be regrouped in parts or as a whole to the southern bank of the Düna, north-west of Titurgas.'[1274]

1269 According to this, the brigade received at least four assault guns as replacements in September 1944, but two assault howitzers were also written off as total losses.

1270 NARA T78, R269 (*General der Artillerie im OKH*), F6217813.

1271 NARA T314, R1022 (*XXXXIII. Armeekorps*), F000628.

1272 NARA T314, R1022 (*XXXXIII. Armeekorps*), F000043.

1273 NARA T314, R1021 (*XXXXIII. Armeekorps*), F000699.

1274 NARA T314, R1022 (*XXXXIII. Armeekorps*), F000055.

To maintain signals communication, the brigade had to order a vehicle fitted with a radio linked to the signals communication centre of the *XXXXIII. Armeekorps.* Apart from that, the assault artillery battery was to be prepared to cross the Düna any time during the withdrawal, and to carry out missions north and south of the river as well as along the roads to Riga.[1275]

6 OCTOBER 1944

At 1000 hours, the forces of the Soviet 268 Rifle Division broke through the defences on the left flank of the *389. Infanterie-Division* with 20 tanks in the area of Vilcini and with nine AFVs near Zilgalvji; these were probably the elements of the 70 Tank Brigade.[1276] The division believed that it would be able to block the penetrations by its own forces. Therefore *Füsilier-Bataillon 225* and the *2. Batterie/ Sturmgeschütz-Brigade 202* were sent to the penetrations from a southerly direction at 1300 hours.

At 1315 hours the division received the other two batteries of *Sturmgeschütz-Brigade 202,* but for the time being they remained in corps reserve. At around noon the Soviet forces penetrated the forest west of Lubkalni. The German assault guns launched a counter-thrust from Jaunstakari against the Soviets and achieved a penetration in the direction of Auzini. At around 1600 hours, elements of *Sturmgeschütz-Brigade 202* carried out a counter-thrust from Vilcini towards north-north-west, but the terrain became more and more disadvantageous for them.[1277]

At 1915 hours the assault guns fighting under the command of the *389. Infanterie-Division* were carrying out a counter-thrust when they ran into a Soviet armoured attack, which it prevented from developing.

In the sector of the division a total of 17 knocked out Soviet tanks were reported that day.[1278] However, a German assault gun was lost during the fighting.[1279]

7 OCTOBER 1944

On the right flank of the *389. Infanterie-Division,* the Soviet troops followed the retreating Germans very slowly. In the northern foreground of Sturisi they managed to break through the defences of the division but they were repelled with the support of the assault guns from *Sturmgeschütz-Brigade 202* thus enabling the former front line to be reoccupied. The Soviets attacked again from the forest north-east of Sturisi, but the Germans smashed this attempt too. Nine Soviet

1275 NARA T314, R1022 (*XXXXIII. Armeekorps*), F000056.

1276 The Soviet 70 Tank Brigade belonged to the 5 Tank Corps' order of battle. *See* NARA T314, R1022 (*XXXXIII. Armeekorps*), F000891.

1277 NARA T314, R1021 (*XXXXIII. Armeekorps*), F000703.

1278 NARA T314, R1021 (*XXXXIII. Armeekorps*), F000705.

1279 NARA T314, R1022 (*XXXXIII. Armeekorps*), F000646.

tanks were knocked out during the fighting[1280] (probably from the 24 and 41 Tank Brigades[1281]).

At 1300 hours, the *389. Infanterie-Division* reported that they were still holding their front line and had knocked out a total of 11 attacking Soviet tanks by then (including one destroyed by a hand-held anti-tank weapon).[1282]

At 2315 hours the commander of the corps reported to the staff of the *16. Armee* that its anti-tank defence was strengthened in depth by occupying anti-tank road blocks as well as by putting assault guns and Jagdpanzer 38(t) tank destroyers on standby for action.[1283] According to this anti-tank defence plan, each battery of *Sturmgeschütz-Brigade 202* took up positions in the depth of the defence of the *389. Infanterie-Division.*[1284]

8 OCTOBER 1944

In the sector of the *389. Infanterie-Division*, another nine Soviet tanks (of the 5 Tank Brigade) that were supporting an infantry attack were knocked out. Including those, the Germans knocked out a total of 38 tanks and three reconnaissance armoured cars inside three days in the sector of the division (most of them were destroyed by the assault guns of *Sturmgeschütz-Brigade 202*).[1285] Their achievement was submitted to the staff of the *16. Armee* for recognition in the *Wehrmacht* daily reports.[1286]

13 OCTOBER 1944

In the sector of the *VI. Waffen-Armeekorps der SS* in the zone of action of the *205. Infanterie-Division,* the Soviet troops launched attacks south of the Düna River during the day that were supported by armoured combat vehicles and ground attack aircraft. In the heavy fighting, the German division repulsed a total of 27 battalion-strength assaults and smashed 14 Soviet assembly areas with the support of the assault guns (including AFVs of *Sturmgeschütz-Brigade 202*) and its own artillery. The Soviets achieved a penetration on the left flank of the *205. Infanterie-Division* but this was blocked by the Germans between Vecgangi and the southern perimeter of Meznicki. In the sector of the *205. Infanterie-Division*, 10 Soviet AFVs were knocked out by German assault guns; an additional seven were disabled by the grenadiers with hand-held anti-tank weapons during the day's fighting.[1287]

1280 NARA T314, R1022 (*XXXXIII. Armeekorps*), F000647.

1281 Both tank brigades belonged to the Soviet 5 Tank Corps. The 24 Tank Brigade had five Soviet-made tanks and 10 self-propelled guns, as well as nine American M3 tanks before the attack on that day. *See* NARA T314, R1022 (*XXXXIII. Armeekorps*), F000891.

1282 NARA T314, R1021 (*XXXXIII. Armeekorps*), F000707, as well as T314, R1022 (*XXXXIII. Armeekorps*), F000650.

1283 NARA T314, R1021 (*XXXXIII. Armeekorps*), F000709.

1284 NARA T314, R1022 (*XXXXIII. Armeekorps*), F000104.

1285 NARA T314, R1022 (*XXXXIII. Armeekorps*), F000654-55.

1286 NARA T312, R628 (*Armeeoberkommando 16*), F8254919.

1287 NARA T312, R628 (*Armeeoberkommando 16*), F8254951.

After 1800 hours, the *VI. Waffen-Armeekorps der SS* received orders from the staff of the *16. Armee* to dispatch *Sturmgeschütz-Brigade 202* to the sector of the *Generalkommando Kleffel*[1288]. *Sturmgeschütz-Brigade 393* was also ordered here, which, having arrived from the *II. Armeekorps,* had to take over the assault guns left from the regrouped *Sturmgeschütz-Brigade 261.*[1289]

However, another order soon arrived according to which the *VI. Waffen-Armeekorps der SS* were to transfer *Heeres-Panzerjäger-Abteilung 731,* equipped with Jagdpanzer 38(t) Hetzers, instead of the assault gun unit.[1290]

15 OCTOBER 1944

Sturmgeschütz-Brigade 202 was subordinated to *Generalkommando Kleffel* after all, together with other units. In the sector of the *19. Waffen-Grenadier-Division der SS,* Soviet troops launched an attack with two battalions at 1315 hours and achieved a minor penetration in the area of Eglites. Eleven Soviet AFVs were fighting in the bulge and rifle infantry were rushing in, carried on trucks. The Germans commenced a counter-thrust here with two battalions and assault guns.[1291]

17 OCTOBER 1944

On the right flank of *Generalkommando Kleffel,* at Point 51.6, the Germans deployed a battalion reinforced by assault guns as cover against the Soviet forces that had broken through on the left flank of their right-hand-side neighbour and to conduct reconnaissance southwards.[1292]

In the course of the day *Sturmgeschütz-Brigade 202,* together with other units, were detached from *Generalkommando Kleffel* and continued fighting under the command of the *VI. Waffen-Armeekorps der SS.*[1293]

18 OCTOBER 1944

The assault guns of *Sturmgeschütz-Brigade 202,* subordinated to *VI. Waffen-Armeekorps,* destroyed six Soviet tanks in the sector of the *24. Infanterie-Division* at Point 70.6, in the southern area of Annenieku.[1294]

1288 This higher command was organized from the staff of the *XVI. Armeekorps* in July 1944, under the command of *General der Kavallerie* Philipp Kleffel. Later the staff of the *XVI. Armeekorps* was reorganized from that.

1289 NARA T312, R628 (*Armeeoberkommando 16*), F8254670.

1290 NARA T312, R628 (*Armeeoberkommando 16*), F8254671.

1291 NARA T312, R628 (*Armeeoberkommando 16*), F8254962.

1292 NARA T312, R635 (*Armeeoberkommando 16*), F8263271.

1293 NARA T312, R635 (*Armeeoberkommando 16*), F8263272.

1294 NARA T312, R635 (*Armeeoberkommando 16*), F8263277.

20 OCTOBER 1944

The *VI. Waffen-Armeekorps der SS* received orders from the staff of the *16. Armee* to detach an assault gun battery of *Sturmgeschütz-Brigade 202* and send it to the sector of the *XXXXIII. Armeekorps* to reinforce the defenders of Sworbe Peninsula.[1295] [1296]

22 OCTOBER 1944

The *2. Batterie / Sturmgeschütz-Brigade 202* arrived at, and was put under the command of, the *XXXXIII. Armeekorps.*[1297]

23 OCTOBER 1944

Three assault guns of *Sturmgeschütz-Brigade 202* were transported to the Sworbe Peninsula.[1298]

24 AND 25 OCTOBER 1944

Oberleutnant Otto Glatzel distinguished himself in the fighting in the peninsula. In recognition of his bravery, he was awarded the certificate of recognition of the Supreme Commander of the German Army.[1299]

26 OCTOBER 1944

The *XXXXIII. Armeekorps* received orders from the staff of the *16. Armee* to establish permanent defence at the isthmus in the northern part of the peninsula and retake blocking position *'Ranna'* to this end.

The operation was codenamed '*Herbstnebel*' (Autumn Fog). To carry out the mission, the corps ordered *Grenadier-Regiment 545* (from the *389. Infanterie-Division*) and 10 assault guns of *Sturmgeschütz-Brigade 202* to Windau by railway transport. Both units were relieved from assignment to *VI. Waffen-Armeekorps der SS* for that reason. Each assault gun set off with one allowance of ammunition and fuel. The attack was planned for 1 November. An additional 12 to15 assault guns of *Sturmgeschütz-Brigade 202*[1300] and the grenadier regiment were planned to be deployed only in this mission and not in the further defensive battles.[1301]

1295 On 19 October 1944 the staff of the *16. Armee* took measures on the defence of the Sworbe-peninsula, so that the German U-boats could be employed most effectively in the Baltic-sea. The *23. Infanterie-Division* received orders to reinforce and hold the peninsula. To this end, the forces of the *XXXXIII. Armeekorps* had to reoccupy position (*Stellung*) *'Ariste'*. For the counterattack, yet another forces were brought forward from the depth of the peninsula.

1296 NARA T312, R634 (*Armeeoberkommando 16*), F8261801.

1297 NARA T312, R635 (*Armeeoberkommando 16*), F8263296.

1298 NARA T312, R634 (*Armeeoberkommando 16*), F8262265.

1299 Scherzer, Veit – Farwick, Werner: *Die Ritterkreuzträger der Sturmartillerie 1939-45*. Band 2: Kranz-Z. Bayreuth, 2012. p. 387.

1300 NARA T312, R634 (*Armeeoberkommando 16*), F8262265.

1301 NARA T312, R635 (*Armeeoberkommando 16*), F8262898.

The assigned assault guns of *Sturmgeschütz-Brigade 202* were to jump off from behind *Grenadier-Regiment 545* and support each *Jäger* regiment of the *12. Luftwaffen-Feld-Division* with an assault gun group.[1302]

The *IV./Artillerie-Regiment 23* and *Pionier-Bataillon 12 (L)* were also included in the forces assigned to attack.

The 10 assault guns of *Sturmgeschütz-Brigade 202* were to arrive at Windau by the evening of 28 October and all of the assigned units – including those transported by sea[1303]– had to be assembled on the peninsula by the evening of 30 October 1944.

About 50 tons of ammunition was to be provided for the assault guns to ensure a successful attack and to repel the anticipated Soviet counter-thrusts.[1304]

Although Operation 'Herbstnebel' was cancelled on the same day,[1305] the re-deployment of the reinforcements (including the assault guns of *Sturmgeschütz-Brigade 202*) was still in force. Most of the brigade was therefore subordinated to *23. Infanterie-Division* which was already fighting in the Sworbe Peninsula.[1306]

27 OCTOBER 1944

The first 10 assault guns of *Sturmgeschütz-Brigade 202* arrived by rail under the command of the *XXXXIII. Armeekorps.*[1307] Only one of the three batteries (probably the *3.Batterie*) remained subordinated to the *VI. Waffen-Armeekorps der SS.*[1308]

28 OCTOBER 1944

Due to the cancellation of Operation 'Herbstnebel', the employment principles for the assault guns of *Sturmgeschütz-Brigade 202* changed. According to these, only the seven assault guns of one battery of the brigade would go to the peninsula. The battery was intended to participate in extended action and a proper maintenance squad capable of performing immediate repairs of any kind was to be assigned to the assault gun unit. The remainder of the brigade was to be sent back by rail and put under the command of the *VI. Waffen-Armeekorps der SS.*[1309]

On the same day, according to the report of the *XXXXIII. Armeekorps,* 10 assault guns (instead of the intended seven) from *Sturmgeschütz-Abteilung 202* were landed on the Sworbe Peninsula. An additional five assault guns of the brigade also arrived and came under the command of the corps, but they were stationed on the mainland.[1310]

1302 NARA T312, R634 (*Armeeoberkommando 16*), F8262541.
1303 NARA T312, R635 (*Armeeoberkommando 16*), F8262905.
1304 NARA T312, R635 (*Armeeoberkommando 16*), F8262906.
1305 NARA T312, R634 (*Armeeoberkommando 16*), F8262548.
1306 NARA T312, R636 (*Armeeoberkommando 16*), F8263926.
1307 NARA T312, R635 (*Armeeoberkommando 16*), F8263322.
1308 NARA T312, R635 (*Armeeoberkommando 16*), F8263323.
1309 NARA T312, R635 (*Armeeoberkommando 16*), F8262915.
1310 NARA T312, R635 (*Armeeoberkommando 16*), F8263327.

However, the elements of *Sturmgeschütz-Brigade 202* not stationed on the peninsula were later subordinated to *Generalkommando Kleffel*, including the batteries that were under the command of the *VI. Waffen-Armeekorps der SS.*[1311]

29 OCTOBER 1944

At 0845, Soviet troops launched an attack with a force of two or three regiments supported by 12 AFVs on the left flank of *Riegel 'Leo'* (blocking position '*Leo*') along the eastern road north of Teesu on the Sworbe Peninsula. The Soviets managed to break through the left flank of *Jäger-Regiment 23 (L).* To eliminate the penetration, the Germans put assault guns into action. However, the Soviets achieved another penetration between the two regimental groups defending the main combat line, in the middle of the blocking position. To eliminate that, two battalions in reserve were deployed with assault guns. The penetration was narrowed from the east towards the west, but its elimination ran into difficulties. Two Soviet tanks were knocked out on that day in the peninsula (one of them by a hand-held anti-tank weapon).[1312] By 2200 hours, the Germans had reoccupied the whole *Leo-Riegel.*[1313]

The *XXXXIII. Armeekorps* ordered the other five assault guns of *Sturmgeschütz-Brigade 202* remaining on the mainland, probably *3. Batterie*, to be placed under the command of *Generalkommando Mellenthin.*[1314] [1315] These assault guns (*3. Batterie*) arrived in the sector of the *Generalkommando Mellenthin* later that same day.[1316]

30 OCTOBER 1944

The second transport of *Sturmgeschütz-Abteilung 202* moved out of the sector of the *XXXXIII. Armeekorps* and came under the command of *Generalkommando Mellenthin.*[1317]

31 OCTOBER 1944

The staff and the *2. Batterie/ Sturmgeschütz-Brigade 202* also arrived in the sector of *Generalkommando Mellenthin.*[1318]

On that day the *16. Armee* issued orders to reduce the actual strength of the troops *(Iststärke)* by 10%. Among others, the assault gun brigades were also granted an exemption from this order.[1319]

1311 NARA T312, R634 (*Armeeoberkommando 16*), F8262265.

1312 NARA T312, R635 (*Armeeoberkommando 16*), F8263333.

1313 NARA T312, R635 (*Armeeoberkommando 16*), F8263336.

1314 The command of *Generalkommando Kleffel* was assumed by *Generalleutnant* Horst von Mellenthin on 20 October 1944, and the staff was renamed as the *XVI. Armeekorps* again.

1315 NARA T312, R635 (*Armeeoberkommando 16*), F8263333.

1316 NARA T312, R635 (*Armeeoberkommando 16*), F8263335.

1317 NARA T312, R635 (*Armeeoberkommando 16*), F8263338.

1318 NARA T312, R635 (*Armeeoberkommando 16*), F8263343.

1319 NARA T312, R634 (*Armeeoberkommando 16*), F8262347.

2 NOVEMBER 1944

The *16. Armee* issued orders to raise grenadier platoons to accompany the assault guns of *Sturmgeschütz-Brigade 202.*[1320] According to which:

> *[...] In general:*
> *In combat, infantry is needed to provide security for the assault guns, especially against tank destroyer squads, since their guns are capable of only limited traverse, and their weak side and rear armour and huge blind spots make them vulnerable to enemy close-combat attacks.*
> *During assault gun attacks, especially through mine barrages and other obstacles, expert pioneer support is frequently needed.*
> *Experience shows that wherever employed in close cooperation with the infantry, they achieved decisive results either in attack or defence. [...]*[1321]

The personnel of the accompanying grenadier platoons had to be selected from distinguished soldiers. The platoons were to be employed only to provide close support for the assault guns and not for securing an occupied sector. A three-vehicle assault gun platoon had to be secured by a squad of 15 men (five soldiers per assault gun). According to these figures, an assault gun brigade with 20 combat-ready assault guns needed two whole platoons for protection. Training for the platoons lasted 14 days.[1322]

Each platoon had a full strength of 61 men (one officer, five NCOs and 55 enlisted men), including 12 soldiers trained as pioneers. Their weaponry was made up of fifty-five Sturmgewehr 44 automatic rifles and three rifles.[1323] Besides these weapons, their equipment included back-packed radio receiver/transmitter units, mines, explosives, mine detectors, flare pistols and large quantities of hand grenades and Panzerfaust anti-tank weapons.[1324] Duties of the accompanying grenadiers were the follows:

- accompanying their 'own' assault gun during combat;
- mutual fire support during advance;
- defence against enemy tank-destroyer squads;
- warning of camouflaged enemy anti-tank guns, mines, obstacles and enemy ground-attack aircraft;

1320 NARA T312, R634 (*Armeeoberkommando 16*), F8262352. The setting up of the accompanying grenadier platoons was also ordered for the assault guns of *Sturmgeschütz-Brigade 393*, the *12. Luftwaffen-Feld-Division* and the *19. Waffen-Grenadier-Division der SS*.

1321 NARA T312, R634 (*Armeeoberkommando 16*), F8262354.

1322 NARA T312, R634 (*Armeeoberkommando 16*), F8262355.

1323 NARA T312, R634 (*Armeeoberkommando 16*), F8262357.

1324 NARA T312, R634 (*Armeeoberkommando 16*), F8262358.

- indicating the sudden appearance of enemy AFVs and other targets by calling out and shooting at them;
- securing disabled assault guns.[1325]

The staffs of the *VI. Waffen-Armeekorps der SS* and *Generalkommando Mellenthin* were required to submit their reports about the status of the platoons – to be set up for the brigade by the 22 of November – to the *16. Armee.*

4 NOVEMBER 1944

Supply echelon soldiers of *Sturmgeschütz-Brigade 202* were assigned to the defence system under construction around Tuckum. The soldiers from the brigade were placed in the combat outpost position of defence Sector 'A' immediately west of the town, together with two anti-aircraft artillery batteries (a total of 225 men, 30×2 cm anti-aircraft machine guns, 10 light machine guns, 23 submachine guns, a hand held anti-tank rocket launcher and 88 Faustpatron).[1326]

7 NOVEMBER 1944

The staff and the *2.* and *3. Batterie/Sturmgeschütz-Brigade 202* were under the command of the *XVI. Armeekorps.*[1327]

9 NOVEMBER 1944

The *16. Armee* issued instructions to its subordinate corps which stated that their tanks and assault guns were to be dug-in at readiness positions established near the front line and that the smallest assault gun sub-unit to be employed was the battery or the tank-destroyer company.[1328]

13 NOVEMBER 1944

In its newly issued instructions, the *16. Armee* ordered every AFV (tanks, assault guns, tank destroyers, self-propelled guns, APCs) to be permitted to move from the combat area to a position deeper than the divisional command post only if it had obtained explicit permission. The ordered destination of the march was to be unambiguously included in the pass.[1329]

From tactical point of view, the Sturmkanone 40 L/48 had proven to be inefficient against enemy AFVs by mid-November 1944. According to the calculations of the German assault artillery at that time, it would soon be impossible to fight down

1325 NARA T312, R634 (*Armeeoberkommando 16*), F8262359. Cooperation in individual combat situations can be observed in the sketch-maps in the *Appendices*.

1326 NARA T312, R636 (*Armeeoberkommando 16*), F8264257, F8264260.

1327 NARA T312, R636 (*Armeeoberkommando 16*), F8263990.

1328 NARA T312, R635 (*Armeeoberkommando 16*), F8263013.

1329 NARA T312, R635 (*Armeeoberkommando 16*), F8263040.

Soviet heavy AFVs (tanks and self-propelled guns) with these guns. The enemy AFVs scored an increasing number of destructive hits from a distance at which assault guns were unable to deliver effective return fire. In response to this problem, the 7.5 cm L/70 guns were to be put into service with the assault artillery.[1330]

The 7:3 employment ratio between the assault guns and assault howitzers also proved effective. Employing assault howitzers *en masse* as an independent force (e. g. at battery level) was not practical. However mixed platoons of two assault guns and one assault howitzer worked well.[1331]

Taking the brigade-level units of the German assault artillery in the eastern theatre in early November 1944 into consideration, the density of the assault guns was at its peak on the 220 km front line of *Heeresgruppe Nord* where only 36.6 km of front line was covered by each assault gun brigade. In comparison, on the 660 km front line of *Heeresgruppe Süd* the distance covered by each unit was 165 km.[1332]

16 NOVEMBER 1944

According to a report by the *16. Armee,* 10,365 German soldiers were fighting in the Sworbe Peninsula with nine assault guns[1333] and a captured T–34 tank.[1334]

17 NOVEMBER 1944

The seven assault guns of the *2. Batterie/ Sturmgeschütz-Brigade 202* was held in anti-tank reserve in the zone of the *XVI. Armeekorps* (in the sector of the *227. Infanterie-Division*) in the southern foreground of Tuckum. The *3. Batterie* of the brigade (also with seven assault guns) was south of the town, behind the *2. Kompanie/ Armee-Panzerjäger-Abteilung 751* which had been assigned with a similar task.[1335]

18 NOVEMBER 1944

At 0840 hours, Soviet troops renewed their attack in the Sworbe Peninsula. Two divisions of rifle infantry and 25 AFVs launched an assault along the whole front line with the support of ground-attack aircraft. At sea, 40 to 50 Soviet surface ships shelled the eastern beach.

Three assault guns of *Sturmgeschütz-Brigade 202* were on standby for action in the eastern half of the peninsula, north-east of Medlise, near a local school. An additional three assault guns were in reserve south-west of Loupollu, near Kiltri

1330 NARA T78, R270 (*General der Artillerie im OKH*), F6217874.

1331 NARA T78, R270 (*General der Artillerie im OKH*), F6217874.

1332 NARA T78, R270 (*General der Artillerie im OKH*), F6217888.

1333 Apart from the AFVs of the 1. battery of *Sturmgeschütz-Brigade 202*, the assault guns of the *12. Luftwaffen-Feld-Division, put into action here, might have been also included.*

1334 NARA T312, R635 (*Armeeoberkommando 16*), F8263049.

1335 NARA T312, R636 (*Armeeoberkommando 16*), F8264111.

and another three were in the depth of the defence, on the eastern side, north-east of Mäebe, also in reserve.

The 20 or so Soviet tanks that had broken through in the morning along the eastern road were halted by the German defence (three assault guns and six anti-tank guns among others) after advancing 500 m. West of there, in the area of Tesu, the German *Füsilier-Bataillon 23* suffered heavy casualties. In that battle, two more assault guns were put into action from the reserve forces.[1336] The Germans tried to force back the Soviets with a counter-thrust, but failed. The Soviet AFVs were attacking continuously. Five of them were soon knocked out by the German assault guns.[1337]

In the middle of the front line, Soviet troops managed to penetrate into the German main combat line. Of the five Soviet tanks that had broken through with desant infantry (infantry mounted on them), the Germans knocked out four in the north-eastern area of Loupollu, at the road fork.[1338] Two of them were fought down by assault guns.[1339]

Leutnant der Reserve Ahrend Höper,[1340] commander of the *I. Zug* (platoon) of the *1. Batterie/ Sturmgeschütz-Brigade 202,* distinguished himself in the day's actions by knocking out four Soviet tanks in a very short period of time. For his achievement he was recommended for the Knight's Cross of the Iron Cross, which he received on 26 November 1944.[1341]

19 NOVEMBER 1944

At around 1130 hours Soviet troops overran the battery positions of the German artillery with the support of 13 AFVs, encircling the *9. Batterie/ Artillerie-Regiment 218* and continuing their advance towards Kaunispe, in the western part of the Sworbe Peninsula.

As a countermeasure the Germans ordered, besides others, two assault guns and the pioneer platoon of *Füsilier-Regiment 68* (carried on the top of the combat vehicles) from the eastern part of the peninsula to the area of Kaunispe.[1342]

1336 NARA T312, R636 (*Armeeoberkommando 16*), F8264286.

1337 NARA T312, R636 (*Armeeoberkommando 16*), F8264338.

1338 NARA T312, R635 (*Armeeoberkommando 16*), F8263796.

1339 NARA T312, R636 (*Armeeoberkommando 16*), F8264338.

1340 Höper was born in November 1921, in Heringsdorf. He joined the German Army in October, 1940. He served in different automobile units. He was promoted to reserve lieutenant on 26 September 1942. In February 1943 he was sent to Jüterbog, where he was retrained as assault artilleryman. He joined the *1. Batterie/Sturmgeschütz-Abteilung 202* on 11 March 1943, where he became a platoon leader at the end of that month. From 12 July 1943 he was the acting commander of the battery. In August 1943 he was transferred to the *3. Batterie* where he became platoon leader again. In November 1943, he was reassigned to the *1. Batterie* as a platoon leader. He was seriously wounded on 19 November 1944, and during his recovery from his wounds, he was transferred to *Sturmgeschütz-Ersatz- und Ausbildungs-Abteilung 300* in mid-December 1944, but he was released from the hospital in May 1945. He died in March 2013. *See* Scherzer, Veit – Farwick, Werner: *Die Ritterkreuzträger der Sturmartillerie 1939-45.* Band 1: A-Krafft. Jena, 2010. pp. 292-294.

1341 Scherzer, Veit – Farwick, Werner: *Die Ritterkreuzträger der Sturmartillerie 1939-45.* Band 1: A-Krafft. Jena, 2010. p. 294.

1342 NARA T312, R636 (*Armeeoberkommando 16*), F8264343.

At around 1430 hours, elements of *Marine-Flak-Abteilung 239,* assembling north of Kulli, received orders to advance towards the east, along with the two assault guns and the pioneer platoon, to relieve the encircled *9. Batterie/ Artillerie-Regiment 218* then establish securing positions between the assault guns and the beach. In the meantime, the assault guns had reached Kaunispe without encountering any Soviet resistance whatsoever. By nightfall the assault guns had also relieved the encircled artillery battery.[1343]

Leutnant der Reserve Höper, leader of *I.Zug/ 1. Batterie/ Sturmgeschütz-Brigade 202*, was seriously wounded.[1344] In the course of his front-line service, he had knocked out 33 Soviet tanks, 21 anti-tank guns, three artillery pieces, and several infantry heavy weapons inside a year.[1345]

20 NOVEMBER 1944

At 0038 hours, the *16. Armee* issued orders to the staff of the *XVI. Armeekorps* to reinforce the German groups fighting in the Sworbe Peninsula with another battalion of the *81. Infanterie-Division* and an additional three assault guns[1346] from *Sturmgeschütz-Brigade 202* which was now under the command of the corps.[1347] The three assault guns were loaded onto the pioneer's ferryboats but the time of their departure was uncertain due to unfavourable weather conditions.[1348] However, according to the situational map of the *16. Armee* for that day, the sea transportation of the assault guns was been completed.[1349]

The intention was to transport disabled assault guns from the peninsula as soon as possible because they were irreplaceable, valuable equipment.[1350] But that never happened.

Meanwhile, fighting continued on the peninsula. Soviet troops occupied the important road fork near Loupollu in the morning. The Germans responded by concentrating all of their combat-ready assault guns in the northern foreground of Joepollu.[1351] After 1200 hours, two assault guns were ordered from there to the road between Joepollu and Järve to keep it open.[1352]

1343 NARA T312, R636 (*Armeeoberkommando 16*), F8264345.

1344 Scherzer, Veit - Farwick, Werner: *Die Ritterkreuzträger der Sturmartillerie 1939-45*. Band 1: A-Krafft. Jena, 2010. p. 294.

1345 Scherzer, Veit - Farwick, Werner: *Die Ritterkreuzträger der Sturmartillerie 1939-45*. Band 1: A-Krafft. Jena, 2010. p. 295.

1346 NARA T312, R635 (*Armeeoberkommando 16*), F8263084. The assault guns were transported to Windau by rail, and they were shipped over to the peninsula from that place. On that day, crews were also requested from *Sturmgeschütz-Brigade 202* enough for three assault guns, who would be transported to Windau by car. It cannot be excluded, that all of the assault guns in the Sworbe Peninsula (including the AFVs of *Panzerjäger-Abteilung 12 [L]*) were planned to be handed over to the elements of *Sturmgeschütz-Brigade 202* fighting there. The latter order, however, was withdrawn on 22 November 1944.

1347 NARA T312, R634 (*Armeeoberkommando 16*), F8261908.

1348 NARA T312, R635 (*Armeeoberkommando 16*), F8263466.

1349 NARA T312, R636 (*Armeeoberkommando 16*), F8264122.

1350 NARA T312, R635 (*Armeeoberkommando 16*), F8263083.

1351 NARA T312, R636 (*Armeeoberkommando 16*), F8264348.

1352 NARA T312, R636 (*Armeeoberkommando 16*), F8264349.

An additional two assault guns supported the counter-thrust launched to retake Lausama, which had been recently lost to the Soviets. A German *Kampfgruppe* (consisting of the staff of *Grenadier-Regiment 67, Pionier-Kompanie 23* and the staff company of *Grenadier-Regiment 397*) commenced its attack at 1520 hours with the support of the assault guns. Three-hundred metres south of Lausama, they ran into the combat outposts of the Soviet 921 Rifle Regiment which they pushed back into the settlement. Here, the assault guns inflicted heavy casualties on the Soviet troops. Finally the *Kampfgruppe* received orders at 1615 hours to withdraw, together with the assault guns, half-way towards Järve and to secure the area. The Soviets did not pursue them.[1353]

21 NOVEMBER 1944

The German troops completed the retaking of their front line on the Sworbe Peninsula.

Four assault guns from *Sturmgeschütz-Brigade 202* were in the western part of the peninsula, in the area of Lülle, another was in the north-western foreground of Hange, and an additional five were in position along the eastern road, north of Mento manor.

Following sporadic attacks in the morning, Soviet troops launched an attack in the noon hours along the whole of the front line, with focal points along the eastern road as well as in the areas of Soodevahe, Torkenhof and Türju. Armoured fighting vehicles were deployed on both flanks. Two minor Soviet penetrations were eliminated by immediate counter-thrusts and in the course of that fighting eight of the 16 Soviet tanks attacking on a wide front were knocked out.[1354]

22 NOVEMBER 1944

By now the Soviet attempts to force a breakthrough on the Sworbe Peninsula had lasted five days. On the 22 November, Soviet assaults occurred at 16 different places with the support of 20 AFVs but they could achieve significant breakthroughs in only two places. One of these was at the road fork near Torkenhof following an attack launched at 1325 hours with the support of seven AFVs. The *I. Bataillon/ Grenadier-Regiment 435* commenced a counter-thrust from the church in Torkenhof with the support of assault guns. During the battle the assault guns knocked out six of the seven Soviet tanks. The struggle led to close quarters combat but, finally, the Germans eliminated the penetration.[1355]

The second Soviet breakthrough was achieved at around 1620 hours,1 km west of Soodevahe where heavy fighting continued throughout the day. The Soviets took

1353 NARA T312, R636 (*Armeeoberkommando 16*), F8264350.

1354 NARA T312, R635 (*Armeeoberkommando 16*), F8263468, F8263471.

1355 NARA T312, R636 (*Armeeoberkommando 16*), F8264356.

a firm stand in the forest south of the German main combat line. Despite the dim moonlight, two assault guns were assigned to the German *Kampfgruppe* carrying out the counter-thrust. The fighting lasted until the next morning, and although they reached their front line again, the Germans were unable to close the gap completely because both of the supporting assault guns were disabled during the battle.[1356]

A total of 11 Soviet tanks were knocked out on the peninsula on that day. The strongest support for the German infantry during this battle came from their own artillery, the assault guns of the *1. Batterie/Sturmgeschütz-Brigade 202* and the anti-aircraft guns and machine guns of a battery of the *Luftwaffe*'s *6. Flak-Division* employed on the main combat line. However, the defenders' chance of success was limited by the fact that they had only sufficient ammunition for one day's fighting.[1357]

According to a report of the *16. Armee* submitted to *Heeresgruppe Nord* at 1215 hours, there were about 7,000 German soldiers and, besides others, 14 assault guns in the Sworbe Peninsula.[1358] Since at that time only three assault guns from the *12. Luftwaffe-Feld-Division* were deployed on the peninsula besides the *1. Batterie/ Sturmgeschütz-Brigade 202,* there is every reason to assume that a total of 16 assault guns were put into action by the brigade.

23 NOVEMBER 1944

At 0730 hours the Soviets achieved yet another penetration in the area of Soodevahe. To support the German counter-thrust, two assault guns were ordered there again, but despite that, the attempt to eliminate the breach failed. Half an hour later, Soviet forces launched another attack with a company-strength force in the area of Mento manor. Artillerymen fighting on foot, anti-aircraft guns and an additional two assault guns were sent against them.[1359]

Soviet troops continued their attack during the day. The assaults of the four rifle divisions,[1360] supported by multiple-rocket launchers and AFVs penetrated into the depth of the German defences in the Torkenhof blocking position and up to the artillery positions. However, the isolated German strongpoints fought on. The Soviet tanks that had broken through were encountered by the German artillery pieces and the assault guns from the *1. Batterie/ Sturmgeschütz-Brigade 202* at Torkenhof and in the area of Tammuna. In the latter place three assault guns fought.[1361]

1356 NARA T312, R636 (*Armeeoberkommando 16*), F8264356-57.

1357 NARA T312, R635 (*Armeeoberkommando 16*), F8263476-77.

1358 NARA T312, R634 (*Armeeoberkommando 16*), F8261918.

1359 NARA T312, R636 (*Armeeoberkommando 16*), F8264357-58.

1360 The following Soviet units fought against the Germans in the Sworbe Peninsula from west to east: 109, 249 Rifle-, 64 Guards-Rifle- and 131 Rifle Divisions. The 109 Rifle Division was supported by the 45 Independent Tank Regiment and the 952 Self-propelled Artillery Regiment, the 249 Rifle Division was supported by the 27 Independent Tank Regiment, the 131 Rifle Division was supported by the AFVs of the 98 Independent Tank Regiment and the 1198 Self-propelled Artillery Regiment.

1361 NARA T312, R636 (*Armeeoberkommando 16*), F8264359.

From the area of Tammuna, the Germans advanced up to the area of Türju and by this means reestablished contact with the German lines.[1362]

The Germans knocked out a total of nine Soviet AFVs on 23 November 1944. Including these, a total of 42 Soviet AFVs were reported to have been knocked out between 18 and 23 November 1944,[1363] most of them T–34/85 medium tanks.[1364] Consequently, the Soviet forces were still not able to break through on the southern side of the peninsula and it was therefore still possible for the Germans to evacuate the area.[1365]

Indeed, the *16. Armee* issued orders to the defenders of Sworbe to evacuate the peninsula by dawn next day. The assault guns were in third place in the order of priority for evacuation, immediately after the wounded and the personnel and before any other equipment or motor vehicles.[1366] In accordance with that, at 2000 hours, the loading of seven assault guns began, then, at 2200 hours, the first pioneer ferry boats put out to sea.[1367] However, some of the assault guns were still fighting in the area of Maantee to secure the evacuation. Those were withdrawn only at 2230 hours to be loaded onto the ferry boats.[1368]

On the same day five new StuH. 42 assault howitzers were dispatched from Germany as replacements for *Sturmgeschütz-Brigade 202.*[1369]

24 NOVEMBER 1944

In the morning, the evacuation of the Sworbe Peninsula was completed. The Germans managed to transport 7,826 soldiers and, besides others, seven assault guns back to Windau. Four of the assault guns pulled out by midnight 23 November[1370] were from the *1. Batterie/ Sturmgeschütz-Brigade 202* and the other three had fought in the *12. Luftwaffen-Feld-Division.*[1371] Therefore, it is the author's opinion that *Sturmgeschütz-Brigade 202* lost a total of 12 assault guns on the peninsula, including the seven combat vehicles lost on the last day. Those were probably blown up,[1372] since their recovery was impracticable.

1362 NARA T312, R636 (*Armeeoberkommando 16*), F8264361.

1363 NARA T312, R635 (*Armeeoberkommando 16*), F8263812.

1364 NARA T312, R636 (*Armeeoberkommando 16*), F8264367. According to this document the Germans knocked out a total of 36 AFVs in the peninsula between 18 and 23 November 1944 (on 18 seven were destroyed and two were disabled, on 21 eight were knocked out, on 22 11 AFVs were knocked out, on 23 eight knock-outs were scored.

1365 NARA T312, R635 (*Armeeoberkommando 16*), F8263485.

1366 NARA T312, R635 (*Armeeoberkommando 16*), F8263101.

1367 NARA T312, R636 (*Armeeoberkommando 16*), F8264363.

1368 NARA T312, R636 (*Armeeoberkommando 16*), F8264363.

1369 NARA T78, R621 (*Oberkommando des Heeres*), F000766. The assault guns were issued to the unit on 10 November 1944, which were to be received via the staff of *Heeresgruppe Nord.*

1370 NARA T312, R635 (*Armeeoberkommando 16*), F8263814.

1371 NARA T312, R635 (*Armeeoberkommando 16*), F8263494.

1372 The squad blowing up the assault guns was among the last to leave the peninsula at 0615 hours on 24 November 1944. They received Soviet infantry fire while going out to sea. *See* NARA T312, R636 (*Armeeoberkommando 16*), F8264324.

Between 18 and 24 November 1944, the *1. Batterie/Sturmgeschütz-Brigade 202* lost five dead and 16 wounded, a total of 21 soldiers, on the Sworbe Peninsula.[1373] During nine days of battle the battery knocked out a total of 54 Soviet AFVs on the peninsula. For that achievement its commander, *Oberleutnant* Gerhard Brandt,[1374] was awarded the Knight's Cross of the Iron Cross on 12 December 1944.

Of the forces transported back to the mainland from the Sworbe Peninsula, elements of *Sturmgeschütz-Brigade 202* (four assault guns[1375]) were sent by rail to the sector of the *XVI. Armeekorps* in the area of Tuckum where they were subordinated to the corps.[1376] The battery moved off the next morning at 0900 hours.[1377]

At the same time *XVI. Armeekorps* received orders to put a battery from other forces subordinated to *Sturmgeschütz-Brigade 202* (the *2. Batterie* with six assault guns) under the direct command of the *16. Armee* in the area of Lielblidiene. The staff of the *L. Armeekorps* was responsible for supplying the battery and forwarding orders to the unit.[1378] The assault gun battery set off at 2115 hours.[1379]

25 NOVEMBER 1944

The *2. Batterie/ Sturmgeschütz-Brigade 202* arrived in the sector of the *L. Armeekorps.*[1380]

26 NOVEMBER 1944

During his inspection tour in the area of *Heeresgruppe Nord*, *Oberstleutnant* Haarberg, a special staff officer responsible for the assault artillery in the German Army, visited *Sturmgeschütz-Brigade 202* in the area of Tuckum.

It turned out that the *16. Armee* had planned to equip each assault gun brigade under its command with two workshop tents because the siting of the workshops, and the working conditions within them, had been rather unfavourable so far. The

---

1373 NARA T312, R636 (*Armeeoberkommando 16*), F8264226.

1374 Brandt was born in September 1919, in Holzminden. He joined *Bau-Bataillon 245* on 28 August 28-án 1939. On 11 November 1939, he was transferred to *Infanterie-Regiment 73*, then, on 1 December to *Artillerie-Ersatz-Abteilung 55* in Braunschweig. Following his service in more artillery units, he joined *Sturmgeschütz-Abteilung 192* on 1 February 1941. On 14 September 1941 he was transferred to the *3. Batterie/ Sturmgeschütz-Ersatz-Abteilung 200*, then he was ordered to Jüterbog very soon, to the artillery school. He joined the *1. Batterie/ Sturmgeschütz-Abteilung 202* on 21 May 1942, but on 15 June he was transferred to the *3. Batterie* as a platoon leader. He was promoted to reserve lieutenant on 1 August 1942. On 1 June 1943, he was classified as a regular soldier. In autumn 1943, he filled the positions of the orderly officer and the adjutant in the battalion. He was promoted to first lieutenant on 1 March 1944. On 28 November 1944 he was transferred to *Sturmgeschütz-Brigade 911*, which was included in *Führer-Grenadier-Division*'s order of battle in early 1945. He was held as a POW by the Allies. He died in November 1957, in Leinfelden. *See* Scherzer, Veit – Farwick, Werner: *Die Ritterkreuzträger der Sturmartillerie 1939-45.* Band 1: A-Krafft. Jena, 2010. pp. 103-106.

1375 The war diary of the *16. Armee* mentions five assault guns, as transported back with the *1. Batterie/Sturmgeschütz-Brigade 202* to the continent. *See* NARA T312, R634 (*Armeeoberkommando 16*), F8261934. However, according to the brigade's own data, only four assault guns had escaped from the peninsula. *See* NARA T78, R270 (*General der Artillerie im OKH*), F6217968.

1376 NARA T312, R635 (*Armeeoberkommando 16*), F8263105.

1377 NARA T312, R635 (*Armeeoberkommando 16*), F8263499.

1378 NARA T312, R635 (*Armeeoberkommando 16*), F8263111.

1379 NARA T312, R635 (*Armeeoberkommando 16*), F8263498.

1380 NARA T312, R635 (*Armeeoberkommando 16*), F8263500.

dimensions of these heated tents were 6 m×4 m×10 m; they had two entrances and could accommodate two assault guns simultaneously.

On that day, *Sturmgeschütz-Brigade 202* had a total of 27 assault guns of which five needed short-term repairs and one was undergoing long-term maintenance. Within the personnel there were three vacant platoon leader positions (assignments to these positions had already been requested). The brigade already had an accompanying grenadier battery of 79 men. The unit was at full strength in special vehicles; as regards wheeled vehicles it had nine fewer than its authorized strength. Of the workshop equipment, only an arc welder was missing.[1381]

In relation to the brigade's previous battles, matters relating to important combat experiences were raised during *Oberstleutnant* Haarberg's visit:

The forces of the brigade evacuated a wooded area next to a highway in the forepart of the defensive sector (obviously an excellent readiness position). The troops left the clearly visible footprints with the track marks of the two assault guns. At night, the sound of armoured vehicles was played through the loudspeakers of two propaganda cars towards the Soviets. Two radio transmitters were employed to generate deceptive radio traffic by using false names. Meanwhile, further from there, the assault guns took up readiness positions. The German artillery preparation covered the whole width of the planned attack, except for a 200-metre-wide gap which remained unnoticed by the enemy. The assault guns, with the infantry carried on top, advanced quickly through that gap during the artillery fire. At the same time one of the flanks was secured behind the penetration while the assault guns turned to one side and broke into the Soviet artillery positions.

In the course of the night, the assault guns arrived at their readiness positions at walking pace, quietly, while maintaining radio silence. When the attack was launched, the assault guns, with the infantry carried by them, dashed at the Soviets at high speed. The infantry was not allowed to send up flare rockets and it was also forbidden to set haystacks and houses on fire in the zone of their advance because they would have illuminated themselves by doing so. Night attacks were not carried out in wide formation *(Breitform)* by the assault guns, but in narrow, deeply echeloned battle formation which made the Soviet guns and mortars, adjusted for night barrage, inefficient against them. Having broken through, the assault guns deployed into wider formations and in sections before turning to attack the Soviet flank. The assault guns continued fighting after nightfall without any targeting whatsoever; they simply fired in the general direction of the sound of battle, supposing that their shells wouldn't hit tree branches or other obstacles that would cause their premature explosion and that nobody would step in front of their gun barrels. During night attacks, it proved advantageous if the

1381 NARA T78, R270 (*General der Artillerie im OKH*), F6217970.

German artillery shelled the identified enemy firing positions with smoke shells. Aiming without relying on reference points didn't work and changing target was difficult. The most suitable time to carry out night attacks was at the end of the night because the enemy positions could be breached in darkness and could be eliminated from behind at dawn.

During the night fighting against tanks, the assault guns should roll at a very low speed (shifted to second gear, they are hardly audible). They had to halt quite often, stop the engine and listen for the sound of enemy combat vehicles. Then the assault guns had to track down the source of the sound until they spotted their target. The next step was rough aiming if that was possible. Then they fired an illuminating shell which enabled the gunners to correct their aim and finally fire at the identified targets.[1382]

Opening fire on the move was employed only during pursuit since it proved inefficient but had a very strong psychological effect on the Soviet infantry.[1383]

Regarding the Sturmhaubitze 42 assault howitzers: the brigade had three barrel explosions in eight weeks. It was found that the cause of those accidents was that the fuse of the 10.5 cm shells was often initiated while screwing in the fuse. Since the batteries drew their ammunition at night, without the supervision of experts from the brigade, tight control was often abandoned.[1384]

It was expected that the assault gun brigades would keep the expended casings of the 10.5 cm shells because they are allegedly reusable even after five times of reuse. However, in the assault howitzers, spent casings could not be reused as often as in the towed guns of the field artillery as this resulted in serious consequences such as jammed casings and dud shells.

There were mechanical problems as well: in four weeks, 15 torsion bars broke without any obvious reason in assault guns that were not in motion. Engines that had undergone complete overhaul were often stored improperly and consequently were delivered to the troops with failures.[1385]

Regarding the replacement parts: aerial masts were requested by the assault gun brigades because these were often shot off during battle.

The brigade drafted recommendations independently or together with other brigades. For example, one such recommendation was that helmets worn by paratroops should become the standard combat helmet of the assault gun commanders as this did not hinder the proper use of scissors binoculars. Furthermore, the paratrooper helmet allowed radio headsets to fit better than the traditional infantry combat helmet. The paratrooper helmet was tried in combat by the assault gun commanders

1382 NARA T78, R270 (*General der Artillerie im OKH*), F6217971-72.

1383 NARA T78, R270 (*General der Artillerie im OKH*), F6217973.

1384 NARA T78, R270 (*General der Artillerie im OKH*), F6217973.

1385 NARA T78, R270 (*General der Artillerie im OKH*), F6217974.

in *Sturmgeschütz-Brigade 202* and this proved to be successful.[1386] An additional recommendation was that the driver of the assault gun should be equipped with a submachine gun or a machine gun in a spherical mount. Because the assault guns almost exclusively delivered shellfire while not in motion, the driver would be available to take part in combat activities.[1387]

The technical inspector of the brigade developed an electric firing system for fixed machine guns.[1388]

Of the assault guns received as a replacements, only every third one was transported with scissors binoculars.[1389]

1 DECEMBER 1944

The staff of the *XVI. Armeekorps* received orders to report the number of Sturmgewehr 44 assault rifles needed to equip the accompanying grenadiers of *Sturmgeschütz-Brigade 202.*[1390]

2 DECEMBER 1944

The *1. Batterie/ Sturmgeschütz-Brigade 202* (with five assault guns) was in the sector of the *227. Infanterie-Division,* in the southern foreground of Tuckum; the *3. Batterie* (with six assault guns) was behind the *2. Kompanie/ Armee-Panzerjäger-Abteilung 751* – both were held as anti-tank reserves. The staff of the brigade with one assault gun remained in the depth of the *281. Infanterie-Division* defences.[1391]

10 DECEMBER 1944

The staff of the *L. Armeekorps* received orders from the *16. Armee* to dispatch the *2. Batterie/Sturmgeschütz-Brigade 202* to the sector of the *XXXVIII. Armeekorps* the following day, where it would form a substitute for the *227. Infanterie-Division's* own assault gun company '*in every respect*'.[1392]

11 DECEMBER 1944

The *2. Batterie/ Sturmgeschütz-Brigade 202* arrived in the sector of the *XXXVIII. Armeekorps.*[1393]

1386 Personnel of *Sturmgeschütz-Brigade 276* also used paratrooper helmets. *See photo* in Scherzer, Veit - Farwick, Werner: *Die Ritterkreuzträger der Sturmartillerie 1939-45.* Band 2: Kranz-Z. Bayreuth, 2012. p. 156.

1387 NARA T78, R270 (*General der Artillerie im OKH*), F6217975.

1388 NARA T78, R270 (*General der Artillerie im OKH*), F6217976.

1389 NARA T78, R270 (*General der Artillerie im OKH*), F6217977.

1390 NARA T312, R635 (*Armeeoberkommando 16*), F8263128.

1391 NARA T312, R636 (*Armeeoberkommando 16*), F8264145.

1392 NARA T312, R635 (*Armeeoberkommando 16*), F8263155.

1393 NARA T312, R635 (*Armeeoberkommando 16*), F8263857.

17 DECEMBER 1944

The *1. Batterie/Sturmgeschütz-Brigade 202* (with five assault guns) was in the sector of the *81. Infanterie-Division,* in the southern foreground of Tuckum; its *3. Batterie* (with seven assault guns) was on the left flank of the *281. Infanterie-Division* – both were in anti-tank reserve. The staff of the brigade was stationed in the depth of the latter division's defences with one assault gun.[1394]

20 DECEMBER 1944

The grenadier accompaniment of *Sturmgeschütz-Brigade 202* were issued 58 Sturmgewehr 44 assault rifles.[1395]

21 DECEMBER 1944

Following a two-hour artillery preparation, Soviet troops launched an attack on the sector of the *XXXVIII. Armeekorps* to break through German defences towards Frauenburg. However, they failed to achieve their aim. The Germans (including the assault guns of the *2. Batterie/ Sturmgeschütz-Brigade 202*) halted the attack late in the morning following a Soviet penetration of about 3 km in depth and reported knocking out 24 Soviet AFVs. During the counter-thrusts, launched in the early afternoon, most of the area that had been lost was retaken.[1396] In the day's fighting, the defenders knocked out a total of 45 Soviet tanks.[1397]

The *16. Armee* issued orders to the staff of the *XVI. Armeekorps* to dispatch the elements of *Sturmgeschütz-Brigade 202* still under its command to the railway station of Broceni after nightfall, putting them under the direct command of the army. The assault guns were to begin their transport by rail at the station in Biksti while their commander had to report to the command post of the *227. Infanterie-Division* at the railway station in Broceni.[1398]

22 DECEMBER 1944

The *16. Armee* subordinated *Sturmgeschütz-Brigade 202* (without its *2. Batterie*) to the *L. Armeekorps,* and dispatched it from Broceni railway station to the command post of the *290. Infanterie-Division.*[1399] The staff of the brigade, as well as its *1.* and its *3. Batterie* arrived in the sector of *L. Armeekorps* later the same day.[1400]

1394 NARA T312, R636 (*Armeeoberkommando 16*), F8264169.
1395 NARA T312, R635 (*Armeeoberkommando 16*), F8263183.
1396 NARA T312, R635 (*Armeeoberkommando 16*), F8263878.
1397 NARA T312, R635 (*Armeeoberkommando 16*), F8263881.
1398 NARA T312, R635 (*Armeeoberkommando 16*), F8263192.
1399 NARA T312, R635 (*Armeeoberkommando 16*), F8263196.
1400 NARA T312, R635 (*Armeeoberkommando 16*), F8263882.

During the day Soviet troops penetrated into the positions of the *II. Bataillon/ Grenadier-Regiment 503* in the sector of the *290. Infanterie-Division* in the area of Ezermali, and occupied Hill 145.1 and Hill 135.2. The division had no reserves left. Thus the *389. Infanterie-Division* lent a pioneer company and three cavalry platoons to them. At 1900 hours the remnants of the *II. Bataillon/ Grenadier-Regiment 503* launched an attack to retake the positions lost during the day. One of the cavalry platoons jumped off against Hill 145.1 with the support of two assault guns (probably from *Sturmgeschütz-Brigade 202*). The *5. Kompanie/ Grenadier-Regiment 503* reached its previous company command post but the cavalry platoon's advance[1401] ground to a halt. Having received a third assault gun, however, the support of the armoured combat vehicles enabled the cavalrymen to retake Hill 145.1 at around 2300 hours. Here, the Soviets left two light anti-tank guns, five light machine guns, field telephone equipment, radio transceivers and large quantities of small arms behind. Following that, the *2. Kompanie/ Pionier-Bataillon 389* took Hill 135.2 with the support of the three assault guns.[1402]

23 DECEMBER 1944

The staff of the *L. Armeekorps* received orders from the *16. Armee* to march a battery of *Sturmgeschütz-Brigade 202* immediately by land to the sector of the *VI. Waffen-Armeekorps der SS.*[1403]

The Soviet troops launched an attack in the sector of that corps and their penetration could be blocked only in the depth of the artillery positions.[1404]

24 DECEMBER 1944

The *I. Armeekorps* ordered the staff of *Sturmgeschütz-Brigade 202* and its last battery under the corps' command to the sector of the *VI. Waffen-Armeekorps der SS* with immediate effect.[1405] The *1. Batterie* of the brigade arrived and was put under command of the *VI. Waffen-Armeekorps der SS* on the same day.[1406]

25 DECEMBER 1944

The *3. Batterie/ Sturmgeschütz-Brigade 202* arrived in the sector of *VI. Waffen-Armeekorps der SS.*[1407]

1401 Cavalry platoon must have been put into action on foot and not on horseback.

1402 Bauer, Josef: *290. Infanterie-Division 1940-1945*. Selbstverlag Kameradenhilfswerk 290. Inf. Div., Delmenhorst, 1960. 412. o.

1403 NARA T312, R635 (*Armeeoberkommando 16*), F8263203.

1404 NARA T312, R635 (*Armeeoberkommando 16*), F8263885.

1405 NARA T312, R635 (*Armeeoberkommando 16*), F8263210.

1406 NARA T312, R635 (*Armeeoberkommando 16*), F8263889.

1407 NARA T312, R635 (*Armeeoberkommando 16*), F8263655.

26 DECEMBER 1944

The *227. Infanterie-Division* and the *2. Batterie/ Sturmgeschütz-Brigade 202*, which had been under the division's command from 11 December, improvised a securing line during the night against the Soviet troops that had broken through. However, these positions were attacked by the Soviets with the support of 60 AFVs and this pushed the front line of the division 2 km back in a north-westerly direction. In the sector of the *VI. Waffen-Armeekorps der SS*, a total of 71 Soviet AFVs were reported as knocked out (including three fought down by German ground-attack aircraft).[1408]

27 DECEMBER 1944

In the sector of the *VI. Waffen-Armeekorps der SS*, Soviet troops launched an attack at around 1100 hours along a wide front with the support of ground-attack aircraft and armoured fighting vehicles. The defenders repulsed the attacks on the front lines of the *19. Waffen-Grenadier-Division der SS* and the *227. Infanterie-Division.* However, the Soviets later penetrated the corps' defences, and were only halted on the Augstkalni–Atmatnieki–Russas–Kiputi–Galenieki line.

The German armoured counter-attack, launched at 1530 hours east of Atmatnieki, met fierce resistance and was called off due to the ensuing nightfall.[1409]

On that day in the sector of the *VI. Waffen-Armeekorps der SS* the following units reported the knock out of a total of 75 Soviet AFVs:

- the assault guns of *Sturmgeschütz-Brigade 202:* 22 AFVs;
- the assault guns and tank destroyers of *Panzerjäger-Abteilung 2:* 21 AFVs;
- *Panzergrenadier-Regiment 5:* eight AFVs (in close combat);
- *Sturmgeschütz-Abteilung 1227:* eight AFVs;
- *Sturmgeschütz-Abteilung 1181:* eight AFVs;
- *schwere Panzerjäger-Abteilung 666:* five AFVs;
- *Grenadier-Regiment 174:* three AFVs (in close combat).[1410]

On that day *Sturmgeschütz-Brigade 202* knocked out its 1,000 Soviet AFV since its establishment. Of that enormous number, 273 AFVs were destroyed after the brigade's reorganization was completed in July 1944. Of the personnel, six soldiers had been awarded the Knight's Cross of the German Iron Cross and another 11 the German Cross in Gold.[1411]

1408 NARA T312, R635 (*Armeeoberkommando 16*), F8263897.
1409 NARA T312, R635 (*Armeeoberkommando 16*), F8263668.
1410 NARA T312, R635 (*Armeeoberkommando 16*), F8263671.
1411 NARA T312, R635 (*Armeeoberkommando 16*), F8263905.

28 DECEMBER 1944

With the support of *Sturmgeschütz-Brigade 202*, the Germans successfully halted the Soviet attempt to break through towards Libau in the sector of the *227. Infanterie-Division*, 1 km from Lestene. The assault guns of *Sturmgeschütz-Brigade 202* knocked out a total of 44 Soviet AFVs and 10 anti-tank guns in three days. The brigade commander, *Hauptmann* Johann Spielmann,[1412] a major by then, was awarded Oak Leaves to his Knight's Cross of the Iron Cross on the 28 March, 1945.[1413]

29 DECEMBER 1944

The assault guns of *Sturmgeschütz-Brigade 202* knocked out an additional two Soviet tanks and a self-propelled anti-tank gun (probably an SU–76 self-propelled gun) in the sector of the *VI. Waffen-Armeekorps der SS*.[1414] Including those, the number of Soviet AFVs knocked out by the unit increased to 1,017.[1415]

By telegram, the commander of the *16. Armee, General der Infanterie* Carl Hilpert, congratulated the personnel and commander of *Sturmgeschütz-Brigade 202, Hauptmann* Spielmann, on the knock out of their 1,000 Soviet AFV two days before. The general also expressed his gratitude for the excellent support the assault guns had provided in the fighting in the area of Dzukste.[1416]

30 DECEMBER 1944

The staff of the *XXXVIII. Armeekorps* received orders from the *16. Armee* to dispatch the *2. Batterie/Sturmgeschütz-Brigade 202* by rail into the sector of the *VI. Waffen-Armeekorps der SS* as soon as the *227. Infanterie-Division*'s own assault gun company arrived.[1417]

1412 Spielmann was born in December 1916, in Laufenburg. He joined *Artillerie-Regiment 5* in November 1937. In October 1939, he was transferred, as a reserve officer-candidate by then, to *leichte Artillerie-Ersatz-Abteilung 5*. In February 1940, as reserve lieutenant and transferred back to *Artillerie-Regiment 5*. Having served in three other artillery regiments, he volunteered for the artillery in November 1940. He was retrained as assault artilleryman from 16 November in Jüterbog. In January 1941 he was assigned to the staff of *Sturmartillerie-* (later re-designated as *Sturmgeschütz-*) *Abteilung 197*. From May 1941, he was a platoon leader in the *1. Batterie*. He was promoted first lieutenant on 1 July. Between 13 and 20 March 1942 he destroyed 49 Soviet AFVs with his platoon in the Kerch Peninsula. For that he was awarded the Knight's Cross of the Iron Cross on 27 March 1942. He was promoted captain on 15 February 1943. On 31 March he was transferred to the armoured troops, as the commander of the *1. Kompanie/schwere Panzerjäger-Abteilung 653*. He was seriously wounded on the first day of the Battle of Kursk and needed medical treatment at the hospital until June 1944. Meanwhile he was in different replacement and training units before being transferred back to the artillery in November 1943. He was acting commander of *Sturmgeschütz-Brigade 202* from 4 September 1944. From 1 January 1945 he was the assigned commander of the unit. On 14 February he was promoted to major. Before the capitulation in Courland in early May 1945, he sailed for Schleswig-Holstein where he was captured as a POW by the British. He died in August 2005, in Laufenburg. *See* Scherzer, Veit – Farwick, Werner: *Die Ritterkreuzträger der Sturmartillerie 1939-45*. Band 2: Kranz-Z. Bayreuth, 2012. pp. 241-246.

1413 Scherzer, Veit – Farwick, Werner: *Die Ritterkreuzträger der Sturmartillerie 1939-45*. Band 2: Kranz-Z. Bayreuth, 2012. p. 246.

1414 NARA T312, R635 (*Armeeoberkommando 16*), F8263680.

1415 Kurowski, Franz – Tornau, Gottfried: *Sturmgeschütze – Die Panzer der Infanterie*. Würzburg, 2008. p. 216.

1416 NARA T312, R635 (*Armeeoberkommando 16*), F8263251.

1417 NARA T312, R635 (*Armeeoberkommando 16*), F8263253.

31 DECEMBER 1944

The *XXXVIII. Armeekorps* dispatched the *2. Batterie/Sturmgeschütz-Brigade 202* by rail into the sector of *VI. Waffen-Armeekorps der SS,* in the area of Biksti.[1418]

The ferocity of the battles in late December 1944 is best illustrated by the fact that from the 60 accompanying grenadiers assigned to the assault guns of the brigade, 40 were killed or wounded. Eight new assault guns were received as replacments for the lost AFVs.[1419]

1945

5 JANUARY 1945

There were only 28 combat-ready assault guns and assault howitzers in *Sturmgeschütz-Brigade 202.*[1420]

13 JANUARY 1945

In the morning, *Sturmgeschütz-Brigade 202* asssembled in the area of Preekuln. *Hauptmann* Zollenkopf temporarily assumed command of the brigade and during that time, the *3. Batterie* was commanded by *Leutnant* Kühn. The assault artillerymen prepared for their mission, together with elements of the *4. Panzer-Division. Hauptmann* Zollenkopf informed the assault gun commanders of their the task.

The commander's assault gun took the lead. The combat vehicles of the brigade had just crossed a narrow valley when, quite unexpectedly, Soviet anti-tank guns opened fire at them. The assault gun of *Unteroffizier* Krämer went up in flames. The crew managed to escape from the vehicle but the driver was killed. Another assault gun received a direct hit: *Unteroffizier* Rau was killed, together with his crew. Following that, four Panther tanks of the *4. Panzer-Division* intervened in the battle and successfully consolidated the situation.[1421]

15 JANUARY 1945

Sturmgeschütz-Brigade 202 had 18 combat-ready StuG. III assault guns out of a total of 26, and eight of the 10 StuH. 42 assault howitzers were operational. An additional five assault guns had been issued previously to the unit and were in transit.[1422]

1418 NARA T312, R635 (*Armeeoberkommando 16*), F8263258.

1419 Kurowski, Franz – Tornau, Gottfried: *Sturmgeschütze – Die Panzer der Infanterie.* Würzburg, 2008. p. 216.

1420 Laugier, Didier: *Sturmartillerie.* Tome I. Bayeux, 2011. p. 203.

1421 Kurowski, Franz – Tornau, Gottfried: *Sturmgeschütze – Die Panzer der Infanterie.* Würzburg, 2008. p. 289.

1422 NARA T78, R621 (*Oberkommando des Heeres*), F000618.

24 JANUARY 1945

Following a short artillery preparation, Soviet troops launched another attack near Preekuln to break through towards Libau. The Soviets penetrated the front line of the German *30. Infanterie-Division* and the *11. SS-Panzergrenadier-Division Nordland,* but the *14. Panzer-Division,* reinforced by the Tiger tanks of *schwere Panzer-Abteilung 510,* eliminated the penetration in 25 hours, knocking out 63 Soviet tanks.

The Soviet attack towards Frauenburg wasn't a great success either. The *205.* and the *215. Infanterie-Divisionen* put up efficient defence along the railroad to Libau. The *205. Infanterie-Division* reported 117 Soviet AFVs as destroyed in five days. The *81. Infanterie-Division* and the *12. Panzer-Division* successfully eliminated a Soviet penetration south of Tuckum. At the end of January the 1 and 2 Baltic Fronts gave up launching further assaults.

25 JANUARY 1945

From 0000 hours, *Heeresgruppe Nord* was redesignated as *Heeresgruppe Kurland.* That did not affect the subordination status of *Sturmgeschütz-Brigade 202.*

2 FEBRUARY 1945

Soviet troops launched an attack on the sector of the *121. Infanterie-Division,* too. *Sturmgeschütz-Brigade 202* was subordinated to the *I. Armeekorps* and drawn forward to the area of Kniveri, just behind the division. At the same time, the multiple-rocket launchers of *Werfer-Regiment 70* were concentrated here. The Soviets overran the German blocking position established between Hill 111.4 and the road crossing west of Audari; this was defended by the forces of *Regiment 405* and *407.* About 300 Soviet soldiers advanced through Utinin towards Adami with the support of five AFVs, and took Hill 111.4. Most of the attacking rifle infantry dashed forwards in a westerly direction through the area of Laci and onwards to Adami. The Germans destroyed six of the 15 attacking Soviet AFVs. In the sector of *Grenadier Regiment 408,* the Soviets also occupied Hill 122. However, the Germans were able to hold Mucenieki where they knocked out an additional three Soviet AFVs.[1423]

During the Fourth Courland Battle, which ended on 3 February 1945, the Soviets – according to German figures – lost 40,000 men, 541 AFVs and self-propelled guns, as well as 178 aircraft.

17 FEBRUARY 1945

The *3. Batterie/ Sturmgeschütz-Brigade 202* fought in a field north of Preekuln. The Soviet troops infiltrated into a wooded area nearby. To clear them out, *Hauptmann* Zollenkopf jumped off with five assault guns from the main combat line. A sixth

---

1423 Haupt, Werner: *Das war Kurland. Die sechs Kurland-Schlachten aus der Sicht der Divisionen.* Eggolsheim, n.d., p. 107.

assault gun –commanded by *Unteroffizier* Heimann – carried out reconnaissance and securing tasks because the Soviets had penetrated 2 km behind the German salient from the right hand side. Having reached an emergency bridge over a four-metre-wide gully with his assault gun, *Unteroffizier* Heimann noticed one of the assault guns of *Sturmgeschütz-Brigade 912* lying in the water with its belly plate up. The NCO got out of his vehicle and went to the unlucky combat vehicle and knocked on it to communicate with anybody inside. Nobody answered. He hurried back to his own assault gun and attempted to contact *Hauptmann* Zollenkopf by radio, without success. He then started back towards the main combat line with his AFV at high speed and in the meantime was finally able to make radio contact with the *Hauptmann,* to whom he reported the upturned assault gun. Following that, *Unteroffizier* Heimann returned to the scene of the accident.

By that time, another assault gun of *Sturmgeschütz-Brigade 912* had arrived at the bridge. The two AFVs tried, but failed, to tow the one that was lying in the water free. *Hauptmann* Zollenkopf's assault gun then arrived and the three assault guns were able to pull the unfortunate vehicle from the ditch with their joint forces. Only two of the crew of the crew of the stricken assault gun survived the accident.[1424]

20 FEBRUARY 1945

In the southern foreground of Preekuln, the Fifth Battle of Courland began. The Soviets attacked the positions of the German *121., 126., 263.* and *290. Infanterie-Divisionen* and the *12. Luftwaffen-Feld-Division* with 21 rifle divisions and several independent tank brigades.

22 FEBRUARY 1945

Soviet troops occupied Preekuln. Their further advance was halted north of the town by the German *11. Infanterie- Division* and the *14. Panzer-Division* with *Sturmgeschütz-Brigade 912* and an additional two German infantry divisions ordered there. However, the German *18. Armee* paid a heavy price for that by losing 5,400 men.

1 MARCH 1945

Soviet troops launched an attack in the direction of Frauenburg. The *122. Infanterie-Division* of the *VI. Armeekorps* was forced back to the Lake of Lemzere by the Soviets, but their attack was halted by the *24. Infanterie-Division,* the *19. Waffen-Grenadier-Division der SS* and *Panzerbrigade Kurland.* Having occupied the town of Dzukste, the Soviets halted their attack on 10 March 1945 due to the spring thaw. According to German figures, Soviet forces lost 70,000 soldiers, 608 AFVs, 438 guns and 178 aircraft during the Fifth Battle of Courland.

1424 Kurowski, Franz – Tornau, Gottfried: *Sturmgeschütze – Die Panzer der Infanterie.* Würzburg, 2008. pp. 289-290.

6 MARCH 1945

Hauptmann Zollenkopf, commander of the *3. Batterie/ Sturmgeschütz-Brigade 202* was killed in the area of Striki.

The Soviet high command worked out a plan in early March to approach the area of Libau from an easterly direction. The 10 Guards Army was to attack westwards through Frauenburg.

18 MARCH 1945

The Soviet attack was commenced and with that, the Sixth Battle of Courland had begun. Soviet artillery shelled the German positions between Dangas and Skutini, then the tank troops jumped off. To repel the Soviet forces that had penetrated into their defences, the Germans put the *11. Infanterie-Division* and the *12.* and *14. Panzer-Divisionen* into action. These units tried to establish blocking positions along the road to Frauenburg. The Soviets lost 92 AFVs on the first day of the battle.

The 10 Guards Army continued its attack. The Soviets shattered the forces of the German *XXXVIII. Panzerkorps* south of Frauenburg but the German *12. Panzer-Division* halted the tank troops that were dashing forward in the area of Mezalazi. The commander of the Soviet 10 Guards Army ordered his troops attacking south of Frauenburg into defence on 23 March.

29 MARCH 1945

At night, the *81. Infanterie-Division* was forced to withdraw its right flank to avoid being encircled as the Soviet troops had reached the railway between Doblen and Frauenburg from the north-east. As elements of the division started to withdraw towards the north, the assault guns of *Sturmgeschütz-Brigade 202* and the *1. Batterie/ Werfer-Regiment 70* arrived. These forces repelled the Soviet 344 Rifle Division which had attacked the right flank of the *81. Infanterie-Division* in the area of Petertale, Rasas and Fapas.[1425]

The collapse of the German defences was prevented by the rear-guard actions of the German *24. Infanterie-Division.*

31 MARCH 1945

The Soviets gave up any further attempts to break through, having lost another 263 tanks and self-propelled guns, 249 machine guns, 185 guns, 29 mortars and 27 aircraft. From then on, the Soviets were content to merely isolate the forces of *Heeresgruppe Kurland* and the fighting became of only local significance.

1425 Haupt, Werner: *Das war Kurland. Die sechs Kurland-Schlachten aus der Sicht der Divisionen.* Eggolsheim, s.a., pp. 133-134.

10 APRIL 1945

Sturmgeschütz-Brigade 202 had a total of 25 assault guns and assault howitzers, as well as one operational towing vehicle. Of the former, two assault guns were in need of repairs and the others were combat-ready.

15 APRIL 1945

Sturmgeschütz-Brigade 202 was operating in the sector of the German *16. Armee,* subordinated to *XXXVIII. Panzerkorps.* At that time it had 29 assault vehicles, including 19 combat-ready assault guns, and six operational assault howitzers.

8 MAY 1945

The personnel of *Sturmgeschütz-Brigade 202,* having destroyed its remaining assault guns and equipment, formally capitulated to the Soviet troops – together with the units of *Heeresgruppe Kurland* – in closed formation at dawn the next day.

SUMMARY

Throughout its existence, from September 1941 until May 1945, *Sturmgeschütz-Abteilung 202* fought in the eastern theatre of war. Its personnel became the third most decorated German assault gun unit. Its subordination changed frequently; at times it had to hold its ground while moving from one place to another even when split into batteries.

The assault gun unit was ordered back to Germany only once for reorganization, in the spring of 1944. Replacement personnel and weaponry were delivered to them in the combat area or in the rear area. Although the unit was frequently issued with new assault guns, its losses were often replaced by way of 'inheritance', that is to say, by the redistribution of combat vehicles left behind by other assault gun units ordered from the theatre to the rear areas. *Sturmgeschütz-Abteilung 202* obtained its first long-barrelled StuG III assault guns in this way in January 1943.

Although *Sturmgeschütz-Brigade 202* knocked out at least 1,017 (confirmed) Soviet tanks and self-propelled guns[1426] in combat in the eastern theatre, it distinguished itself not only by carrying out '*Panzerjäger*' tasks but also by successfully carrying out other significant tasks such as:

- providing close support to planned German infantry attacks;
- providing close support to assaults with small numbers of personnel and with limited aims;
- providing close support to German counter-thrusts against enemy penetrations;
- substituting for tanks that were lost or subordinated to a *Panzer-Division* or a *Panzer-Regiment;*
- conducting combat reconnaissance in mixed formations;
- conducting combat reconnaissance assigned to an advance squad;
- in static battles, delivering slot or pinpoint fire on machine gun or heavy weapons firing positions and bunkers to eliminate them;
- 'tank-killing' (destroying previously disabled enemy AFVs in the vicinity of the front line);
- repulsing tank attacks with fire from the main combat line;
- individual 'hunting down' of enemy AFVs that had broken through into the depth of the German defences by acting as a mobile anti-tank reserve.

1426 Unfortunately very few German archival records survived about the actions of the unit in 1945. In our opinion, *Sturmgeschütz-Brigade 202* might have knocked out a total of 1,100 Soviet tanks and self-propelled guns from autumn 1941 to the capitulation in May 1945.

Although the performance of *Sturmgeschütz-Brigade 202* was not unique, it was characteristic of most of the German assault artillery units. Between 22 June 1941 and the end of 1944, German assault artillery knocked out a total of 20,709 tanks and self-propelled guns. Thus each assault gun crew member (a total of 6,052 men) could 'claim' an average of 3.4 knocked out enemy AFVs.[1427]

It is also true, however, that the gunners of the German assault guns used binoculars that magnified five times while in German tanks, the binoculars supplied on the most widely used aiming device magnified by just two-and-a-half times. Also by way of comparison, the commander of a German assault gun could reconnoitre the surrounding terrain through scissors binoculars that magnified ten times whereas a tank commander had ordinary 6×30 binoculars at his disposal. This is comparable to the difference between the German snipers' telescopic sight and the simple open sight on the rifles of the ordinary grenadiers.[1428]

Interestingly, a statement drawn up in August 1944 (based on documented information on the 23 assault gun batteries operating in the eastern theatre between 1 December 1943 and 31 May 1944) concluded that enemy AFVs represented less than 12% of the total number of targets fought down by German assault guns. The assault guns (about 88% of the time) fired at enemy infantry, anti-tank guns, mortars, artillery pieces and motor vehicles in support of infantry. They only turned against enemy AFVs if their attacks penetrated the German defences. During the period mentioned above, the assault guns fired a total of 51,595 shells at 6,574 AFVs; of these, 70.5% of were armour-piercing, 21.2% HEAT(high explosive anti-tank) shells and 8.3% HE(high explosive) shells.[1429]

Sturmgeschütz-Brigade 202, like other German assault artillery units, formed the steely backbone – and was sometimes the saviour – of the German infantry. With its outstanding achievements in combat, it contributed not only to the success of the German troops but also to the procrastination of the inevitable, final defeat.

1427 NARA T78, R270 (*General der Artillerie im OKH*), F6218041.

1428 NARA T78, R620 (*Oberkommando des Heeres*), F000021.

1429 NARA T78, R270 (*General der Artillerie im OKH*), F6217413-15. Much less were produced from HEAT-shells and tungsten core AP-shells, then the larger calibre common versions. Even a 7.5 cm HE-shell could have a devastating effect on the softer shelled light tanks and self-propelled guns, built on the chassis of the previous vehicles. Running out of AP and HEAT shells, they could be used in emergency against medium tanks and self-propelled guns because they could be disabled by a lucky hit.

APPENDIX 1

Commanders of *Sturmgeschütz-Abteilung/Brigade 202*

- 10 September 1941–30 December 1941: *Major* Dr. Hans Marder (KIA)
- January 1942–November 1942: *Oberstleutnant* Karl Evers
- November 1942–14 March 1943: *Hauptmann* Hans Handrik (acting)
- 15 March 1943–5 September 1943: *Major* Martin Buhr
- 6 September 1943: *Hauptmann* Vollrad Kutscher (KIA)
- 7 September 1943–24 October 1943: *Major* Martin Buhr
- 25 October 1943–3 September 1944: *Hauptmann* Gerhard Essigke
- 4 September 1944–8 May 1945: *Major* Johann Spielmann

APPENDIX 2

Award holders of *Sturmgeschütz-Abteilung/Brigade 202*

I. Knight's Cross of the Iron Cross with Oak Leaves (*Eichenlaub zum Ritterkreuz des Eisernen Kreuzes*)
- *Major* Johann Spielmann, on 28 March 1945, as commander of *Sturmgeschütz-Brigade 202.*

II. Knight's Cross of the Iron Cross (*Ritterkreuz des Eisernen Kreuzes*)
- *Wachtmeister* Fritz Amling, 11 December 1942, in *3. Batterie/Sturmgeschütz-Abteilung 202*;
- *Oberwachtmeister* Richard Schramm, 23 December 1942, in *1. Batterie/ Sturmgeschütz-Abteilung 202*;
- *Major* Martin Buhr, 11 September 1943, as commander of *Sturmgeschütz-Abteilung 202*;
- *Wachtmeister* Heinz Scharf, 17 August 1944, in *3. Batterie/ Sturmgeschütz-Abteilung 202*;
- *Leutnant* Ahrend Höper, 26 November 1944, in *1. Batterie/Sturmgeschütz-Abteilung 202*;
- *Oberleutnant* Gerhard Brandt, 12 December 1944, in *1. Batterie/ Sturmgeschütz-Abteilung 202.*

III. German Cross in Gold (*Deutsches Kreuz in Gold*)
- *Oberleutnant der Reserve* Dr. Georg Meyer, 12 August 1942, in *Sturmgeschütz-Abteilung 202*;
- *Oberwachtmeister* Siegfried Preis, 8 December 1942, in *1. Batterie/ Sturmgeschütz-Abteilung 202*;
- *Hauptmann* Hans Handrik, 11 February 1943, in *3. Batterie/ Sturmgeschütz-Abteilung 202.*;
- *Hauptmann* Josef Brandner, 16 September 1943, in *2. Batterie/ Sturmgeschütz-Abteilung 202;*
- *Wachtmeister* Albert Krämer, February 1944, in *3. Batterie/Sturmgeschütz-Abteilung 202*;
- *Wachtmeister* Heinz Scharf, 28 May 1944, in *3. Batterie/ Sturmgeschütz-Abteilung 202*;

- *Oberwachtmeister* Heinrich Sponsel, 27 July 1944, in *3. Batterie/ Sturmgeschütz-Abteilung 202.*;
- *Hauptmann* Gerhard Essigke, 7 August 1944, as commander of *Sturmgeschütz-Abteilung 202*;
- *Oberleutnant* Rudolf Bayer, 3 October 1944, in *1. Batterie / Sturmgeschütz-Abteilung 202*;
- *Hauptmann* Franz Rieger, 9 October 1944, in *2. Batterie / Sturmgeschütz-Abteilung 202*;
- *Leutnant* Gerhard Jansen, 23 November 1944, in *2. Batterie/ Sturmgeschütz-Abteilung 202*;
- *Wachtmeister* Michael Sitzberger, 27 November 1944, in *3. Batterie / Sturmgeschütz-Abteilung 202*;
- *Oberwachtmeister* Paul Jacobi, 12 December 1944, in *2. Batterie/ Sturmgeschütz-Abteilung 202*;
- *Leutnant* Wolfgang Kühn, 22 December 1944, in *3. Batterie/ Sturmgeschütz-Abteilung 202*;
- *Wachtmeister* Hermann Brunträger, date and unit unknown;
- *Hauptmann* Martin Zollenkopf, 8 February 1945, in *3. Batterie/ Sturmgeschütz-Abteilung 202*;
- *Obergrefreiter* Johann Fischer, 18 March 1945, in *3. Batterie/Sturmgeschütz-Abteilung 202*;
- *Wachtmeister* Erich Waldner, unknown date, in *1. Batterie/ Sturmgeschütz-Abteilung 202.*

IV. Names recorded in the Roll of Honour of the German Army (*Ehrenblatt des Heeres*)

- *Oberwachtmeister* Heinrich Osterhage, 15 July 1942, in *2. Batterie/ Sturmgeschütz-Abteilung 202*;
- *Hauptmann* Josef Brandner, 7 September 1944, in *2. Batterie/ Sturmgeschütz-Abteilung 202*;
- *Oberleutnant* Martin Zollenkopf, 25 September 1944, in *3. Batterie/ Sturmgeschütz-Abteilung 202*;
- *Oberwachtmeister* Erich Waldner, 25 December 1944, in *1. Batterie/ Sturmgeschütz-Abteilung 202.*

V. Certificate of recognition from the Supreme Commander of the *Heer* (*Anerkennungsurkunde des Oberbefehlshabers des Heeres*)

- *Leutnant* Helmut Weirich, 10 April 1942, in *2. Batterie/ Sturmgeschütz-Abteilung 202*;

- *Leutnant* Benno Schindowski, 5 September 1942, in *1. Batterie/ Sturmgeschütz-Abteilung 202*;
- *Oberleutnant* der Reserve Otto Glatzel, 25 November 1944, in *2. Batterie/ Sturmgeschütz-Abteilung 202*.

Commanders: three high awards
In *1. Batterie*: eight high awards
In *2. Batterie*: eight high awards
In *3. Batterie*: ten high awards

APPENDIX 3

Combat-technical data sheet of the assault guns

	Sd.fz. 142	Sd.fz. 142/1	Sd.fz. 142/2
Combat weight	20,2 t	22,4 t	23,9 t
Main armament	7.5 cm L/24 gun	7.5 cm L/48 gun	10.5 cm L/28 howitzer
Secondary weapons	1 × 7.92 mm machine gun with 600× 7.92 mm ammunition	1 × 7.92 mm machine gun in turret with 600×7.92 mm ammunition	
Crew	Assault gun commander, gunner, loader, driver		
Total length	5,380 mm	6,170 mm	6,140 mm
Total height	1,960 mm	2,160 mm	1,960 mm
Ground clearance	380 mm		
Climbing capacity	800 mm		
Elevation	+20° -10°	+20° -9°	+20° -6°
Traverse	Right and left 12.5°	Right and left 11°	Right and left 10°
Firing height	1,500 mm		1,530 mm
AP-shell muzzle velocity	580 m/s	750-930 m/s	-
HE-shell muzzle velocity	450 m/s	550 m/s	540 m/s
Allowance of ammunition	44 (in practice up to 120)	42 (in practice up to 100)	36 (in practice up to 90)
Engine	Maybach HL 120 TRM		
Number of cylinders	12		
Cylinder volume	11,900 cm³		
Fuel capacity	320 litre Otto		
Number of gears	Six forward, one reverse		
Maximum speed on road	47 km/h	44 km/h	40 km/h
Range (cross-country)	80-110 km		
Armour Hull **front** **side and rear** **top** **bottom**	 50 mm/69-80° 30 mm/90° 11-20 mm/0-15° 16-30 mm/0°		

APPENDIX 4

Comparison of TOE strengths of *Sturmgeschütz-Abteilung/Brigade 202*[1430]

	Abteilung, February 1942	Brigade, July 1944
Officers	24	17
NCOs and enlisted men	564	416
Personnel in total[1]	588	433
Assault guns	21	31
Rifles and carbines	323	255
Submachine guns	66	86
Pistols	251	166
Machine guns	31	40
Motorcycles/tracked motorcycles	N/A	9
Cars	27	23
Trucks	68	62
Halftracks	21	8

1430 It is not the complete TOE, only based on the main strength an equipment.

APPENDIX 5

Excerpt from the report of the German *9. Armee* on an experimental gunnery carried out by an assault gun at a railway station near Rschew

Date: 3 March 1942.
Weather: Sunny, temperature: 12 to15 C° below zero
Assault gun with 7.5 cm L/24 tank gun

Type of target and direction of fire	Distance of target	Angle of impact	Ammunition type and quantity	Hit rate	Effect on target
KV-1 side	150 m	45 degrees	3 Pz. Gr. 2 Gr. AZ 23 3 Gr. AZ 38	100%	The tower clogged, otherwise only surface damage
KV-1 front	80 m	N/A	4 Gr. AZ 38	50% (two shells detonated prematurely, due to their impact on tree branches)	1. hit: opening in front armour torn away. 2. hit: clear ricochet mark on front armour
T-34 side	70 m	about 60 degrees	4 Gr. AZ 38	100%	Forward driving wheel shattered, track damaged.
T-34 front	80 m	N/A	3 Pz. Gr. 4 Gr. AZ 38	100%	Penetration in the turret: entrance hatch of the driver and turret lid torn away. Two rounds through the entrance hatch into the fighting compartment. Track slightly damaged. Two clear ricochet marks on the slant plate of front armour.

Source: NARA T314, R1315 (LIII. Armeekorps), F000221.

APPENDIX 6

Combat experiences of *296. Infanterie-Division* during the fighting of summer 1942, supported by *Sturmgeschütz-Abteilung 202*

(excerpt)

The assault gun is an offensive weapon. It must be used accordingly even in defence. In order to be ready for counter-thrusts and counter-attacks as soon as possible, the assault guns must be put on standby for action in covered positions two or three kilometres behind the main combat line. Roads must be surveyed minutely. If we put them in readiness in the main combat line or immediately behind it, we deprive ourselves of any chance of carrying out a surprise attack on the enemy. We must survey as many firing positions for them as possible in the main combat line and behind it.

Employing single assault guns proved incorrect. They should be deployed in platoon formations at least. Every effort should be made to use them in battery formation.

During assaults before the main combat line, pioneers should be assigned to them for mine clearing.

In battle the sides and the rear of the assault gun must be covered by the infantry. Close cooperation between the infantry and the assault guns is important especially in urban fighting. Here the infantry must neutralize enemy effects of fire from above (snipers in roof openings). Ricochet shots with delay fuses and smoke ammunition could be especially effective, mainly in streets of stone buildings.

In wooded areas assault guns are almost always ineffective (too small sector-of-fire, premature detonation on tree trunks and branches, snipers in trees, and mechanical failures due to frequent shunting).

Since after nightfall neither the gun commander nor the gunner NCO is able to identify targets, and because the risk of making mistakes and of threatening our own infantry by friendly fire, assault guns are not to be deployed at night.

In battle against tanks, if the enemy AFVs are accompanied by infantry, it is essential to secure the assault guns by own infantry. If it is a forgone conclusion that the assault guns will be deployed against tanks, positions of readiness must be chosen next to a highway if possible, from where the territory of combat involvement can be reached in favourable conditions (paved roads and passable terrain in every season).

Assault guns must not be drawn forward into the main combat line either singly or in formation for a long time, or emplace them there as tank destroyers concealed. They are quickly discovered and fought down.

It's no use to dig in the assault guns (as the Russians do with certain tanks), since traverse is highly reduced that way.

To ensure fluent cooperation between the two branches, it is essential that the assault artillery commander and the commander of the infantry establish personal contact with each other.

Since the *Sturmgeschütz-Abteilung* has no communications equipment [to provide communication with the infantry], infantry subunits must expand the field-telephone network to assault gun subunits subordinated to, or ordered to cooperate with, them.

Source: NARA T315, R1961 (296. Infanterie-Division), F000690-691.

APPENDIX 7

The assault gun inventory of *Sturmgeschütz-Abteilung 202*
and *Sturmgeschütz-Brigade 202*
between 1942 and 1945

Datum (MM/DD/YY)	7,5 cm L/24			7,5 cm L/43			7,5 cm L/48			10,5 cm L/28			Total	
	OH	CR	IR	OH	CR	IR	OH	CR	IR	OH	CR	IR	OH	CR
06. 30. 1942	9	6	3	-	-	-	-	-	-	-	-	-	9	6
07. 15. 1942	11	8	3	-	-	-	-	-	-	-	-	-	11	8
07. 21. 1942	11	8	3	-	-	-	-	-	-	-	-	-	11	8
07. 28. 1942	10	5	5	-	-	-	-	-	-	-	-	-	10	5
08. 04. 1942	13(+1)	13	0	-	-	-	-	-	-	-	-	-	13(+1)	13
08. 11. 1942	?	9	?	-	-	-	-	-	-	-	-	-	?	9
08. 12. 1942	12	7	5	-	-	-	-	-	-	-	-	-	12	7
08. 19. 1942	18	8	10	-	-	-	-	-	-	-	-	-	18	8
08. 26. 1942	16	12	4	-	-	-	-	-	-	-	-	-	16	12
09. 02. 1942	16	9	7	-	-	-	-	-	-	-	-	-	16	9
09. 09. 1942	15	14	1	-	-	-	-	-	-	-	-	-	15	14
09. 15. 1942	15	14	1	-	-	-	-	-	-	-	-	-	15	14
09. 17. 1942	15	15	0	-	-	-	-	-	-	-	-	-	15	15
09. 18. 1942	15	14	1	-	-	-	-	-	-	-	-	-	15	14
09. 20. 1942	18	14	4	-	-	-	-	-	-	-	-	-	18	14
09. 22. 1942	18	16	2	-	-	-	-	-	-	-	-	-	18	16
09. 23. 1942	18	17	1	-	-	-	-	-	-	-	-	-	18	17
09. 24. 1942	18	17	1	-	-	-	-	-	-	-	-	-	18	17
09. 30. 1942	12	11	1	-	-	-	-	-	-	-	-	-	12	11
10. 01. 1942	12	11	1	-	-	-	-	-	-	-	-	-	12	11

Datum (MM/DD/YY)	7,5 cm L/24			7,5 cm L/43			7,5 cm L/48			10,5 cm L/28			Total	
	OH	CR	IR	OH	CR	IR	OH	CR	IR	OH	CR	IR	OH	CR
10. 03. 1942	16	11	5	-	-	-	-	-	-	-	-	-	16	11
10. 05. 1942	17	11	6	-	-	-	-	-	-	-	-	-	17	11
10. 06. 1942	17	14	3	-	-	-	-	-	-	-	-	-	17	14
10. 07. 1942	26	16	10	-	-	-	-	-	-	-	-	-	26	16
10. 08. 1942	26	15	11	-	-	-	-	-	-	-	-	-	26	15
10. 12. 1942	23	15	8	-	-	-	-	-	-	-	-	-	23	15
11. 27. 1942	21	21	0	-	-	-	-	-	-	-	-	-	21	21
01. 01. 1943	10	8	2	-	-	-	-	-	-	-	-	-	10	8
01. 04. 1943	11	9	2	-	-	-	-	-	-	-	-	-	11	9
01. 05. 1943	9	7	2	-	-	-	-	-	-	-	-	-	9	7
01. 07. 1943	9	7	2	-	-	-	-	-	-	-	-	-	9	7
01. 08. 1943	11	7	4	-	-	-	-	-	-	-	-	-	11	7
01. 09. 1943	11	7	4	-	-	-	-	-	-	-	-	-	11	7
01. 10. 1943	11	8	3	-	-	-	-	-	-	-	-	-	11	8
01. 11. 1943	11	8	3	-	-	-	-	-	-	-	-	-	11	8
01. 12. 1943	13	9	4	3	3	-	-	-	-	-	-	-	16	12
01. 13. 1943	12	8	4	4	4	-	-	-	-	-	-	-	16	12
01. 14. 1943	13	9	4	4	4	-	-	-	-	-	-	-	17	13
01. 15. 1943	12	9	3	6	6	-	-	-	-	-	-	-	18	15
01. 17. 1943	13	9	4	7	6	-	-	-	-	-	-	-	20	15
01. 19. 1943	14	9	5	5	5	-	-	-	-	-	-	-	19	14
01. 20. 1943	13	10	3	6	6	-	-	-	-	-	-	-	19	16
01. 23. 1943	15	11	4	8	8	-	-	-	-	-	-	-	23	19
01. 24. 1943	15	10	5	8	8	-	-	-	-	-	-	-	23	18
01. 26. 1943	14	4	10	7	7	-	-	-	-	-	-	-	21	11

Datum (MM/DD/YY)	7,5 cm L/24			7,5 cm L/43			7,5 cm L/48			10,5 cm L/28			Total	
	OH	CR	IR	OH	CR	IR	OH	CR	IR	OH	CR	IR	OH	CR
01. 27. 1943	15	8	7	8	5	3	-	-	-	-	-	-	23	13
03. 31. 1943	9	7	2	13[1431]	10	3	-	-	-	-	-	-	22	17
04. 10. 1943	9	3	6	14	13	1	-	-	-	-	-	-	23	16
04. 20. 1943	9	3	6	14[1432]	14	-	-	-	-	-	-	-	23	17
04. 30. 1943	9	5	4	10	9	1	4[1433]	4	-	-	-	-	23	18
05. 10. 1943	9	5	4	10	8	2	12	12	-	-	-	-	31	25
05. 20. 1943	9	5	4	10	8	2	14	14	-	-	-	-	33	27
05. 30. 1943	9	7	2	10	10	-	14	14	-	-	-	-	33	31
06. 10. 1943	7	5	2	10	9	1	14	13	1	-	-	-	31	27
06. 20. 1943	7	6	1	10	9	1	14	13	1	-	-	-	31	28
06. 30. 1943	7	6	1	10	9	1	14	13	1	-	-	-	31	28
07. 10. 1943	7	7	-	10	10	-	14	14	-	-	-	-	31	31
07. 20. 1943	7	7	-	10	9	1	14	12	2	-	-	-	31	28
07. 30. 1943	7	7	-	10	10	-	14	14	-	-	-	-	31	31
08. 10. 1943	7	5	2	10	10	-	14	14	-	-	-	-	31	29
08. 20. 1943	3	2	1	8	6	2	13	11	2	-	-	-	24	19
08. 30. 1943	3	1	2	8	7	1	13	10	3	-	-	-	24	18
09. 10. 1943	3	-	3	7	6	1	11	5	6	-	-	-	21	11
09. 20. 1943	2	-	2	6	3	3	12	6	6	-	-	-	20	9
09. 30. 1943	2	1	1	6	2	4	12[1434]	7	5	-	-	-	20	10
10. 10. 1943	2	1	1	6	2	4	18	10	8	-	-	-	26	13
10. 20. 1943	1	-	1	5	2	3	13	8	5	-	-	-	19	10

1431 Further one StuG. III L/43 was allocated to the unit.
1432 Further 12 StuG. IIIs L/43 were allocated to the unit.
1433 Further 8 StuG. IIIs L/48 were allocated to the unit.
1434 Further 6 StuG. IIIs L/48 were allocated to the unit.

Datum (MM/DD/YY)	7,5 cm L/24			7,5 cm L/43			7,5 cm L/48			10,5 cm L/28			Total	
	OH	CR	IR	OH	CR	IR	OH	CR	IR	OH	CR	IR	OH	CR
10. 30. 1943	1	-	1	5	2	3	13	8	5	-	-	-	19	10
11. 10. 1943	1	-	1	5	4	1	13	8	5	-	-	-	19	12
11. 20. 1943	1	-	1	3	3	-	23[1435]	9	14	-	-	-	27	12
11. 30. 1943	1	-	1	3	-	3	30	18	12	-	-	-	34	18
12. 10. 1943	1	-	1	3	3	-	30	20	10	-	-	-	34	23
12. 20. 1943	1	-	1	3	1	2	30	23	7	-	-	-	34	24
12. 31. 1943	1	-	1	3	1	2	30	23	7	-	-	-	34	24
08. 01. 1944	-	-	-	-	-	-	19	12	7	8	6	2	27	18
09. 01. 1944	-	-	-	-	-	-	18	14	4	7	4	3	25	18
10. 01. 1944	-	-	-	-	-	-	22	14	8	5	4	1	27	18
01. 15. 1945	-	-	-	-	-	-	26[1436]	18	8	10	8	2	36	26
03. 15. 1945	-	-	-	-	-	-	22	20	2	9	8	1	31	28
04. 15. 1945	-	-	-	-	-	-	20	19	1	9	6	3	29	25
05. 01. 1945	-	-	-	-	-	-	?	?	?	?	?	?	?	28

OH = on hand

CR = combat ready

IR = in repair

1435 Further 9 StuG. IIIs L/48 were allocated to the unit.

1436 Further 5 StuG. IIIs L/48 were allocated to the unit.

INDEX

C

D

E

M

R

S

MAPS AND DOCUMENTS

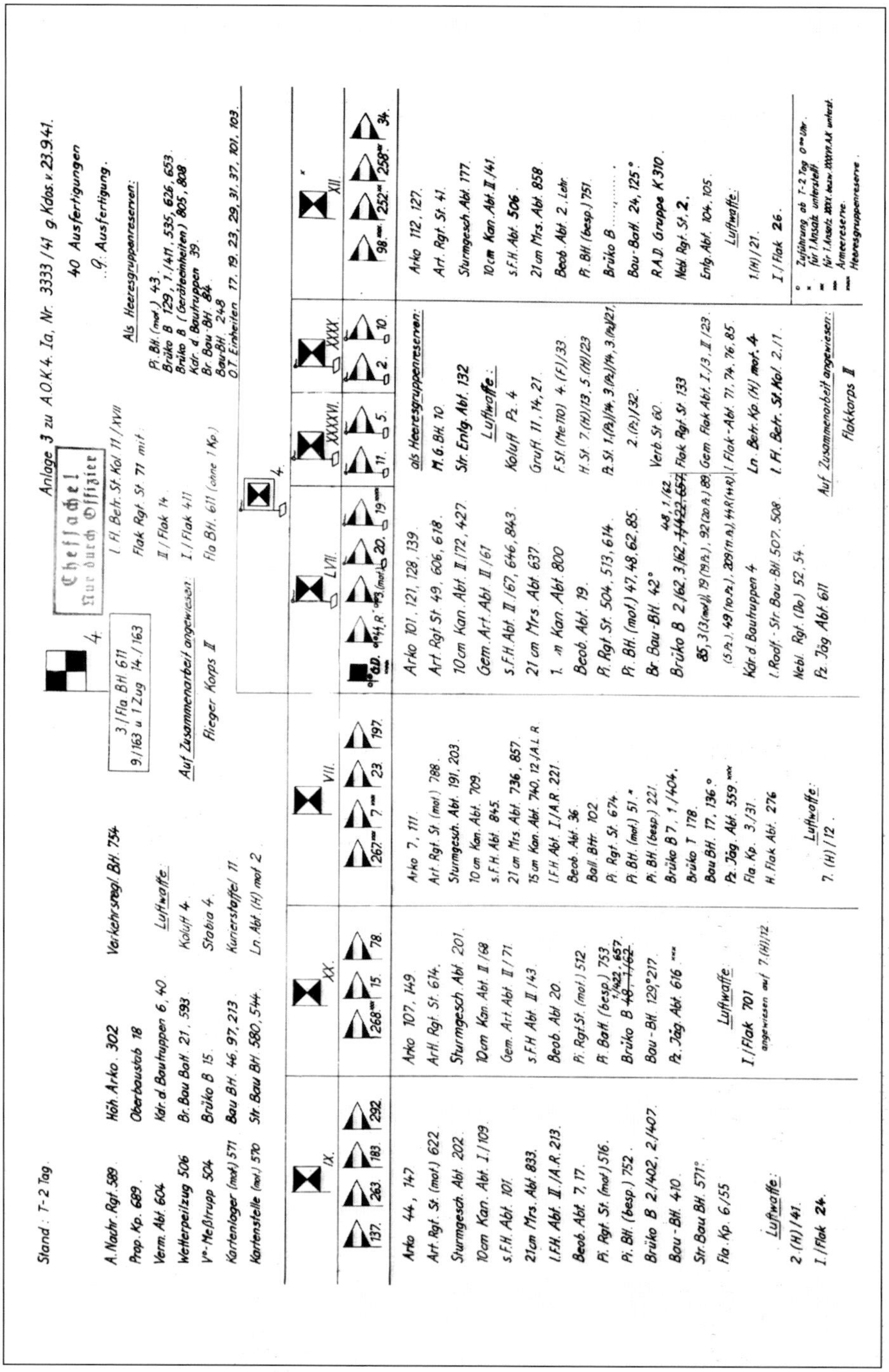

The order of battle of the German *4. Armee,* 23 September, 1941, including *Sturmgeschütz-Abteilung 202,* subordinated to the *IX. Armeekorps* (NARA).

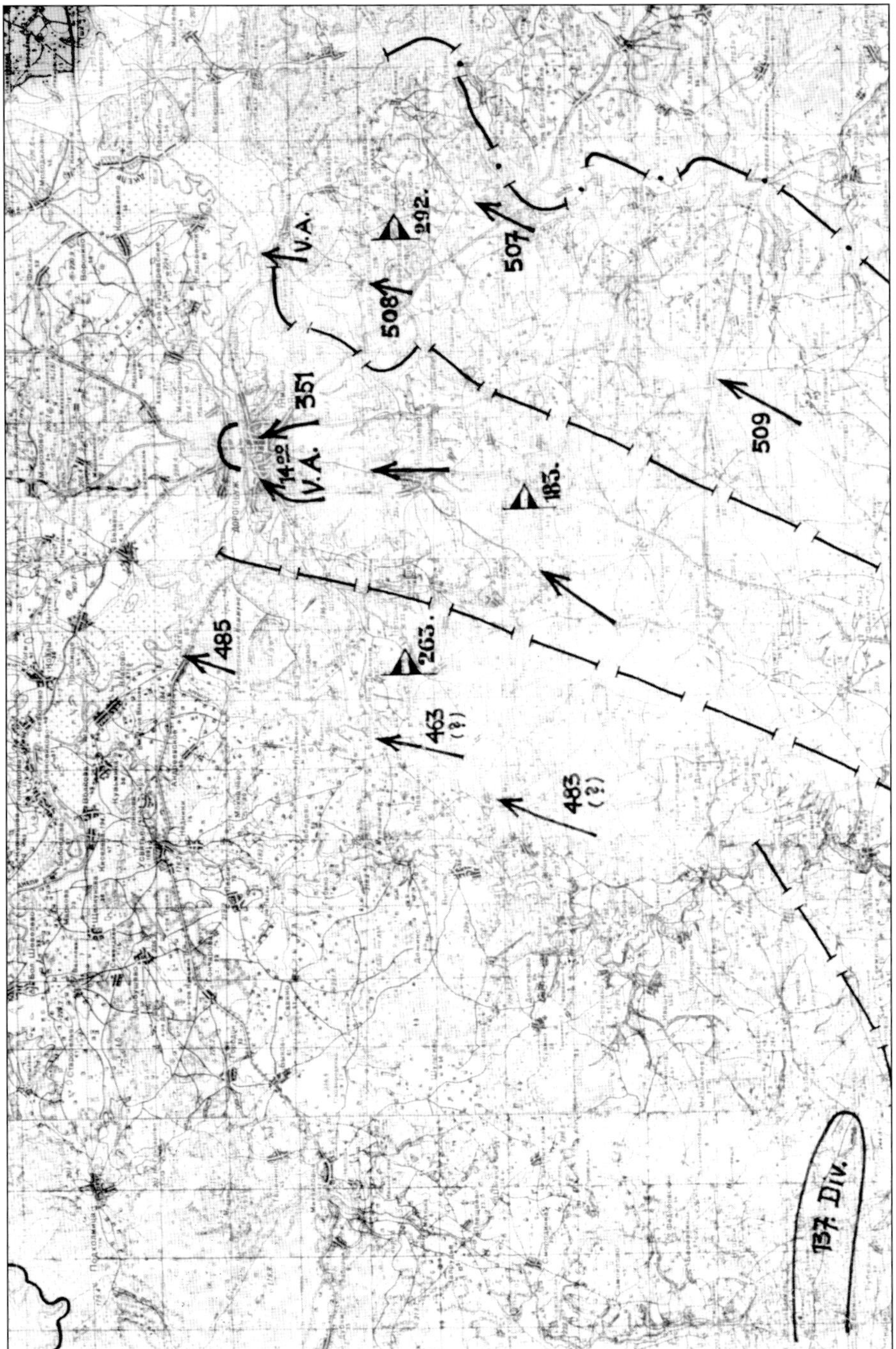

Advance detachment (*Vorausabteilung*) of the *183. Infanterie-Division*, including elements of *Sturmgeschütz-Abteilung 202*, in the area of Dorogobusch, in the evening, 7 October 1941 (NARA).

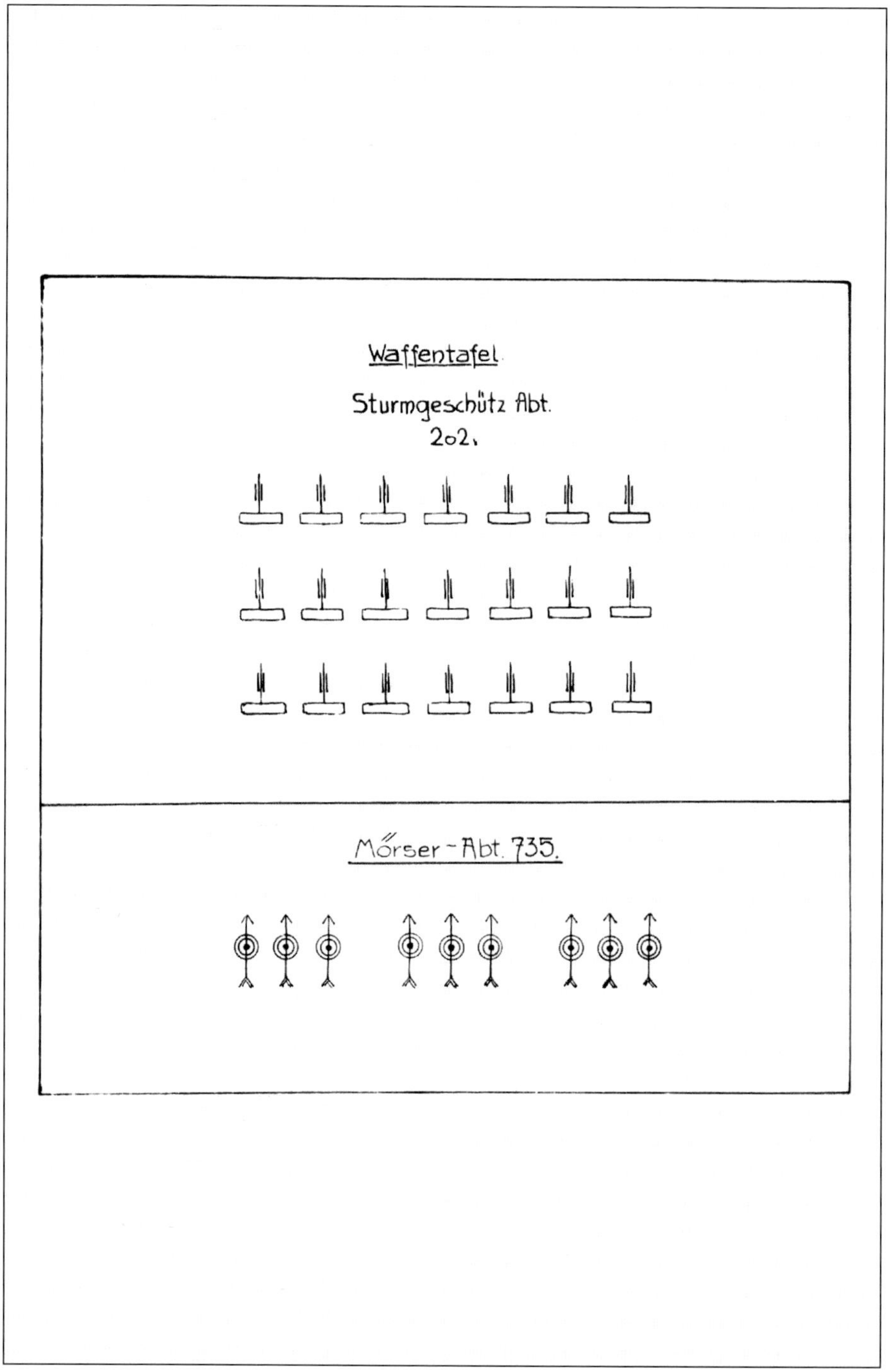

Authorized gun strengths of *Sturmgeschütz-Abteilung 202* and *Mörser-Abteilung 735,* 25 November 1941. (NARA).

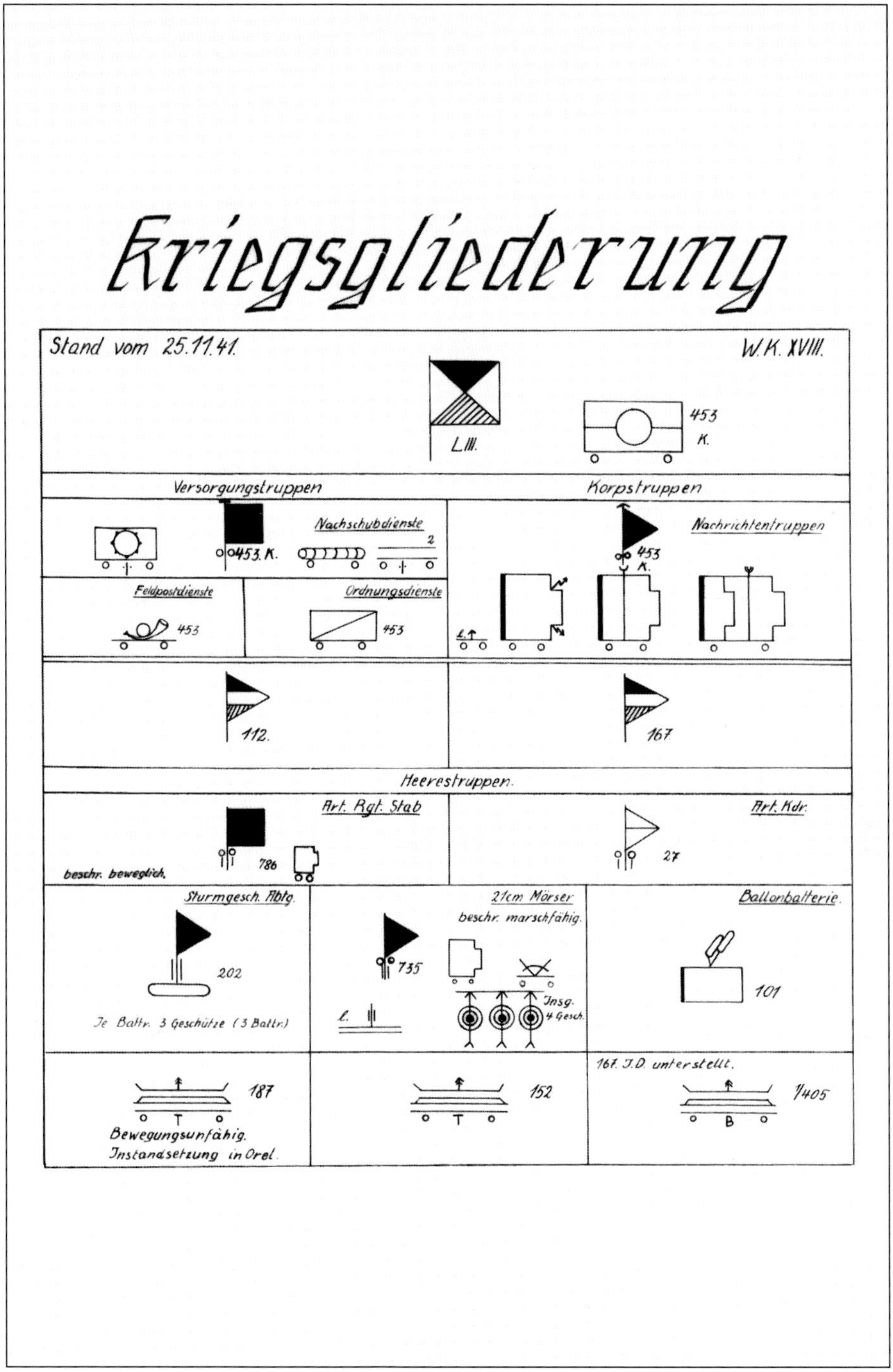

Actual gun strength of *Sturmgeschütz-Abteilung 202,* 25 November 1941, under command of the *LIII. Armeekorps* (NARA).

Sturmgeschütz-Abteilung 2o2 O.U., den 29. Januar 1942.
Abt. Ia

Bezug: Generalkommando LIII. A.K. Abt. Ia vom 28.1.1942.
Betr.: Fernschreiben Pz.A.O.K. 2, Ia vom 27.1.1942.

Dem

Generalkommando LIII. A.K.

Zu o.a. Bezug meldet die Abteilung:

1.) personell bedingt einsatzfähig,
gerätemässig einsatzfähig,
kraftfahrzeugmässig nicht einsatzfähig.

2.) Die Abteilung meldet folgende Soll- und Ist-Stärke:
Zu a)

	Offiziere	Unteroffiziere	Mannsch.
Soll-Stärke:	24	137	427
Ist -Stärke:	17	83 x)	352. x)

x) Da 122 Unteroffiziere und Mannschaften durch Krankheit, Erfrierung und Verwundung ausgefallen sind und in absehbarer Zeit nicht wieder dienstfähig werden, beträgt die für den Einsatz in Frage kommende tatsächliche Ist-Stärke:

17 Offiziere = 71% der Sollstärke,
59 Unteroffiziere = 43% der Sollstärke,
254 Mannschaften = 59% der Sollstärke

Zu b)

Soll an Sturmgeschützen = 21
Ist an Sturmgeschützen = 7 (beweglich) einsatzbereit
5 mit größeren Schäden von längerer Reparaturdauer. Wiederherstellung teilweise nur im Heimatkriegsgebiet möglich.
3 völlig unbrauchbar; zum Abtransport in die Heimat gemeldet.

	M.G.:	M.P.:	Pistolen:	Karabiner:
Soll-Stärke:	31	66	251	323
Ist -Stärke:	23	41	175	279.

Status report of *Sturmgeschütz-Abteilung 202,* 29 January 1942 (NARA).

73

Ia

Aufstellung über abgeschossene Feindpanzer

Dat.	Anzahl	abgeschossen durch
16.2.	1	7./A.R. 25
	2	2. Pz.Jg. 25 (5 cm Lt. Kämmerle, Obergefr. Binder)
17.2.	2	5./K. 25 (1.J.G. Uffz. Kaps, Obergefr.Straub
	1	1./Pz.Jg. 529
	2	2./Pz.Jg. 25 (einer durch 5 cm Obergefr. Binder einer durch 3,7 cm)
	2	1./Pz.Jg. 529
	2	2./Pz.Jg. 25 (3,7 cm Uffz. Deschauer)
	1	10./J.R. 35 (Fldw. Scheibele mit geballter Ladung)
	4	St.Gesch.Abt. 202 (Lt. Weirich)
18.2.	2	1./Pz.Jg. 529 (Uffz. Hake)
	5	2./Pz.Jg. 25 (zwei durch Uffz. Deschauer, zwei durch Uffz. Eckenwalder, einer durch Obergefr.Gruber)
	1	13./J.R. 35 (1.J.G. Uffz. Friedrich)
	1	J.R. 35 (le. Flak)
	2	6. Pz.Rgt. 39
	4	St.Gesch.Abt. 202 (Lt. Weirich)
19.2.	2	St.Gesch.Abt. 202 (Oberwchtm. Schirmer)
	14	6. Pz.Rgt. 39
	1	S.R. 40 (3,7 cm Pak)
20.2.	1	6. Pz.Rgt. 39
21.2.	5	St.Gesch.Abt. 202 (Lt. Weirich)
22.2.	1	St.Gesch.Abt. 202 (Lt. Weirich)
	3	Artilleriefeuer, (vermutl. 4./A.R. 25)
	59	

__Bemerkungen für 6. Pz.Rgt. 39:__

Sämtliche Abschüsse wurden durch die Kompanie durch 3 Panzern IV und 5 Panzern III erzielt. Dabei zeichnete sich Oblt. Kaiser, Oblt. Graf Douglas mit Richtschütze Obergefr. Saufert und Lt. Schlumberger besonders aus.

23.2.	2	6./Pz.Rgt. 39
26.2	2	
27.2	1	[illegible]
	3.	
28.2	1	[illegible]
	68	

Inventory of Soviet AFVs knocked out in the sector of the *LIII. Armeekorps*, between 16 and 28 February 1942 (NARA).

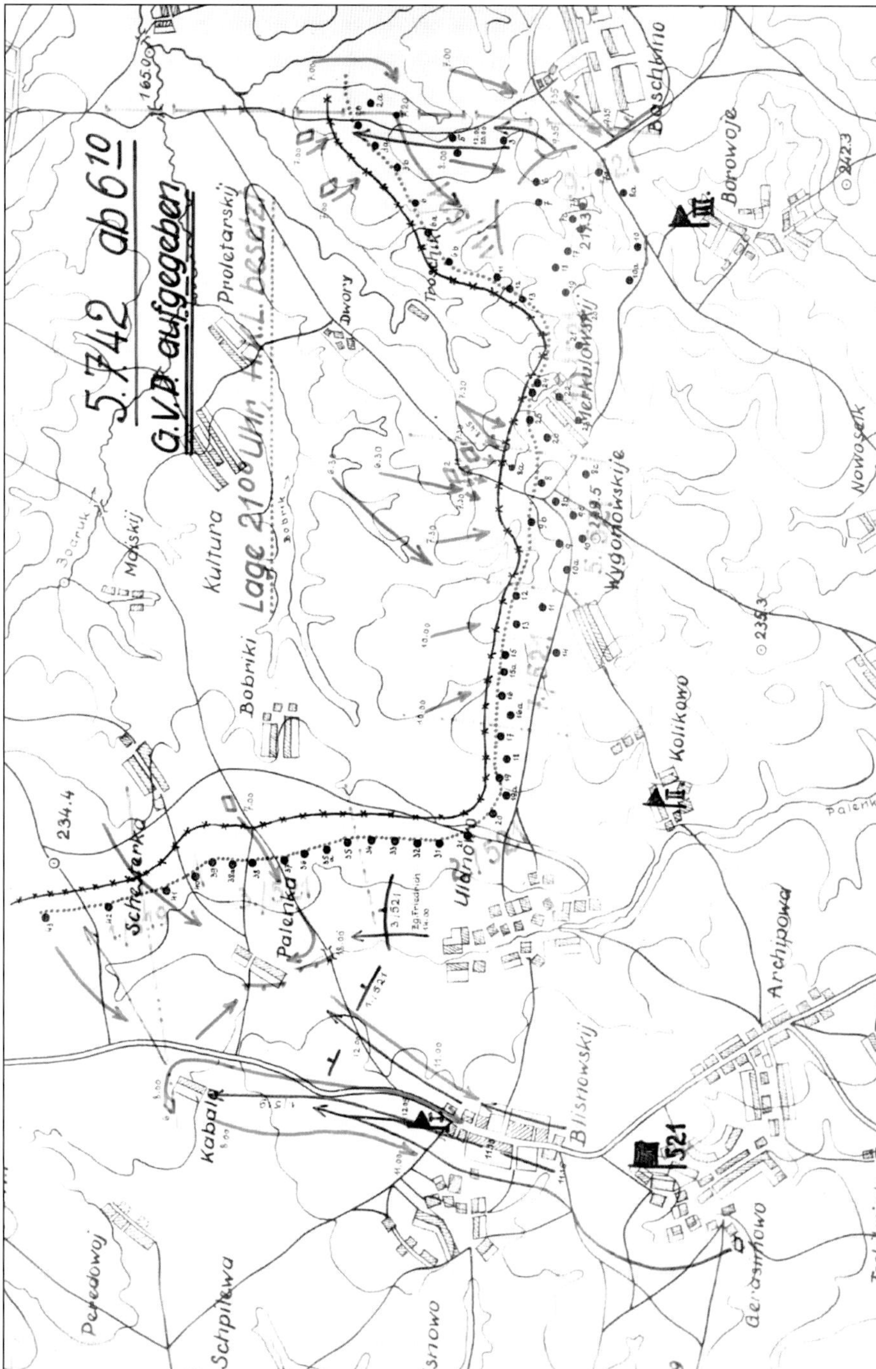

Sketch map of the battle fought in the area Blisnowskij, 5 July 1942 (NARA).

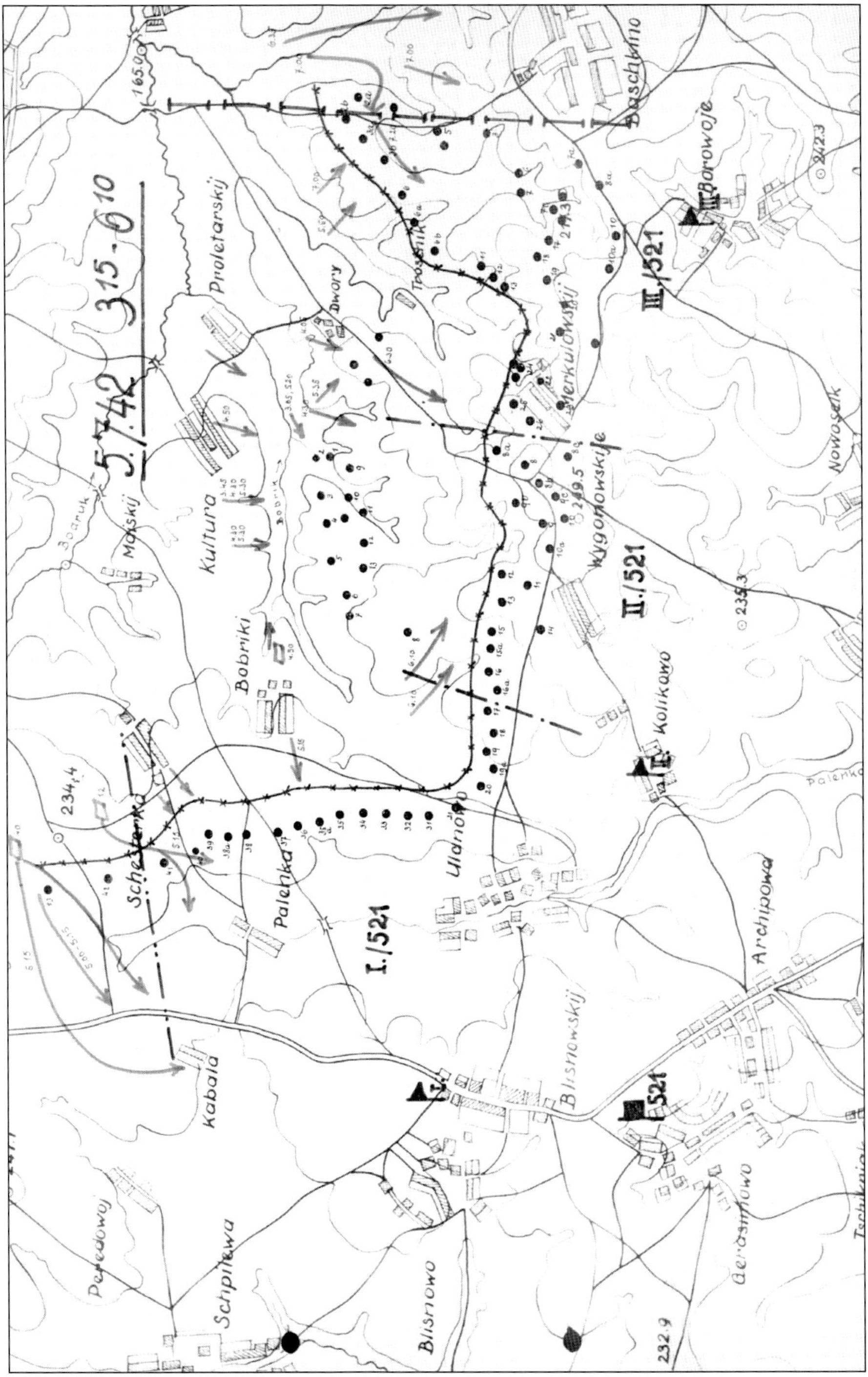

Sketch map of the battle fought in the area Blisnowskij, 5 July 1942 (NARA).

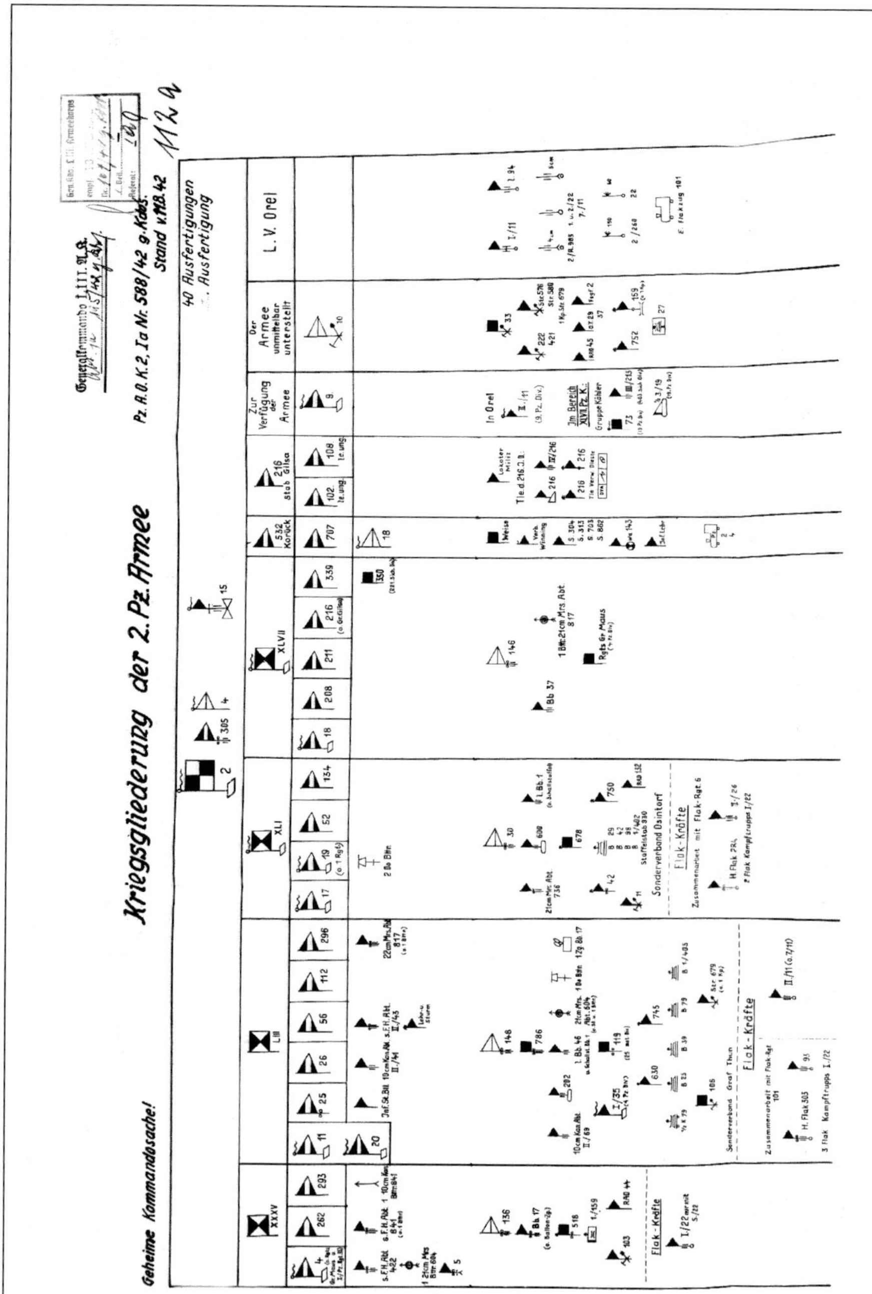

The order of battle of the German *2. Panzerarmee* 11 August 1942, including *Sturmgeschütz-Abteilung 202,* subordinated to the *LIII. Armeekorps* (NARA).

Generalkommando LIII. A.K. , 11. September 1942.
Der Kommandierende General

16

An die

Sturmgeschütz - Abteilung 202.

In bewährter Einsatzfreudigkeit hat die Sturmgeschütz-Abteilung 202 seit November 1941 Anteil an fast allen größeren Kämpfen des LIII.A.K.

Durch die Schlacht von Teploje, die Abwehrkämpfe des Winters, bei denen der erste Kommandeur der Abteilung, Hauptmann Dr. Marder, den Heldentod fand, das Gefecht von Sholesinski, den Abwehrsieg des Juli gegen starken Panzerfeind und die Angriffs- und Abwehrschlachten des August, in denen Teile des Korps eine feindliche Panzerarmee zerschlugen, ist die Abteilung für alle Zeiten eng mit dem Kampfgeschehen des LIII.A.K. verbunden.

Am Tage ihres Ausscheidens aus dem Korpsverband spreche ich der tapferen Sturmgeschütz-Abteilung 202 meine Anerkennung und meinen Dank für die erfolgreiche Unterstützung in zahlreichen Gefechten aus. Jeder Infanterist meines Korps wird diesen Dank für die durch die braven Männer der Sturmgeschütz-Abteilung, oft in letzter Stunde, gebrachte Hilfe in seinem Herzen mit sich forttragen und dabei mit mir vor allem der Sturmgeschützsoldaten gedenken, die bei diesen Einsätzen ihr Leben für Deutschland gaben.

Für die Zukunft gelten der Abteilung meine besten Wünsche. Ich bin überzeugt, daß auch jeder weitere Einsatz ein erfolgreicher sein wird.

Nach dem Abgang:

25.I.D. (mot.)
26.I.D.
56.I.D.
112.I.D.
296.I.D.

Farewell orders of *General der Infanterie* Heinrich Clößner, commander of the *LIII. Armeekorps* to *Sturmgeschütz-Abteilung 202,* 11 September 1942 (NARA).

Panzerabschusstafel der 78.Inf.Div.

Datum	Truppenteil	vernichtet	erbeutet	bewegungsunf.	Panzer-Typ.
26.11.	Art.Rgt.178	14			
	Gren.Rgt. 14 / Schn.Abt.178	5			
	II./116	5			2 KWI, 3 T34
	7./33	4			
	Flak	1			
		29			
27.11.	Schn.Abt.178	17		4	
		2		1	
		19		5	
28.11.	Gren.Rgt. 14	11	1	1	
		4			
	Schn.Abt.178	3			
		18			
29.11.	Gren.Rgt. 14 / Schn.Abt.178	1			
		5			
	Gren.Rgt.215 / Sturmgeschütze / Pak.-Sfl.	15			
		2			
		23			
3o.11.	Gren.Rgt.215	23			1 KWI,16 T34 6 T6o
1.12.	Art.Rgt.178	1			
	Gren.Rgt.215	5			
		6			
2.12.	Gren.Rgt. 14 / Pz.G.R. 13	11			2 KWI, 3 T34
	Gren.Rgt. 14 / Schn.Abt.178	2			2 T34
	Art.Rgt.178	3			1 T34
		16			
4.12.	Gren.Rgt.215	32			1 KWI, 10 T34 14 T6o
	Art.Rgt.178	1			
		33			
5.12.	Gren.Rgt. 14 / s.F.H.	1			1 KWI,
	s.Pak(Sfl.)	2			2 T34
	s.Pak	4			4 T6o
	Gren.Rgt.215 / Flak	7			T34 und T6o
		3			
		17			

Inventory of Soviet AFVs knocked out in the sector of the *78. Infanterie-Division,* between 26 November 1942 and 16 December 1942, including knock-outs scored by the assault guns of *Sturmgeschütz-Abteilung 202* (NARA).

- 2 -

Datum	Truppenteil	vernichtet	erbeutet	bewegungsunf.	Panzer-Typ.
6.12.	Gren.Rgt.215	5	-	-	T 34
	Pz.G.R. 13	-	-	1	T34 auf Mine
		5		1	
11.12.	Gren.Rgt.215				
	Flak	15			
	Pz.Kp.33	5			
	Nahkampf	13			
		33			
	Gren.Rgt. 14	11			
	Flak	14			
	Art.Rgt.178	10			
	Sturmgesch.	67			
		135			
12.12	Sturmgesch.	21			
	II./Pz.Rgt.3	40			3 KWI,34 T34 3 T6o
		61			
13.12.	Gren.Rgt.215 Sturmgesch.	10			2 KWI,7 T34 1 T6o
	III./33	2			1 KWI, 1T34
	erbeutet		1	1	T6o
	Gren.Rgt. 14 Schn.Abt.178	1			KW I
		13		1	
14.12.	G.R. 215	7			
15.12.	"	3 + 13 ([illegible])			T 34
16.12.	"	10			T 34
		431	2	78	

Inventory of Soviet AFVs knocked out in the sector of the *78. Infanterie-Division,* between 26 November 1942 and 16 December 1942, including knock-outs scored by the assault guns of *Sturmgeschütz-Abteilung 202* (NARA).

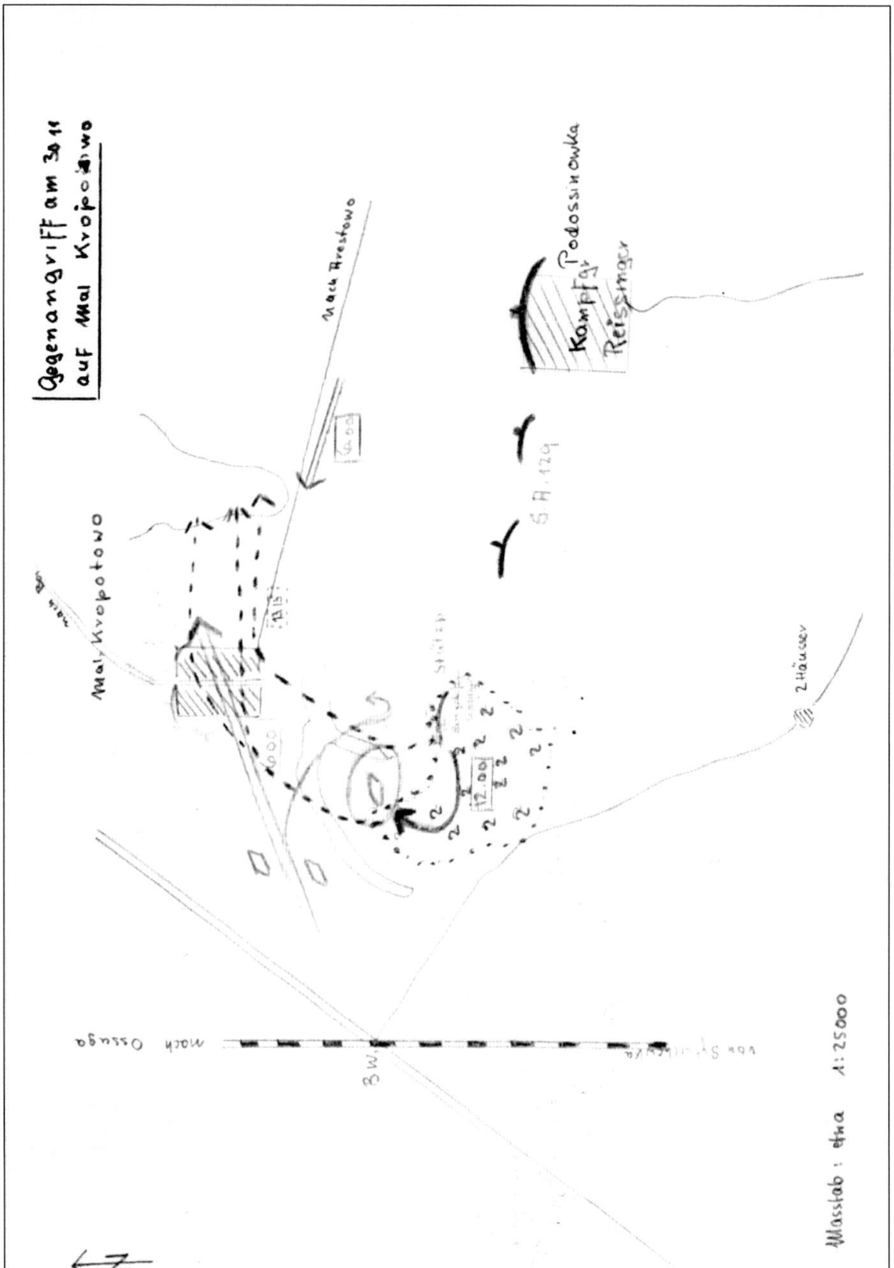

Sketch of the German attack on Mal. Kropotowo, 30 November 1942 (NARA).

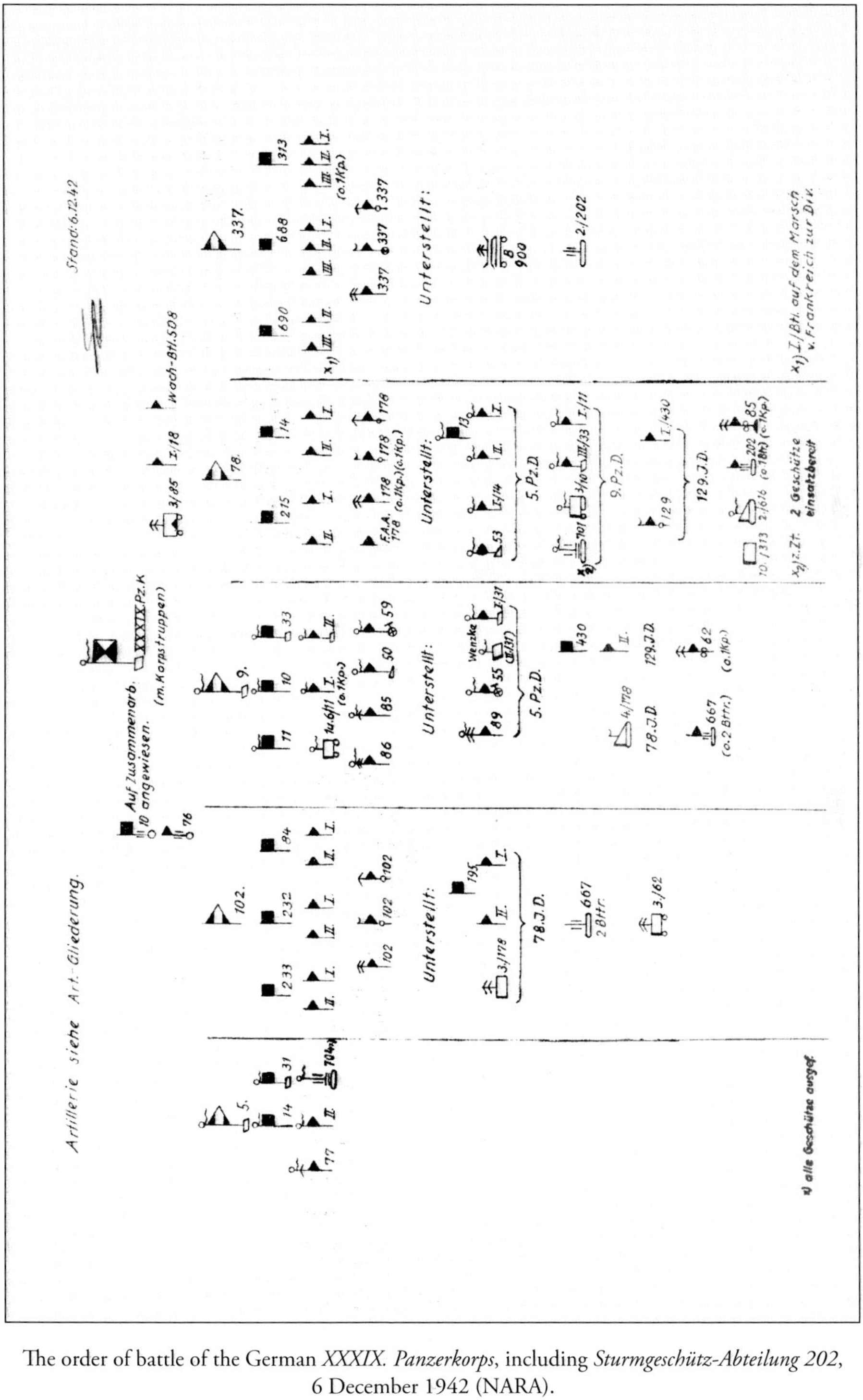

The order of battle of the German *XXXIX. Panzerkorps*, including *Sturmgeschütz-Abteilung 202*, 6 December 1942 (NARA).

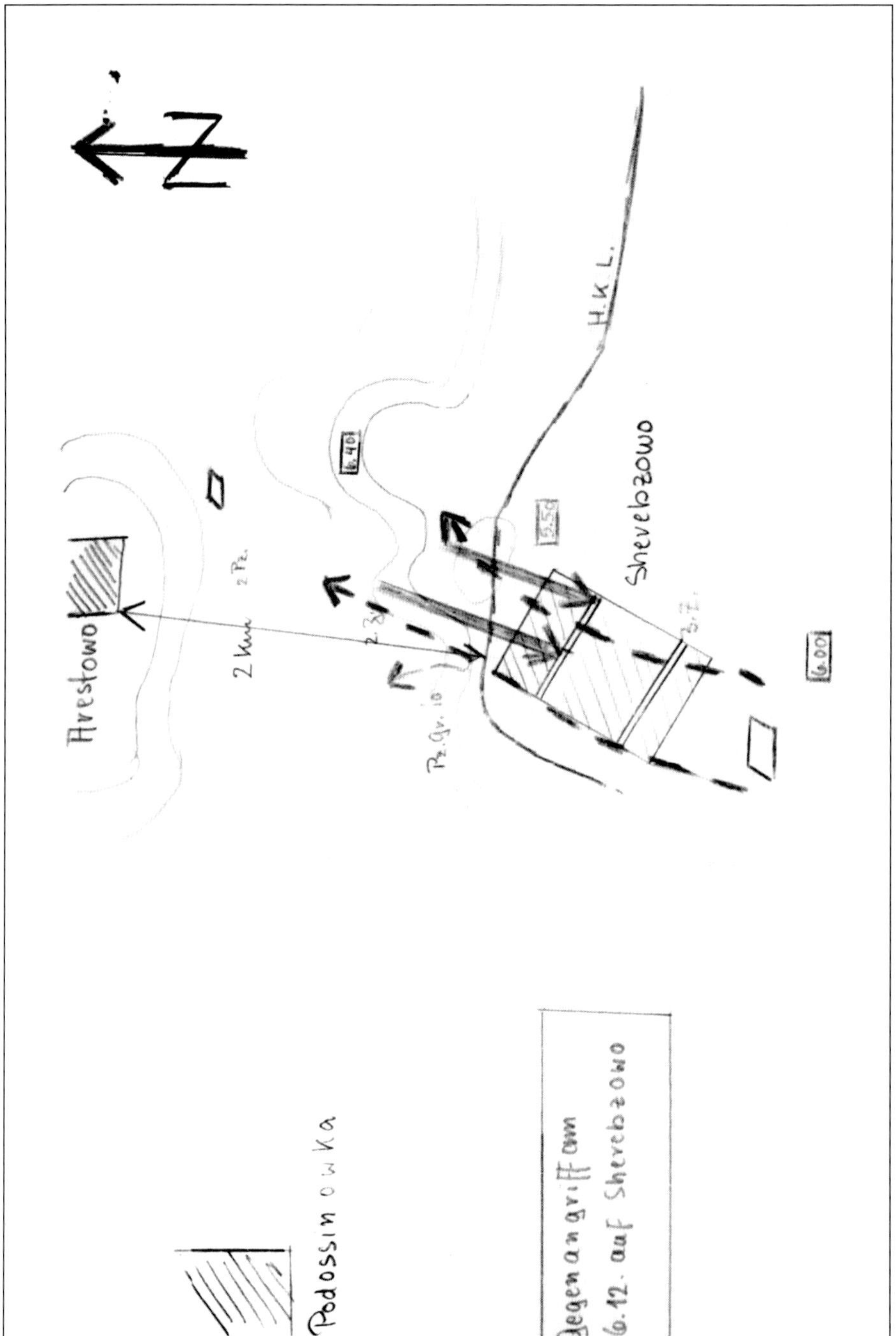

Sketch of the German attack on Sherebzowo, 6 December 1942 (NARA).

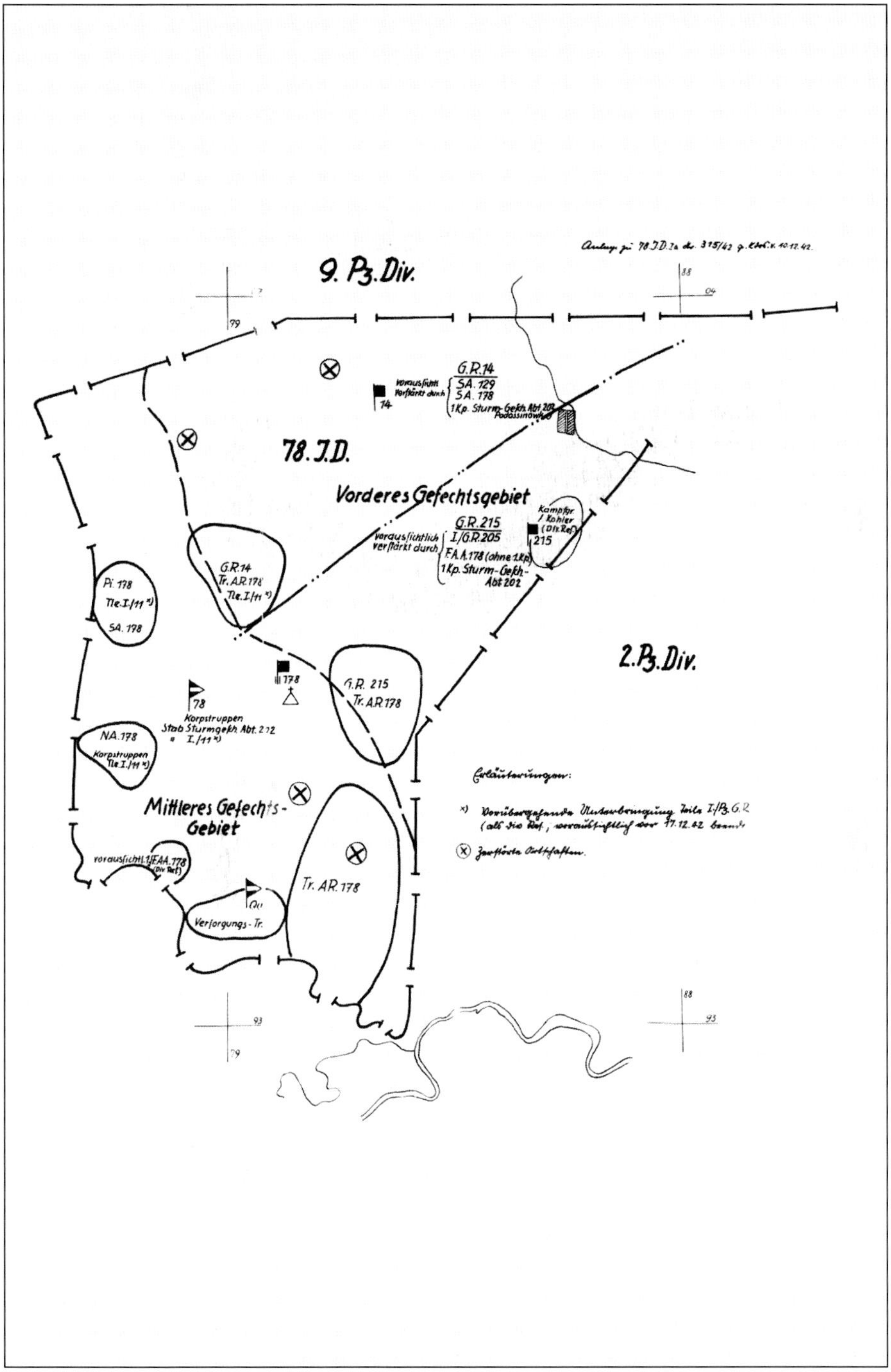

Disposition of German units in the defensive sector of the *78. Infanterie-Division*, 10 December 1942. Settlements marked with encircled Xs were destroyed (NARA).

78. Infanterie-Division Div.Gef.Stand, 10.12.1942.
Ia

Betr.: Panzerabschußerfolge der Sturmgeschütz-Abt. 202.
- 1 - Anlage.

An
Generalkommando XXXIX. Pz.K. /Ia

In der Anlage wird eine Meldung der Sturmgeschütz-Abt. 202 über Panzerabschußerfolge vorgelegt.

Da die Feindpanzer sowohl im Abschnitt der 78. Inf. Division als auch bei der 337. Inf. Div. abgeschossen wurden, konnte eine Einzel-Nachprüfung nicht erfolgen. Die gemeldeten Zahlen dürften aber den tatsächlichen Abschußerfolgen entsprechen.

In Anbetracht der Erfolge und der vorbildlichen Einsatzbereitschaft der Sturmgeschütz-Abt. 202 wird gebeten, eine Nennung dieser Abteilung im Wehrmachtsbericht erwirken zu wollen.

Der Divisions - Kommandeur

Presentation of the *78. Infanterie-Division* to the staff of the *XXXIX. Panzerkorps* in relation to Soviet AFVs knocked out by *Sturmgeschütz-Abteilung 202* between 28 November 1942 and 5 December 1942 (NARA).

Sturmgeschütz-Abt.202 O.U.den 5.12.1942
Ia

Betrifft:Abschußerfolge
Bezug:Ohne
Anlage:-0-

D e r

78. Infanterie-Division

Die Abteilung meldet für die Zeit vom 28.11.-5.12.42 folgende Abschusszahlen an feindlichen Panzerkampfwagen:

28.11.	3	Pzkpfwg.
29.11.	11	"
30.11.	11	"
1.12.	3	"
2.12.	1	"
3.12.	-	
4.12.	25	"
5.12.	7.	"
insgesamt	61	"

Davon schoss der Uffz. A m l i n g mit seinem Sturmgeschütz am 4.12. aus einem mit zehnfacher Übermacht geführten feindlichen Panzerangriff in kurzer Zeit allein 10 Panzer,der Wm. T a n t i u s innerhalb 3 Tagen 15 Panzer ab.

i.V.

Hauptmann

Presentation of the *78. Infanterie-Division* to the staff of the *XXXIX. Panzerkorps* in relation to Soviet AFVs knocked out by *Sturmgeschütz-Abteilung 202* between 28 November 1942 and 5 December 1942 (NARA).

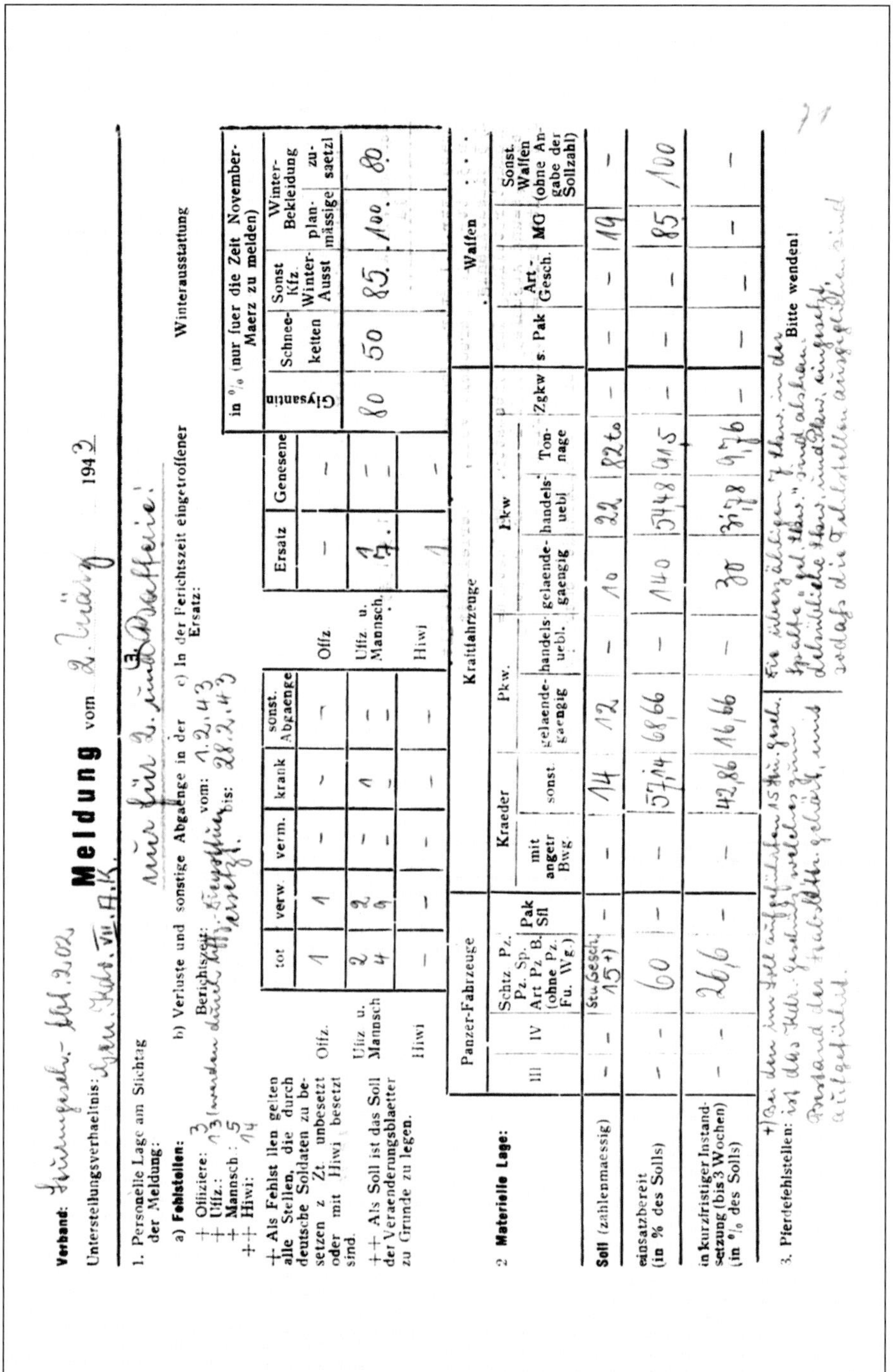

Verband: Sturmgesch.-Abt. 202

Meldung vom 2. März 1943

Unterstellungsverhaeltnis: Gen. Kdo. VII. A.K.

nur für 2. und 3. Batterie!

1. Personelle Lage am Stichtag der Meldung:

a) **Fehlstellen:**

\+ Offiziere: 3
\+ Uffz.: 13 (werden durch Uffz.-[illegible] ersetzt.)
\+ Mannsch.: 5
++ Hiwi: 14

\+ Als Fehlstellen gelten alle Stellen, die durch deutsche Soldaten zu besetzen z. Zt. unbesetzt oder mit Hiwi besetzt sind.

++ Als Soll ist das Soll der Veraenderungsblaetter zu Grunde zu legen.

b) Verluste und sonstige Abgaenge in der Berichtszeit: vom: 1.2.43 bis: 28.2.43

	tot	verw.	verm.	krank	sonst. Abgaenge
Offz.	1	1	–	–	–
Uffz. u. Mannsch.	2 4	2 9	– –	1 –	– –
Hiwi	–	–	–	–	–

c) In der Berichtszeit eingetroffener Ersatz:

	Ersatz	Genesene
Offz.	–	–
Uffz. u. Mannsch.	1 7.	– –
Hiwi	1	–

Winterausstattung

in % (nur fuer die Zeit November-Maerz zu melden)				
Glysantin	Schneeketten	Sonst Kfz. Winter-Ausst.	Winter-Bekleidung plan-mässige	Winter-Bekleidung zusaetzl.
80	50	85.	100.	80.

2. **Materielle Lage:**

	Panzer-Fahrzeuge: III	IV	Schtz Pz. Pz. Sp. Art Pz B. (ohne Pz. Fu. Wg.)	Pak Sfl	Kraftfahrzeuge: Kraeder mit angetr. Bwg.	Kraeder sonst.	Pkw. gelaende-gaengig	Pkw. handels-uebl.	Lkw gelaende-gaengig	Lkw handels-uebl.	Lkw Ton-nage	Zgkw	Waffen: s. Pak	Art.-Gesch.	MG	Sonst. Waffen (ohne Angabe der Sollzahl)
Soll (zahlenmaessig)	–	–	Stu.Gesch. 15+)	–	–	14	12	–	10	22	82 to	–	–	–	19	–
einsatzbereit (in % des Solls)	–	–	60	–	–	57,14	68,66	–	140	54,48	91,5	–	–	–	85	100
in kurzfristiger Instandsetzung (bis 3 Wochen) (in % des Solls)	–	–	26,6	–	–	42,86	16,66	–	30	31,78	9,76	–	–	–	–	–

3. Pferdefehlstellen: +) Bei den im Soll aufgeführten 15 Stu. Gesch. ist das Kdr.-Geschütz, welches zum Bestand der Stabsbttr. gehört, mit aufgeführt.

Die überzähligen 7 Lkw. in der Spalte „gel. Lkw." sind als handelsübliche Lkw. und Pkw. eingesetzt, sodaß die Fehlstellen ausgeglichen sind

Bitte wenden!

Status report of the *2.* and *3. Batterie/Sturmgeschütz-Abteilung 202*, 2 March 1943 (NARA).

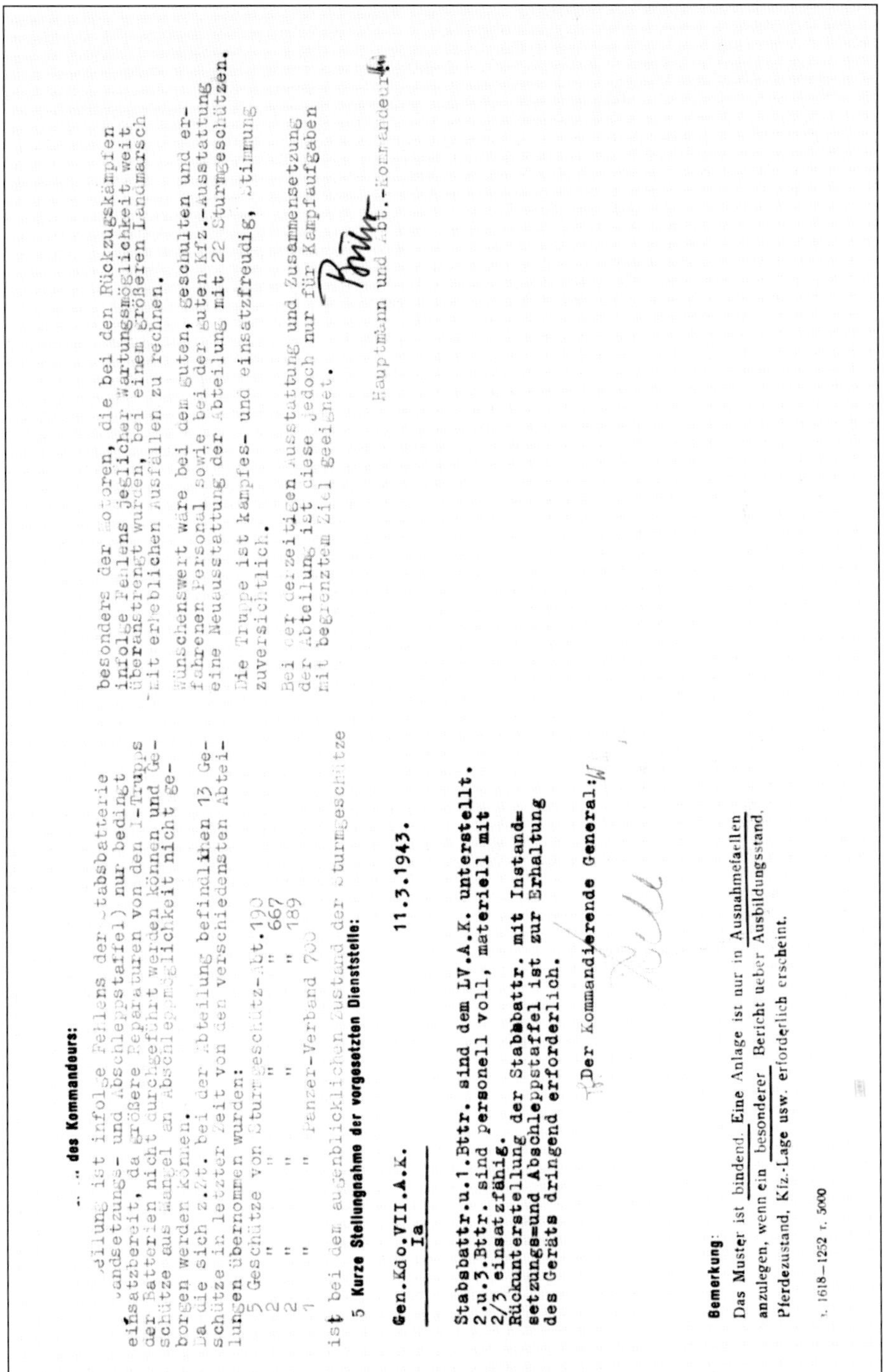

.. .. **des Kommandeurs:**

.eilung ist infolge Fehlens der Stabsbatterie (Instandsetzungs- und Abschleppstaffel) nur bedingt einsatzbereit, da größere Reparaturen von den I-Trupps der Batterien nicht durchgeführt werden können und Geschütze aus Mangel an Abschleppmöglichkeit nicht geborgen werden können.
Da die sich z.Zt. bei der Abteilung befindlihen 13 Geschütze in letzter Zeit von den verschiedensten Abteilungen übernommen wurden:

5	Geschütze von Sturmgeschütz-Abt.	190
2	" " " "	667
2	" " " "	189
1	" " Panzer-Verband	700

ist bei dem augenblicklichen Zustand der Sturmgeschütze besonders der Motoren, die bei den Rückzugskämpfen infolge Fehlens jeglicher Wartungsmöglichkeit weit überanstrengt wurden, bei einem größeren Landmarsch mit erheblichen Ausfällen zu rechnen.

Wünschenswert wäre bei dem guten, geschulten und erfahrenen Personal sowie bei der guten Kfz.-Ausstattung eine Neuausstattung der Abteilung mit 22 Sturmgeschützen.

Die Truppe ist kampfes- und einsatzfreudig, Stimmung zuversichtlich.

Bei der derzeitigen Ausstattung und Zusammensetzung der Abteilung ist diese jedoch nur für Kampfaufgaben mit begrenztem Ziel geeignet.

Hauptmann und Abt.-Kommandeur.

5 **Kurze Stellungnahme der vorgesetzten Dienststelle:**

Gen.Kdo.VII.A.K. **11.3.1943.**
Ia

Stabsbattr.u.1.Bttr. sind dem LV.A.K. unterstellt.
2.u.3.Bttr. sind personell voll, materiell mit 2/3 einsatzfähig.
Rückunterstellung der Stabbattr. mit Instand=setzungs=und Abschleppstaffel ist zur Erhaltung des Geräts dringend erforderlich.

Der Kommandierende General:

Bemerkung:
Das Muster ist bindend. Eine Anlage ist nur in Ausnahmefaellen anzulegen, wenn ein besonderer Bericht ueber Ausbildungsstand, Pferdezustand, Kfz.-Lage usw. erforderlich erscheint.

r. 1618–1252 r. 5000

Status report of the *2.* and *3. Batterie*/*Sturmgeschütz-Abteilung 202*, 2 March 1943 (NARA).

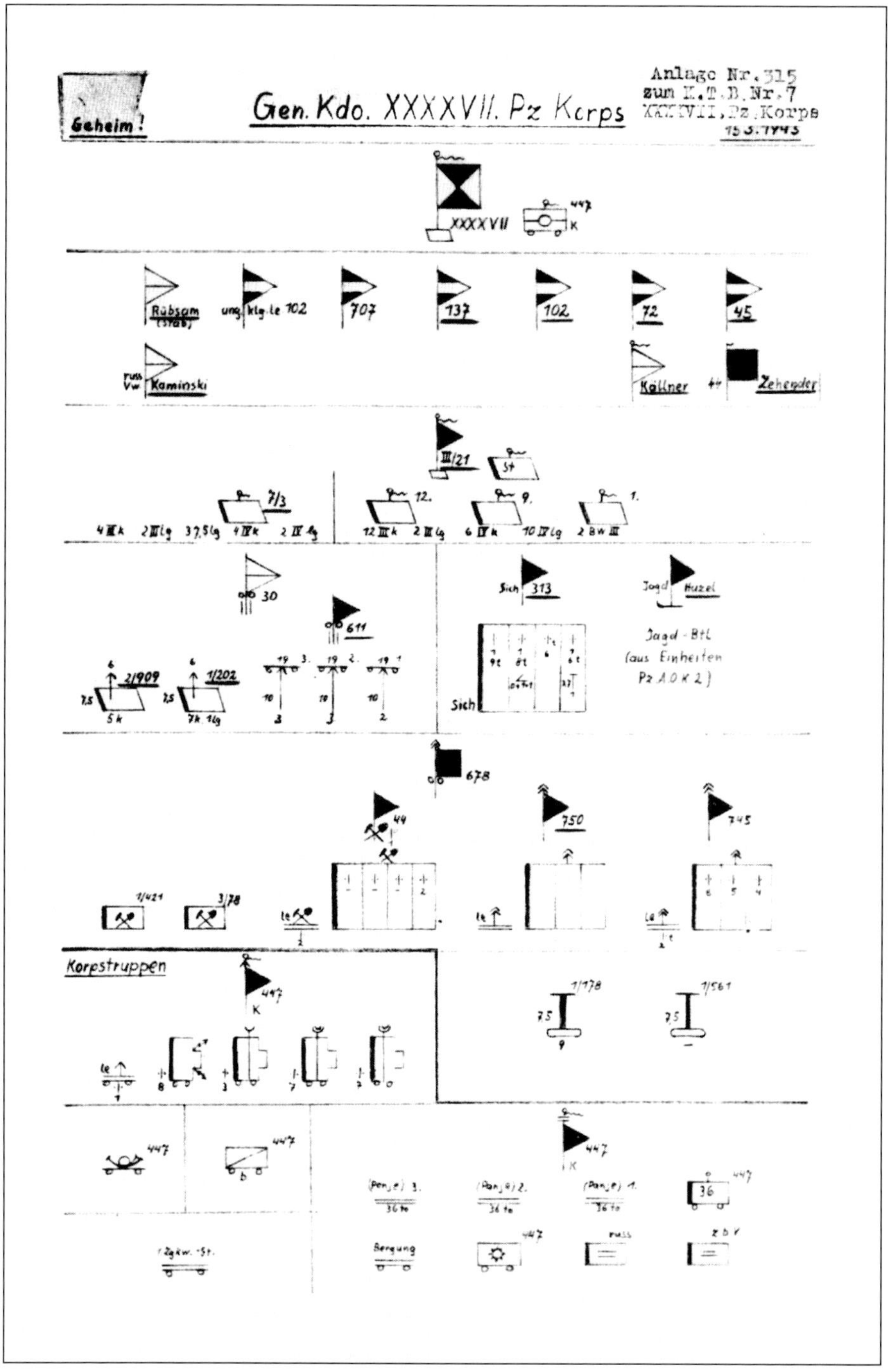

The order of battle of the *XXXXVII. Panzerkorps*, including
the *1. Batterie/Sturmgeschütz-Abteilung 202*, 15 March 1943 (NARA).

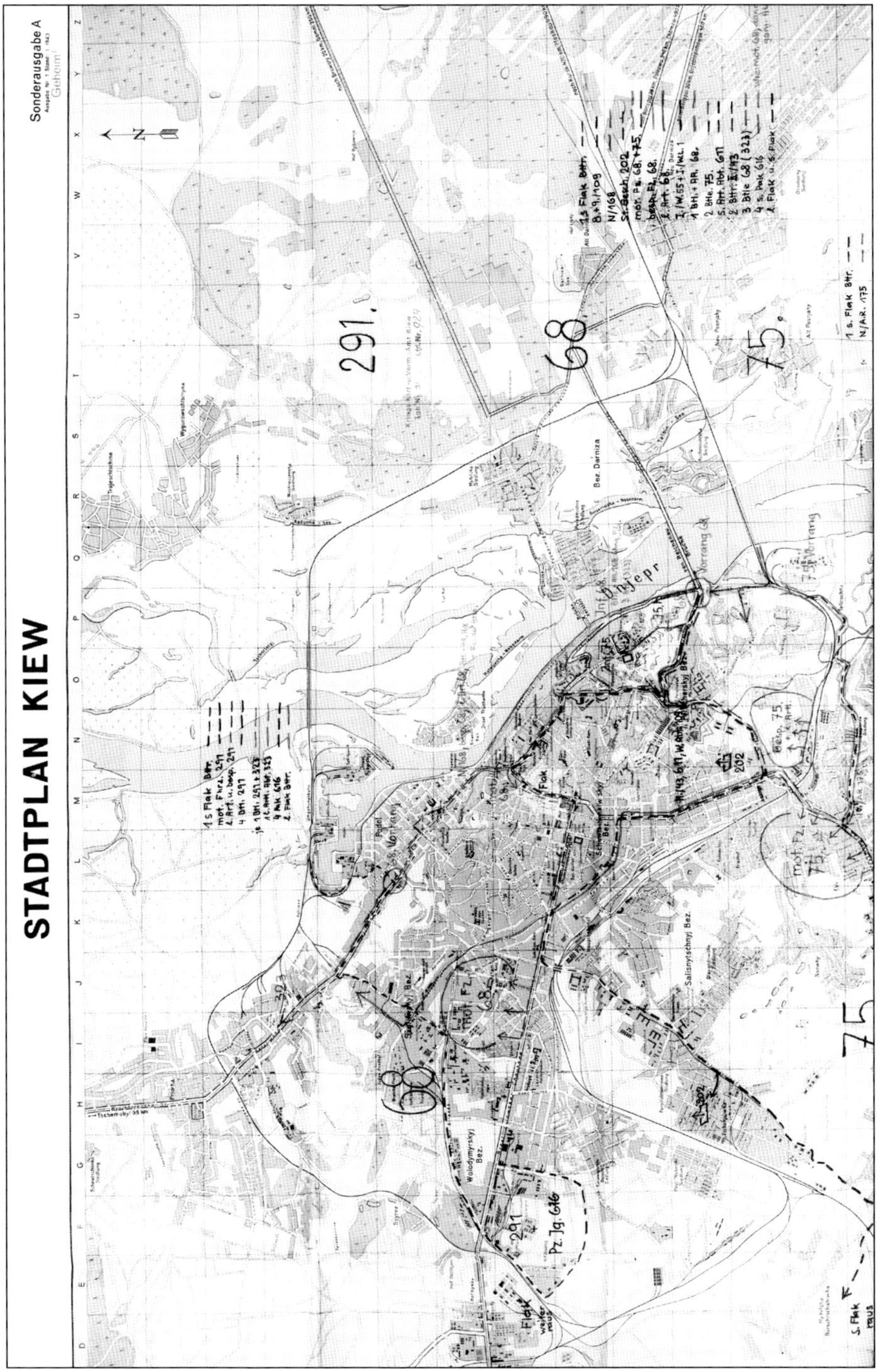

Defence system of Kiew, including *Sturmgeschütz-Abteilung 202*, 25 September 1943 (NARA)

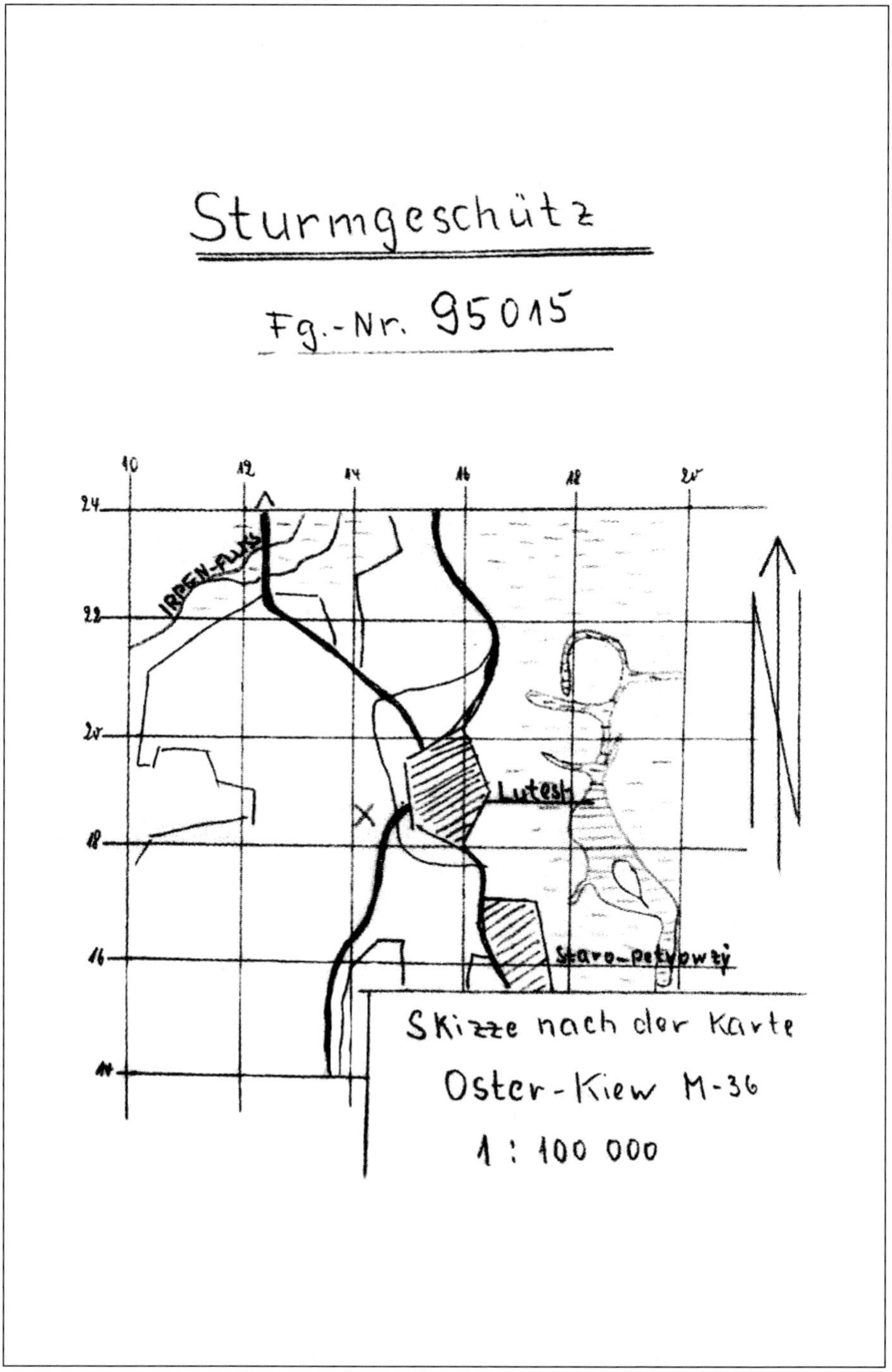

Position of the assault gun of *Sturmgeschütz-Abteilung 202* with chassis number '90015', written off as a total loss, 12 October 1943 (NARA)

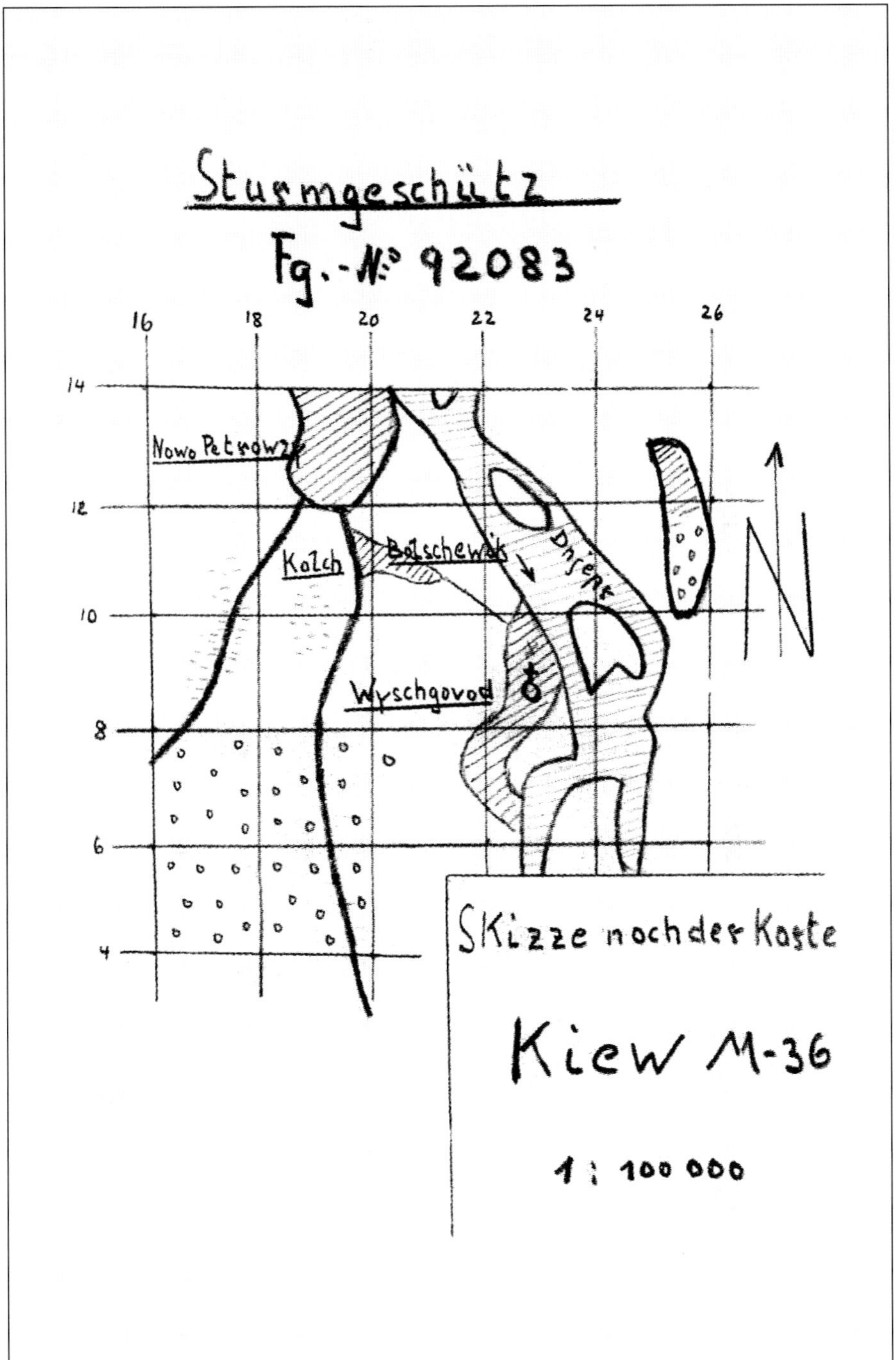

Position of the assault gun of *Sturmgeschütz-Abteilung 202* with chassis number '92083' written off as a total loss, 18 October 1943 (NARA).

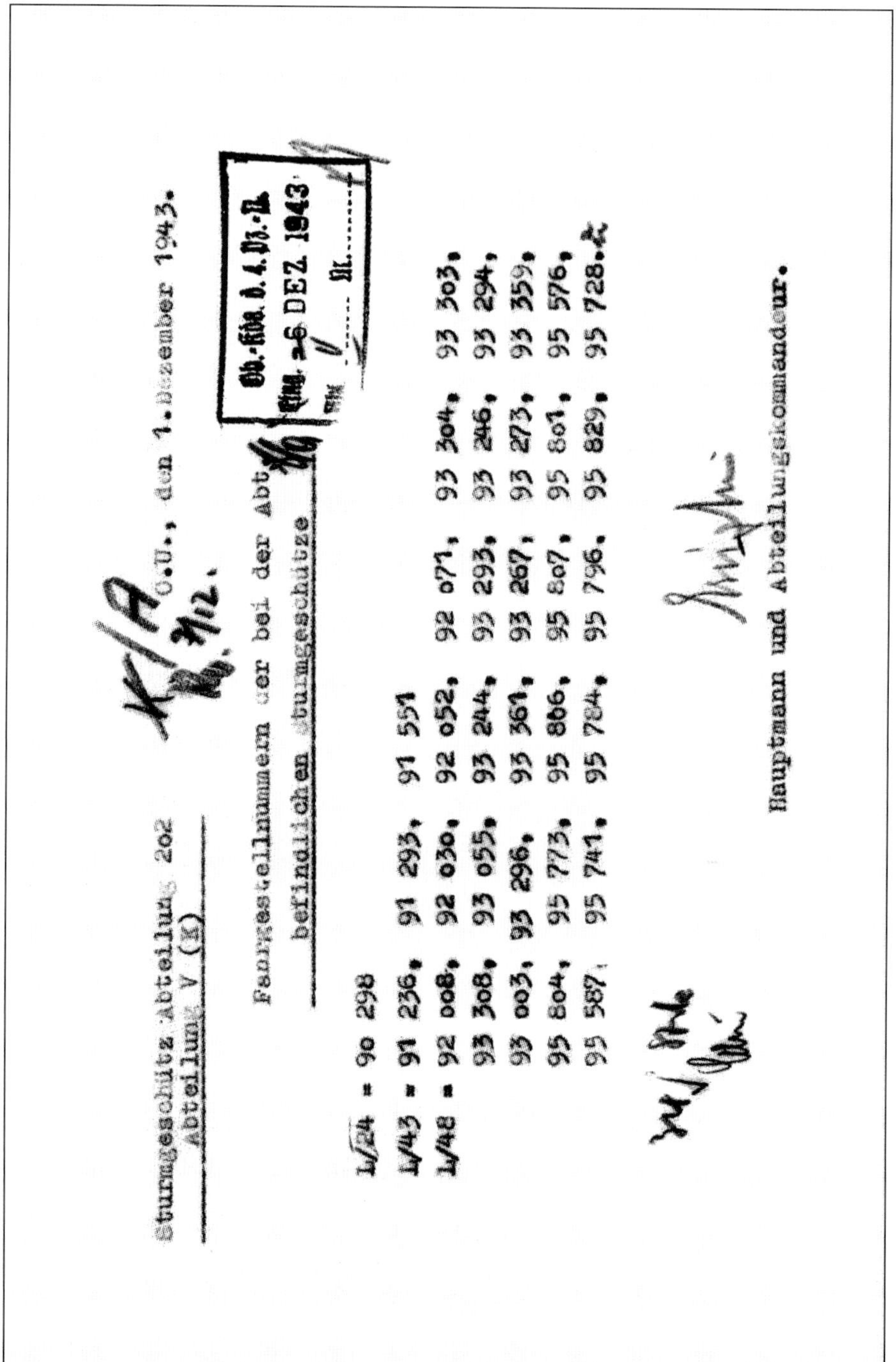

Sturmgeschütz Abteilung 202
Abteilung V (K)

O.U., den 1. Dezember 1943.

Ob.-Kdo. d. 4. Pz.-A.
Eing. 6 DEZ 1943
Nr. ......

Fahrgestellnummern der bei der Abt. befindlichen Sturmgeschütze

L/24 = 90 298

L/43 = 91 236, 91 293, 91 551

L/48 = 92 008, 92 030, 92 052, 92 071, 93 304, 93 303,
93 308, 93 055, 93 244, 93 293, 93 246, 93 294,
93 003, 93 296, 93 361, 93 267, 93 273, 93 359,
95 804, 95 773, 95 806, 95 807, 95 801, 95 576,
95 587, 95 741, 95 784, 95 796, 95 829, 95 728.

Hauptmann und Abteilungskommandeur.

Assault guns of *Sturmgeschütz-Abteilung 202* according to their chassis numbers and calibre length of their guns, 1 December 1943 (NARA).

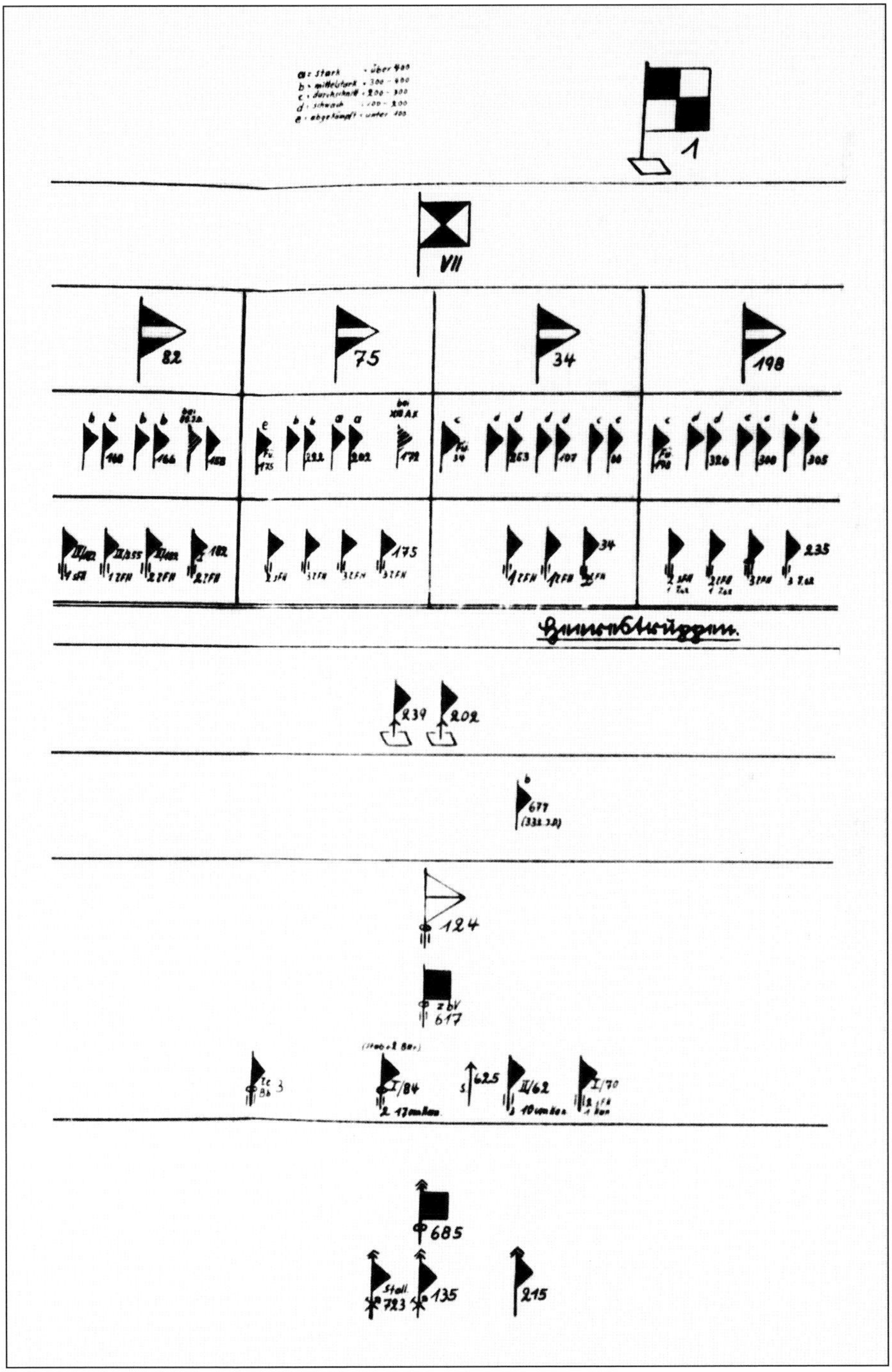

The order of battle of the German *1. Panzerarmee* including *Sturmgeschütz-Abteilung 202,* under command of the *VII. Armeekorps,* 14 January 1944 (NARA).

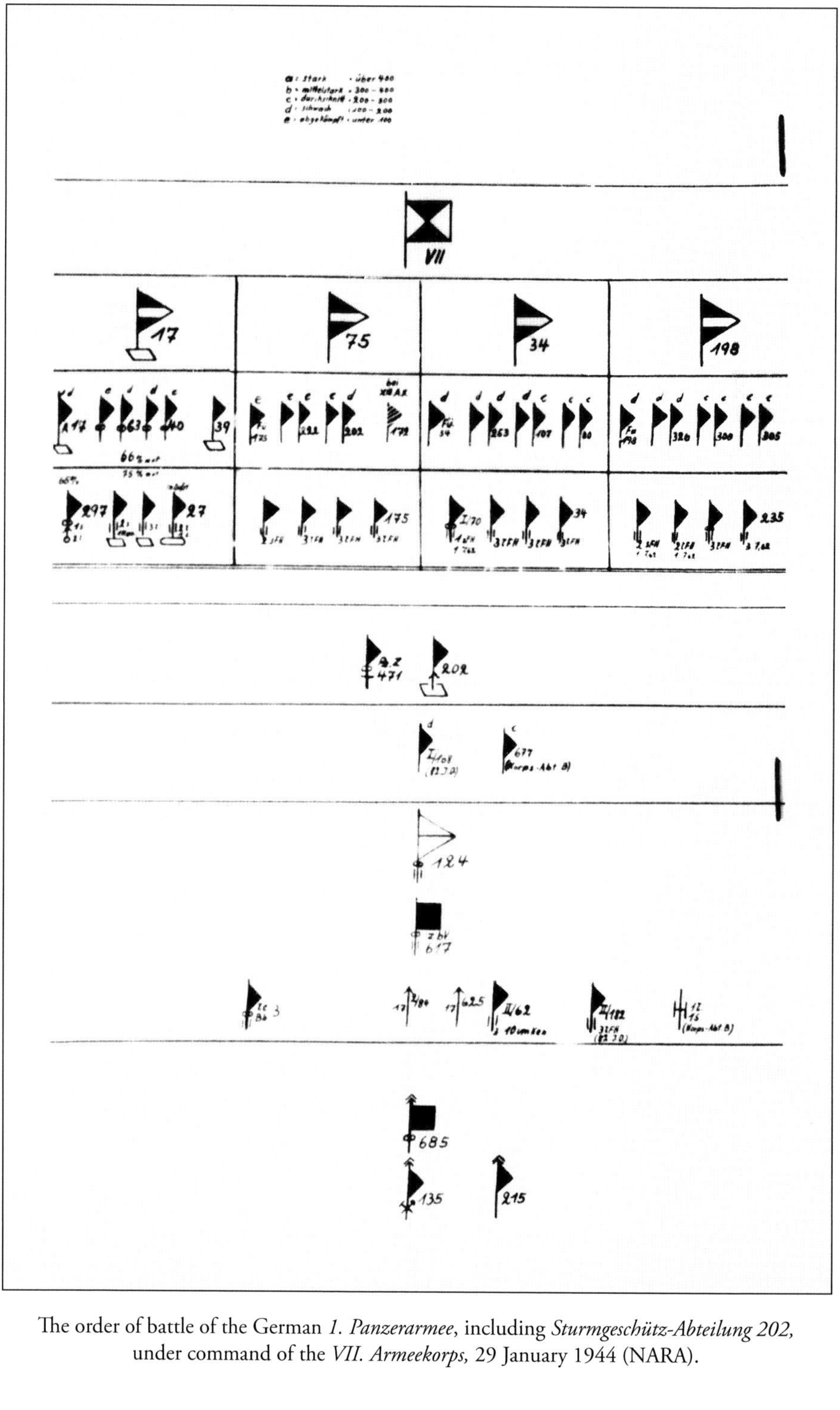

The order of battle of the German *1. Panzerarmee*, including *Sturmgeschütz-Abteilung 202*, under command of the *VII. Armeekorps*, 29 January 1944 (NARA).

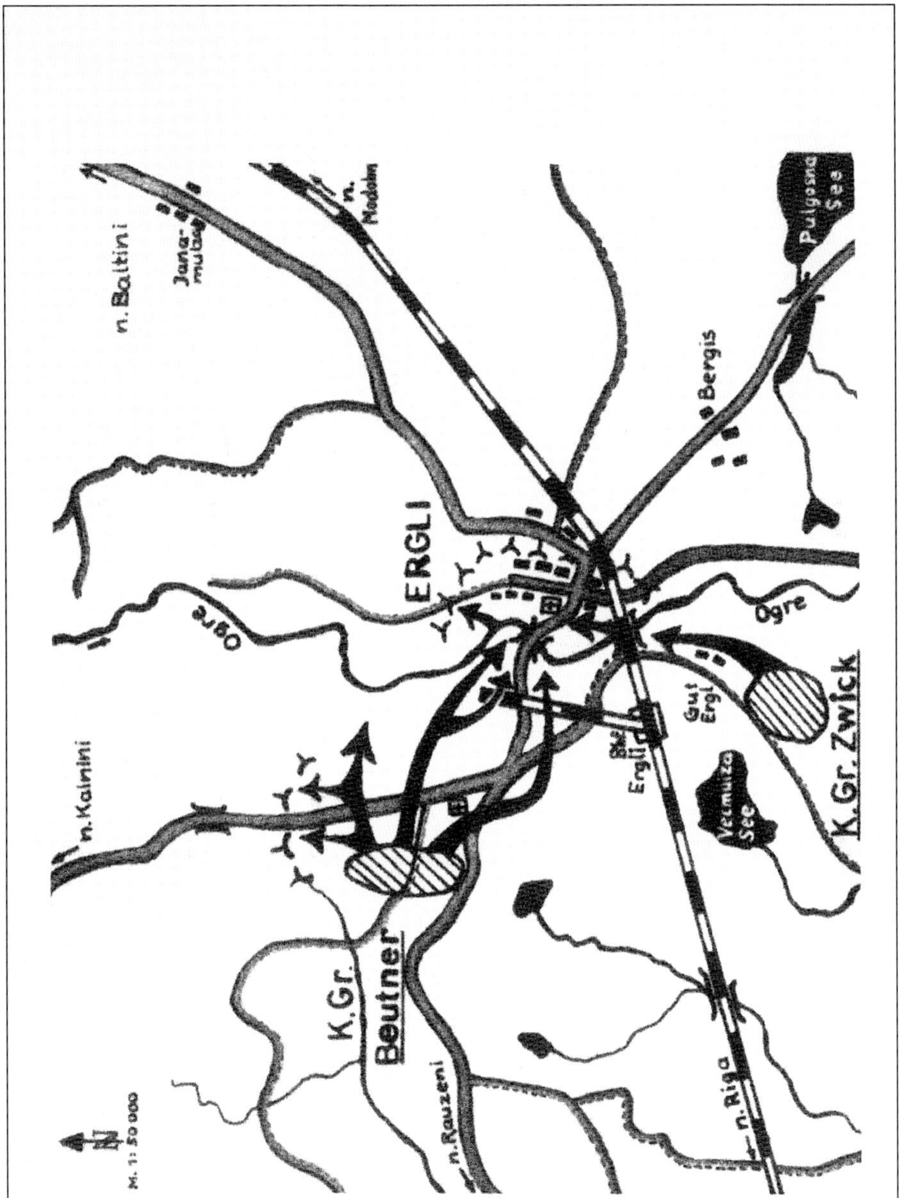

Recapture of Ergli by the Germans, 20 August 1944. The *3. Batterie/Sturmgeschütz-Abteilung 202* also fought in *Kampfgruppe ‚Beutner'* (Photograph in Pape, Klaus: *329. Infanterie-Division. Cholm – Demjansk – Kurland.* Jena, 2007. p. 169).

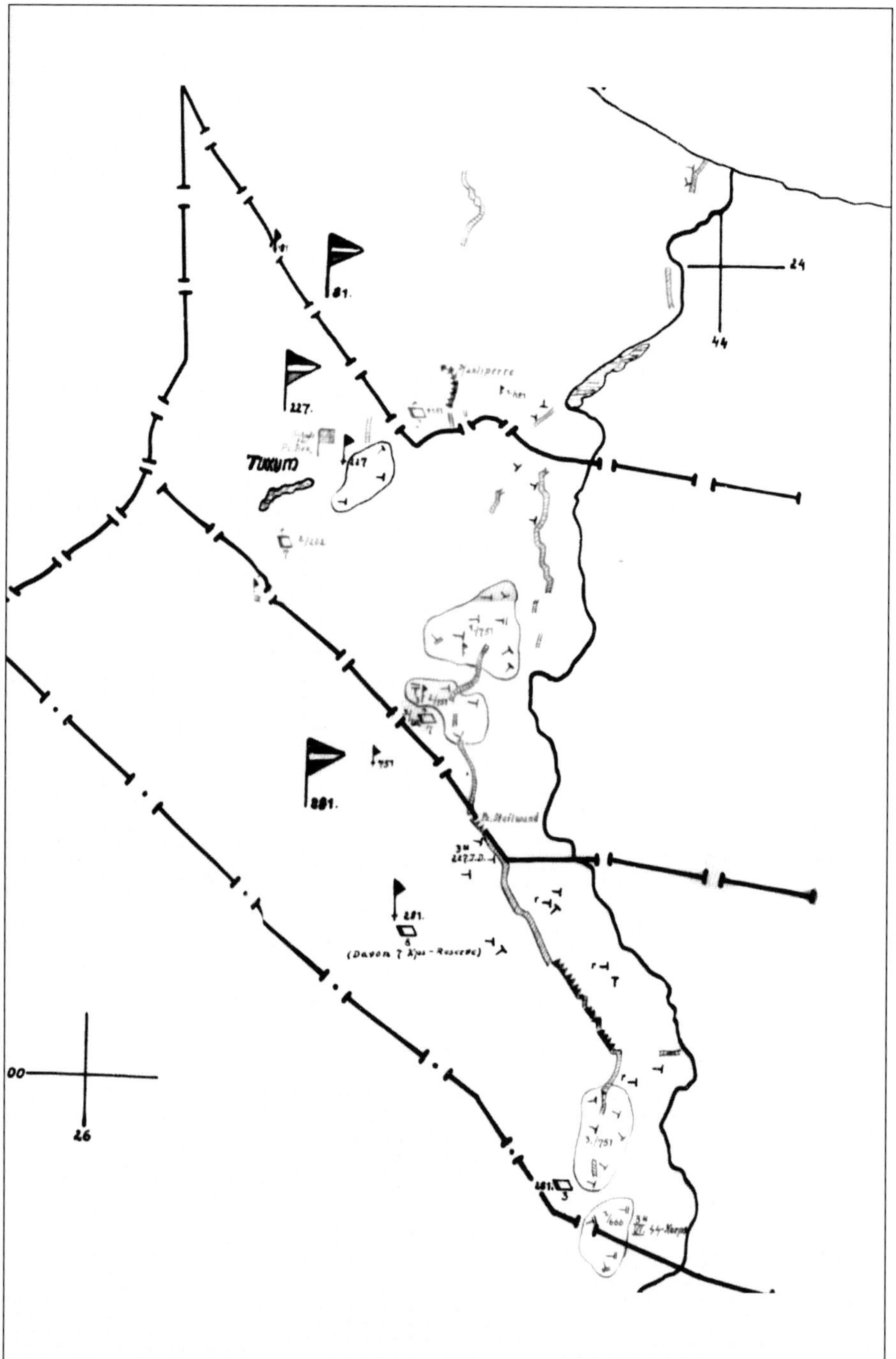

Anti-tank plan of fire of the *XVI. Armeekorps*, including assault guns of *Sturmgeschütz-Brigade 202,* in the area of Tuckum, 17 November 1944 (NARA).

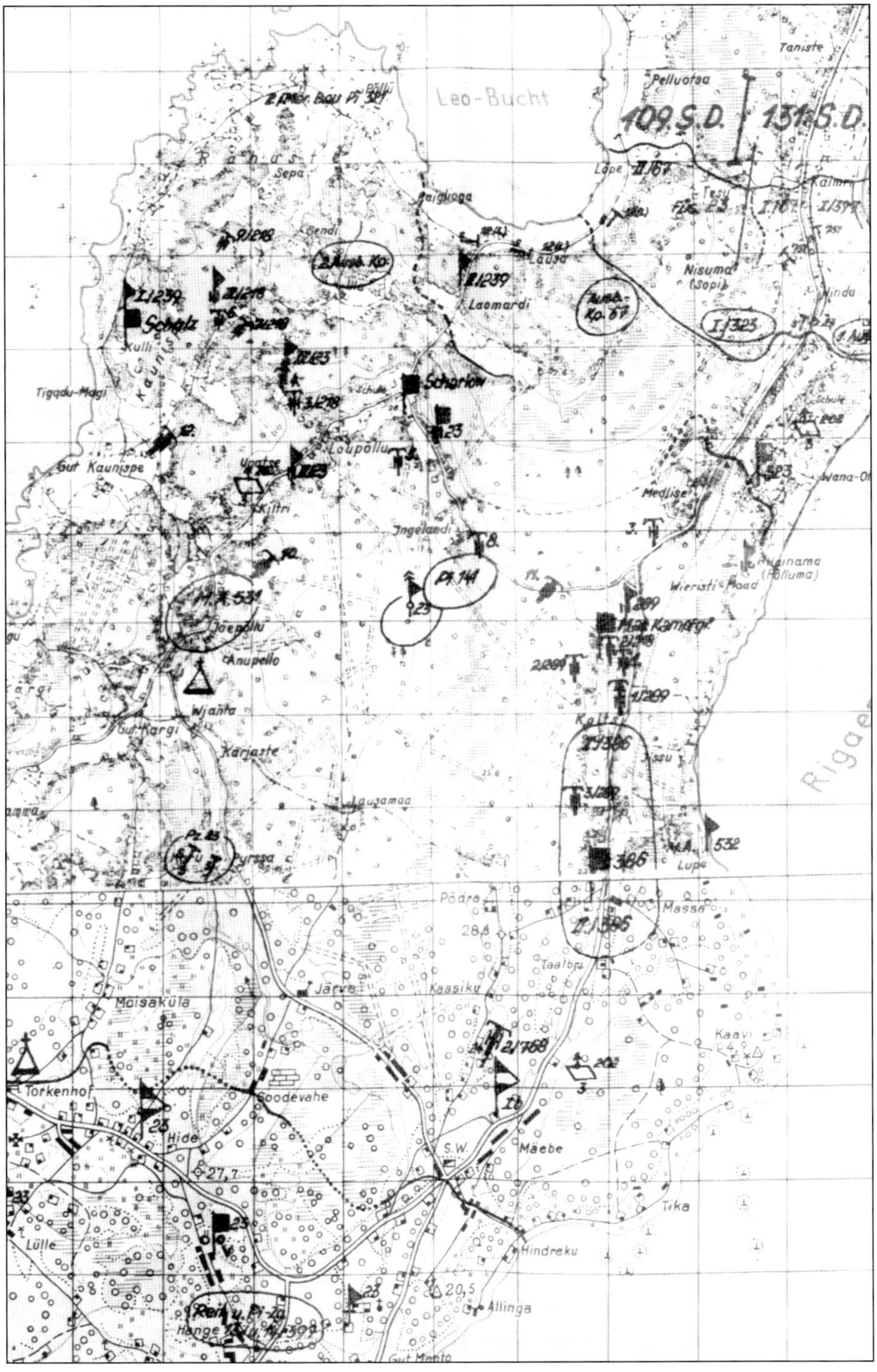

Elements of *Sturmgeschütz-Brigade 202* in the Sworbe Peninsula, 18 November 1944 (NARA).

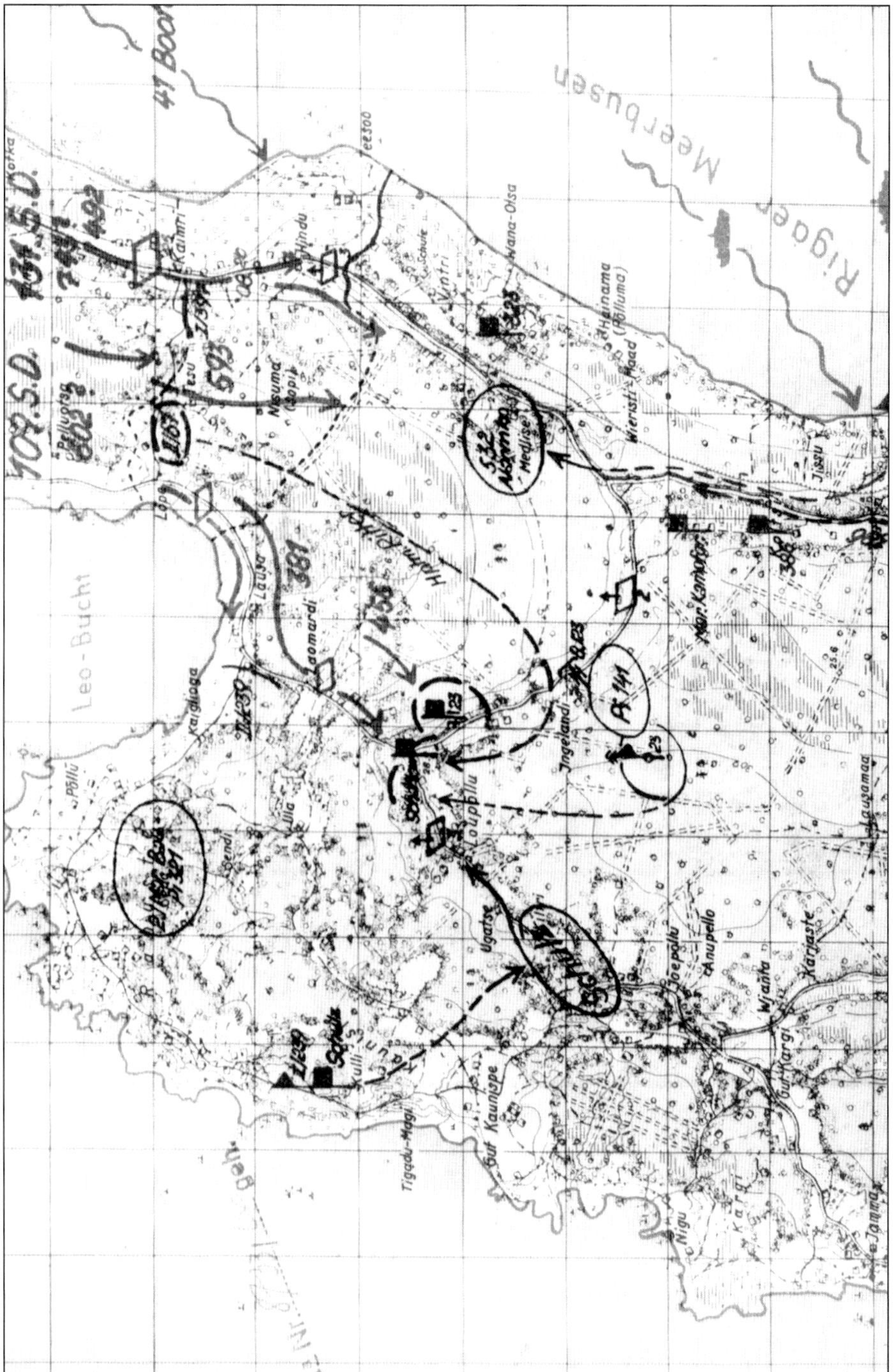

Elements of *Sturmgeschütz-Brigade 202* in the Sworbe Peninsula, 18 November 1944 (NARA).

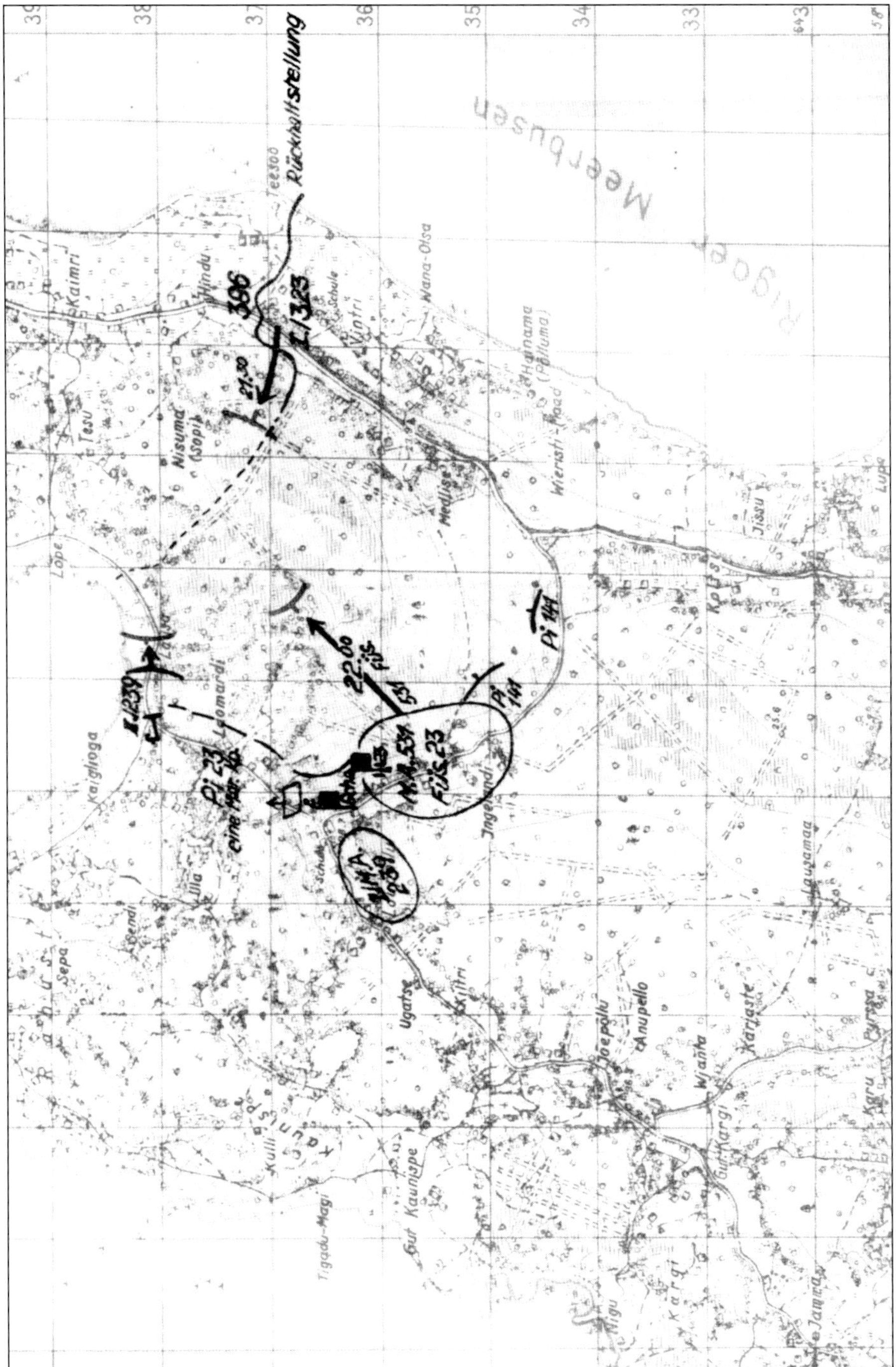

Elements of *Sturmgeschütz-Brigade 202* in the Sworbe Peninsula, 19 November 1944 (NARA).

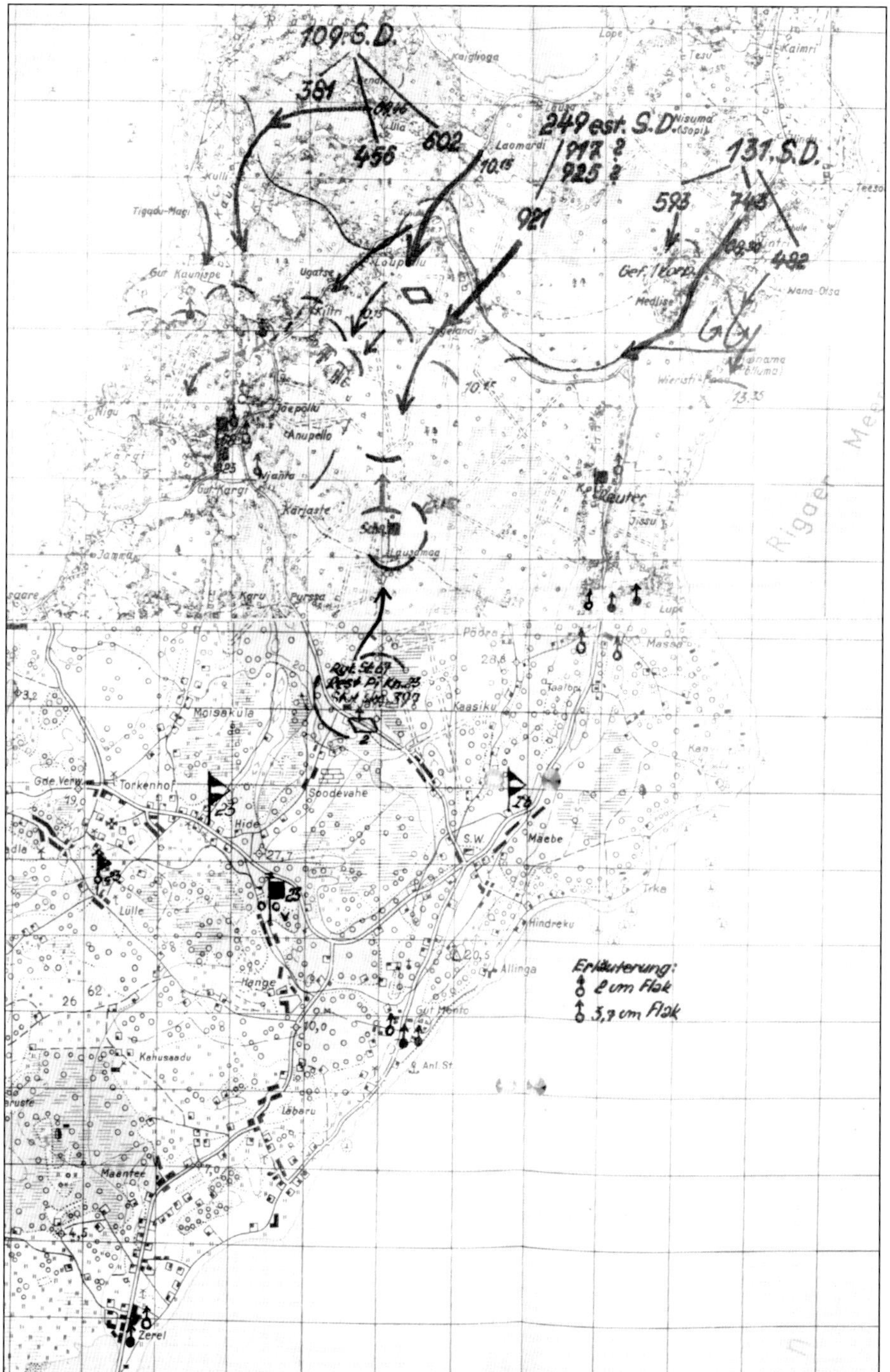

Elements of *Sturmgeschütz-Brigade 202* in the Sworbe Peninsula, 20 November 1944 (NARA).

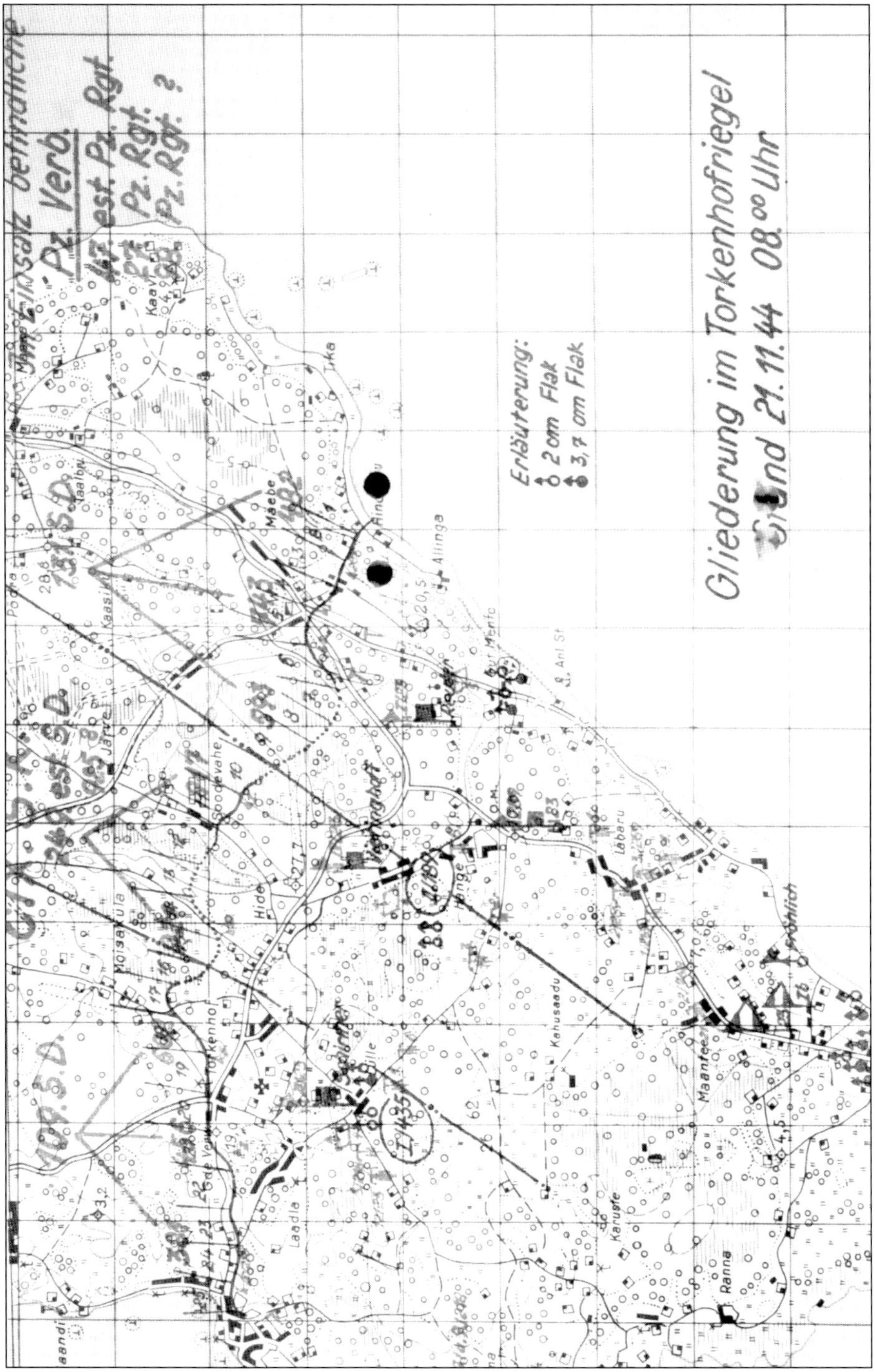

Elements of *Sturmgeschütz-Brigade 202* in the Sworbe Peninsula, 21 November 1944 (NARA).

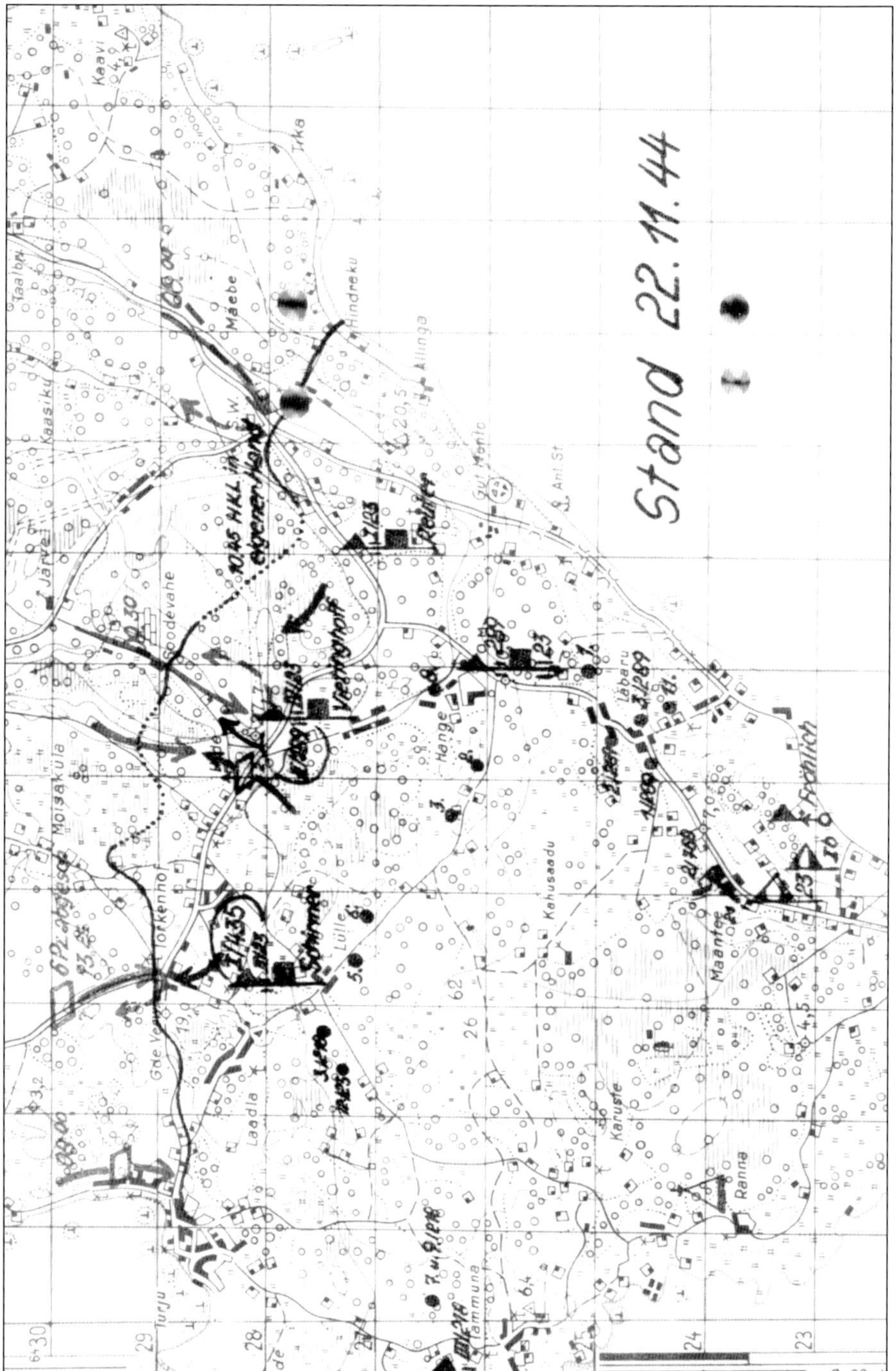

Elements of *Sturmgeschütz-Brigade 202* in the Sworbe Peninsula, 22 November 1944 (NARA).

391.

29.12.

1.) H.Sturm-Gesch.Brig.2o2
2.) Gen.Kdo.roem.6. SS-Korps(nachr.)   AOK 16, Ia

Ich beglückwünsche die Heeres-Sturmgeschütz-Brigade 2o2 und ihren Kommandeur, Hptm.Spielmann zum 1ooo Panzerabschuss, und sage gleichzeitig meinen Dank für die ausgezeichnete Kampfhilfe bei den schweren Kämpfen der letzten Tage im Raume von Dzukste.

Der OB der 16.Armee:
gez. H i l p e r t,
Geneal der Jnfanterie.

Nach Abgang:
Stopak,
Harko,
KTB,
Ia.

- 1 -

Telegram of praise from the commander of the *16. Armee, General der Infanterie* Carl Hilpert sent to *Sturmgeschütz-Brigade 202* on the occasion of their knocking-out the 1000th Soviet AFV (NARA).

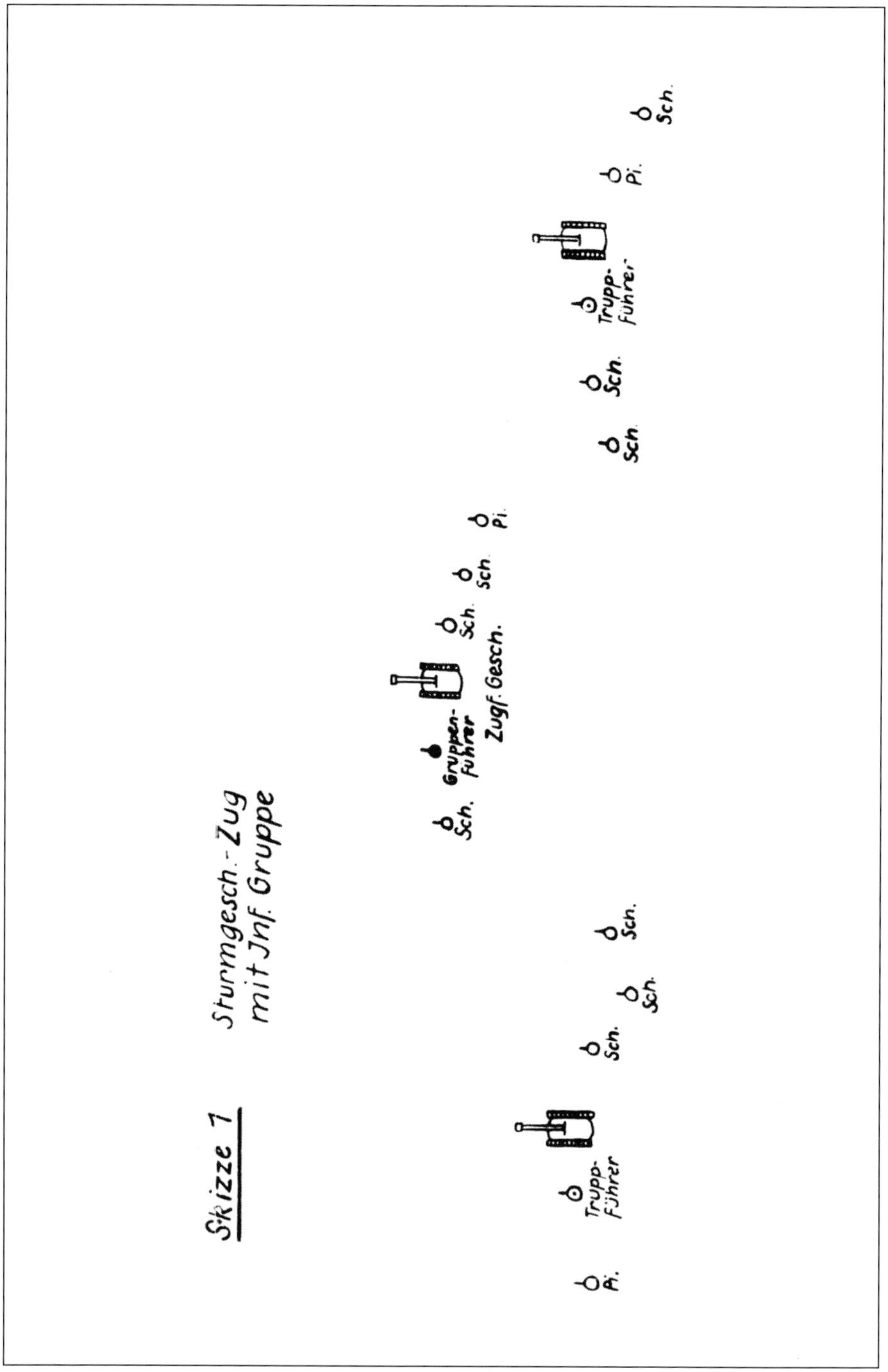

Cooperation of the assault gun platoon with the accompanying grenadiers in open ground (NARA).

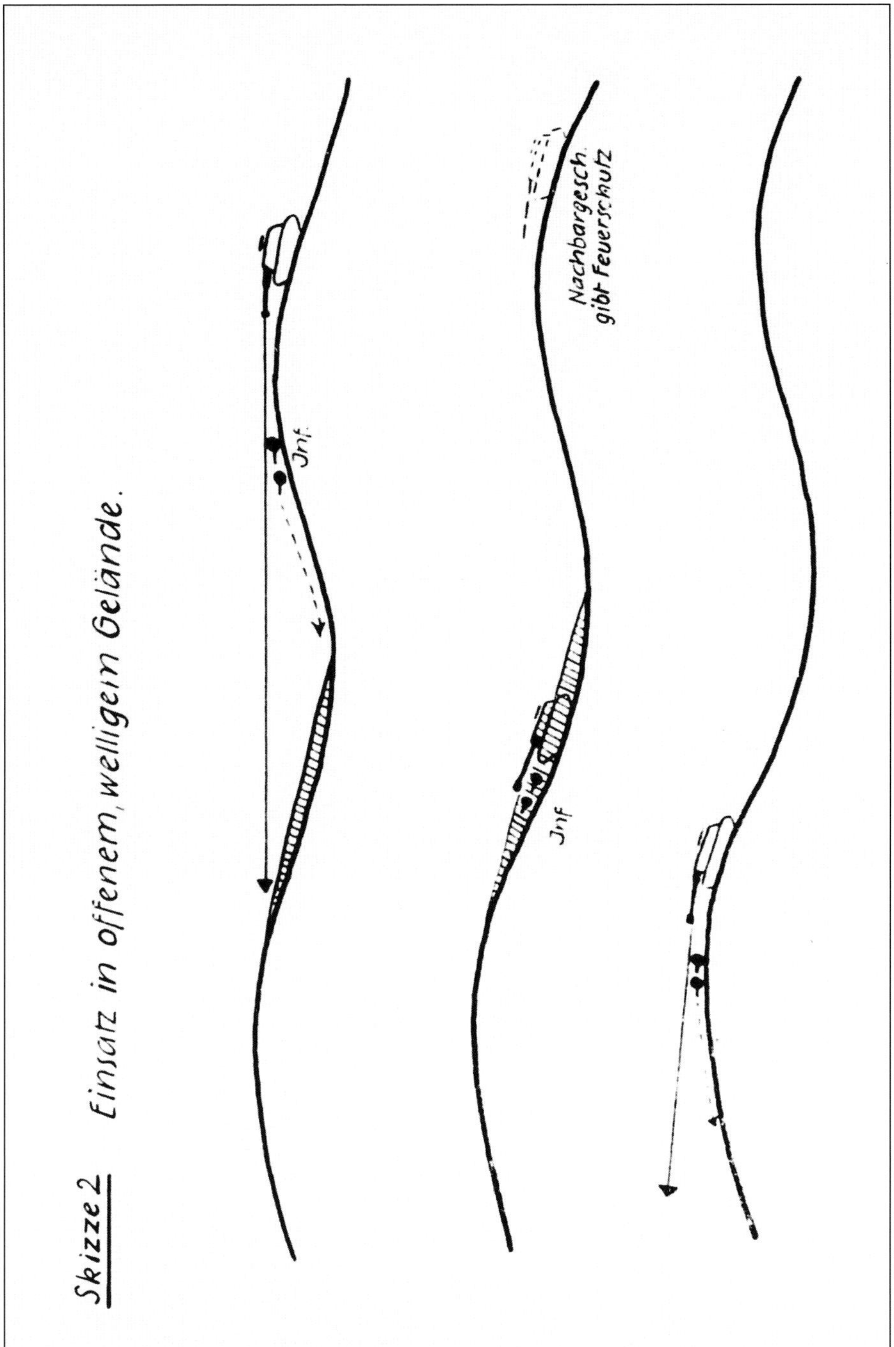

Cooperation of the assault gun platoon with the accompanying grenadiers on rugged terrain (NARA).

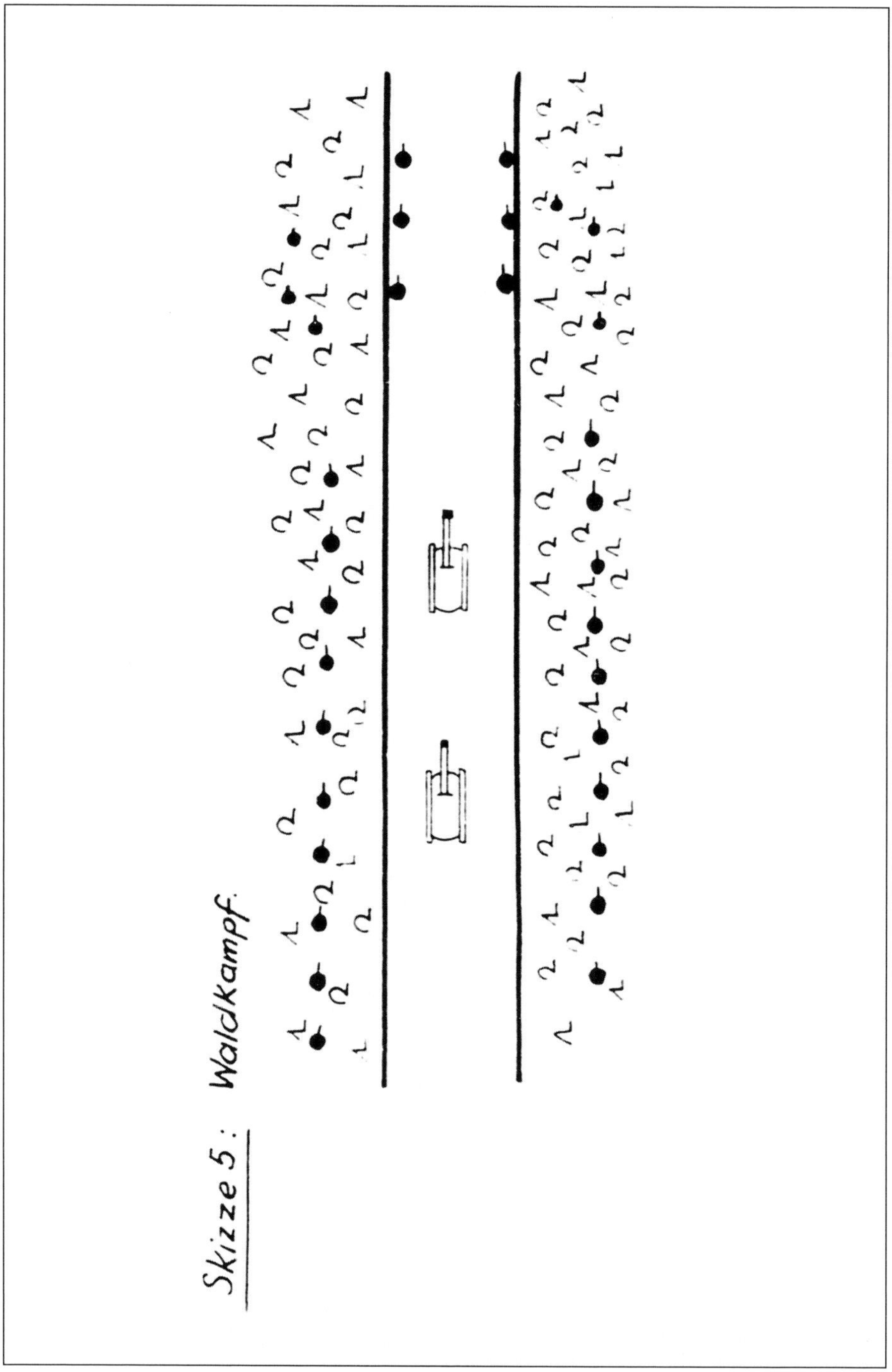

Cooperation of the assault gun platoon with the accompanying grenadiers during fighting in wooded terrain (NARA).

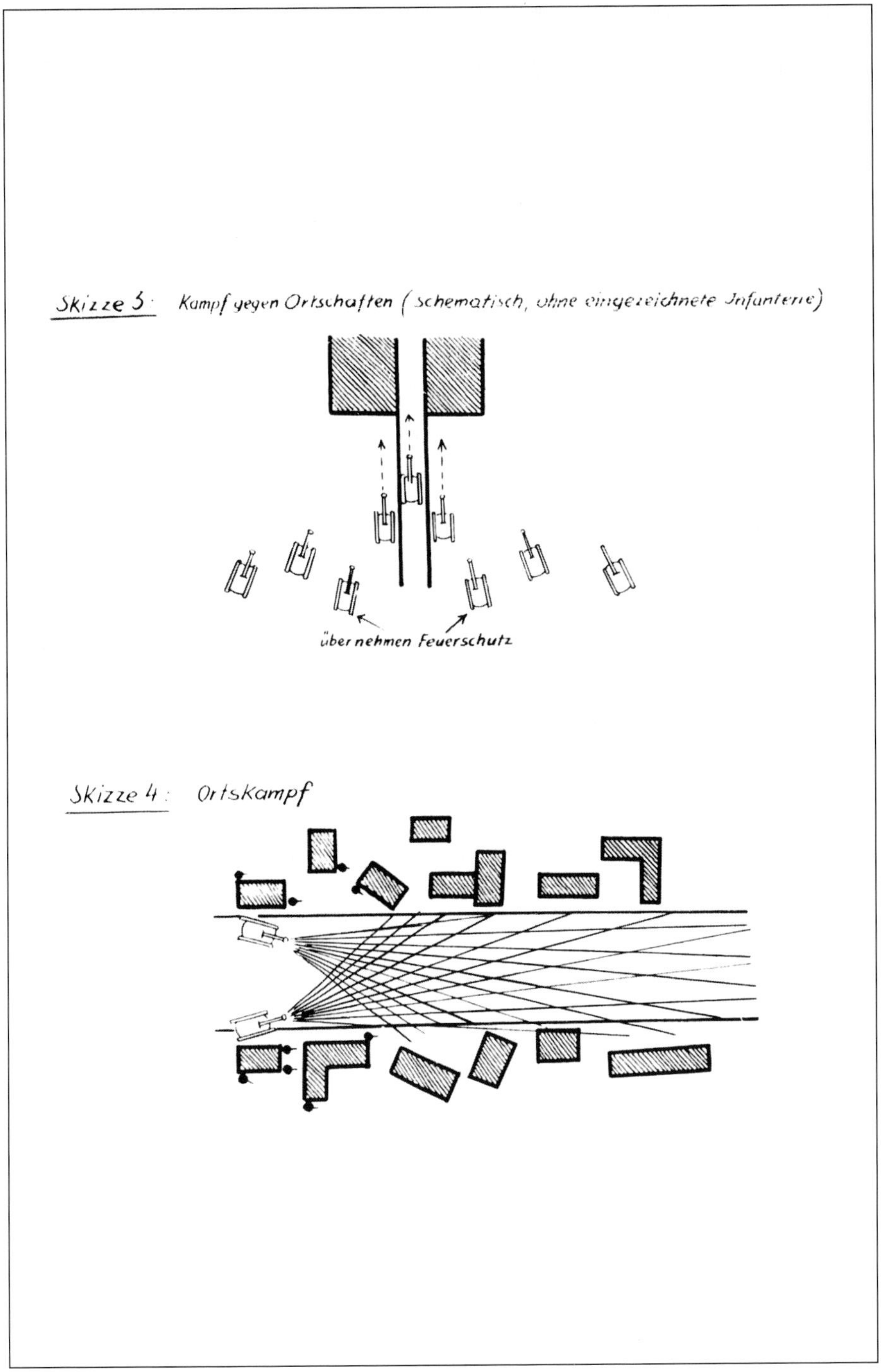

Cooperation of the assault gun platoon with the accompanying grenadiers during urban fighting (NARA).

PHOTOS

Rail shipment of the StuG. III assault guns of *Sturmgeschütz-Abteilung 202*; probably in autumn 1941.

An Sd.Kfz. 252 armoured ammunition carrier halftrack of *Sturmgeschütz-Abteilung 202*; probably in winter 1941-1942.

The StuG. III Ausf. D assault gun named 'Tiger' (produced by Alkett during May-September 1941) from the *3. Batterie / Sturmgeschütz-Abteilung 202*; probably in spring 1942.

One of the Klöckner-Humboldt-Deutz S330 diesel trucks of *Sturmgeschütz-Abteilung 202*. The unit insignia can be clearly seen on the right-side mudguard.

The StuG. III Ausf. E assault gun, named 'Leopard' (produced by Alkett during October-November 1941) from the *3. Batterie /Sturmgeschütz-Abteilung 202*, in a Soviet settlement not far from the unit's CP, in winter 1942.

The assault gun of the *2. Batterie/ Sturmgeschütz-Abteilung 202*, named 'Habicht' (Harrier), whitewashed for camouflage effect, in winter 1942-1943.

Recovery of the assault gun 'Leopard' in late 1942; the Pz.Kpfw. III Ausf. J tank lending a hand is probably an AFV of the *5. Panzer-Division.*

StuG. III assault gun 'Puma' of the *3. Batterie/Sturmgeschütz-Abteilung 202* in winter whitewash camouflage.

Wachtmeister Fritz Amling, an assault gun commander in the *3. Batterie* of *Sturmgeschütz-Abteilung 202* (with a bandage around his head) on 24 December 1942, just after receiving the Knight's Cross of the German Iron Cross while next to the assault gun 'Lowe' (Lion) of the *3. Batterie*. Amling was the first soldier of the assault artillery unit to be awarded this prestigious decoration.

A StuG. III Ausf. F/8 (produced by Alkett during September-December 1942) of *Sturmgeschütz-Abteilung 202*; spring 1943. Notice the curious cross symbol behind the German *Balkenkreuz*. It is not impossible that this identifies the battery command vehicles in the unit.

Close-up of the same assault gun. The soldier is standing in the place of the commander.

Close-up of the place of the gunner in the assault gun. The SflZF1a gun sight's reticle had a 5× magnification.

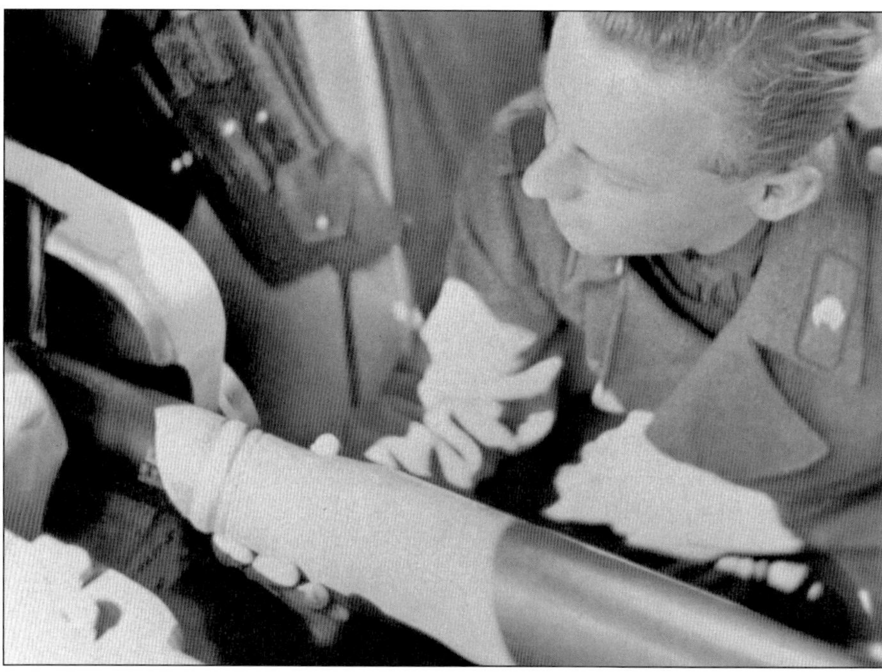

Close-up of the loader's position. In the background, an ammunition pouch for an MP 40, the standard issue submachine gun for the assault gun crews, can be seen.

The same assault gun with the pennant of the battalion commander, a strangely shaped loudspeaker and a good-luck horseshoe.

Hauptmann Buhr (third from the left, wearing a coat) in front of a battery CP of *Sturmgeschütz-Abteilung 202*, probably in spring 1943.

Hauptmann Martin Buhr assumed command of *Sturmgeschütz-Abteilung 202* in March 1943. Previously he had proved himself worthy of the task as commander of the *3. Batterie.*

A StuG. III Ausf. F (produced by Alkett during June-August 1942) L/48 assault gun of *Sturmgeschütz-Abteilung 202*. Notice the curious wooden side skirt, as well as the front hull armour. It could be that the AFVs equipped with wooden skirts were 'inherited' from another *Sturmgeschütz-Abteilung*. So far that kind of makeshift modification has only been seen in photos of StuG. IIIs of *2./Sturmgeschütz-Abteilung 202*. Notice also the *Luftwaffe* soldiers on the assault guns.

The Sd.Kfz. 252 armoured ammunition carrier halftrack of *Sturmgeschütz-Abteilung 202,* named 'Moritz'; probably taken in late spring 1943. The assault gun unit still had eight of these vehicles in late 1943.

The assault gun 'Alligator' belonging to the *1. Batterie/Sturmgeschütz-Abteilung 202* in summer 1943, in the area of Ssumy. This StuG. III, the AFV of *Oberwachtmeister* Schramm, was destroyed by a direct hit by Soviet artillery on 12 October 1943.

The assault gun 'Krake' (Octopus) of *1./Sturmgeschütz-Abteilung 202*; summer 1943, in the area of Ssumy.

Close-up of the assault gun 'Alligator'. *Oberwachtmeister* Schramm is in the commander's cupola.

A StuG. III assault gun of *Sturmgeschütz-Abteilung 202* in a repair base located in the area of Ssumy during summer 1943. Notice the track links attached to the hull to increase protection.

The assault gun 'Tigerhai' (Tiger Shark) of *1./Sturmgeschütz-Abteilung 202*, in summer 1943, in the area of Ssumy. Though the added tank links improved the armoured protection of the AFV, they also increased its total weight and therefore reduced its manoeuvrability.

Tigerhai

In this photo, taken at closer range, the StuG. III assault gun ‘Tigerhai’, provides a stylish background for commemorative photos; summer 1943, in the area of Ssumy.

A close-up photo of ‘Nilpferd’, at the same location.

The StuG. III Ausf. F assault gun 'Nilpferd' (Hippopotamus), probably of late production (by Alkett during June-October 1942), is equipped with a L/48 gun; it belonged to the *1. Batterie/Sturmgeschütz-Abteilung 202.* In front of the combat vehicle we can see *Oberwachtmeister* Schramm (in the middle); taken during summer 1943, in the area of Ssumy.

An assault gun (probably the 'Triton') of the *1. Batterie/Sturmgeschütz-Abteilung 202* in summer 1943, in the area of Ssumy. The slanted armour plating of the fighting compartment of the StuG. III Ausf. E (produced by Alkett during September 1941-February 1942) was cast with concrete on both sides and was reinforced with the addition of spare track links and drive wheels. Four hand grenades can be seen on the roof armour.

The assault gun 'Triton' of *1./Sturmgeschütz-Abteilung 202*, at the same location. The name of the combat vehicle is clearly legible in this photo.

The *1. Batterie* of *Sturmgeschütz-Abteilung 202* lined up in Ssumy.
The StuG. III 'Tigerhai' can be seen on the extreme left of the first line; summer 1943.

The same battery photographed from behind. The Sd.Kfz. 252 armoured ammunition carrier halftracks are clearly recognizable in the background.

Repair base of *Sturmgeschütz-Abteilung 202* in Ssumy; summer 1943. On the left hand side of the picture the assault gun 'Löwe' of the *3. Batterie* can be seen.

The photo of the repair base of the assault artillery unit taken from another angle. Notice the large number of track links added to the AFVs to improve armour protection.

Mechanics performing repair on the Sd.Kfz. 252 armoured ammunition carrier 'Moritz'.

The relatively calm period in Ssumy gave the unit an opportunity to improve training, as well as to conduct extensive maintenance on the AFVs. In this extremely rare photo we can see a late production StuG. III Ausf. F assault gun with side skirts, and an Ausf. G assault gun of *Sturmgeschütz-Abteilung 202* conducting gunnery training. The photo was taken just after the StuG. III had opened fire. It was moderately camouflaged by its crew; its early made skirting must have been attached to the sides in the field, then camouflage-painted by the troops.

The assault gun 'Seeteufel' (Anglerfish) of *1./Sturmgeschütz-Abteilung 202*, in summer 1943.

Battalion command assault gun of *Sturmgeschütz-Abteilung 202* in summer 1943.

The assault gun 'Adler' (Eagle) of *2./Sturmgeschütz-Abteilung 202* disabled a T–34 tank of the 26th Tank Brigade of the Soviet 2nd Tank Corps by overrunning it near the church in Nish. Ssyrowatka on 17 August 1943. The German StuG. III Ausf. G assault gun was built on a Pz.Kpfw. III Ausf. M chassis in April-May 1943 at the MIAG factory. The wooden side-skirting protected mainly the running gear of the combat vehicle when hit by shells.

The engagement with the Soviet tank from a different angle: the immense forces of the collision had flung off the turret of the Soviet AFV.

The assault guns of *2./Sturmgeschütz-Abteilung 202*; probably late in summer 1943. The 'Greif' (Griffin) is presumably a StuG. III Ausf. G (produced by Alkett/MIAG during April-December 1943). Behind it two earlier-production, wooden-skirted StuG. III Ausf. F (L/48, produced by Alkett during June-September 1942) AFVs can be seen. The assault guns are well concealed from the view of Soviet reconnaissance and ground attack aircraft by the coppice. Notice the curious steps cut into the side-skirt of the StuG. III assault gun 'Greif'. The circle sign denotes the position of the vehicle within the platoon: this was probably a platoon command AFV.

Investiture ceremony of *Major* Martin Buhr, commander of *Sturmgeschütz-Abteilung 202*, in September 1943, near Kiev. The personnel of the unit are lined up for the bestowal of the Knight's Cross of the Iron Cross. In the background, the battalion command assault gun can be seen with three crew members but without its commander.

Major Buhr marches by the lined-up personnel. Note the victory rings around the barrel of the StuG. III in the background.

In the presence of the commander of the *VII. Armeekorps, General der Artillerie* Ernst-Eberhard Hell (left), the Knight's Cross of the Iron Cross is placed around the neck of the commander of *Sturmgeschütz-Abteilung 202.*

General der Artillerie Hell inspects the battalion command assault gun.
Notice the commander's pennant on the left mudguard of the StuG. III.

Major Buhr is chatting with the general in front of the battalion command assault gun.
Behind him, the name 'Condor', given to one of the StuG.
IIIs of the *2./Sturmgeschütz-Abteilung 202,* is clearly decipherable.

And now the whole crew: *Major* Buhr takes his place as the commander of the battalion command gun.

A close-up of the battalion command StuG. III assault gun. Of course, the ever-present track links to improve protection are not missing from this combat vehicle either.

Soviet soldiers examine the assault gun 'Tigerhai' of *1./Sturmgeschütz-Abteilung 202* in autumn 1943. The assault gun, commanded by *Unteroffizier* Prietsch, was knocked out by a Soviet KV-1 heavy tank in early November 1943, probably south-west of Saborje.

The assault gun 'Tigerhai', captured by the Soviets; this picture is taken from a different angle but at the same location.

StuG. III assault gun of *2./Sturmgeschütz-Abteilung 202* in the sector of the *82. Infanterie-Division;* in early 1944.

The assault gun 'Bussard' of *2./Sturmgeschütz-Abteilung 202* with soldiers from the *82. Infanterie-Division*; early 1944.

Bussard

The assault gun 'Bussard' is waiting for its mission orders while in readiness position. The three bars (III) on the StuG. III's gun mantlet and rear armour plate probably denote the vehicle's position within the platoon.

Assault guns of *2./Sturmgeschütz-Abteilung 202* are assembling in snow-covered terrain to support the *82. Infanterie-Division*; early 1944.

Engine replacement for 'Bussard' (Buzzard), a StuG. III Ausf. F/8 (produced by Alkett during September-December 1942) belonging to *2./Sturmgeschütz-Abteilung 202*; in the area of Ssumy, March 1943. A crane with a lifting capacity of 3 tons is used to handle the StuG's engine which weighs almost 1 ton.

A StuG. III Ausf. G of *Sturmgeschütz-Abteilung 202* with a coat of winter white-wash is conducting a vehicle recovery mission with another StuG. III Ausf. G. On the assault gun in the foreground, the wooden hoist supporting bracket was installed on the front of the right-hand-side mudguard. Despite the presence of supporting brackets, its side skirting is missing. The machine gun shield of the loader was originally designed for the MG 42. The metal luggage rack of the rear AFV is a field improvisation. The large wooden boxes on each of the vehicles were probably for carrying personal equipment.

An intriguing photograph of a StuG. III Ausf. G of *Sturmgeschütz-Abteilung 202* involved in an accident in early 1944. This version was produced by Alkett between December 1943 and September 1944. Notice the non-penetrating hit to the lower front hull plate. Among the pieces of equipment scattered around the vehicle, a StuK40 cannon can also be seen but the reason for its presence is not known.

A StuG. III Ausf. G (produced by Alkett between October 1943 and March 1944) in a covered shelter – built to provide protection against winter weather – with its crew posing in front of it.

Sturmgeschütz-Brigade 202 was reorganized in the area of Ziegenhals and Langendorf in Upper-Silesia. At this time, the unit also received StuH. 42 assault howitzers (see the two AFVs to the right in the picture). The assault guns are still carrying (among others, on their side skirts) the geometrical markings denoting their position within the platoon.

Sturmgeschütz-Brigade 202 received its new combat vehicles only in the first half of July 1944. After the assault guns arrived, different military exercises began. In the picture the AFVs are pulling into the column in the area of Ziegenhals in early July 1944.

The assault gun already seen in the previous photo probably slipped off the road. Its recovery is being organized in this picture.

A column of StuG. III Ausf. G assault guns of *Sturmgeschütz-Brigade 202*, probably in Ziegenhals. These AFVs also received extra concrete-protection and additional track links. The lead assault gun, produced by Alkett, was installed with a wooden hoist supporting bracket on the front of the right-hand-side mudguard, in contradiction to agreed specifications, since other field-modified storage racks (e. g. for 20 litre fuel cans) had been fitted to its original place on the rear part of the fender.

The personnel of *Sturmgeschütz-Brigade 202* lined up during a parade in the main square of Ziegenhals before their next mission.

eph Kappel
Gegr. 1899
KAPP

Adler Drogerie

A column of StuG. III Ausf. G assault guns of *Sturmgeschütz-Brigade 202* on parade. It is conceivable that all of the AFVs of the brigade underwent field modifications to improve their protection with concrete cast onto the slanting front armour, additional track links, and new camouflage paint. Note that the forward side-skirt section is cut out in the line of the sprocket wheel – probably to simplify servicing.

The armoured protection of the command StuG. III Ausf. G – in contradiction to agreed specifications – was strengthened by a layer of concrete in the field. By 1944, the protection of the assault guns had become inferior to that of the modern Soviet tanks and self-propelled guns. The superior officer welcoming the parade drill is standing with his staff on a platform improvised from an Sd.Ah. 116 low-loading trailer.

A command StuG. III Ausf. G assault gun (probably 'Puma') of the *3./Sturmgeschütz-Brigade 202* parading in Ziegenhals. Fixing wires are attached to the forward sections of the mudguards, but the track links – presumably due to the parade – are missing.

The new assault gun 'Tigerhai' (of *1./Sturmgeschütz-Brigade 202*) during the parade. Individual names were usually given to the assault guns in this unit. The dark cross on the side-skirt is probably the symbol of the battery commander.

Entrainment and send off of *Sturmgeschütz-Brigade 202* at the railway station of Ziegenhals on 14 July 1944. Curiously, the assault guns are decorated with flowers – clearly seen on the muzzle brake of the closest AFV.

Assault gun 'Tigerhai' having entrained. On top of the StuG. III, *Oberleutnant* Rudolf Bayer, commander of *1./Sturmgeschütz-Brigade 202*, is sitting in the middle.

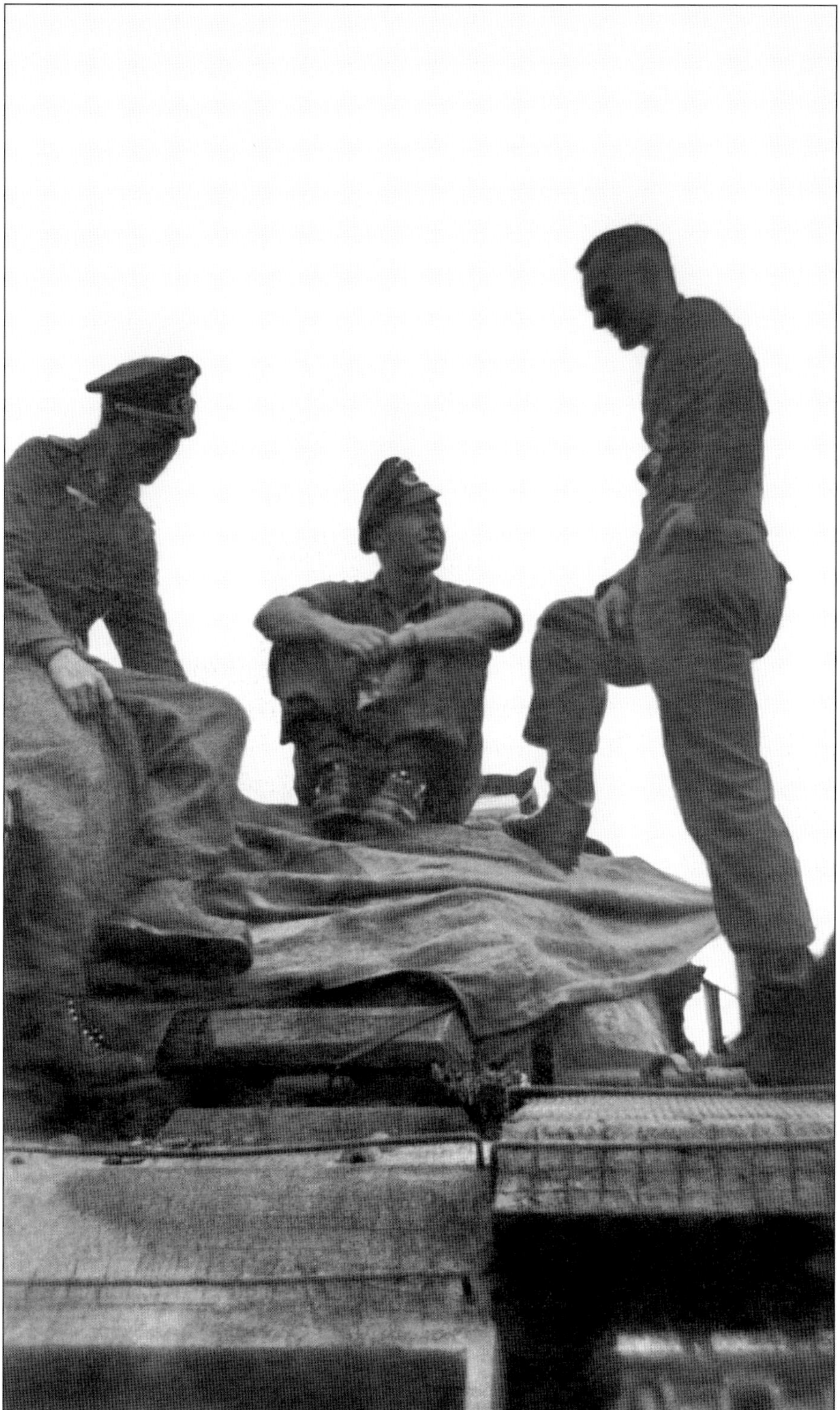

A StuH. 42 assault howitzer of *Sturmgeschütz-Brigade 202* crossing a stream in summer 1944. Two wooden boxes are on the luggage rack. Due to that the two road wheels were placed onto the slanting rear hull armour and a storage rack fitted to the rear part of the fender for two 20 litre cans. Because of the task given to them, the vehicle was moderately camouflaged.

The StuH. 42 assault howitzer 'Kranich' (Crane) of *2./Sturmgeschütz-Brigade 202* in July or August 1944; with German grenadiers. According to the marking (II) on the side-skirt, this AFV is the second one within the platoon.

Three assault guns of the *Sturmgeschütz-Brigade 202* (probably from the *2. Batterie*) on march in the Baltic region in late summer 1944. According to the circles on the rear armour plates, all three belong to the same platoon. The last AFV is probably 'Bussard'.

The assault gun 'Sperber' (Sparrowhawk) of *2./Sturmgeschütz-Brigade 202* in August 1944. Notice the soldiers of a German TD-squad with hand-held Panzerschreck rocket launchers to the left in the picture.

The assault gun 'Tigerhai' of *1./Sturmgeschütz-Brigade 202* in a standby position, camouflaged. The battery commander, *Oberleutnant* Bayer, is the second from the left. The lettering on the board: Bayer echelon.

Another assault gun, 'Krokodil' (Crocodile) of *1./Sturmgeschütz-Brigade 202*, heavily camouflaged is waiting for its next mission in August 1944. To the right, only the cover on the muzzle brake of the other camouflaged assault gun can be seen.

The assault guns of *Sturmgeschütz-Brigade 202* embarking in the port of Ventpils (German Windau) for Sõrve (German Sworbe) Peninsula in October 1944.

Blown-up assault guns of *1./Sturmeschütz-Brigade 202* at the southernmost end of Sõrve (German Sworbe) Peninsula, late November 1944.

The assault gun 'Tigerhai' of *1./Sturmgeschütz-Brigade 202,* left-behind and destroyed, photographed from different angles, in the southernmost end of Sõrve (German Sworbe) Peninsula; late November 1944.

The building in the previous photos in the early 2010s, at the foot of the lighthouse of Sõrve (German Sworbe) Peninsula.

Two StuG. III Ausf. G assault guns of *3./Sturmgeschütz-Brigade 202* in winter whitewash camouflage near the end of the war, probably in spring 1945. The one in the front is the AFV named 'Panther'. Second from the right is probably *Wachtmeister* Scharf, one of the NCOs of the brigade, who was awarded the Knight's Cross of the Iron Cross. Note the cleats fixed on the tracks. It is also interesting, that different (normal and winter) track links are attached to the side armour of the fighting compartment.

Probably the assault gun 'Panther', now disabled.

The last commander of a *Sturmgeschütz-Brigade 202, Major* Johann Spielmann, in spring 1945. Notice the Oakleaves decoration to his Knight's Cross of the Iron Cross around his neck, which he earned with his unit in late December 1944.

Portrait photograph of *Wachtmeister* Amling.

Oberwachtmeister Richard Schramm, a platoon leader of the *1. Batterie/Sturmgeschütz-Abteilung 202*, the second member of the unit to receive the Knight's Cross of the Iron Cross on 23 December 1942.

Wachtmeister Heinz Scharf, an assault gun commander of *3./Sturmgeschütz-Brigade 202* earned the Knight's Cross of the Iron Cross for knocking out eight Soviet AFVs on 6 August 1944.

Leutnant der Reserve Ahrend Höper earned the Knight's Cross of the Iron Cross during the battles fought in the Sõrve (German Sworbe-) Peninsula in November 1944.

Oberleutnant Gerhard Brandt, commander of *1./Sturmgeschütz-Brigade 202* earned the Knight's Cross of the Iron Cross for his achievements in the Sõrve (German Sworbe-) Peninsula.

Oberwachtmeister Joseph Rohrbacher served as an assault gun commander in *1./Sturmgeschütz-Abteilung 202* between May and December 1942. He was awarded the Knight's Cross of the Iron Cross as a platoon leader of *Sturmgeschütz-Brigade 245* on 4 May 1944.

Hauptmann Johann Friedrich Hoering commanded the *2. Batterie* of *Sturmgeschütz-Abteilung 202* from July to December 1942 then from November 1942 became the commander of the *1. Batterie*. He earned the Knight's Cross of the Iron Cross as one of the battery commanders of *Sturmgeschütz-Brigade 277* in summer 1944, which he received on 8 August 1944. He was killed in action in East-Prussia on 19 October 1944.

Stabswachtmeister Erich Zillmann was assigned to *2./Sturmgeschütz-Abteilung 202* as a platoon leader in March 1942, where he served until he was wounded in November 1942. He was awarded the Knight's Cross of the Iron Cross as a platoon leader of *Sturmgeschütz-Brigade 245* on 8 August 1944.

COLOR PLATES

FELIPERODNA

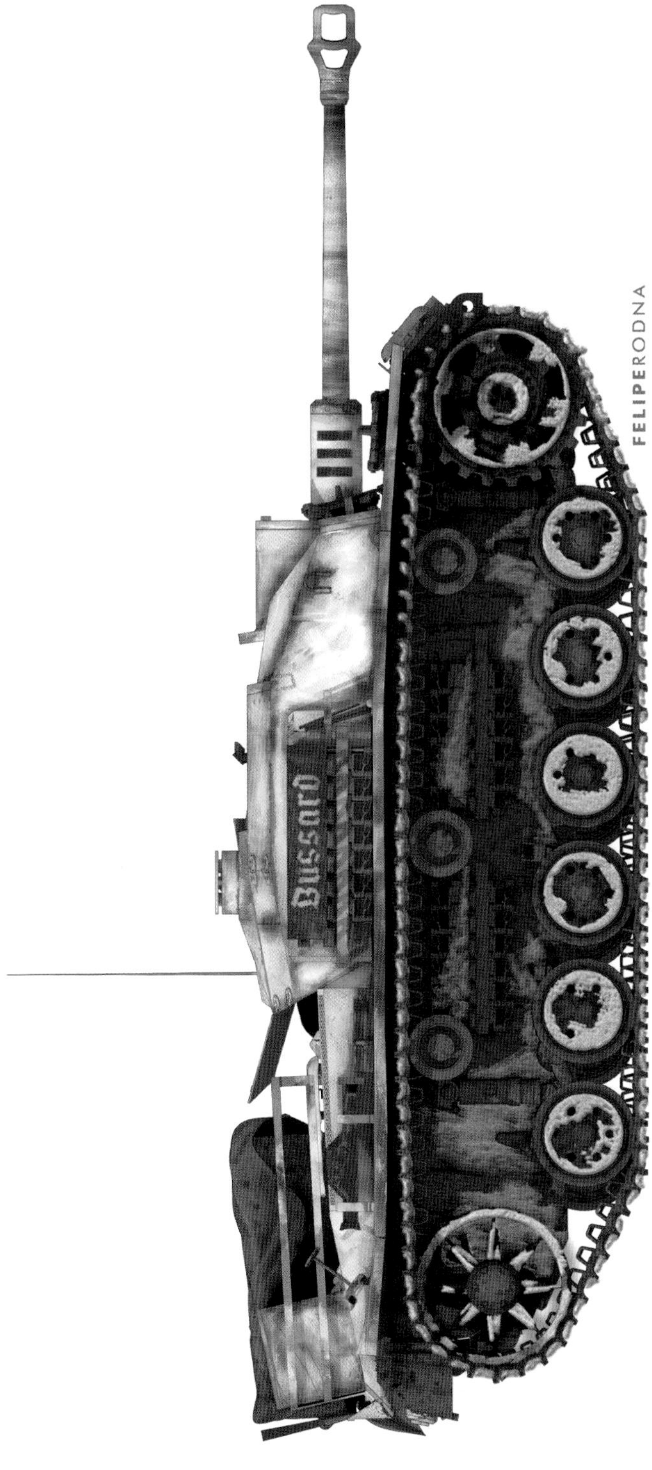
Bussard
FELIPERODNA

FELIPERODNA

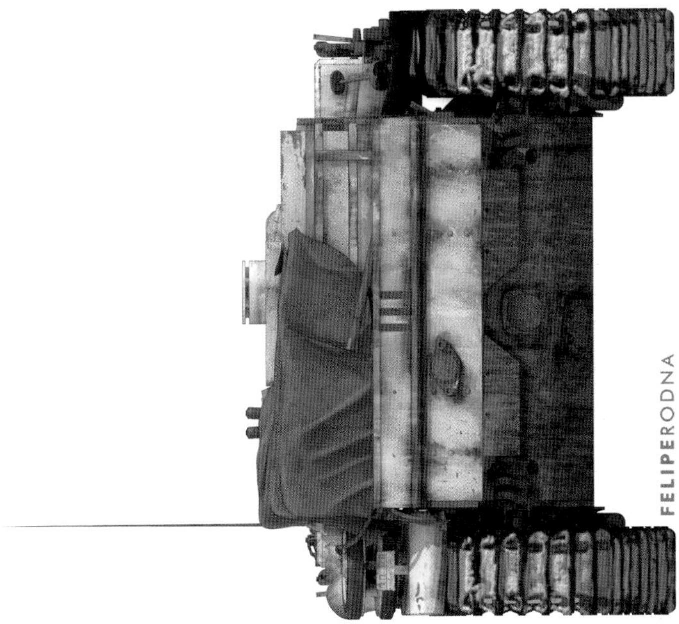
FELIPERODNA

FELIPERODNA

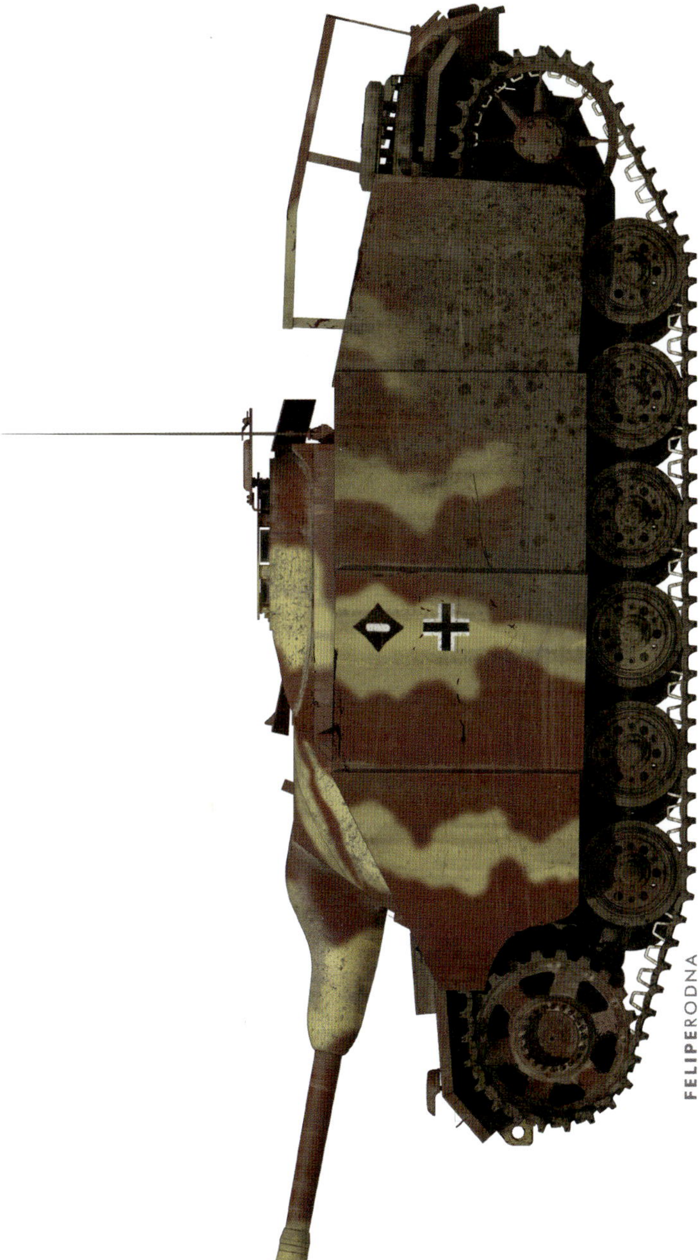
FELIPERODNA

Kranich
FELIPE RODNA

FELIPE RODNA

TIGERHAI
FELIPERODNA